CROSSING HISTORIES AND ETHNOGRAPHIES

Methodology and History in Anthropology

Series Editors:
David Parkin, Fellow of All Souls College, Oxford
David Gellner, Fellow of All Souls College, Oxford
Nayanika Mathur, Fellow of Wolfson College, Oxford

Recent volumes:

For a full volume listing, please see the series page on our website:
http://berghahnbooks.com/series/methodology-and-history-in-anthropology

CROSSING HISTORIES AND ETHNOGRAPHIES

Following Colonial Historicities in Timor-Leste

Edited by
Ricardo Roque and Elizabeth G. Traube

berghahn
NEW YORK • OXFORD
www.berghahnbooks.com

First published in 2019 by

Berghahn Books

www.berghahnbooks.com

Library of Congress Cataloging-in-Publication Data

Names: Roque, Ricardo, editor. | Traube, Elizabeth G., editor.
Title: Crossing Histories and Ethnographies: Following Colonial
    Historicities in Timor-Leste / edited by Ricardo Roque and Elizabeth G.
    Traube.
Description: First edition. | New York: Berghahn, 2019. | Series:
    Methodology and History in Anthropology; volume 37 | Includes
    bibliographical references and index.
Identifiers: LCCN 2019010117 (print) | LCCN 2019011115 (ebook) |
    ISBN 9781789202724 (ebook) | ISBN 9781789202717
    (hardback:alk. paper)
Subjects: LCSH: Timor-Leste--History. | Timor-Leste—Colonization. |
    Ethnology—Timor-Leste.
Classification: LCC DS649.5 (ebook) | LCC DS649.5 .C76 2019 (print) |
    DDC 959.87—dc23
LC record available at https://lccn.loc.gov/2019010117

British Library Cataloguing in Publication Data

A catalogue record for this book is available from the British Library

ISBN 978-1-78920-271-7 hardback
ISBN 978-1-80539-114-2 paperback
ISBN 978-1-80539-368-9 epub
ISBN 978-1-78920-272-4 web pdf

https://doi.org/10.3167/9781789202717

CONTENTS

ILLUSTRATIONS

ACKNOWLEDGMENTS

This volume was inspired by Crossing Histories and Ethnographies: Anthropology and the Colonial Archive in East Timor hosted by the Instituto de Ciências Sociais, Universidade de Lisboa. The concept for this book evolved from our exchanges since 2013, through mutually enriching conversations and many emails over six years. We thank the Fundação para a Ciência e Tecnologia, Portugal (FCT) for funding the research projects that led to this volume (grant references HC/0089/2009 and PTDC/HAR- HIS/28577/2017).

Our dear colleague Claudine Friedberg passed away in 2018. All the contributors to this volume join with the editors in expressing our profound gratitude to Claudine for her lifelong example of scholarship, for her intellectual guidance, and for her contagious joy of living. We know she would be pleased to see this collection finally materialize.

We thank Chris Ballard and the anonymous reviewers for commentaries and advice on earlier versions of the manuscript. James J. Fox generously agreed to join the project in its final stages. During these years, it was a pleasure to work with Duncan Ranslem, Molly Mosher, and Ann DeVita; and with Marion Berghahn, Harry Eagles, Elizabeth Martinez, and Tom Bonnington at Berghahn.

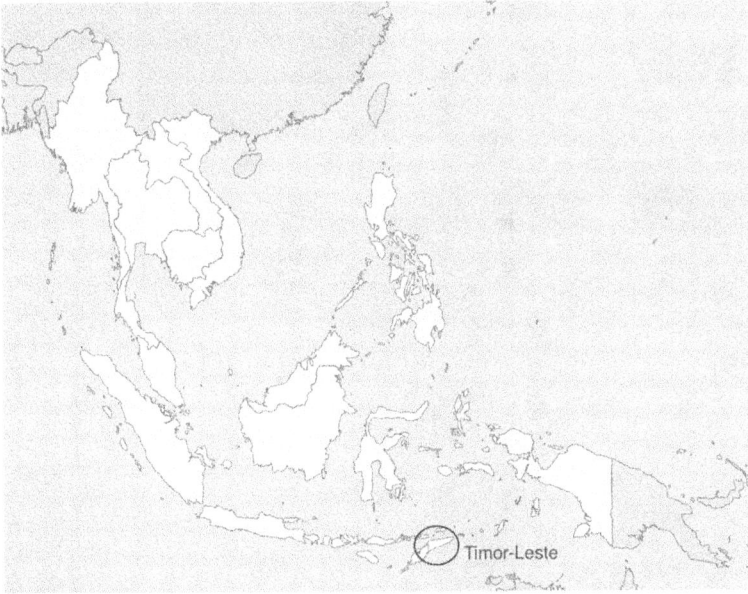

Map. Timor-Leste in Southeast Asia. Map created by "Hariboneagle927," adapted by the authors. Wikimedia Commons, public domain.

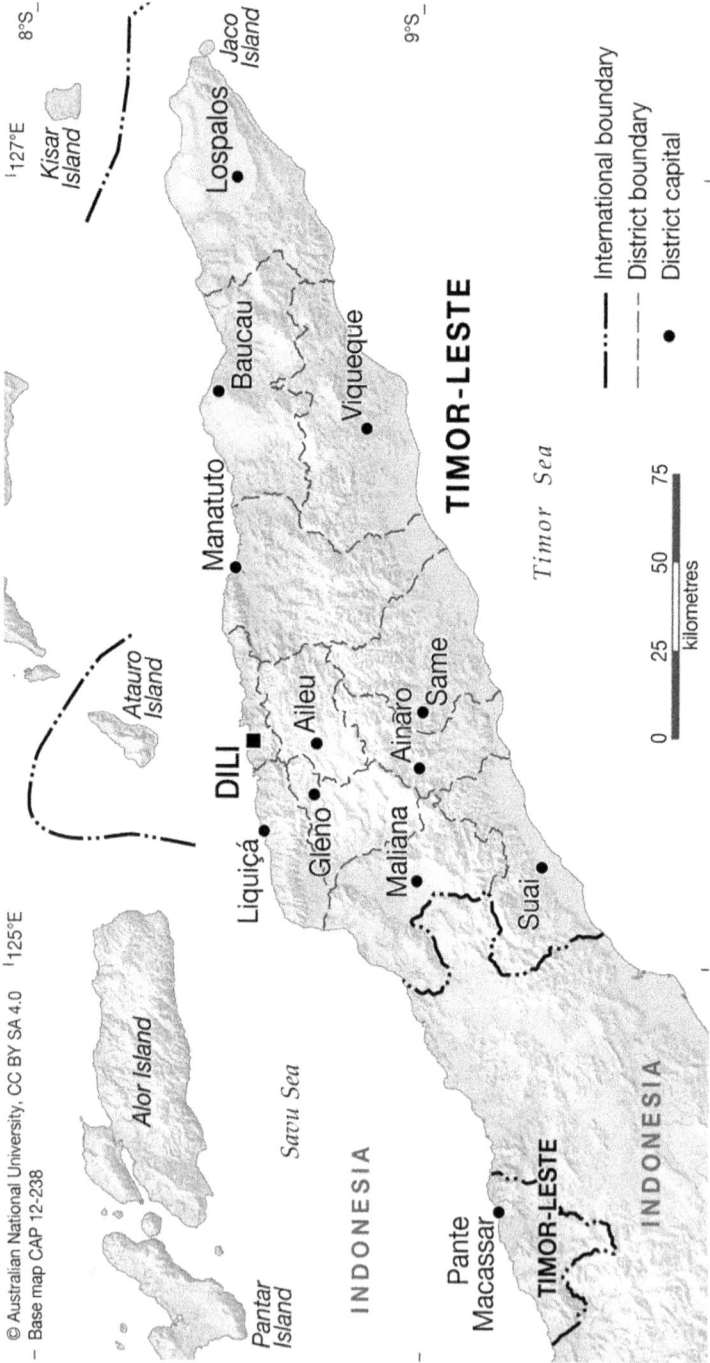

127°E
125°E
8°S
9°S

Kisar Island

Lospalos
Jaco Island

Baucau

Viqueque

Manatuto

TIMOR-LESTE

Atauro Island

Aileu

Same

DILI

Ainaro

Liquiçá

Gleno

Maliana

Suai

Alor Island

Savu Sea

INDONESIA

Pantar Island

Pante Macassar

TIMOR-LESTE

INDONESIA

Timor Sea

Timor Sea

0 25 50 75
kilometres

International boundary
District boundary
District capital

Map. Timor-Leste. Map reproduced with the permission of CartoGIS Services, ANU College of Asia and the Pacific, The Australian National University.

INTRODUCTION

CROSSING HISTORIES AND ETHNOGRAPHIES

Ricardo Roque and Elizabeth G. Traube

Mutual engagements between anthropology and history have become common if not standard practices within both disciplines. The key question for many anthropologists and historians today is not whether to cross the boundary between their disciplines but how—or indeed, if—the very idea of a disciplinary boundary should be sustained. The field and the archive, methodological spaces that traditionally stood for anthropology and history respectively, no longer belong exclusively to either discipline. Today few anthropologists and historians will contest this viewpoint. While the methodological spaces may still be differentially prioritized (an anthropologist who does no fieldwork remains almost as marginal within anthropology as a historian who never entered an archive would be in history), there is an emerging consensus that the field and the archive are mutually constitutive and that each can in certain circumstances be approached as a version of the other—the field as a kind of archive, the archive as a kind of field.

Timor-Leste, this volume argues, constitutes a particularly compelling case for the interdependence of ethnographic and archival research in contemporary anthropological and historical practice. We take the rich and complex history of colonialism and anthropology in Timor-Leste as an exemplary site for a general reflection on the encounters between the archive and the field, and between European and indigenous historicities. This country's unique and unusually long colonial history—combining centuries of singular Portuguese colonialism with two decades of dramatic military occupation by and East Timorese resistance to Indonesian forces—offers a vantage point (beyond the common and hegemonic British, German, French, and Dutch examples of colonial states) from which to reflect upon the interdependences between history and anthropology. In 2002,

Timor-Leste, comprising the eastern half of the island of Timor, became the first new nation-state of the twenty-first century. This was the outcome (unexpected, except, perhaps, to the East Timorese) of a long and complicated history of colonial entanglements. Over some five hundred years, local communities on Timor have engaged with increasingly intrusive outsiders; they have responded in various ways, reflecting local conditions as well as the particular projects of the colonizers, by selectively incorporating and adapting elements of the foreign systems, by reworking preexisting social and cultural forms, and by actively and more and more collectively resisting foreign political domination.

Timorese encounters with Europeans date back to the sixteenth century, when Portuguese traders and missionaries first visited the island. After the conquest of Malacca in 1511, the Portuguese expanded their military influence and trading networks throughout maritime Southeast Asia while simultaneously confronting Dutch rivalry. By the mid-sixteenth century, Portuguese soldiers, traders, and missionaries had settled in the islands of Solor and Flores—and afterward Timor, attracted there by the imagined wealth of its most famous local product, sandalwood. European presence in Solor and Flores gave rise to a powerful mestizo ruling class, the so-called Topasses (also known as "Black Portuguese"). The Topasses dominated the early settlements, either independently or on behalf of Portugal, and strongly expanded their authority over parts of Timor in the seventeenth and eighteenth centuries. There, meanwhile, Catholic missionaries had successfully Christianized some indigenous rulers, who saw in their alliance with European foreigners and their conversion to Christianity an opportunity to increase their powers. Following the Portuguese victory over the prestigious realm of Wehali in 1642, Portuguese influence in western Timorese domains increased, and finally in the early 1700s the first governor was appointed to Lifau. Portuguese expansionism, however, was limited by competition with the Dutch (established firmly in Kupang since the 1650s) as well as by Topass claims to de facto overlordship in the island. In 1769, pressed by both Dutch and Topasses, the Portuguese governor abandoned Lifau and retreated to Dili, where a small but durable Portuguese stronghold was established in eastern Timor. By then, however, the Portuguese position in the region had steadily deteriorated; in Timor it had contracted dramatically. Dutch hegemony prevailed across the archipelago; the golden days of Portugal's Asian Empire had come to an end. In the 1800s, Portugal's domains in Southeast Asia were reduced to scattered settlements in Solor, Flores, Oecussi, and East

Timor. In 1851, in an act seen by many as a marker of imperial decline, Solor and Flores were sold to Holland. Thereafter, based in Dili, the Portuguese laid their territorial claims over East Timor and the Oecussi enclave alone.

Portuguese colonial authority was extended and consolidated over the late nineteenth century through a series of violent military campaigns, but Portugal remained a relatively weak though long-lasting colonial state. First in 1859 and finally in 1913, after almost three centuries of struggle for control of Timor, the Portuguese and Dutch governments reached agreement over colonial borders, thereby stabilizing a longstanding division of the island, with the Portuguese in the east and the Dutch in the west. In 1912–13, the kingdom of Manufahi and its allies led the largest and most devastating anti-Portuguese uprising in East Timor. The Portuguese military emerged victorious, after which a series of important changes in the structure of colonial administration and its relations with indigenous systems was enacted. Previously recognized as indigenous polities within Portuguese administration, the *reinos* (kingdoms) and their Timorese rulers holding royal titles were replaced by a new administrative ordering, which was based on a network of *sukus* that, nonetheless, continued to integrate native ruling lineages. The tribute system that formerly structured the colonial state and its galaxy of *reinos* was abolished and replaced by a head tax. Coffee cultivation in state-controlled plantations expanded. This process, however, was interrupted during World War II. In 1941–42, the country was invaded by Allied and then Japanese forces, and only in 1945, following the Japanese defeat, did Portuguese administration resume. After the war the Portuguese Estado Novo dictatorship invested in the "reconstruction" of the country. It also gave former nationalistic ideologies of imperial grandeur a new impetus and continued to claim East Timor—then renamed Timor Português (Portuguese Timor)—as an integral part of Portugal's national empire. Anticolonialist ideologies, the Cold War, and the long shadow of the new Republic of Indonesia, independent from the Netherlands since 1949, fell over the isolated colony and put Portugal's administration under growing international and regional political pressure. Decolonization, however, began only in 1974, following the overthrow of the Salazar/Caetano regime in Portugal, and was disrupted in August 1975 by a brief bout of civil fighting, during which the Portuguese colonial administration physically abandoned the province, only to be replaced by a militarized Indonesian occupation that lasted until 1999.

International interest in the inhabitants of the island of Timor first emerged during the nineteenth century, in the context of inquiries into the racial and civilizational condition of Oceanic peoples. Travelers and observers were fascinated and intrigued with the human social, linguistic, and physical heterogeneity that was contained in such a relatively small territory. Thus, in spite of its remoteness and size, Timor epitomized for decades the puzzlement of Europeans with the ethnoracial and ethnolinguistic complexities of the "Malay Archipelago." Notwithstanding this long, multifaceted history of early ethnological and colonial engagements, however, eastern Timor first became known in the modern anthropological literature later in the twentieth century for the internal complexity and resilience of its social and cultural systems. The structuralist-inspired ethnographers who conducted fieldwork in Portuguese Timor over the 1960s and early 1970s were oriented primarily toward the synchronic, and while they acknowledged that extralocal forces had long penetrated local lives, their accounts tended to foreground the stability and resilience of the indigenous systems. Anglophone anthropologists could be acquainted with Evans-Pritchard's motto—a central methodological question, Evans-Pritchard suggested provocatively in 1950, is "whether social anthropology . . . is not itself a kind of historiography" (Evans-Pritchard 1950: 121; see Hicks, this volume)—but in practice their studies gave little or no attention to colonial history and archival documents; instead they followed the then-fashionable approaches of structural analysis. History, when addressed at all, appeared largely in the form of (potentially) disruptive events from outside that were "absorbed" within local cultural orders, such that, as Lévi-Strauss had put it, these cultures could experience change as continuity. The synchronic emphasis reflected a wider tendency within the discipline, one that was coming under scrutiny and would be challenged with mounting intensity over the ensuing decades. A number of anthropologists and historians began to use archival sources (dominantly Dutch language materials) together with oral traditions and indigenous texts to explore colonial history in Bali (Wiener 1995; Schulte-Nordholt 1996) and the Lesser Sundas (Fox 1971, 1977; Barnes 2013), including Timor (Fox 1982; McWilliam 2002). But most of these mutual engagements of anthropology and history coincided with the closure and isolation of Timor-Leste. Between 1975 and 2000, Indonesian occupation of Timor-Leste restricted access to the country and impeded researchers from outside from conducting systematic research there, creating what has been described by Gunn as an "ethnographic gap" (Gunn 2007). With the end of the occupation in 1999–2000 and the restoration of Timor-Leste's independence, a new generation of anthropologists has been re-exploring the country as an ethnographic field site, resulting in many rich and creative works (for overviews see McWilliam and Traube 2011; Nygaard-Christensen and Bexley 2017; Viegas and Feijó 2017). Earlier interest in Austronesian topics has been renewed, and new themes emerge, reflecting the epistemic and political issues posed by nation-building, postconflict challenges, social change, and "development," to form what is now a lively inter-disciplinary field of Timor-Leste studies.

In the historical literature on eastern Timor, however, an anthro-pological turn has been slow to arrive. Throughout the twentieth century, historical writing on Timor was a gauge of imperialist and na-tionalist interest, or else of anticolonial motivations. At the same time as anthropologists were emphasizing synchrony, the historians' pri-mary orientation toward the diachronic was expressed in approaches based on written documents alone that largely overlooked Timorese cultural understandings to the privilege of nation-oriented histo-ries, while tending to over-represent—except perhaps for occasional historical curiosity surrounding the case of the mixed "Portuguese-Indigenous" rulers, the Topasses (Boxer 1947; but cf. Hägerdal 2007, Andaya 2010)—the imprint of European "presence" in the island. In Portuguese historiography, in particular, documentary evidence and accounts of past events abound, but too often their significance is read from a Luso-centric perspective, in some cases ideologically nationalist and colonialist until at least 1974 (Leitão 1948, 1952; Oliveira 1949–52; but compare with Matos 1974; Figueiredo 2011; especially the wider Asianist perspective of Thomaz 1994). Besides, with exception made perhaps to the poet, colonial official, and eth-nographer Ruy Cinatti, Lusophone writings on "Timor Português" in the late colonial period were loosely connected to the main themes that fueled the Francophone and Anglophone debates on the anthro-pology of Eastern Indonesia (cf. Castelo 2017). Kelly Silva's chapter in this volume, for example, documents the utter lack of familiarity with the anthropological literature on the part of both Portuguese and Timorese "anti-barlaque" intellectuals in the early 1970s, while even the intellectual defenders of indigenous exchange practices seemed to ignore international literature that would have supported their posi-tion. From 1975 to the end of Indonesian occupation in 1999–2000, "anticolonial" historical accounts critical of Portuguese rule retold colonial chronology, only to emphasize European wrongdoings, ne-glect, and brutality over time, and thereby celebrate the longevity of Timorese opposition and "resistance" to foreigners (Pélissier 1996; Gunn 1999). Notwithstanding its valuable documentary revelations, such historiography was rarely in dialogue with ethnographic accounts. Moreover, the hiatus in field research during the Indonesian occupation of Timor-Leste was accompanied by a gap of another sort: an archival ethnographic gap, a scarcity of archive-grounded studies on the country's colonial history. After independence, a new wave of historical studies appeared, and scholars now show stronger concern with the oral record and the multiple and different forms of accounting for Timorese history (cf. Gunter 2008, 2010; Hägerdal 2012a, 2012b, 2015, 2017; Kammen 2016; Barnes, Hägerdal, Palmer, 2017; Roque 2017). With regard to Timor-Leste, the field and the archive until quite recently remained distinct disciplinary provinces; anthropology and history seemed to lead separate lives.

The current volume gives expression to a growing recognition of the irrelevance of this separation. It both reflects and contributes to an ongoing process of cross-disciplinary reciprocities within and beyond the study of Timor-Leste, and it moves that process forward, addressing the achievements, limitations, and promises of field and archival research for anthropology's future as a discipline. Combining analytical insight and solid empirical research, the authors reflect on the inextricable historicity of field research, while offering original perspectives on the significance of reading colonial archives and events in connection with oral accounts and field data, and of reading current ethnographies in relation to colonial knowledge and archival records. Together they reconsider these broader issues in relation to a diversity of critical topics, including the production and interpretation of colonial ethnographies, the encounter between documentation and oral histories, the enduring presence of memories of colonial warfare, and the meanings of Timorese sacred heirlooms to their Timorese owners and European collectors.

Crossings

Ricardo Roque is a historian-turned-anthropologist, developing a new understanding of Portuguese colonialism in Timor in the form of a historical ethnography of colonial encounters (Roque 2010). In Elizabeth Traube's ethnography (Traube 1986), based on research conducted in the early 1970s, he had found a valuable resource for recovering indigenous voices that were largely suppressed in Portuguese colonial documents. But while he appreciated Traube's work for its ethnographically grounded attention to indigenous agency, he also called attention to its incompleteness: observing that indigenous political practice had long been entangled with the Portuguese colonial regime, he insisted on the need to use colonial sources as well as ethnographic ones in order to gain access to the historical encounters that had provided the matrix within which the cultural discourses described in Traube's ethnography had been formed. Although Roque is not a field ethnographer, his research visits to Timor-Leste have provided him with interpretive energy for reading the colonial archives. In his dissertation, inspired by Traube's insights, he was moved by the idea of treating the colonial archive ethnographically; more recently he is also exploring "the field" as a generative site for the historical imagination. In 2012, as part of a team project on the history of colonial anthropology in Timor-Leste, he used Portuguese documents from archives in Lisbon to prompt interactions with concrete East Timorese places, stories, and people in the field. These interactions complicated his prior assumptions about the Portuguese historical record itself, feeding back into archival work at home. His chapter in this volume, as well as the chapter in collaboration with Lúcio Sousa, is an effort at thinking through these intersections, experimenting with a kind of field-based historiography.

Traube was not an utter stranger to the Portuguese *arquivo*. She had visited several of the collections in Lisbon as a graduate student in preparation for conducting fieldwork. Yet this archival research (the basis for a master's paper on colonial history) was not closely connected to the field-based project on "social and symbolic dualism" that she came to Portuguese Timor to pursue in 1972, and her dissertation presented an overwhelmingly synchronic perspective on Mambai society (Traube 1977). The occupation prevented her from returning to the field before publishing her dissertation-based monograph. In the milieu of the 1980s, a return to the archives would have been a plausible alternative to follow-up fieldwork and might have encouraged a more historical anthropology reflective of the wider disciplinary turn that was by then underway. She did not, however, make that turn, and the book, like the dissertation, relied almost exclusively on ethnographic material. In her case, at least, the disjuncture between ethnography-as-fieldwork and archival research that McWilliam and Shepherd call attention to in this volume reflected a gradual withdrawal from Timor research rather than any sense that colonial history was irrelevant to contemporary social formations. Indeed, the book ended with a critical acknowledgment of its lack of historical understanding. After political events made new fieldwork possible, Traube returned to Timor-Leste where the neglected historicity of the discourses and practices she had previously studied seemed to confront her at every turn. One index of her perspectival shift was her belated recognition that a narrative tradition she had received as a "tale" in the early 1970s appeared to have both shaped and been shaped by historical events. Her chapter in this volume represents an effort to rethink ethnographic materials in relation to historical processes. It relies heavily on Roque's work, which was in turn indebted to her earlier ethnography.

These personal stories about our intellectual passages to each other's work are indicative of the kind of crossings between historiography and ethnography that this volume intends to navigate and address. We emphasize the active term "crossing" in our title since we are seeking to explore the *mutual* productivity of archival research and ethnographic fieldwork. We ask how fieldwork is inherently a journey into colonial archives; how archival work with colonial documents is, also, inherently a fieldwork undertaking. In the zone of intersection between the field and the archive, ethnography and historiography can intimately combine and productively short-circuit each other. Hence our concern is not simply with using archival documents in the context of ethnographic methods, as in otherwise valuable literature on ethnographic methodology (cf. Hammersley and Atkinson 1995; Brettell 1998; Gracy 2004). Our concern is to put forward an approach to archive-as-field and field-as-archive as one encompassing research and analytical endeavor. Moving in, with, and across archival and field data; written and oral materials; European and indigenous epistemologies; dusty colonial documents and face-to-face encounters, we seek to generate the sort of detailed and intimate understanding of temporally situated social worlds, and of time itself as a social artifact, that anthropology and history commonly pursue. Thus, this volume argues for a specifically blurred genre of "historical anthropology" (cf. Axel 2002; Dube 2007). It makes a case for a form of ethnography that implies a form of historiography, the writing of history/ies, based in the field and in the archive simultaneously.

In what follows we contextualize the chapters in relation to our reading of anthropology's engagement with history, temporality, and the knowledge politics of colonial archives in the last four or five decades (for surveys, see also, for example, Faubion 1993; Axel 2002; Brettell 2015: 11–35; Roque and Wagner 2012). We identify three main directions, or "turns," in this sustained process of engagement between history and anthropology with regard to colonialism: a wider disciplinary turn to *history* and temporality as analytical and methodological sensitivity; a turn to colonial *archives* as a politically charged field site and as historical subject in its own right; and a turn to indigenous agency and the ethnographic study of *historicities* in the plural, the manifold social and cultural ways of being conscious of, and performing, (colonial) pasts, presents, and futures. We then introduce the chapters in relation to what we propose as three research strategies for translating these concerns into concrete studies of the historicities of colonialism through field and archive methodologies: following stories; following objects; following cultures through archives.

Historical Turns in Anthropology

In a programmatic essay, Bernard S. Cohn presented a conjuncture between history and anthropology as a means of self-realization for both disciplines. "I am going to suggest," he wrote, "that history can become more historical in becoming more anthropological, that anthropology can become more anthropological in becoming more historical" (Cohn 1980: 216). On the anthropological side of the chiasmus, Cohn argued that the change would redefine the object of knowledge. Rather than objectifying non-Western cultures as static, atemporal systems that had persisted largely unchanged, historical anthropologists would approach them as dynamic outcomes of temporal processes, mutable products of human actions and events; they would shift "away from the objectification of social life to a study of its constitution and construction" (Cohn 1980: 217).

Evans-Pritchard had urged anthropology to mend its "breach with history," but Cohn articulated conceptual foundations for rapprochement. His emphasis on the processual character of social life resonated with a wider tendency that was gathering force in anthropology and other disciplines at the time, what Sherry Ortner (1984) subsequently dubbed the "practice turn." The rubric included a set of approaches aimed at developing less rigidly deterministic models of social life; premised on an interplay between systems or structures and action and events, they sought to accommodate agency and contingency and to account for change as well as continuity over time. Practices, culturally patterned sequences of social action that could be concatenated into events, were defined as sites where culture is continually made, remade, and sometimes transformed by the participants. The practice turn was implicit in Cohn's assertion: "Since culture is always being constituted and constructed, so it is also always being transformed" (Cohn 1980: 217). But if practice was a key concept in historical anthropology, not all versions of practice theory emphasized history. Temporality, Nicholas Thomas observed, had come to be regarded "as constitutive of rather than marginal to social and cultural systems," but diverse scales of time were under consideration (Thomas 1996 [1989]; see also Fabian 1983). In *Outline of a Theory of Practice*, a work that helped solidify the practice turn, Pierre Bourdieu sought to recover the time of lived experience as it was manifested in strategic manipulations of the tempo of social action, such as delaying or speeding up responses to provocations embodied in challenges and gifts. "But there are other time scales," Thomas noted, "such as the time of historic entanglements with intrusive systems, or the longer time of prehistoric social evolution" (Thomas 1996: 102).

Historic entanglements were Cohn's focus. Dialogue between anthropologists and historians was to generate a common subject matter as well as a common epistemology, and Cohn identified colonialism as a primary subject. He proposed a focus on the cultural dynamics of colonial encounters, defined as the interactions between colonizers and colonized as each engaged in representing the other and themselves to the other within what was to be viewed as one analytic field (Cohn 1980: 217–18). A key charge for historical anthropology was thus to overcome the discipline's "strange reluctance," as Talal Asad had put it, "to consider seriously the power structure within which their discipline has taken shape" (Asad 1973: 159).[1]

Heightened attention to colonialism and its consequences was not limited to anthropology and history. Cohn's emphasis on the cultural dynamics of colonial encounters suggested both the influence and the limits of Edward Said's *Orientalism*, a work that helped to initiate a discourse-centered critical postcolonial tradition and ultimately laid the basis for a novel interest in the investigation of colonial archives (Said 1978). Colonial knowledge, in Said's critique, is constructed by the colonizers who represent the colonized as the West's inferior Other, and its force is such that the colonized come to see themselves in its terms. "Culture" or "discourse" thus came to be seen as a central (if not *the* central) aspect of the domineering power apparatus of Western empires. Postcolonial criticism then emphasized the condition of colonial records as inherently power-saturated locations where knowledge and power met for the sole benefit of European colonial rule. This has sometimes led to excessive textualism, to skeptical visions of the possibility of history as a knowledge project focused on the past, and to strong critiques that deny colonial records the possibility of providing signs of the agency and voices of the colonized and the "subaltern" subjects (Spivak 1985; Chakrabarty 1992; Dirks 2015; but cf. O'Hanlon and Washbrook 1992; Young 2002). Yet in Cohn's programmatic formulations, by contrast, the colonized can use indigenous cultural resources to represent the colonizers and to reimagine themselves in a colonial world. Nevertheless, even Cohn focused his historical anthropology of colonial India on the ways in which state-authorized forms of knowledge both misrepresented and transformed Indian culture (Cohn 1987, 1996). Rather than as ways to access the past or retrieve indigenous voices, colonial documents, images, and texts were approached as discursive formations that made manifest "the categories and operations of the [colonial] state itself," as political expressions of Western desires to master the world (Dirks 2002: 58; cf. Foucault 1972: 145; Ballantyne 2001; Mathur 2000).

The Anthropology of Colonialism and the "Archival Turn"

A voluminous field of studies then prospered around the study of colonialism and its forms of knowledge in the wake of Cohn, Said, Foucault, and the postcolonial critiques. Many anthropologists shifted focus from conventional ethnohistory and "precolonial" societies to the historical study of Western colonialism's cultures as revealed in and through its archives. Anthropological field sites expanded to include the vast documentation generated by Europeans and by the knowledge-hungry machineries of the colonial state. South Asianist scholarship on the British Empire in India epitomizes this focus on colonial archives as the heart of European knowledge as power. In this vein, anthropology's historical turn equaled a critical inquiry into the politics of the archival legacies of colonialism. This orientation was championed by Nicholas B. Dirks, who had been Cohn's student. "Colonial knowledge," as Dirks asserted in a characteristically polemical statement, "both enabled conquest and was produced by it; in certain important ways, knowledge was what colonialism was all about" (Dirks 1996: xi). Dirks developed his approach along Foucauldian lines, arguing that the colonial state in India made ethnographic knowledge into one of its primary cultural technologies of rule; in British India, a "revenue state" gave way to a type of "ethnographic state" (Dirks 2002, 2001). Dirks's most detailed and extended case is the colonial engagement with caste (Dirks 2001). He argues persuasively that caste was the vehicle by which British colonial officials and ethnologists detached Indian society from history and recast it as a timeless system fundamentally different from the West. By defining caste as religious rather than political (obscuring how it straddled the European distinction) and as the paramount source of Indian social identity (rather than one mode of identification among others), colonial ethnologists constructed Indians as an essentially "spiritual" people with no rational political system of their own, dependent on

Europeans to bring them into modern history. Dirks attributes enduring consequences to the colonial construction of caste. Anticolonial
nationalists, he argues, absorbed the idea of India's essential difference into their demands for independence, while twentieth-century
scholarship continued to treat caste as what defines and differentiates
postcolonial Indian society.[2]

Yet caste "as we know it," Dirks reiterates, is not a timeless traditional reality but the product of colonial history. Dirks has forcefully
established the colonial state's investment in an "ethnographic archive" as a form of governmentality, and his case for anthropology's
complicity with colonialism merits attention. However, his position is,
in many respects, too extreme.

Dirks's critics have seen a tendency to elide colonial constructions
of caste with indigenous articulations (see Sivaramakrishnan 2005;
Dube 2004). Even orientalist knowledge and categories (including the
caste category), some scholars have argued, can also to some extent
be regarded as an indigenous product (Bayly 1999; Bayly 1996; Wagoner 2003). In subordinating the diverse and fluid meanings of caste
in Indian social life to a monolithic, supposedly determining European
vision, Dirks's theory arguably overestimates both the unity and effects of colonial knowledge forms. It is by now well-established that
"European" discourse and the archival record cannot be approached
as a homogenous whole (see Thomas 1994; Bayly 1996; Cooper and
Stoler 1997). Hans Hägerdal's contribution to this volume is a useful
reminder of this point. Although "the written materials for periods
of colonial domination [in East Timor] were frequently produced in a
Western or Western-derived context," Hägerdal notes, the European
accounts of the early days of conquest in Timor are far from homogenous. Portuguese and Dutch agents, for instance, produced strikingly
different versions of conquest events, which need to be evaluated
against one another. Colonial ethnographies are also not simply manifestations of colonial strength and state imperatives; to presume this
would be a reductionism of the variety, richness, and even contradictory nature of colonial ethnographic knowledge, as Rosa's and Viegas
and Feijó's chapters, for instance, here demonstrate.

Arguments for the internal incongruences of colonial archives
have been strongly articulated in works framed by the so-called "archival turn." In recent years the tendency to treat colonial archives
(and consequently colonialism itself) as coherent blocs has been coun-
tered by a new wave of archival ethnographies of colonialism, representing what some scholars have termed an "archival turn" (Stoler
2009; Geiger, Moore, and Savage 2010: 4; see also Ladwig et al.

2012). Ann Stoler, in particular, has argued that this new orientation implies a "move from archive-as-source to archive-as-subject" (Stoler 2009: 44). In contrast with both positivist research and postcolonial discourse analysis, ethnographies of colonial archives oppose totalizing, monolithic, and textualist approaches with an emphasis on the fragmented, ineffectual, and tensional aspects of colonialism and its forms of knowledge. Record keeping was often "thin," erratic, and episodic, and the colonial production of knowledge was marked by fluidity and complexity. Furthermore, in these approaches the archive becomes not simply a place where information is stored, fixed, and extracted but a space that has a specific history and agency. Rather than mere *objects* and depositories for historiographical retrieval, archives come to count as active *subjects* of history in their own right; "not as sites of knowledge retrieval" as Stoler writes, "but of knowledge production" (Stoler 2002: 90). "Ethnography in and of the colonial archives," Stoler adds, "attends to processes of production, relations of power in which archives are created, sequestered, and rearranged" (Stoler 2009: 32). It is to ethnographies of specific documents and records that one is called to turn attention; to ethnographies of archival fragments and tensions, and to what these fragments and tensions produce and make visible—as well as what they hide and conceal. Such ethnographies of colonial archives make manifest not simply the strength but also the anxieties, vulnerabilities, and failures of colonialism. A fine-grained engagement with records counters excessive weight given to Western knowledge as a form of domination. Rosa's and Roque's chapters in this volume provide further examples of this point. As Roque demonstrates, Portuguese imaginaries of Timorese war magic in the *Arbiru* ceremony stemmed from a sheer sense of extreme isolation and political fragility. In Rosa's chapter, the Portuguese records may reveal colonial prejudice and practices of theft and destruction of Timorese sacred objects, but the same records also allow for destabilizing readings of the colonial endeavor: for the missionary impetus to eradicate indigenous appropriations of Catholicism was also inherently "self-destructive."

Attention to the incomplete and fragmentary condition of colonial texts, words, and categorizations, their vulnerability to failure, is a crucial part of treating colonial histories across the archive and the field. By contrast, excessive emphasis on a direct connection between knowledge and domination can result in the attribution to archival materials of a kind of uncontested and absolute power that some colonizers' fantasies presumed but that actual documents and words in fact never possessed. This volume, therefore, adopts a critical but more nuanced approach to the epistemological and political potential of European-authored colonial archives. To borrow freely from Carlo Ginzburg's methodological encouragements (1999), we see documents neither as "open windows" (as in the positivist credo) nor as "walls" (as some postcolonial skeptics would have it), but as conceptually generative materials that, after careful and critical perusal, can pave the way for a variety of fresh understandings. The chapters by Traube, Viegas and Feijó, and Silva, for instance, show plentiful examples of how Portuguese colonial writings might be reread productively and put to generative use in new anthropological interpretations. In her contribution, Kelly Silva unearths a colonial ethnographic debate on the East Timorese social institution of marriage exchange (*barlake*) and acknowledges its value for her own ethnography in contemporary Dili. Viegas and Feijó similarly revisit the valuable ethnographic texts of Father Rodrigues on the king of Nári, while Elizabeth Traube, in her turn, finds in the Portuguese missionary Barros Duarte's accounts precious and unexpected elements to understand her own ethnographic encounters with Timorese stories of outsiders. In addition, the chapters included here offer abundant evidence of the inscription of Portuguese colonial archives in dynamics of violence, exploitation, and coercion—but also of the vulnerability of colonial formations themselves. They do so without losing sight of the contextual nature of power relations; without dismissing a priori the interpretive potential of Portuguese-authored records; and without withholding the possibility of reading in these same records Timorese cultural notions and forms of agency, including their complex entanglements with colonial outsiders.

The critique of colonial records, we believe, should include considerations of the active role of indigenous people and cultures in the making of both actual historical events and the written records themselves. In some cases, colonial records express entangled intercultural processes that—notwithstanding their inextricable political nature— can include both European and indigenous conceptions, agents, and social worlds. Archival records, in other words, open up rich ethnographic spaces that do not simply mirror the European mindset (Roque and Wagner 2012; see also Ladwig et al. 2012). However, to effectuate this methodological gesture requires a move *away* from colonial archives as mere demonstrations of European culture and power and a move *toward* archives as potential holders of indigenous signs. In this respect, anthropological scholarship on the Asia-Pacific region has been pursuing an approach that emphasizes the "entangled" character of colonial archives and of the historical encounters between colonizers and colonized; it provides a valuable complement to the above tenets of the so-called "archival turn."

Anthropology of Entanglements in the Asia-Pacific

In the history and anthropology of the Pacific Islands, a differently inflected approach to colonial encounters has emerged since the 1980s. Adapted to the geographical reality of what Bronwen Douglas calls an "island sea," it starts from the assumption that long histories of population movements, expansion, contacts, and exchanges had shaped the cultures that European colonizers encountered (Douglas 2015a).[3] The cultural distance in colonial encounters was far greater than in precolonial intra-island contacts, and the European colonizers became increasingly committed to transforming the local cultures; nevertheless, for islanders, colonialism was a new engagement with an outside world that had always been recognized within local cultural schemes.[4] Such engagements unfolded in various ways, conditioned by both the particular projects and the material and symbolic resources of the competing European powers who entered the region and on those of the diverse, internally divided indigenous groups. The approach is particularizing rather than totalizing, aimed at understanding colonialism as a global phenomenon through what Nicholas Thomas calls local "histories of entanglement," produced by both the colonized and the colonizers in concrete moments of encounter (Thomas 1991).

As even a cursory survey of the field is beyond the scope of this introduction, we use an argument between Nicholas Thomas and Marshall Sahlins to illustrate one of its characteristic concerns: the role of indigenous agency in colonial encounters. In a pair of articles published in 1992, Thomas set out to debunk the essentializing and dehistoricizing tendencies that were still pronounced in the anthropology of the Pacific (Thomas 1992a, 1992b). His focus was on traditional customs by which villagers collectively defined themselves in opposition to Westerners, to which ethnographers and villagers alike were prone to attribute a timeless quality. Like Dirks, Thomas argued that ethnographic phenomena of this sort have been historically shaped in colonial encounters. One of his primary examples was a Fijian custom of exchange known as *kerekere*, widely regarded as emblematic of "the Fijian way." Based on his reading of colonial archives, Thomas argued that *kerekere* only became an emblematic custom over the latter half of the nineteenth century, in the course of the establishment of indirect rule, when the British, who translated it as "begging," began to call for its abolition on the grounds that it discouraged individualism. In reaction, according to Thomas, Fijian chiefs embraced the newly objectified custom as a positive marker of collective identity, opposing their noble generosity to the selfish practices of the whites who buy and sell. On the Fijian side, this re-articulation of a preexisting practice involved a "work of imagination" in which some Fijians participated more than others (Thomas 1992b: 220).[5] Thomas saw it as an "invention of culture," not in the sense of conscious manipulation by which Hobsbawm and Ranger had differentiated "inauthentic tradition" from "true custom," but rather in Roy Wagner's sense of culture as creative process (Hobsbawm and Ranger 1983; Wagner 1975; on the contrastive notions of cultural invention, see Clifford 2013).

Sahlins, however, as the ethnographer who had supposedly overestimated the custom's longevity, took issue with Thomas's historiography and what he took to be its theoretical implications (Sahlins 1993, [1993] 2000). He faulted Thomas's time-line, using early 19th century references to *kerekere* as distinctively Fijian to argue that Fijians themselves had initiated the process of objectification prior to their contact with the Europeans. In this reading, a collective identity that revolved around reciprocity was not a product of the colonial encounter, but something brought to it by Fijians, who then further elaborated it. As Sahlins put it, this reading accords Fijians "an autonomous, positive role in their self-representation" and in the negative assessment of European habits that it evoked (Sahlins 1993: 860).

This was an argument between intellectual allies, and each took pains to acknowledge the importance of the other's contributions. Nevertheless, Sahlins charged Thomas with overestimating the impact of colonialism and underestimating indigenous agency and autonomy, and he concluded with a strong warning: "We cannot equate colonial history simply with the history of the colonizers" (Sahlins 1993: 864; [1993] 2000: 486). Thomas, who had made this very point numerous times, was understandably vexed, and he strongly denied both charges in his response (Thomas 1993, 1991; see also 1997: 29). However, he posited a difference in their respective understandings of the cultural dynamics of colonial encounters. Sahlins, he argued, had elevated to a general principle the idea that indigenous people had sufficient agency and autonomy to assimilate "external offerings and impositions" into pre-existing cultural schemes, whereas the effect or lack of effect of colonial intrusions, he asserted, must be a matter of historical inquiry. Thomas argued further that assimilation

of the new to pre-existing forms presupposed a type of situation restricted to the early stages of colonial contact, when European power
was relatively restrained by limited interests as well as by local resistance.[6] With sustained contact and the establishment of a formal colonial state, the conditions of cultural reproduction change, and a new
dynamic emerges in which external offerings are understood in something closer to the terms in which they are presented; or, as Thomas
also put it, indigenous people learn from their contact experiences,
as when they couch their own identity and resistance in terms made
available by the dominant. Sahlins, who has indeed focused on early
contact in much of his best known work, acknowledged that conditions of local cultural reproduction change "for the worse" under a
colonial state that mobilizes both coercive and persuasive techniques
of control. However, invoking Ranajit Guha's characterization of the
subaltern period in South Asia as a "dominance without hegemony,"
he portrayed the state's persuasive power as limited and emphasized
the capacity of the colonized to evade or subvert coercive restrictions
by adapting their cultural traditions (Sahlins 2000 [1993]: 491–92;
Sahlins 1993: 864; Guha 1989).

What differentiates these positions is not the relative importance
accorded to indigenous agency but the particular forms of agency
they foregrounded. Thomas's distinction between assimilation to prior
categories and what people learn from contact experiences elucidates,
for instance, the difference between incorporating Catholic icons and
practices into indigenous ritual systems (see Rosa, Traube, Viegas and
Feijó, this volume), and the indigenization or creative appropriation
of Christianity by self-avowed converts (see Hoskins 1993; Douglas
1995; Keane 2007; Bovensiepen 2016; Traube 2017). In the first
case, the foreign origins of the incorporated elements are likely to
be symbolically marked, while in the second they tend to be effaced.
Both, however, attest to a capacity for cultural inclusion characteristic
of Pacific peoples who, as Margaret Jolly has argued, are "accepting
of both indigenous and exogenous elements as constituting their culture" (Jolly 1992). A certain openness toward outsiders was implicit
in indigenous systems of rule, or "stranger king formations" as Sahlins (2012) calls them (see also Biersack 1991: 13; Douglas 1992;
Henley and Caldwell 2008), which treat the incorporation of external
authority as a principle of political life. In the Timor region, we argue
below, stranger kingship provides a critical lens for understanding
historical interactions between indigenous political systems and colonial rule.

Indigenous and European Strangers

In island Southeast Asia and throughout the Austronesian-speaking world, rulers are widely represented as descendants of outsiders whose arrival (often from overseas) and interactions with the people of the land (identified as autochthons or as earlier settlers) alter the structure of the realm (Fox 2008). There are many variations in the pattern, with regard to the origins of the strangers, the roles they assume, and the relative statuses of outsiders and insiders, which are highly contested and often fluctuate according to the positions from which the narrated events are viewed; for instance, those who claim "outside" origins may define the arrival of their ancestors as the founding event in the formation of the realm, whereas descendants of "insiders" may valorize an earlier time and state when their own ancestors presided (see Reuter 2002: 24). If, as Henley and Caldwell observe (2008: 165), the pattern can legitimize rule of actual foreigners (including, in some cases, colonial powers), it is also a charter for the representation of indigenous (or assimilated) rulers as foreign.

On Bali, for instance, the rulers of the precolonial *negara* are represented as descendants of Javanese ancestors who conquered Bali long before the Europeans arrived and established their sovereignty, embodied in such regalia as the *keris*. On the basis of largely ethnological materials, Clifford Geertz (1980) formulated his model of the nineteenth century Balinese *negara* as a "theater-state" in which royal rituals were spectacular performances of a power that rulers did not actually possess; this is illustrated in his much quoted phase, "power served pomp, not pomp power" (13). Margaret Wiener (1995) has suggested that Geertz's sharp distinction between imaging power and exercising it reproduces historically particular Dutch colonial perceptions of Balinese rulers as mere "spiritual overlords" with little actual influence. Using sources that include colonial archives, Balinese *babads*, and ethnographic interviews, the historian Henk Schulte-Nordholt (1966) has replaced Geertz's notably atemporal model with a historical account of the rise and fall of the kingdom of Mengwi. Like Wiener, he presents ritual not as an alternative to but one aspect of royal power, and he challenges Geertz's portrayal of Balinese kings: rather than remote and passive icons of the sacred, they were practical actors who actively cultivated extensive networks of personal relations with both subordinate satellites and allied rulers of other *negara*. While large-scale rituals were one way of maintaining their influence, warfare was equally important. Represented as the protectors of the *negara*, Balinese kings defended it against human enemies as well as hostile spiritual beings.

On Bali before colonial conquest, stranger king ideologies seem to have underwritten elite attitudes of condescension toward the Dutch; the *puputans* (ritual suicides) of 1906 were arguably less acknowledgments of Dutch superiority than dramatic recognitions that Balinese kings had somehow lost the support of their spiritual allies. East of Bali, in the Lesser Sundas, the early colonial period was lengthy, the level of political integration was relatively low, and the presence of mutually hostile competing colonial powers complicated the situation. Multiple arenas of interaction emerged between indigenous polities and colonial groups around trade, war, religion, and justice. In his master study of the early colonial period on Timor, Hans Hägerdal (2012a) draws on both Dutch and Portuguese archives, as well as oral histories, to explore the extent of European influences and the culturally mediated interests of local rulers in both resisting the strangers and allying with them. On the one hand, offering martial resistance to powerful foreigners indexed the power of local rulers, many of whom appear to have represented themselves as indigenous strangers. On the other hand, the colonizers were donors of regalia and titles, external signs of sovereignty that elevated the recipients, and they could be drawn into the indigenous systems as stranger kings themselves. The title of Hägerdal's book is an allusion to rulers allied with the Dutch from the 1650s until the twentieth century; they represented themselves as lords of the land who paid deference to the lords of the sea (2012a: 5).

Neither the Dutch nor the Portuguese fully understood the political relations among the indigenous polities, but from the seventeenth century there was a notion that many of them paid some form of allegiance to the rulers Sonbai in the west and the Great Lord (*Nai Boot*) of Wehali in south-central Belu. These figures are referred to as "Emperor" or "Kaiser," and their prestige was sufficiently recognized to justify a (Topass-led) Portuguese attack in 1640–41, in which the centers of both realms were burned and the rulers forcibly converted to Christianity. But if the position of these polities (whatever its nature) was weakened, their prestige endured; descendants of Sonbai continued to be a source of opposition to the Dutch, while Wehali accepted titles and other signs of recognition from both colonial powers (Fox 1982: 31). Narrative traditions recorded by anthropologists in the twentieth and twenty-first centuries attest to the enduring importance of these and other realms in local regard.[7]

While indigenous myths cannot be projected backward as historical fact, they do suggest certain enduring principles of organization that appear to have both informed and been transformed over the course of colonial history. Ethnographic research has documented a variety of stranger king traditions that tend to align in various ways with "diarchic" divisions between ritual and executive functions of rule (see Cunningham 1965; Schulte-Nordholt 1971; Therik 2004; Fox 2008; Traube 2011 and this volume; Bovensiepen 2014). Roles that Balinese kings combined are more often divided on Timor, and preeminence is in many cases attributed to ritual authority. But ritual authority on Timor has assumed distinctive forms. Balinese stranger kings claimed a great and powerful empire as their source, represented as a repository of limitless power; on Timor, various ruling houses to the west and east claim descent from male ancestors who were sent out from Wehali; or in a variant of the theme, their ancestors acquire spears from Wehali (Bovensiepen 2016). Unlike Majapahit, however, Wehali, in its own self-representations (see Therik 2004) gives away the power of rule, retaining only ritual authority; as the ultimate "navel" of the land, Wehali is the center of centers, like the royal court of a *negara*, but the center was symbolically empty; the Great Lord of Wehali was dark, immobile, and symbolically female; he was surrounded by active male executives who regulated external affairs; they were responsible for warfare and for annual delivery of harvest tribute to the center, in return for the ritually maintained fertility of the land.

Polities associated with Wehali are often represented as female centered, like their source, organized around similarly passive ritual figures whose counterparts are active, masculine executives. Such origin narratives recount a process that Fox (2008) has described as the "installation of the outsider inside," wherein indigenous strangers from Wehali arrive in a new realm; displace, or in some cases drive out, the presiding "lords of the land"; marry their daughters; and come to represent the inside. A classic expression is when Sonbai, represented as the younger brother of the Wehali executive ruler, is installed in Oenam as the immobilized "sleeping lord" (*atupas*). Further west, however, the femininity of the centers becomes less pronounced in myth and, by extension, in political life (Schulte-Nordholt 1971: 372–74). Andrew McWilliam (2002), in a meticulously detailed historical ethnography of the Atoni domain of Amanuban in the southwest of present-day West Timor, has elucidated the political process underlying the symbolism. He shows how over the nineteenth century the Nope clan ruler of Amanuban had attenuated the diarchic division within the center by combining male governance with ritual control of fertility; when one of his satellites, the head of a warrior clan, rebelled and established his own center (a common strategy in symbolically centered but weakly integrated and unstable Southeast

Asian polities), he did so as a strongly masculine ruler who combined political power with control over the cult of warfare, the masculine pole of ritual life, while delegating fertility ritual to a subordinated "lord of the land," the one whose role the Nope ruler had usurped. In Amanuban, McWilliam argues (1996: 164), leaders were able to use headhunting to consolidate political power.

R. H. Barnes (2013) detects an analogous pattern in status relations on Flores, where the ancestor of the raja of Larantuka, another stranger king who traced descent to Wehali, remained external and mobile in relation to an indigenous lord of the land over whom he claimed superiority. Barnes suggests, on the one hand, that legends about stranger kings from Timor can be taken as evidence of historical inter-island contacts that date back before the advent of the Portuguese and Dutch. On the other hand, he observes (51), "they are remarkably reminiscent of events during the period of European contact that closely affected the buildup of Black Portuguese influence on Flores and Timor." Indeed, the Topasses aggressively inserted themselves into local polities as stranger kings of a distinctive sort: light-skinned, speaking a foreign language and practicing a foreign religion, they contracted alliances with native rulers by marrying their daughters, but without giving up their superiority as active, masculine, martial leaders. E. Douglas Lewis (2010), on the basis of a careful review of the evidence for stranger-king traditions throughout the Timor area, has argued that their occurrence, along with that of the associated diarchic divisions, correlates with areas of Topass influence. According to Lewis, diarchic divisions between ritual and executive rule were not a fundamental feature of eastern Indonesian cultures; they were contingent historical effects, which developed in some societies but not in others, strongly conditioned by interactions with "real" foreigners.

Lewis's argument is suggestive, and his characterization of diarchy as a division between "religious" (or "ritual") versus "secular" rule is clearly appropriate in the case of the Topasses, who presented themselves as the temporal defenders of Christianity. Twentieth-century relations between "traditional" ritual authorities and colonially appointed native administrators might also be characterized in this way. But we would see this as a transformation of earlier indigenous schemes based in concrete idioms such as gender, space, mobility, and luminosity. In other words, the "active" (male, outer, mobile, shining, celestial) pole of indigenous Timorese polities is not well translated as "secular" (any more than is the warrior aspect of Balinese kingship), though it would seem that executive rulers were historically "secularized," to the same degree that colonial officials constructed (and largely dismissed) indigenous ritual leaders as "religious." Indigenous executives better fit with European notions of rule, and their functions (especially warfare, pre-pacification, but also justice) could be both emphasized and gradually detached from the complementary functions of ritual authorities. But if native rulers would gradually become more like European ones, the Europeans also seem to have partially modeled themselves on indigenous stranger kings. Stranger kingship, Henley and Caldwell emphasize (2008: 165–66), has a practical as well as a cultural logic, particularly evident in adjudication: because of their greater impartiality and lack of involvement in local conflicts and rivalries, strangers may make good mediators, and colonial officials frequently cultivated this potential attraction. In Sulawesi, the VOC not only institutionalized but ritualized their role as judicial arbiters (172–73; see also Henley 2004: 99–100). On Timor, Portuguese colonial officials engaged in what Roque has described as a kind of parasitic colonial mimesis: having appropriated headhunting as a military strategy (Roque 2012, 2018), they devised over the second half of the nineteenth century a colonial system of justice and a form of mimetic governmentality that incorporated indigenous elements, implicitly framing themselves as a more dignified version of indigenous executive rulers (Roque 2015).

In sum, stranger kingship, to our minds, exemplifies the complex processes of entanglement that characterize colonial encounters across different periods. In the regional context of Eastern Indonesia, it is an important analytical framework for understanding colonial histories and the effects of European imperialism, on local cultural terms. Thus, in research strategies concerned with crossing oral records and archival sources, the contingent patterns of mutual incorporation within outside-inside cultural idioms of power must be taken into account. On Timor, indigenous peoples incorporated colonial outsiders into cultural schemes, while colonial officials actively inserted themselves into indigenous systems as they understood them, becoming so entangled, as Thomas would say, that, contra Thomas, no clear line can be drawn on the indigenous side between assimilation of the foreign into preexisting schemes and understanding the foreign in the terms in which it presents itself.

Ethnographies of Historicity

Ethnographic histories use field and archival sources to construct less Eurocentric perspectives on colonial contacts as they were, and sometimes still are, experienced by indigenous people. But there are other histories. "The same event," Greg Dening contends, "is possessed in culturally different ways" (1995: 24); or, in Marshall Sahlins's phrasing, "The different cultural orders studied by anthropology have their own historicities" (1985: 53). "Why" therefore, asked postcolonial scholar and historian Dipesh Chakrabarty, "*must* one privilege the ways in which the discipline of history authorizes its knowledge? . . . It is a question asked seriously by many historians today" (italics in original; 1998: 22). Ethnographic historians challenge the equation of history with written texts by recognizing other modes of archiving the past, including oral traditions, places, artifacts, and dances (see also e.g., Rosaldo 1980; Fox 2006 [1997]; Shorter 2009). Expanding the archive in such way expands the concept of history to include diverse cultural forms, different ways of linking, or combining, past, present, and future, what Francois Hartog calls "regimes of historicity" (Hartog 2015). Consequently, the assumption that not only the ways of remembering the past but also the very notions of history and time are culturally diverse has inspired a wealth of scholarship concerned with "historicity" as an ethnographic object in its own right. "Whereas [the Western conception of] 'history' isolates the past," propose Hirsch and Stewart in a similar vein, "historicity focuses on the complex temporal nexus of past-present-future. Historicity in our formulation concerns the ongoing social production of accounts of pasts and futures" (Hirsch and Stewart 2005: 262). Pacific scholars and Amazonianists, in particular, have engaged with the rich performative realm of indigenous and vernacular historicities by which people understand and articulate their own sense of time—including events of colonial contact (see Ballard 2014; Whitehead 2003). The turn toward historicity as plural offers a valuable critique of Western notions of historiography as one culturally specific form of making past-present-futures rather than a universal mode and thus questions conventional history writing in colonial studies (see Chakrabarty 1998). "An anthropology of history," Stephan Palmié and Charles Stewart also recently suggested, "extends the exploration of how history is conceived and represented to take in non-Western societies, where ethnographic study can reveal local forms of historical production that do not conform to the canons of standard historiography" (Palmié and Stewart 2016: 208).

Several chapters in this volume explore this mode of ethnographic sensibility toward indigenous historicities of the colonial. They do so by bringing up tensions as well as juxtapositions and coexistences between and across Portuguese and Timorese forms of addressing colonial pasts. Colonial histories are not simply contained in Portu-

guese texts and archival documentation; they are continuously pro-
cessed, changed, and organized by East Timorese people, on their own
cultural terms. East Timorese forms of imagining, narrating, and
performing past, present, and future do not always conform to the
Portuguese orderings of time and events. Judith Bovensiepen's contribution on "different perspectives" on colonial warfare especially
brings this point into light: in Portuguese and Timorese records one
finds sharply contrasting notions of "destruction" and "victory" of
the kingdom of Funar in the colonial period. But relation as well as
difference can also be found. For example, in his account of the Portuguese myth of *Arbiru*, Roque similarly exposes the disjunctions between European and indigenous versions of death and victory while
also exhibiting the relational nature of such nonetheless distinct ways
of conjuring up the colonial past. Yet these chapters also make a point
of further general significance for the ethnographic study of historicity in what "colonial" processes are concerned. The study of Timorese understandings must not be divorced from an engagement
with the Portuguese written record. Indigenous perspectives need
to be complemented by or interwoven with histories from the colonizers' perspectives that elucidate not only their disciplinary projects
and condescension to the colonized but also the "anxieties of rule,"
moments of uncertainty, disorder, and elision when boundaries are
unstable (see also Dening 1996, 2004; Fabian 2000; Stoler 2009;
Roque 2012). Central to these histories is, then, the question of their
relation to the archives. On the one hand, ethnographic historians
have showed the multiple ways through which the colonial past can
be stored, arranged, and performed, beyond conventional archival
texts and Western historiographies. On the other hand, we argue, inasmuch as colonial archives remain a primary destination for field
researchers, the exploration of indigenous forms of history cannot
simply do without European documentation.

Especially in what concerns societies marked by processes of colonization, the anthropology of history requires ethnographic fieldwork
as much as it requires ethnography of the archive as site of production of colonial knowledge. The ethnography of colonial historicity, in
other words, cannot give the colonial archive away. It does not oppose
archival to vernacular, nonetheless; it does not presume the priority or
privilege of one form of historicity over another, for it does not mean to
sift "truth" from "fiction"; instead it seeks to articulate their reciprocal
dis/connections, fissures, and juxtapositions. This volume therefore
proposes that following historicities of "the colonial" in East Timor
and elsewhere requires attention to the junctures, the gaps, and the

relationships between, and within, European and indigenous cultural forms of crossing past, present, and future. From distinct standpoints, all chapters in this volume embrace this challenge.

Following Colonial Historicities

This volume brings field and archive together as part of one single analytical and methodological strategy. It points toward a form of historical anthropology that is concerned, on the one hand, with tracing colonial historicity and its varied cultural and political manifestations—as embodied in written documents, in oral narratives, in bodily practices, and in material culture, for example—and, on the other hand, with combining archival methods (the study of written documents) with field methods (the direct observation of people's "cultures" and social lives) in the creation of such descriptions. The organization of the volume also expresses our concern with identifying and proposing distinct ways of exploring this historical anthropological sensitivity. As such, the volume is organized into three parts that are representative of three methods or approaches for studying colonial historicities with and across archival and field materials. Though we present them as analytically distinct, they can obviously be variously combined in research design and practice.

Following Stories

Part I, "Following Stories," approaches the field as an archival zone saturated with storytelling, and of origin stories, in particular. On Timor, local knowledge of the past is organized in narratives that recount how the world as a whole or some contemporary social formation (such as a house group, a village, or higher-level political unit) originated and came to assume its present organization. The protagonists are not always human: rocks, trees, and cultigens, for instance, as well as sacred heirlooms of various sorts, may have origin stories that are similar in form to ancestral narratives. A common form is what James J. Fox (2006 [1997]) calls "topogeny," a recitation of an ordered sequence of place names: these provide condensed accounts of the travels of the various narrative protagonists, their winding journeys, itineraries, or paths across the land, passing through named places, some empty and others already inhabited. Inasmuch as such narrated place names may be attached to specific locations, topogeny shapes a distinctive regime of historicity wherein the past is always in a sense potentially present, inscribed in inhabited space; a topogeny, as Fox puts it, "represents a projected externalization of memories that can be lived as well as thought about" (2006 [1997]: 8). Verbal and nonverbal forms of memory are mutually implicated, as narratives of the past give significance to the lived landscape of place, and named places can evoke accounts of past events. Time and space are also interwoven within ancestral narratives, where protagonists are distinguished in terms of their temporal order of appearance, as elder/younger, autochthonous inhabitants/immigrants, or first settlers/late arrivals. Precedence in time does not always confer precedence in status in origin narratives; rather, narrative interactions between the ancestors, often involving the display of sacred heirlooms, provide models for contemporary status relations, which are spatially embodied in the layout of houses and settlements. Whether articulated in narratives or materially embodied, such constructions of the past are dynamic and contested; what is shared is not a single version of the past but an idea that knowing the past is critical to understanding the present.

Ethnographers encounter indigenous stories in various forms, ranging from formal verbal performances to informal, allusive comments about how a given title or heirloom was acquired, or about what happened in some particular setting. All these stories have complex relations with written archival documents, of tension and contradiction, as well as connection. The chapters in this section cross a variety of oral narratives with written accounts. This method unravels multiple historicities, conflicting perspectives on the past, the contemporary politics of historical narration; it does so by bringing archival and field data into contact and into dialogue, in a sort of cross-cultural analysis of distinct practices of historicity.

Elizabeth Traube focuses on two narrative traditions that were repeatedly recounted to her as part of the histories of two Mambai villages where she conducted much of her research. One is an origin story that she had been following since her first fieldwork in the early 1970s; the other is a story that had in effect been following her over this same period, despite her stubborn efforts to ignore it. The first, known as the "walk [journey] of the flag," incorporates Portuguese colonialism into an ancestral origin narrative about the acquisition of regalia of rule and the establishment of political order; the other describes what is presented as the first encounter of the indigenous people with foreign missionaries and its unfortunate aftermath involving the execution of one of the foreigners. In the chapter, Traube approaches both narrative traditions as devices for incorporating outsiders into local cultural orders. But rather than positing and foregrounding a preexisting cultural system capable of absorbing external "events," as she had done in her monograph, she emphasizes the "eventful" character of storytelling itself as a situated practice embedded in contested status relations. To this end, she endeavors to historicize both narrative traditions by crossing her ethnography with archival texts, including accounts of Portuguese colonial practices highlighted in Roque's work, accounts of missionary activities in the region over the late nineteenth century, and Portuguese missionary records of Timorese cult practices in the 1960s and 1970s.

Claudine Friedberg revisits her remarkable collection of Bunaq origin narratives to argue for the intrinsically political nature of Timorese ancestral traditions. Bunaq speaking populations occupy an area in central Timor that spans both sides of the colonially created border; Bunaq are one of several peoples on Timor who speak a non-Austronesian language, but whereas the others (Fatuluku, Makassae and Makalero) are located in a contiguous area in the east, Bunaq are surrounded by speakers of Austronesian languages. Both Friedberg and Antoinette Schapper (2011) emphasize that Bunaq see themselves (and are seen) as different from their neighbors, Kemak to the north, Mambai to the east, and Tetum to the south and west; nevertheless, their linguistic and cultural practices attest to a long history of engagement in which Bunaq have extensively borrowed and adapted Austronesian concepts and cultural forms. Indeed, their designation of their ancestral narratives as *Bei Gua*, literally "footprints" or "itineraries of the ancestors," suggests that Bunaq have adapted the topogeny, a cultural form that occurs throughout the Austronesian world.

Friedberg, who first did research between 1966 and 1973 in Bunaq regions on the Indonesian side of the border, received multiple versions of these ancestral narratives from their acknowledged guardians, "masters of the word." The itineraries she follows begin in a celestial realm, where the primordial ancestors are born and receive power tokens from their parents; the ancestors descend to earth, where they scatter across the land of Timor. According to Friedberg, many of the places they visit, including those ostensibly located on Timor, are not geographically identifiable (a contrast with Austronesian topogenies), and several of the ancestors also make trips to "other-worldly" realms overseas where they acquire wealth and wives. Friedberg cautions against trying to reconstruct historical reality from the texts, that is, reading them as simple reflections of the westward migration and expansion of Bunaq speakers out from a "core region," which Schapper locates in the northeast of their contemporary territory (Schapper 2011: 168). Rather, the texts give access to themes and principles that would have shaped and been shaped in historical interactions among Bunaq houses and between Bunaq and other ethnic groups. There is some dispute over whether non-Austronesian speakers anteceded the Austronesians on Timor (the conventional view) or arrived after them (as McWilliam has argued for Fataluku), though linguistic evidence from place-names supports the former view in the case of Bunaq, according to Schapper (2011: 182). Be that as it may, Friedberg shows how some contemporary Bunaq regard themselves as descended from mythic immigrants and assert claims to status on that basis, in effect appropriating the Austronesian mythology of the stranger king.

Ricardo Roque examines stories about a more recent past, oral and written stories concerning a Portuguese colonial officer who was killed by Timorese in 1899, to explore how Timorese cultural materials became incorporated into colonial mythologies of conquest. For the Portuguese storytellers, of course, "myth" was the discourse of the Other; their own stories constituted truthful praise of a martyred hero, an accurate chronicle of the event. Roque shows that maintaining the distinction between "myth" and "history" entailed denigrating the version of the event attributed to the Timorese while elevating the official Portuguese version and erasing the processes of its formation. In what the Portuguese recognized as the indigenous "mythic" version, Timorese adhered to "magical beliefs" in the potency of the heroic victim and were so overwhelmed by his death that they surrendered posthaste, snatching defeat out of victory; Portuguese versions of the events affirm their own "historical" character by explicitly rejecting this "popular belief" in magical agency while selectively and partially incorporating elements from Timorese oral traditions, including the poetics of place so central to indigenous discourse on the past. The making of "the *Arbiru*" (a name supposedly attributed to Duarte by Timorese, from a Tetum term connoting power and disorder) was an intercultural process in which Portuguese poached on local stories and ritual practices. The site where the officer was said to have died was commemorated in an official ceremony created over half a century after the event, in the wake of an abortive 1959 uprising against the colonial state. Grounded in oral stories that had been circulating for decades within the Portuguese community, the ceremony projected a mythic story of colonial supremacy and Timorese loyalty into an uncertain political present.

Methodologically, Roque crosses archival records of Duarte's death with memories and oral history that he collected from former colonial officers in Lisbon. He subsequently followed the story in post-independence Timor-Leste, where he met with Timorese descendants of some of the protagonists. These conversations, supported by findings of other ethnographers, make clear that the mythmaking process was never controlled by the Portuguese; its ritualization notwithstanding, the colonial "myth of conquest" did not prevent Timorese from understanding Duarte's death in other terms, for instance, by incorporating it into a narrative of resistance to foreign rule.

Contrasting accounts of the past also figure in Judith Bovensiepen's chapter, which focuses on the village of Funar in the mountains of central Timor. According to Portuguese sources, Funar was the object of at least one and possibly two colonial campaigns mounted by Governor Celestino da Silva, who launched and presided over the "pacification" of the interior in the late nineteenth century. Although Celestino himself seems to have left relatively scant correspondence regarding Funar, there is one surviving reference to an attack on it as motivated by the rebellious and generally unruly nature of its inhabitants. But one of his strongest critics, an ardent Republican who wrote under the pen name of "Zola," depicted the charge of rebellion as a mere pretext. According to Zola, Celestino had attacked Funar for personal profit, and the village had been utterly destroyed in the ensuing campaigns. Bovensiepen, who conducted fieldwork in post-independence Funar, is less concerned with the disparity between the two archival accounts than with the way both were contradicted by stories told to her in Funar, which made no mention of either a local rebellion or colonial persecution. Whereas Roque encountered Kemak Timorese who proudly associated themselves with an ancestral tradition of resistance, Bovensiepen received accounts broadly reminiscent of what Traube had found among neighboring Mambai, insofar as many people in Funar represented the Portuguese colonial period as a time of relative peace in which Funar had benefited politically, a situation usually associated with "loyal allies" rather than unruly rebels.

Bovensiepen's strategy is to treat both Portuguese and Timorese accounts as hybrids of what are conventionally distinguished in Western culture as "myth" and "history." Thus, while Zola's melodramatic account of a clash between a corrupt colonial regime and innocent Timorese reflected and reinforced antimonarchical Republican mythmaking, the story may nevertheless preserve traces of events that have been suppressed in Funar oral traditions. Those traditions, moreover, are no more homogeneous than the written accounts. The first story that Bovensiepen was told about Funar's amicable interactions with the Portuguese colonial state legitimized the authority of the current ruling house; but one day, a certain place she happened to pass by prompted her companion to refer to a story that seemed to contradict much of what she had been told by local elites. Once alerted to the variation, Bovensiepen went on to elicit a counternarrative to the official version of Funar's historical relations with the colonial state. Triangulating Zola's written account of Funar's destruction with the divergent local narratives, Bovensiepen is able to relate competing accounts of the past to an enduring conflict over the distribution of rule that was exacerbated by colonial policies of indirect rule.

Following Objects

Part II, "Following Objects," represents a specific modality of our "following stories" approach that grants methodological priority to material culture or the natural environment as materializations of different forms of historicity of colonial encounters. Here the focus is less on the way verbalized stories emerge, circulate, and change than on the ways through which "ancient" things and landscape become mediators between past and present, embodiments of certain narratives and conceptions of time. It focuses on objects and features of the landscape—such as scepters, flags, or houses, but also trees, rocks, or cultivated plants—that embody conceptions of time and are endowed with certain agencies for articulating the past, present, and future. Just as the field is saturated with storytelling, it is also saturated with a material world of things that condense and precipitate stories—a material world that, in some instances, can itself constitute a form of storytelling, in its own right. In the context of East Timorese cultures and their encounters with the Portuguese colonizers, ancestral objects and sacred heritage, frequently endowed with spiritual qualities and potent agencies, are especially good to think about the performance of colonial historicity in this manner. Many of these material objects can be approached as intercultural products, as kinds of entangled objects (Thomas 1991). A wealth of things that the East Timorese were to understand as powerful autochthonous materials in their origin stories, such as flags and drums, for example, were Portuguese in origin.

In his chapter, Frederico Delgado Rosa follows the Portuguese missionaries' violent clash with the Timorese appropriations of Catholic objects as *lulik* materials in the 1930s–50s. By revisiting the archive of early twentieth-century missionary ethnographies, Rosa explores the Catholic priests' obsessive rejection of religious syncretism, while aiming at the "historical reconstruction" of an untouched "precolonial" native religion. Central to these imageries of radical alterity was the pejorative vision of Timorese religion as immoral, savage and virtually orgiastic, a vision of which the ultimate embodiment, in the missionary view, was the Timorese cult of *lulik* objects. Accordingly, in contrast with the then-current theories of Catholic missiology, missionary authorities in Portuguese Timor (notably Father Abílio Fernandes) followed an inquisitorial practice of abduction and "systematic destruction of some of the most tangible elements of the 'Timorese religion,'" including setting *lulik* houses and objects on fire. Timorese converts were forced to hand over their precious *lulik* items, sacred heirlooms that constituted important connections to ancestry and spirituality. Yet, as Rosa demonstrates, such acts amounted as well to a gesture of "self-destruction." For among the *lulik* objects stored in the burned houses were such things as images of Catholic saints and statues of the Virgin that at some point in the past had been integrated into the communities' sacred heritage. Although missionaries saw the treatment of such objects as a horrifying "degeneration" of Catholicism in native hands, their presence is in fact indicative of complex forms of religious syncretism. A prime example of such complexity, Rosa argues, was the Timorese cult of Saint Anthony in Manatuto, known as "Amo Deus Coronel Santo António." An ancient figure of this saint had been transformed into a *lulik* possession that was customarily revered by the Manatuto *moradores*, indigenous companies of auxiliary soldiers who served the colonial government in the event of war. Father Ezequiel Pascoal in the 1930s studied this cult in a series of rich ethnographic vignettes. In contrast to Fernandes's destructive approach to *lulik*, however, Pascoal claimed such indigenous appropriation of the saint constituted a victory of Portuguese colonization, and as such the Manatuto cult was not persecuted. The underlying theme of these approaches to religious materiality, however, was the systematic denial of any sort of blending between Catholicism and Timorese conceptions: "The problem of the centuries-old interaction between 'Timorese religion' and Christianity was resolved," Rosa concludes, "through its negation."

Combining their own field ethnography with a reanalysis of the works of a distinct group of missionaries—the Salesians among the Fataluku in the 1940s–50s—Viegas and Feijó offer a complementary counterpoint to Rosa's reflections on the tensional religious exchanges in colonial Timor-Leste. The authors start from their field observations of a recurrent presence of both Fataluku ritual funerary posts and Christian crosses in indigenous mortuary practices and cemeteries. Viegas and Feijó then trace the origins of this form of "parallel coexistence" back to the negotiated nature of the historical encounters between Salesian missionaries and the Fataluku after World War II. In this remote eastern region, the Catholic missionaries were latecomers, and the relationship they ended up establishing with local communities was characterized by "ambivalence and tension" but also, above all, by "negotiations" and mutual concessions. The authors concentrate on the fascinating case of Father Rodrigues's published studies on the king of Nári in the late 1940s. In this work, they argue, one can find a form of colonial ethnographic encounter marked by conversation, in which a mode of cohabitation between Catholicism and Fataluku religiosity was encouraged rather than denied. Although instances of burning and destruction of *helura* (equivalent to *lulik*) objects also occurred in the region, the authors suggest indigenous cooperation could be involved, such that destruction of *helura* "may have constituted a rite of separation, resolving dubious situations regarding the true owner of the objects." Through following crosses and funerary posts across archival records and field encounters, Viegas and Feijó finally put forward an interpretive hypothesis about "structures of coexistence" between different (rather than syncretic) religious formations in Timor-Leste: "The post and the cross can be seen as an index to that structure, where world-views are partially integrated but also kept side by side on parallel."

The colonial engagements with Timorese *lulik* material culture is the theme of Roque and Sousa's chapter, centered on an enigmatic Timorese display of *lulik* heritage in the context of interactions between Portuguese colonial anthropologist António de Almeida and the ritual keepers of the house of Afaloicai that took place in Baguia in 1957. In particular, the authors consider the complex texture of entangled meanings concerning the *lulik* stones that the Timorese keepers brought to Almeida's attention in that encounter. By moving between fieldwork in Baguia and the analysis of Almeida's records and publications, Roque and Sousa revisit that field encounter to address the dissonances between the interpretation of the stones as prehistoric evidence by the anthropologist in the 1950s and the local cultural understandings of these materials as potent ritual objects and signs of power. In 1960, a few years after his return from Timor, António de Almeida published a scientific article reporting on his discovery of certain archaeological evidence of prehistoric cultures in "Portuguese Timor": a set of so-called "Neolithic stones" from the village of Afaloicai. In the article, Almeida described in some detail the encounter that led to his examining and photographing of the stones, and he gave details of the names and ritual status of their Timorese keepers. The authors thus reconsider the entangled meanings of this historical encounter, both in the light of Almeida's scientific interests in archaeology and the convoluted local political struggles of the late 1950s in "Portuguese Timor." While the anthropologist's peculiar fixation with the stone objects (in detriment of other ancient sacred objects displayed, such as Portuguese flags) can be regarded as an instantiation of his theories of an untouched East Timorese prehistoric racial past, the ritual keepers' presentation of the stones, by contrast, possibly made manifest an autonomous claim of the Afaloicai to ritual and political power. The authors finally reconsider Almeida's encounter in relation to contemporary field materials and ask what sort of histories about the past the Afaloicai stones (or else their surviving photographic representations) may still mediate and elicit in the present.

Following Cultures

Part III, "Following Cultures through Archives," represents approaches that treat the archive as a field site, or else as an important extension of ethnographic fieldwork inquiries, that can give access to indigenous sociocultural life in colonial exchanges. It starts from the assumption that traces of European cultural conceptions as well as traces of indigenous cultures populate colonial written records (cf. Douglas 2015b). Here archival records become locations in which signs of indigenous agency can be unearthed, indigenous cultural concepts and social institutions can be read, and where they can be traced in connection with their relative embroilment with European conceptions and colonizing preoccupations. "Following Cultures" thus involves a consideration of both European and indigenous understandings and their intercultural dynamics and power inequalities as they appear in written records. This approach also elucidates the diversity of cultural meanings of recorded events, with emphasis on the plurality of perspectives, and on how entanglements are experienced by the people involved. This implies attention to differences within each subject category of colonizers and colonized. "European" written accounts and understandings, for instance, were often multivocal and thus—just like indigenous recollections—should be considered as situated, partial perspectives that cannot be reduced to any single and homogeneous vision. This approach brings to light certain methodological challenges, including how to articulate different, and sometimes contradictory, accounts and subject positions *within* European written records; how to use archival registers in anthropological analysis of indigenous cultures; and how to connect polyphonic archival registers to indigenous forms of telling the past.

The first chapter in this section addresses this latter point by proposing an approach to the study of Timorese historicity that implies crossing archival records from different European languages and subject positions. The question of "how to formulate a Timorese history of Timor," asks historian Hans Hägerdal, must consider the contribution of early modern Western-authored accounts, in which "indigenous voices" can also often be found. However, a Timor-centered historiography should also not be reduced to European accounts. In the case of Timor-Leste, a full answer to that question, the author proposes, resides in a work of "triangulation of source materials": triangulation between Portuguese and Dutch written documents; between these and the East Timorese oral record (as this can be retrieved from ritual keepers, such as the *lian na'in*); or still between the latter and the findings of archaeology and linguistics. Thus countering a tradition of mutual ignorance between Portuguese and Dutch historiographies, the author reveals the traps of reconstructing East Timorese history with either Portuguese or Dutch records alone, arguing for the advantages of crossing Portuguese and Dutch written sources. To this purpose, Hägerdal reflects critically on the virtues and limitations of early modern records concerning the "conquest phase" of Timor in the seventeenth century. He finds striking contrasts in the themes and events of conquest that were selected and put on written record by Portuguese and Dutch authors respectively—a disjunction that must take into account the distinct political and commercial interests of the two European powers at the time. "Events of obvious importance in one archive," Hägerdal observes, "are passed over in silence in the other. In order to appreciate them we must read the texts along the grain, elucidating their role in the early colonial milieus of maritime Asia." And yet crossing written sources is not enough, even for the early modern period of Timor-Leste. Hence Hägerdal argues that the historian may also find valuable materials in the accumulated wealth of oral "genealogical history" that survives within Timorese lineages and houses, sometimes referencing events as far back as three hundred years. Not only can such oral stories register encounters with Europeans, they can also, again, lead to subversive shifts of historiographical emphasis on the protagonists of the conquest phase. Historians may be led to write different histories of conquest. What, one may ask, would histories of early modern colonial conquest of Timor look like if henceforth the Makassarese, rather than the Europeans, appear as central characters; or if the Topasses, the so-called "Black Portuguese," rather than the invading white foreigners, are described as the driving force of processes of conquest and claims for governance in that historical period?

A concern with the Portuguese colonial archive's potential for both enriching and being enriched by contemporary ethnographic research traverses McWilliam and Shepherd's contribution. Andrew McWilliam and Chris Shepherd's ethnographic work has sought to understand social change, with emphasis on how rural livelihoods were disrupted by war, by Indonesian occupation, and by the United Nations and the establishment of an independent state government. In contrast with the early wave of foreign anthropologists, who lacked systematic engagement with Portuguese records and history in general, McWilliam and Shepherd undertake their ethnographic projects while conscious of the need to articulate contemporary questions with past events. In their case, the Portuguese colonial government's efforts to establish a state-based agriculture and plantation system in Timor in the twentieth century becomes a significant benchmark for understanding current issues. The chapter thus offers an insightful reading of the Portuguese colonial plantation archive during and after the important Republican period, 1910–26. Even if they tend to efface Timorese voices, the colonial records can be read against the grain, to reveal traces of colonial land exploitation and labor coercion as well as signs of indigenous agency. "Reading against the grain not only leads to an appreciation of Timorese agency," they argue, "but also to one of the colonial propensity for dissembling and hubris." Timorese agency, the authors further argue, can include not just resistance but also an effective engagement with colonial projects, as in the dramatic cases of destruction and clearing of *lulik* lands for the purpose of establishing coffee plantations. Portuguese records allow an understanding of a colonial culture of power invested in the control, appropriation and transformation of Timorese traditional management of land and natural resources. In addition, they contain a relevant interpretive potential for field studies on sociocultural "change" in Timor-Leste today. Accordingly, McWilliam and Shepherd argue for the pressing need to engage in "historicized ethnographic inquiry" in a kind of "retrospective ethnography of plantation practice," in which both colonial records and living cultural memories play a productive analytical role. In this sense the colonial archive becomes not simply a source for extracting data but also an agent that shapes the very nature of field research.

From a distinct anthropological angle, David Hicks's contribution addresses the issue of how to integrate fragmentary colonial records-as-sources in original research inquiries concerned with the analysis of Timorese social institutions. Here the focus is on field-based ethnography rather than archive-grounded historiography. In a retrospective and autobiographical essay (an effort at self-historicizing one's ethnographic work in its own right), Hicks reconsiders both his neglect and his use of Portuguese administrative records, census data, and even origin legends collected by Portuguese officers as sources of ethnographic "information" during his different fieldwork stays in Timor-Leste, since 1966. In the 1960s, under the influence of Rodney Needham and structural analysis, Hicks was involved in a kind of social anthropology in which history and the use of colonial documentation were minor and secondary to concerns with the social study of "authentic" indigenous institutions—such as, notably, marriage exchange, *barlake*. Hicks also reveals that in his case—notwithstanding the way that actual analysis ended up masking colonial "sources"—the information networks of Portuguese colonial administration did play a significant role in fieldwork practice. In 1966, Hicks collected and used Portuguese census data extensively (even working as a census officer himself); he also realized that, in some cases, Portuguese administrators and missionaries themselves had already produced an array of ethnographic data in the form of accounts of Timorese legends and origin stories. Although he considered this data too "fragmentary," it was his contact with a local colonial archive that prompted his interest in collecting Tetum myths. Upon his return to the field in 1999, the author resumed and reinforced the use of administrative documentation as method to understand differences between population distributions in the Portuguese period and later on, in the 2000s. Anglophone and Francophone ethnographies from the 1960s tended to simply overlook Portuguese colonial texts or else leave them in the shadow. Hicks's recollection, however, provides an example of the hidden importance of firsthand crossings between social anthropology and the Portuguese colonial ethnographic archive as a "source" for the study of Timorese social life.

Kelly Silva's chapter directs our attention to another way of engaging retrospectively with the potential of the colonial ethnographic record. In the chapter that closes this collection, Silva unearths a controversy from the late years of the Portuguese colonial period— the so-called "*barlake* war" (guerra do barlaque)—concerning the meaning of "traditional" marriage practices, and shows that this dispute informed East Timorese nationalism and continues to influence present-day understandings of marriage alliances. Silva's retrospective examination of the colonial archives was triggered primarily by her own ethnography on *barlake* in contemporary Dili, during which the "*barlake* war" was evoked as a foundational moment in local East Timorese intellectual history. Thus, following *barlake* as a distinctive cultural trait in Timorese self-perceptions of "tradition" led to an investigation of a colonial controversy preserved in the Portuguese written records. In the 1970s, a public debate on the relative value, meaning, and moral significance of *barlake* in Timorese culture occupied the pages of the main newspapers in "Portuguese Timor." Several Portuguese colonial officials and missionaries devalued *barlake* as no more than a commodity transaction, while a group of Catholic-educated East Timorese intellectuals—among whom were soon-to-be prominent pro-independence political leaders and resistance fighters—highlighted its social and ritual meanings and praised its positive value as an essential Timorese "traditional" institution. Although addressing a theme (marriage exchange) that was critical to foreign ethnography in Timor and elsewhere, this debate was grounded mostly on Portuguese colonial knowledge and as such developed parallel (and largely unconnected) to contemporary developments in European social anthropology. Yet the debate also reveals the vibrancy of local colonial intellectual circles and the political centrality that "nativist" concerns with establishing cultural authenticity, identity, and "tradition" around emblematic practices (such as *barlake*) played in the early phase of Timorese nationalism. The *barlake* war, Silva contends, stimulated nationalist feelings and encouraged some indigenous intellectuals to do "research on Timorese traditional forms," as opposed to their involvement with Portuguese culture and education.

Coda: The Past in the Present

Suddenly they spoke at the same time about stories ancient and different. They only coincided when they spoke about the Manufahi war. . . . It was as if they wanted to become reconciled again concerning the war that had put a definitive end to the wars of pacification. . . . As if they were resurrected beings from the past.
— Luís Cardoso, *Crónica de uma Travessia. A Época do Ai-Dik-Funam* [*The Crossing: A Story of East Timor*], 1997, our translation.

This volume calls attention to how colonial historicity can be followed in research practice and how it can be turned into a field and archival object of history and ethnography simultaneously. In East Timor—as well as in many other places strongly marked by histories of colonization—colonial history can be instantiated in documentation and in vernacular materials, in written as well as in oral, bodily, and performative practices. The "colonial past" can be read in distinct materials and heard in a variety of cultural idioms; it can belong simultaneously to distinct and yet coexistent, partially juxtaposed forms of historicity. Our epigraph, from East Timorese writer Luís Cardoso's 1997 autobiographical novel *The Crossing*, is inspiring and evocative of this point—and it provides an eloquent close to our introduction. The novel, originally written in Portuguese, is justly celebrated for its elegant rendering of the tensional intersections between Timorese historicities and chronological orderings of time (Moutinho 2012: 103–7). Cardoso recalls above how his late father blended rumor and fact, imagination and events, in accounts of colonial pasts. His disruption of linear chronology makes visible wider East Timorese practices of folding together past and present. In his recollections, more or less remote colonial events are made to bear upon the present as if they were one and same condensed moment: the Manufahi rebellion of 1911–13, the Japanese occupation of 1942–44, resistance fighting in 1970s, and, in the end, the very moment of storytelling. And yet even among Cardoso's East Timorese interlocutors—let alone between them and the Portuguese intruders—the potential for dissonance in conversation about "old and different stories" is high. Such is the fascinating world of proliferated historicities in which the chapters in this volume dwell. We hope the stories they tell will inspire other researchers to make new crossings between histories and ethnographies.

Ricardo Roque is research fellow at the Institute of Social Sciences of the University of Lisbon (Instituto de Ciências Sociais da Universidade de Lisboa) and currently an honorary associate in the Department of History of the University of Sydney. He works on the history and anthropology of human sciences, colonialism, and cross-cultural contact in the Portuguese-speaking world. He has published extensively on the colonial history of Timor-Leste. Current research interests include the comparative history of twentieth-century racial sciences and the theory and ethnography of colonial archives and biological collections. He is the author of *Headhunting and Colonialism* (2010), and coeditor (with K. Wagner) of *Engaging Colonial Knowledge* (2012) and (with W. Anderson and R. Ventura Santos) of *Luso-tropicalism and Its Discontents* (2019).

Elizabeth G. Traube is professor of anthropology at Wesleyan University (USA). She began her research with Mambai-speaking people of Aileu when Timor-Leste was still under Portuguese rule and has returned to Aileu several times since renewing her research there in 2000. She is the author of *Cosmology and Social Life: Ritual Exchange among the Mambai of East Timor* (1986) and coeditor (with Andrew McWilliam) of *Land and Life in Timor-Leste: Ethnographic Essays* (2011). Recent publications have focused on Mambai perspectives on the legacy of resistance and the independence struggle.

Notes

1. Ortner was somewhat dismissive of the 1970s critiques of the link between anthropology and colonialism; she included domestic social movements (the counterculture, the antiwar movement, the women's movement) among the "real-world events" that had unsettled the discipline but made no mention of anticolonial nationalist movements that proliferated over the same period (1984:138).
2. Louis Dumont's theory of caste as exemplifying a non-Western orientation toward hierarchy is a focus of Dirks's critique (2001, 1987); on the orientalizing aspect of Dumont's sociology, see also Peter van der Veer (1993).
3. Bronwen Douglas includes Island Southeast Asia within a broad definition of the Pacific Islands (or "Oceania").
4. The Pacific provides a particularly vivid case of Eric Wolf's argument (Wolf 1982) that ethnographic models of bounded, separate systems did not adequately depict the situation before European expansion, let alone the global system of links that expansion would create.
5. One of his main arguments in that article is that objectification makes it possible for traditions to be rejected by modernist Fijians.
6. Thomas has reiterated this argument numerous times (see Thomas 1996: 112–13; 1997: 37–38).
7. A significant but still underresearched case concerns the realm of Luca to the east of Belu. Combining oral and archival records, Barnes, Hägerdal and Palmer (2017) recently called attention to the lasting significance of claims to political and ritual centrality over eastern Timor (perhaps even the whole island) by the ruling lineages of Luca (see also Roque and Sousa, this volume).

References

Andaya, L. Y. 2010. "The 'Informal Portuguese Empire' and the Topasses in the Solor Archipelago in the Seventeenth and Eighteenth Centuries." *Journal of Southeast Asian Studies* 41(3): 391–420.

Asad, T. 1973. *Anthropology and the Colonial Encounter*. New York: Humanities Press.

Axel, Brian Keith. 2002. "Introduction: Historical Anthropology and Its Vicissitudes." In *From the Margins: Historical Anthropology and Its Futures*, edited by B. K. Axel, 1–45. Durham, NC: Duke University Press.

Ballantyne, T. 2001. "Archive, State, Discipline: Power and Knowledge in South Asian Historiography." *New Zealand Journal of Asian Studies* 3(1): 87–105.

Ballard, C. 2014. "Oceanic Historicities." *The Contemporary Pacific* 26(1): 96–124.

Barnes, R. H. 2013. "The Power of Strangers in Flores and Timor." In *Excursions into Eastern Indonesia: Essays on History and Social Anthropology*, monograph 63, 38–52. New Haven, CT: Yale University Southeast Asia Studies.

Barnes, S., H. Hägerdal, and L. Palmer. 2017. "An East Timorese Domain: Luca from Central and Peripheral Perspectives." *Bijdragen Tot de Taal-, Land- en Volkenkunde* 173: 325–55.

Bayly, C. A. 1996. *Empire and Information: Intelligence-Gathering and Social Communication in India, 1780–1870*. Cambridge: Cambridge University Press.

Bayly, S. 1999. *Caste, Society and Politics in India from the Eighteenth Century to the Modern Age*. Cambridge: Cambridge University Press.

Biersack, A. 1991. "Introduction: History and Theory in Anthropology." In *Clio in Oceania*, edited by A. Biersack, 1–36. Washington, DC: Smithsonian Institution Press.

Bovensiepen, J. 2014. "Installing the Insider 'Outside': House Reconstruction and the Transformation of Binary Ideologies in Independent Timor-Leste." *American Ethnologist* 41(2): 290–304.

———. 2016. *Land of Gold: Post-Conflict Recovery and Cultural Revival in Independent East Timor*. Southeast Asia Program Publications, Ithaca: Cornell University Press.

Boxer, C. R. 1947. *The Topasses of Timor*. Amsterdam: Koninklijke Vereeniging Indisch Instituut.

Brettell, C. B. 1998. "Fieldwork in the Archives: Methods and Sources in Historical Anthropology." In *Handbook of Methods in Cultural Anthropology*, edited by H. R. Bernard, 513–46. Walnut Creek, CA: Altamira Press.

———. 2015. *Anthropological Conversations: Talking Culture across Disciplines*. London: Rowman & Littlefield.

Castelo, C. 2017. "Ruy Cinatti, the French-Portuguese Mission and the Construct of East Timor as an Ethnographic Site." *History and Anthropology*, 1–23.

Chakrabarty, D. 1992. "Postcoloniality and the Artifice of History: Who Speaks for 'Indian' Pasts?" *Representations* 37: 1–26.

———. 1998. "Minority Histories, Subaltern Pasts." *Postcolonial Studies* 1(1): 15–29.

Clifford, J. 2013. "Indigenous Articulations." In *Returns: Becoming Indigenous in the Twenty-First Century*, 50–67. Cambridge, MA: Harvard University Press.

Cohn, B. S. 1980. "History and Anthropology: The State of Play." *Comparative Studies in Society and History* 22(2): 198–221.

———. 1987. "The Census, Social Structure, and Objectification in South Asia." *An Anthropologist among the Historians and Other Essays*, 224–54. Delhi: Oxford University Press.

———. 1996. *Colonialism and Its Forms of Knowledge: The British in India*. Princeton, NJ: Princeton University Press.

Cooper, F., and A. L. Stoler (eds.). 1997. *Tensions of Empire: Colonial Cultures in a Bourgeois World*. Berkeley: University of California Press.

Cunningham, C. E. 1965. "Order and Change in an Atoni Diarchy." *Southwestern Journal of Anthropology* 21(4): 359–82.

Dening, G. 1995. *The Death of William Gooch: A History's Anthropology*. Carlton South: Melbourne University Press.

———. 1996. *Performances*. Chicago: University of Chicago Press.

———. 2004. *Beach Crossings: Voyaging across Times, Cultures, and Self*. Philadelphia: University of Pennsylvania Press.

Dirks, N. B. 1987. *The Hollow Crown: Ethnohistory of an Indian Kingdom*. Cambridge: Cambridge University Press.

———. 1996. "Foreword." In B. S. Cohn, *Colonialism and Its Forms of Knowledge: The British in India*, ix–xvii. Princeton, NJ: Princeton University Press.

———. 2001. *Castes of Mind: Colonialism and the Making of Modern India*. Princeton, NJ: Princeton University Press.

———. 2002. "Annals of the Archive: Ethnographic Notes on the Sources of History." In *From the Margins: Historical Anthropology and Its Future*, edited by B. K. Axel, 47–65. Durham, NC: Duke University Press.

———. 2015. *Autobiography of an Archive: A Scholar's Passage to India*. New York: Columbia University Press.

Douglas, B. 1992. "Doing Ethnographic History: The Case of Fighting in New Caledonia." In *History and Tradition in Melanesian Ethnography*, edited by J. Carrier, 86–115. Berkeley: University of California Press.

———. 1995. "Power, Discourse and Appropriation of God: Christianity and Subversion in a Melanesian Context." *History and Anthropology* 9(1): 57–92.

———. 2015a. "Pasts, Presents and Possibilities of Pacific History and Pacific Studies: As Seen by a Historian from Canberra." *Journal of Pacific History* 50(2): 224–28.

———. 2015b. "Agency, Affect, and Local Knowledge in the Exploration of Oceania." In *Indigenous Intermediaries: New Perspectives on Exploration Archives*, edited by S. Konishi, M. Nugent and T. Shellam, 103–29. Canberra: ANU Press.

Dube, S. 2004. "Colonial Casts." *Economic and Political Weekly* 39(18): 1800–1801.

———. 2007. "Introduction: Anthropology, History, Historical Anthropology." In *Historical Anthropology*, edited by S. Dube, 1–73. Delhi: Oxford University Press.

Evans-Pritchard, E. E. 1950. "Social Anthropology: Past and Present; The Marett Lecture, 1950." *Man* 50: 118–24.

Fabian, J. 1983. *Time and the Other: How Anthropology Makes Its Object*. New York: Columbia University Press.

———. 2000. *Out of Our Minds: Reason and Madness in the Exploration of Central Africa*. Berkeley: University of California Press.

Faubion, J. D. 1993. "History in Anthropology." *Annual Review of Anthropology* 22: 35–54.

Figueiredo, F. 2011. *Timor: A Presença Portuguesa (1769–1945)*. Lisboa: Centro de Estudos Históricos/Universidade Nova de Lisboa.

Foucault, M. 1972. *The Archaeology of Knowledge*. New York: Pantheon Books.

Fox, J. J. 1971. "A Rotinese Dynastic Genealogy: Structure and Event." In *The Translation of Culture: Essays to E. E. Evans-Pritchard*, edited by T. O. Beidelman, 37–77. London: Tavistock.

———. 1977. *Harvest of the Palm: Ecological Change in Eastern Indonesia*. Cambridge, MA: Harvard University Press.

———. 1982. "The Great Lord Rests at the Centre: The Paradox of Powerlessness in European-Timor Relations." *Canberra Anthropology* 5(2): 22–33.

———. 1995. "Installing the 'Outsider' Inside: The Exploration of an Epistemic Austronesian Cultural Theme and Its Social Significance." *Indonesia and the Malay World* 36(105): 201–18.

———. 2006 [1997]. "Place and Landscape in Comparative Austronesian Perspective." In *The Poetic Power of Place: Comparative Perspectives on Austronesian Ideas of Locality*, edited by J. J. Fox, 1–21. Canberra: ANU Press.

Geertz, C. 1980. *Negara: The Theater State in Nineteenth Century Bali*. Princeton, NJ: Princeton University Press.

Geiger, T., N. Moore, and M. Savage. 2010. "The Archive in Question." CRESC Working Paper no. 81, 23. www.cresc.ac.uk/medialibrary/workingpapers/wp81.pdf

Ginzburg, C. 1999. *History, Rhetoric and Proof*. Hanover and London: University Press of New England.

Gracy, K. F. 2004. "Documenting Communities of Practice: Making the Case for Archival Ethnography." *Archival Science* 4: 335–65.

Guha, R. 1989. "Dominance without Hegemony and Its Historiography." In *Subaltern Studies*, edited by R. Guha, 210–309. Oxford: Oxford University Press.

Gunn, G. 1999. *Timor: 500 Years*. Lisboa: Livros do Oriente.

———. 2007. "The State of East Timor Studies after 1999." *Journal of Contemporary Asia* 37(1): 95–114.

Gunter, J. 2008. "Communal Conflict in Viqueque and the 'Charged' History of '59." *Asia Pacific Journal of Anthropology* 8(1): 27–41.

———. 2010. "Kabita-Kakurai, de cada dia: Indigenous Hierarchies and the Portuguese in Timor." *Portuguese Literary and Cultural Studies* 17/18: 281–301.

Hammersley, M., and P. Atkinson. 1995. "Documents." In *Ethnography: Principles in Practice*, edited by M. Hammersley and P. Atkinson, 157–74. London: Routledge.

Hartog, F. 2015. *Regimes of Historicity: Presentism and Experiences of Time.* New York: Columbia University Press.

Henley, D. 2004. "Conflict, Justice and the Stranger King: Indigenous Roots of Colonial Rule in Indonesia and Elsewhere." *Modern Asian Studies* 38(1): 85–144.

Henley, D., and I. Caldwell. 2008. "Kings and Covenants: Stranger Kings and Social Contract in Sulawesi." *Indonesia and the Malay World* 36(105): 269–91.

Hirsch, E., and C. Stewart. 2005. "Introduction: Ethnographies of Historicity." *History and Anthropology* 16(3): 261–274.

Hobsbawm, E., and T. Ranger (eds.). 1983. *The Invention of Tradition.* Cambridge: Cambridge University Press.

Hoskins, J. 1993. *The Play of Time: Kodi Perspectives on Calendars, History, and Exchange.* Berkeley: University of California Press.

Hägerdal, H. 2007. "Colonial or Indigenous Rulers? The Black Portuguese of Timor in the 17th and 18th Centuries." *IIAS Newsletter* 44(26).

———. 2012a. *Lords of the Land, Lords of the Sea: Conflict and Adaptation in Early Colonial Timor.* Leiden: KITLV.

———. 2012b. "The Colonial Official as Ethnographer: VOC Documents as Resources for Social History in Eastern Indonesia." *Wacana, Journal of the Humanities of Indonesia* 14: 405–28.

———. 2015. "Eastern Indonesia and the Writing of History." *Archipel* 90: 75–98.

———. 2017. "Timor and Colonial Conquest: Voices and Claims about the End of the Sonba'i Realm in 1906." *Itinerario* 41: 581–605.

Jolly, M. 1992. "Specters of Inauthenticity." *Contemporary Pacific* 4(1): 49–72.

Kammen, D. 2016. *Three Centuries of Conflict in East Timor.* Singapore: NUS Press.

Keane, W. 2007. *Christian Moderns: Freedom and Fetish in the Mission Encounter.* Berkeley: University of California Press.

Ladwig, P., R. Roque, O. Tappe, C. Kohl, and C. Bastos. 2012. "Fieldwork between Folders: Fragments, Traces and the Ruins of Colonial Archives." Max Planck Institute for Social Anthropology Working Paper no. 141, http://www.eth.mpg.de/cms/de/publications/working_papers/.

Leitão, H. 1948. *Os Portugueses em Solor e Timor de 1515 a 1702.* Lisbon: Tipografia da Liga dos Combatentes da Grande Guerra.

———. 1952. *Vinte e oito anos de história de Timor, 1698–1725.* Lisbon: Agência Geral do Ultramar.

Lewis, E. D., 2010. *The Stranger Kings of Sikka.* Verhendelingen van het Koninklijk Instituut voor Taal-, Land- en Volkenkunde, no. 257. Leiden: KITVL Press.

Mathur, S. 2000. "History and Anthropology in South Asia: Rethinking the Archive." *Annual Review of Anthropology* 29: 89–106.

de Matos, A. T. 1974. *Timor Português 1515–1769: Contribuição para a sua história.* Faculdade de Letras da Universidade de Lisboa: Instituto Histórico Infante Dom Henrique. Lisboa. 1974.

McWilliam, A. 1996. "Severed Heads That Germinate the State: History, Politics and Headhunting in Southwest Timor." In *Headhunting and the Social Imagination in Southeast Asia*, edited by J. Hoskins, 127–66. Stanford, CA: Stanford University Press.

———. 2007. "Austronesians in Linguistic Disguise: Fataluku Cultural fusion in East Timor." *Journal of Southeast Asian Studies* 38(2): 355–75.

———. 2002. *Paths of Origin, Gates of Life: A Study of Place and Precedence in Southwest Timor*. Leiden: KITLV Press.

McWilliam, A., and E. G. Traube. 2011. "Land and Life in Timor-Leste: Introduction." In *Land and Life in Timor-Leste: Ethnographic Essays*, edited by A. McWilliam and E. Traube, 1–21. Canberra: ANU Press.

Moutinho, I. 2012. "Historicity and Storytelling in East Timorese Fiction in Portuguese." *Ellipsis* 10: 101–22.

Nygaard-Christensen, M., and A. Bexley. 2017. "Introduction: Fieldwork in a New Nation." In *Fieldwork in Timor-Leste: Understanding Social Change Through Practice*, M. Nygaard-Christensen and A. Bexley, 1–31. Copenhagen: NIAS Press.

O'Hanlon, R., and D. Washbrook. 1992. "After Orientalism: Culture, Criticism and Politics in the Third World." *Comparative Studies in Society and History* 34(1): 141–67.

de Oliveira, L. 1949–52. *Timor na História de Portugal*. 3 vols. Lisboa: Agência Geral das Colónias.

Ortner, S. 1984. "Theory in Anthropology since the Sixties." *Comparative Studies in Society and History* 26(1): 126–66.

Palmié, S., and C. Stewart. 2016. "Introduction: For an Anthropology of History." *Hau—Journal of Ethnographic Theory* 6(1): 208–36.

Pélissier, R. 1996. *Timor en guerre: le crocodile et les portugais, 1847–1913*. Orgeval: Ed. Pelissier.

Reuter, T. 2002. *The House of Our Ancestors: Precedence and Dualism in Highland Balinese Society*. Leiden: KITLV Press.

Roque, R. 2010. *Headhunting and Colonialism: Anthropology and the Circulation of Human Skulls in the Portuguese Empire 1870–1930*. New York: Palgrave Macmillan.

———. 2012. "Entangled with Otherness: Military Ethnographies of Headhunting in East Timor." In *Engaging Colonial Knowledge: Reading European Archives in World History*, edited by R. Roque and K. A. Wagner, 254–78. Basingstoke: Palgrave Macmillan.

———. 2015. "Mimetic Governmentality and the Administration of Colonial Justice in Timor, ca. 1860–1910." *Comparative Studies in Society and History* 57(1): 67–97.

———. 2017. "Lost Traces: Hunting the Past in the Colonial Archives of Timor-Leste." In *Fieldwork in Timor-Leste: Understanding Social Change Through Practice*, M. Nygaard-Christensen and A. Bexley, 58–79. Copenhagen: NIAS Press.

———. 2018. "Dances with Heads: Parasitic Mimesis and the Government of Savagery in Colonial East Timor." *Social Analysis* 62(2): 28–50.

Roque, R., and K. A. Wagner. 2012. "Introduction: Engaging Colonial Knowledge." In *Engaging Colonial Knowledge: Reading European Archives in World History*, edited by R. Roque and K. A. Wagner, 1–32. Basingstoke: Palgrave Macmillan.

Rosaldo, R. 1980. *Ilongot Headhunting, 1883–1974: A Study in Society and History*. Stanford, CA: Stanford University Press.

Rutherford, D. 2012. *Laughing at Leviathan*. Chicago: University of Chicago Press.

Sahlins, M. 2000 [1993]. "Goodbye to Tristes Tropiques: Ethnography in the Context of Modern World History." In *Culture in Practice: Selected Essays*, 471–500. Cambridge, MA: MIT Press.

———. 1985. *Islands of History*. Chicago: University of Chicago Press.

———. 1993. "Cere Fuckabede." *American Ethnologist* 20(4): 848–62.

———. 2012. "Alterity and Autochthony: Austronesian Cosmographies of the Marvelous." *Hau: Journal of Ethnographic Theory* 2(1): 131–60.

Said, E. 1978. *Orientalism*. New York: Pantheon Books.

Schapper, A. 2011. "Finding Bunaq: The Homeland and Expansion of the Bunaq in Central Timor." In *Land and Life in Timor-Leste: Ethnographic Essays*, A. McWilliam and E. G. Traube, 163–86. Canberra: ANU Press.

Schulte-Nordholt, H. G. 1971. *The Political System of the Atoni of Timor*. The Hague: Martinus Nijhoff.

———. 1996. *The Spell of Power: A History of Balinese Politics, 1650–1940*. Verhendelingen van het Koninklijk Instituut voor Taal-, Land- en Volkenkunde, no. 60. The Hague: Nijhoff.

Shorter, D. 2009. *We'll Dance Our Truth: Yaqui History in Yoeme Performances*. Lincoln: University of Nebraska Press.

Sivaramakrishnan, K. 2005. Review of *Castes of Mind: Colonialism and the Making of Modern India* by Nicholas B. Dirks. *American Anthropologist* 107(1): 146.

Spivak, G. 1985. "The Rani of Sirmur: An Essay in Reading the Archives." *History and Theory* 24(3): 247–72.

Stoler, A. L. 2002. "Colonial Archives and the Arts of Governance." *Archival Science* 2: 87–109.

———. 2009. *Along the Archival Grain: Epistemic Anxieties and Colonial Common Sense*. Princeton, NJ: Princeton University Press.

Therik, T. 2004. *Wehali, the Female Land: Traditions of a Timorese Ritual Centre*. Canberra: Research School of Pacific and Asian Studies/The Australian National University, in association with Pandanus Books.

Thomas, N. 1991. *Entangled Objects: Exchange, Material Culture and Colonialism in the Pacific*. Cambridge, MA: Harvard University Press.

———. 1992a. "Substantivization and Anthropological Discourse: The Transformation of Practices into Institutions in Neotraditional Pacific Societies." In *History and Tradition in Melanesian Anthropology*, edited by J. G. Carrier, 64–85. Berkeley: University of California Press.

———. 1992b. "The Inversion of Tradition." *American Ethnologist* 19: 213–31.

———. 1993. "Beggars Can Be Choosers." *American Ethnologist* 20(4): 868–76.

———. 1994. *Colonialism's Culture: Anthropology, Travel and Government.* Princeton, NJ: Princeton University Press.

———. 1996 [1989]. *Out of Time: History and Evolution in Anthropological Discourse.* 2nd ed. Ann Arbor: University of Michigan Press.

———. 1996. *Outside Time: History and Evolution in Anthropological Discourse.* Ann Arbor: University of Michigan Press.

———. 1997. *In Oceania: Visions, Artifacts, Histories.* Durham, NC: Duke University Press.

Thomaz, L. F. 1994. *De Ceuta a Timor.* Lisbon: Difel.

Traube, E. G. 1977. "Ritual Exchange among the Mambai of East Timor: Gifts of Life and Death." Unpublished thesis, Department of Anthropology, Harvard University, Cambridge, MA.

———. 1986. *Cosmology and Social Life: Ritual Exchange Among the Mambai of East Timor.* Chicago: University of Chicago Press.

———. 2011. "Planting the Flag." In *Land and Life in Timor-Leste: Ethnographic Essays*, edited by A. McWilliam and E. G. Traube, 117–40. Canberra: ANU Press.

———. 2017. "Returning to Origin Places in an Expanding World." In *Transformations in Independent Timor-Leste*, edited by R. Feijó and S. M. Viegas, 45–60. London: Routledge.

Van der Veer, P. 1992. "The Foreign Hand: Orientalist Discourse in Sociology and Communalism." In *Orientalism and the Postcolonial Predicament: Perspectives on South Asia*, edited by C. A. Breckenridge and P. van der Veer, 23–44. Philadelphia: University of Pennsylvania Press.

Viegas, S. M., and R. G. Feijó (eds.). 2017. *Transformations in Independent Timor-Leste: Dynamics of Social and Cultural Cohabitations.* London: Routledge.

Wagner, R. 1975. *The Invention of Culture.* Chicago: University of Chicago Press.

Wagoner, P. B. 2003. "Precolonial Intellectuals and the Production of Colonial Knowledge." *Comparative Studies in Society and History* 45(4): 783–814.

Whitehead, N. L. (ed.). 2003. *Histories and Historicities in Amazonia.* Lincoln: University of Nebraska Press.

Wiener, M. J. 1995. *Visible and Invisible Realms: Power, Magic and Colonial Conquest in Bali.* Chicago: University of Chicago Press.

Willford, A., and E. Tagliacozzo (eds.). 2009. *Clio/Anthropos: Exploring the Boundaries between History and Anthropology.* Stanford, CA: Stanford University Press.

Wolf, E. 1982. *Europe and the People without History.* Berkeley: University of California Press.

Young, R. J. 2002. *Postcolonialism: An Historical Introduction.* London: Blackwell.

PART I

Following Stories

Chapter 1

OUTSIDE IN

MAMBAI EXPECTATIONS
OF RETURNING OUTSIDERS

Elizabeth G. Traube

Introduction

The people of Timor-Leste have proved themselves adept at incorporating outsiders into local cultural orders. They have had considerable
practice. Over the past century, three foreign powers—Portugal, Ja-
pan, and Indonesia—have occupied their land. The violent departure
of Indonesia in 1999 brought in a multinational peacekeeping force
(INTERFET), followed by a UN transitional administration (UNTAET),
which oversaw the transition to full independence in 2002. After having been effectively cut off from the outside world during the Indonesian occupation, Timor-Leste has seen a huge influx of outsiders
during the transitional and postindependence periods—UN administrators and police, international development organizations, NGOs,
and returning Timorese diasporans, not to mention anthropologists,
a few of whom, like me, were also returnees.

I first went to what was then Portuguese Timor in 1972 to do fieldwork for my doctoral dissertation during what turned out to be the
last years of Portuguese colonial rule. After three months of indeci-
sion, spent mainly in the town of Laleia on the northern coast, I relo-
cated to the district of Aileu, in the mountains thirty-two kilometers
south of Dili. Aileu is part of the Mambai zone, which extends from the
north to the south coast across the approximate center of the island.
Laleia is in the Galoli region, one of the few in which Catholicism had
been the majority religion since the early twentieth century, but in

Aileu converts were still a small, primarily elite minority. The Mambai, moreover, had a collective reputation as a people fiercely committed to traditional ways. They were the archetype of what East Timorese call *kaladi*, a term used to distinguish the peoples in the western interior from more cosmopolitan coastal townsfolk, as well as from the supposedly more enterprising peoples in the east, called *firaku*.[1] Neighboring ethnic groups, *kaladi* themselves, regard the Mambai as the original, autochthonous people of the land (Molnar 2011: 101, 104).

This collective identity, I learned, was a source of pride among many Mambai—especially those from origin villages that claimed ritual authority over the invisible spirit powers of the land. Over the course of my first fieldwork I became closely associated with two such places, paired ritual centers named Hohul and Raimaus. My ties to these origin villages were mediated by two men: Mau Balen of Raimaus and Mau Bere of Hohul. Mau Balen was introduced to me by the wife of the *liurai* of Seloi, in whose household I resided. His deceased father had been a head priest of Raimaus, but, according to Mau Balen, he had resigned his position (for reasons I failed to explore). Mau Balen took me to Raimaus and later to Hohul, where I met Mau Bere, the eldest son of a Hohul priest. I spent most of my second year in their company, attending a variety of ritual events.

I left Timor in late 1974, a year before the Indonesian invasion. I returned for the first time in late 2000, during the transition. I rejoined the household in which I had lived, and I also renewed my relationships with Hohul and Raimaus. Mau Bere had died two years previously in Dili, where he had moved, according to his younger brother, to avoid punishment for his participation in the early stage of the armed resistance. Mau Balen was living in the village of Malere, just outside Aileu town. People came out to watch me as I walked down the road to his house for the first time, and I heard children excitedly telling one another, "She's the one who was here before, the one who was here before!"

In ways I continue to work through, my protracted association with Hohul and Raimaus has been interwoven with preexisting stories of Mambai relationships with outsiders. One of these is an origin narrative, referred to as the "walk of rule" or the "walk of the flag." First narrated to me by Mau Balen and Mau Bere as part of a larger creation myth, it represents the *Malai Butin*, white overseas foreigners, as returning outsiders whose ancestor was born on Timor and who come back to their homeland, summoned by Hohul and Raimaus ancestors, to establish a "heavy rule and a weighty ban" (*ukun rihu nor badun mdeda*). The other story, set in a recognizable historical past, involves a figure named Felix whose outsider character is more elusive. He is, all tellers insisted, "black, like us," not a Malai, yet nonetheless a foreign stranger who comes to Aileu with the first missionaries. When hostile chiefs drive the missionaries away, he remains behind and settles in Hohul, where he too arouses enmity. Sentenced to death for sorcery, he survives a series of attempted executions and disappears.

I have written about these narrative traditions separately (Traube 1995, 2007, 2011), but in this chapter I consider them together, in relationship to overlapping initiatives undertaken by the colonizers during the late nineteenth century: the extension of colonial authority and a renewed effort at evangelization. To the Portuguese, these processes engaged respectively with the political and religious spheres of indigenous life, but Timorese political systems confounded that division, as they were based on a distinction between executive power and the ritual or spiritual authority that legitimates it.[2] The latter position was marginalized by the expanding colonial presence, and Mambai narrative traditions, I will argue, both reflect and protest this history of marginalization.

Representing foreign rulers as returning ancestors is an incorporative response to outside intervention that is not limited to Timor. In a study of Andean responses to Spanish colonialism, Peter Gose calls it a "worldwide indigenous strategy" that articulates a "politics of connection," of "recognition, solidarity, and reconciliation" (2008: 6). The colonized, Gose argues, use preexisting cultural resources to recast the colonial relationship as an intercultural alliance, a pact of reciprocity; in treating invaders as ancestors, they seek to make them subject to indigenous social claims. Such a strategy can justify defiance as well as submission, since it holds outsider rulers up to moral standards that they rarely meet.

I cannot say when this way of representing the Portuguese developed among the Mambai. Portuguese colonialism on Timor was characterized by a long lag between colonial presence and colonial control, and various ideas about the foreigners must have circulated over the extended interval. Portuguese involvement with Mambai people increased after 1769, when the embattled Portuguese moved their capital from Lifao to Dili, which was then part of the Mambai zone. Mambai responses to the newcomers were far from uniform. Ermera, just west of Aileu, oscillated between alliance and revolt until 1911, when a final rebellion was put down (Almeida 1965: 30), and Manufahi to the south led the last two major anticolonial rebellions. Aileu, however, proved more reliable; Aileu chiefs participated as "loyal allies" in the military "pacification" campaigns of the late nineteenth and early twentieth centuries, including the two Manufahi wars (Pélissier 1996).[3] A preexisting construction of kinship with the foreigners could have mediated and facilitated the alliance, or it could have been developed subsequently to justify it.

The question of authorship is similarly complex. Gananath Obeyesekere (1992), in his polemical critique of Sahlins (1985), has argued that it was the Europeans rather than the Hawaiians who initially deified Captain Cook, and he largely discounts the importance of pre-existing cultural categories in shaping indigenous responses to foreign invaders.[4] Without entering into the particular debate over Cook, I appreciate and share Sahlins's (2000) insistence on the role of the colonized in colonial history, and the general tendency of Timorese peoples to cast outside influences in indigenous cultural terms has been well-documented (see McWilliam 1999: 378).

In eastern Indonesia, moreover, interest in absorbing foreign powers anteceded the arrival of the Europeans and was reflected in the potency attributed to regalia of office; throughout the region a variety of imported objects, including ceramics, weapons, musical instruments, and golden jewelry, became inextricably entangled with local claims to rule (Hoskins 1997).[5] The Dutch as well as the Portuguese colonizers depended on and reconfigured such ideologies in contracting alliances with local rulers. On Timor, the Portuguese deliberately sought to substitute their own regalia for traditional heirlooms and to redefine the offices of their recipients.[6] They also took pains to enhance their own dignity through symbolic displays that surely contributed to their aura.

But what most disturbs Obeyesekere about the deification of Cook is his assumption that any ideology that elevates colonial rulers would necessarily denigrate the indigenous peoples, and this anxiety seems to me misplaced. In incorporating foreigners as ancestors, indigenous peoples dignify rather than demean their own position; as Gonzalo Lamana observes, they use cultural frames "to produce *respectable selves*," opening up a space "in which the non-Western subject is coherent by being different *and* equal" (2008: 79, emphasis in original).

Whereas Obeyesekere sees European colonizers in the Pacific manipulating native beliefs in order to glorify themselves, Ranajit Guha (1983, 1997) argues that the British made little effort to win ideological support from the majority of the colonized population in India. Controlled by coercive mechanisms, the subalterns experience colonial rule as "dominance without hegemony," and their local cultural forms retain autonomy from elite culture, both colonial and national. Inasmuch as subalterns nurture grievances rooted in experiences of exploitation, they have a predisposition to rebel and can be mobilized by nationalist elites; but such subaltern participation, Guha emphasizes (1983: 4), is motivated by an autonomous "politics of the people" which leaves its imprint on nationalist movements. While I agree with and have pursued this last proposition (Traube 2011), I believe that subaltern responses to colonial rule are often more ambivalent than Guha supposes. In this chapter I approach colonialism as an intercultural production in which both colonizers and indigenous peoples engage in a socially located politics of incorporation. Rather than posing an obstacle to nationalist sentiment, I will suggest, the legitimacy colonial rule acquired among Mambai could help to nurture it, by providing a standard against which both particular Portuguese policies and the imposition of Indonesian rule were critically judged.

The Narrative Traditions

Claiming kinship with foreigners does not require but is consistent with a cosmogonic tradition in which all phenomena are related through descent from a common source. Mambai cosmogony is of this type.[7] Origin narratives represent inanimate and animate beings alike as descended from the primal couple, Father Heaven and Mother Earth, whose original union on Mount Tat Mai Lau centers the world. "Timor and Malaia," speakers would declare in ritual chants and formal greetings, "we two have one mother, we two have one father" (*it ru inan id, it ru aman id*); such formulaic assertions of kinship were also common in ordinary speech, both before and after the Indonesian occupation, although the origin narratives that elucidate them are viewed as specialized knowledge.

Many cosmogonies deal with the question of unity and division by recounting the separations that make human life possible (Schrempp 1992). In Mambai cosmogonic narratives, Father Heaven orders the world by differentiating it into separate categories and imposing the terms for their interaction. He is the source of the order of rule (*ukun*), which has two manifestations. The oldest is known as the "ban of the night" (*badun hoda nin*), the primordial period of origins when the deities bring forth their children; imposed by Heaven, the ban silences the nonhuman world, removing the power of speech from all but his youngest, human children, who are henceforth entitled to appropriate their "silent" (*molu*) elder kin: "We eat our older brothers," as Mambai say, but in return they perform sacrificial rituals to "repay their fatigue" (*seul ro ni kolen*). Heaven also differentiates his human sons, who include three brothers. The two elder brothers draw black water and remain black, while the youngest draws white water, with which he "bathes white, washes clean" (*luk buti, riu mo*). The eldest brother receives the knowledge and tools of metalwork as his patrimony, and he goes off into the west; to the middle brother go "luck and fortune" (*ubdaida nor fortuna*), in the form of sacred ornaments and other articles of ritual dress, which he seizes from Father Heaven; he and his descendants eventually found houses in Raimaus and Hohul. But the youngest lays hold of "rule and ban" (*ukun nor badun*), the second modality of law that belongs to "the daylight" (*ada nin*) and is designed to regulate human affairs; it is embodied in an assortment of regalia that includes the flag, and he vanishes with these objects across the water and the sea.[8] On Timor, the absence of tokens of sovereignty results in anarchy: people neither "tremble nor fear" (*ba rih ro, ba tmau ro*) and "they stab one another and they kill one another" (*ro sa ro, ro tar ro*). To end the chaos, the middle brother (or in some variants, his descendants) uses his mystical powers to transport himself over the seas to Portugal, where his Malai younger brother presents him with regalia of office: staffs, drums, and a flag named Raimundo (literally, "land of the outside world," from whence it came). With these tokens, which inspire "fear and trembling," he establishes his realm (*reinu*), an association of origin groups that recognize the supremacy of Hohul and Raimaus.[9] In this account, as tellers would emphasize, their ancestors once held political power (rule over women and men), together with the older authority "of the night"(*hoda nin*) to regulate interactions between human beings and the nonhuman world; but at some point in the past, they would say, their ancestors grew weary and "surrendered the rule" (*sra ukun*), embodied in the flag and other regalia, delegating power over human affairs to indigenous newcomers and devoting themselves to their ritual guardianship of the land; "they sat down to watch over the rock and to look after the tree" (*kde oid deiki hauta nor aia*), immobilizing themselves like their iconic charges. In this account, the newcomers who become the active executives are the rulers of the kingdom of Aileun, named for a twisted tree (*ai-leun*) located in their origin village, which has also given its name to the larger, colonially established administrative district (Aileu). Later, the Malaia themselves return from overseas and take up their place on the coast, in Dili, as the supreme upholders of justice. In this ritually centered view, the Malaia on the coast and Hohul and Raimaus in the mountains mark the two poles of the political system, while the indigenous political rulers of Aileun are the mobile mediators who "go down (north) to the sea" (*du ni taisa*), to report to the Malai, and "go up (south) to the interior" (*sai ni hoha*), to report to the lords of rock and tree.[10]

As narrated to me by Hohul and Raimaus people, the "walk of rule" (or "walk of the flag") recounts the establishment of a diarchic political system based on a division between an older, inalienable form of ritual or spiritual authority and a younger, more mobile (and mobilizing) power to regulate human affairs.[11] One expression of diarchy is in the mythology of the stranger king: the widespread Austronesian idea that rulers were originally strangers who came from outside the realm (often from overseas) and were installed as sovereigns over the original people of the land.[12] The origin of the outsider is variously constructed, as James J. Fox (1995) observes in a comparative analysis of eastern Indonesian versions of the mythology. In many cases he is a "complete outsider" from another realm or from overseas, but some versions identify him as an earlier ancestor who leaves for a period of time and is received back into society as a "returning outsider"; in a variant of this set, the returning outsider is a relative—a brother or son who was exiled or went away.[13]

Viewed as a version of the stranger king mythology, the Hohul/Raimaus tradition is not distinguished by the indigenous provenance of the foreign stranger but by the nature of his "installation": on the coast, as a jural-political ruler. A common pattern on Timor involves what Fox (1995) calls the "installation of the outsider inside"; in this pattern the (returning) outsider is installed as insider and often displaces the original ruler as the realm's supreme spiritual authority; the displaced leaders may then take on the active/executive role of defending the realm, while the immobilized stranger "just sits."[14] The Malaia undergo no such functional transformation; they return as the supreme representatives of political order, counterparts, on the north-south axis, of the spiritual authorities in the interior highlands. They are, however, symbolically immobilized in relationship to the indigenous jural rulers of Aileun, who are viewed from ritual centers as the mobile mediators between the poles.[15] Moreover, the story of the journey overseas to acquire tokens of rule arguably constructs the Hohul/Raimaus ancestors as stranger kings of a sort, who subsequently delegate the powers they brought back from overseas to Aileun and install (or re-install) themselves on the inside.[16] A visible trace of that represented act is maintained in Hohul in the form of a wooden pole, identified with the pole of the original flag: "We hold the base [trunk] of rule," Hohul people say, and Aileun "holds the tip," that is, the flag.[17] Hohul and Raimaus people take great pride in both their ancestors' represented role as founders of the realm and in their contemporary ritual responsibilities; to my knowledge, however, only the latter is acknowledged by Aileun rulers.

The Tat Felix story, so far as I could tell, is universally known in Aileu; it was recited to me on many occasions in the 1970s, and on my postoccupation visits it sometimes seemed as if every topic I broached led back to Felix. As an oft-told tale, it has many variants, but there is a relatively stable core. It describes the people's first encounter with missionaries, one of whom is named Jacob; Felix, who accompanied and assisted them, was a Christian (*sarani*), though neither a Malaia nor a priest; their conversionary efforts meet resistance from chiefs in both Aileun and Hohul, that is, from indigenous jural and ritual authorities, whose common fear is that the newcomers will "usurp their rule";[18] Father Jacob leaves and goes to Soibada, which becomes a center of learning;[19] Felix stays behind and eventually settles in Hohul; he starts to build a chapel just outside the origin village, in a place that becomes known as Tutreda;[20] besides preaching the new doctrine, he performs assorted miracles, and, in some accounts, he also settles disputes regarding ritual prestation obligations; one or more of these acts antagonize the Hohul leaders, who accuse him of being a sorcerer (*sauba*); the charge leads to his arrest by the Aileun ruler and appearance before the Malai military commandant of the colonial court; he is condemned to death (either by the Malaia or the Aileun ruler), but he cannot be killed; after surviving a series of attempted executions, he disappears (*lako*), but he reappears (*mosu*) at different times and places, in a variety of forms.

Among the contested points (and tellers tended to be familiar with and to refute other versions) is the precise nature and distribution of fault. In most accounts there are two priests, and one of them (Diakobi) is killed by the Aileun chief—something that descendants of the latter strongly deny.[21] While most people I asked seemed to regard Felix as a saintly martyr, others (including Mau Balen) identified him with Jesus and accused the Hohul ancestors who turned against him of having "killed God." In Hohul versions, Felix disappears after riding his horse into the church in Aileu town, while Mau Balen and others said he assumed the form of a young boy named Mau Bere. When, where, and how often he has "reappeared" (*mosu*) are disputed, but his story is always unfinished. Whereas the "walk of the flag" represents the foundations of order, the advent of outsiders in the Felix tradition precipitates an ancestral fault (the murder of the priest and/ or the mistreatment of Felix) that is transmitted through time and demands redress.

The Intercultural Dynamics of Colonialism

Not all East Timorese regard the Malaia as returning ancestors, but interest in European insignia of office was widespread among Timorese rulers, from both poles of the local diarchies. With roots in indigenous ideologies of rule in which power comes from outside, such interest was also promoted by the historical strategies and practices of the Portuguese colonizers, which Ricardo Roque (2010) has elucidated. While he generally accepts my ethnographic analysis of the incorporation of the foreigners as legitimate jural rulers, Roque argues cogently that legitimation was the product of interactions between the colonizers and the colonized; and whereas I had focused on a discourse carried on among themselves by ritual leaders, he has foregrounded Portuguese dealings with indigenous representatives of the jural-political plane.

Central to Roque's analysis is the weakness of Portuguese colonial rule, even as it was extended over the second half of the nineteenth century. Chronically underfinanced and understaffed, concentrated in Dili with an uneven presence in the interior, surrounded by often hostile kingdoms, the Portuguese relied on alliances with indigenous rulers. The peculiar strength of such weak forms of rule, Roque argues, depends upon the colonizers' capacity to incorporate elements of the colonized other. Inasmuch as the colonized simultaneously pursue their own interests by incorporating elements of the colonizers' system of rule, Roque characterizes the dynamic as "mutual parasitism" (2010: 36).

With their military and judicial responsibilities, the active executive figures of indigenous diarchic polities better fit European conceptions of rule than did symbolically immobile spiritual authorities, and Portuguese colonial officials dealt primarily with the former. They distributed military patents, ranked from colonel to lieutenant, and insignia of rule, including staffs, military drums, and flags, in return for pledges of loyalty to the crown.[22] The recipients agreed to amass and send to Dili an annual tribute in kind (the *finta*), a tax instituted by the Portuguese in the early eighteenth century modeled on preexisting tributary structures, and to serve the government by providing workers in peacetime and by raising troops (*arraiais*) to assist in punitive expeditions against rebellious rulers and to serve in colonial garrisons. In receiving foreign titles and regalia, local rulers acquired heightened prestige within their own realms. The possibility of leveraging an alliance with the Portuguese to defeat a rival chief was not insignificant; but arguably as important as material support was the cosmological legitimacy that foreign regalia traditionally bestowed on military force.

The Portuguese colonial authorities, as Roque demonstrates, were no less preoccupied with symbolic displays of power than were their Timorese allies. Many of them sensed that the Timorese were intensely invested in persons and objects representative of colonial authority. The governor and the flag, in particular, seemed to be regarded as embodiments of a mystical power worthy of veneration, and encouraging that attitude became a goal of colonial practices. Many of the colonizers came to see preserving and enhancing Portuguese prestige through regular displays of symbolic power as essential to colonial rule. Annual delivery of the *finta* to Dili provided one totalizing performance, with the colonial administration positioned as the great "mother and father" who are reciprocated for the order they maintain. But the ordering power that the colonial government sought to enforce as well as to embody was associated primarily with warfare and the exercise of justice, and in both these institutional spheres the Portuguese depended on their indigenous allies well into the twentieth century.

Warfare was framed as a display of punitive violence against kingdoms that resisted the extension of colonial power. Waged by the Portuguese and their "loyal allies," military campaigns were critical performances and tests of colonial power, which was enhanced by victory and diminished by defeat. In indigenous conceptions, moreover, the power of combatants is indexed by the degree of "heat" generated through forms of ritualized violence such as headhunting. To channel that power, Roque argues, Portuguese-led "pacification" campaigns incorporated the very "barbarities" they would later be portrayed as eliminating (2010: 37). Similarly, in the exercise of justice, a pragmatic politics of tolerance for indigenous custom prevailed, a sense that efficient government of the "natives" required the colonizers to embrace Timorese manners, while the indigenous rulers, in turn, depended on tokens of office and titles bestowed by the governor for their legitimacy.

Through such military and judicial performances of power, Portuguese colonial authorities and indigenous jural rulers became increasingly intertwined and mutually dependent, while indigenous ritual authorities, perceived as religious rather than political functionaries, were largely ignored and increasingly marginalized. An overall effect of the extension of colonial authority was to weaken the diarchic organization of the local polities.

Whereas colonial administrators generally respected taboos on what they saw as the "religious" sphere of native life, the project of the missionaries was to transform it. Catholicism has a long history on Timor, dating back to the arrival of the Portuguese Dominicans in the late sixteenth century. Nevertheless, when the colonial administration began to expand over the latter half of the nineteenth century, Christianity was still but weakly implanted. Frédéric Durand (2004: 50) suggests a number of reasons for the slow progress of missionization, including the desire of the Portuguese governors to limit Dominican influence, and the transfer of the capital to Dili, which meant that missionary efforts had to begin all over again with a new population; a virtual absence of missionaries between 1834 and 1874 further impeded those efforts.

A new initiative began in 1877, when six missionaries spread out across the districts. One of these was a Timorese priest, Jacob dos Reis e Cunha, who had been educated and ordained abroad and returned to Timor in the 1860s (Pélissier 1996: 55). Father Jacob was assigned to Luca and Same on the southern coast; from there he went to Aileu, where sluggish conversion rates indicate he had little success.[23] Nevertheless, as the vitality of the Felix tradition attests, the early encounter with the missionary project made a deep and lasting impression on the inhabitants, and Christianity became part of local realities in a variety of ways. Durand (2004: 36) suggests that dualism has allowed Timorese converts to accept and integrate the Christian rites without having to deny their local religions; in my experience, many Mambai Catholics alternate between fulfilling duties "to the church" and "to rock and tree," treating them as two sets of contextualized practices rather than as irreconcilable doctrines. Conversely, those who identify primarily with indigenous ritual practice, who have come to be called and to call themselves *sentiua* (from Portuguese *gentios*, heathens or pagans), incorporate Christian symbols and practices into their ceremonies. In Hohul, this incorporative tendency is especially pronounced; in partial redress for the fickle Hohul ancestors who received Felix only to turn against him, subsequent generations have hosted Christians at indigenous ceremonies.

The Incorporation of Christianity

From a structural perspective, Mambai rituals reverse the processes of separation and division represented in origin narratives: at multiple levels, they bring together and reunify divided wholes. The underlying

principle, I have argued elsewhere (Traube 1989), is that the hosts
are the part of a divided totality that represents the original whole
prior to division; they both oppose and include their counterparts,
as, for instance, the eldest branch of an origin house represents the
"old mother and old father" in welcoming back members of younger
branches. I suspect a version of this principle is at work in the way
that Christianity has been incorporated into indigenous ritual life; as
the religion of the "younger brothers," its followers are symbolically
invited to attend indigenous rituals, and the inclusiveness of the cel-
ebrations indexes the hierarchical status of the hosts. But it is Hohul
that has most dramatically incorporated Christianity as the religion
of Felix.

Like other Timorese peoples, Mambai identify Father Heaven, the
transcendent figure in the pantheon, with the Christian God. In both
Hohul and Raimaus, the "white" house dedicated to Heaven is referred
to by the Tetum term Maromak (from *naroma*, "to grow light"), which
the missionaries used to translate "God." The white "God house" (Fad
Maromak) is opposed to the "black" house of Mother Earth, as well as
to other, more worldly manifestations of celestial maleness. In Hohul,
its masculine counterpart is a house called Liurai (the Tetum term for
a ruler) which is represented as the house of justice within the ritual
sphere, the place where disputes relating to ritual obligations are resolved; people say that Felix used to frequent this house when he came
to Hohul, and it was dedicated to him in the wake of the conflict. Its
unique status is evident in its design. A central hearth running east-
west divides other sacred houses (*fad lulin*) into an outer, northern section, where guests are received, and an inner, southern section, where
sacra are kept and offerings are made; by contrast, Liurai is divided
into western and eastern halves, associated respectively with *sentiua*
and *sarani*. On the *sentiua* side, indigenous ritual practice prevails:
there are rocks for placing shaved offerings to the spirits, and ritual
meals are served to human guests in black bowls made from coconut
shells; on the *sarani* side, there is only one rock, where candles are lit,
and no spirit offerings are made. Prayers are recited by a man who
is not a convert but knows how to pray (*resa*), after which a meal is
served on white tin or ceramic plates to Christian guests, if any attend,
or else to house masters who represent them. Having expelled Felix in
the past, Hohul now unites followers of both religions in his house.

In a valuable essay on the Felix tradition and its afterlife, the mis-
sionary-ethnographer Jorge Barros Duarte (1987/88) describes these
and other Hohul practices as the "paganizing of Christianity." I think
the phrase is misleading, as cult practice in Hohul is based on op-

position and inclusion rather than blending. In *liurai*, for instance, Christian cult objects and practices are treated as symmetric complements of their indigenous counterparts. Similarly, when Mambai refer to particular stages of the annual cycle of agricultural rituals as "Timorese Christmas" or "Timorese Easter," they are not referencing efforts to imitate the Christian festivals, as Duarte implies, but rather acknowledging parallels between two coexisting ritual systems, each of which addresses phenomena of life and death in its own way.

Most jarring to me was Duarte's account of one Maria Isabel, whom he describes as a native of Laleia and former student of the Canossian nuns.[24] Not unlike Felix, she is said to have set up residence in Hohul, where she halted the "paganizing of Christianity" by means of her apostolic work. This, according to Duarte's (unidentified) informant, involved translating into Mambai and Tetum the religious books she had brought with her. But her presence and its enlightening influence were temporary. After her departure, Duarte writes, Hohul reverted to its syncretizing ways and "submerged itself again in the paganizing of the Catholic cult" (1987/88: 44).

Isabel is the Mambai rendering of Elizabeth, and it was widely known that I had lived in Laleia before coming to Aileu; my affiliation with Hohul was also common knowledge in Aileu and beyond. Having never heard of any Catholic woman taking up residence in Hohul, I assume that the diligent and pious Maria Isabel is someone's version of me, as Duarte received it in the mid-1980s. Like me, Maria Isabel is defined by her mastery of the technology of literacy; ours is the "book and pen" (*libru nor labis*), tokens that Mambai regularly associated with the Malaia and opposed to "rock and tree" (*hauta nor aia*), the silent icons of indigenous ritual life. We are both transcribers of sacred texts, but with different purposes. I positioned my project in terms of the preservation of indigenous knowledge, and people often said that my work was to use "book and pen" to write down the "walk of rock and tree," whereas Isabel is a would-be agent of spiritual transformation who seeks to bring the Word into the silent realm. But her success (like mine) is limited. The "paganizing" process she interrupts is renewed in the "nativist movements" that Duarte goes on to describe.

With respect to these movements, I am much in his debt, for Felix's charismatic afterlife had long eluded me. In fact, throughout my first fieldwork, I experienced the story (which was told to me repeatedly) as a distraction from my concerns. Trained in a variety of structuralist traditions, I understood my object as a cosmological order that manifested itself in ritual practices, objects, spatial arrangements, and social relations and was articulated in a language of dual categories.

The pervasive dualism of the flag narrative delighted me, as did its apparent absorption of colonial history into structure. By contrast, the Felix story, told in prose rather than poetic language, seemed overwhelmingly eventful; there was a plot, of course (the miraculous donor whom the people fail to recognize), but narrative performances often struck me as incoherent, one sequence flowing into another, and another, with no clear end to it. What I stubbornly failed to grasp was that in recounting the story, people were telling me about a chain of events that was still unfolding, and to which my own arrival (and departure) could be assimilated. Mau Balen narrated the story on the night we first met, and he returned to it many times over, yet I never reflected on the possible implications of the narrative act. I never wondered why he was so intent on telling this story *to me* or whether he was hoping to elicit some response. I imagine my indifference frustrated him.[25] In 2001, both Mau Balen and his younger brother told me (on separate occasions) that shortly before their father, Tat Beis, died, only a few years before I first appeared, he had told Mau Balen to expect the arrival of a young Malai woman who would help them to resolve the injustice done to Felix. And Tat Beis, they told me, had heard this from none other than Felix himself.

Mau Balen's father, I now realize, had been involved in one of the "nativist movements" that Duarte describes, and I suspect that is what led to his "giving up" his priestly role in Raimaus. "Syncretic" does seem an accurate characterization of these phenomena, which blend Christian with indigenous practices in ways that elicit disapproval from representatives of both the church and the traditional cult. They were, as best as I can tell, relatively small in scale and short in duration. Recurrent features include a mystically gifted leader (in some cases a young boy), identified with Felix and/or Jesus, transported by his followers on a palanquin (*ador*) similar to those used for making prestations to ritual authorities in the traditional cult. According to retrospective accounts I gathered on my return visits, the leaders claimed assorted supernatural powers, performed acts of prestidigitation, and bestowed blessings in return for payment (in cash or kind).[26] Duarte associates these movements with Hohul, and Hohul members were among the participants, although mainly from "branch" houses rather than Hohul itself, according to my informants.[27] Hohul people tended to be critical of movement practices, which they described as "making a false prophet" (*fun frofetu falsu*), and several people charged past movement leaders with improperly "using Hohul's name."

At least some of these movements had anticolonial dimensions. Let us recall that although Felix is allied with the missionaries, the colonial administration participates in his punishment. The Malai military commander either imposes the sentence or becomes the Pilate figure, handing the matter back to the indigenous jural rulers of Aileun who had lodged the sorcery complaint.[28] In either case, the Felix of Mambai oral tradition has no reason to trust in the colonial government and could become a vehicle for resistance to it. In the 1970s, when attributing anticolonial sentiments to Felix (or his reincarnations), people cited perceived violations in the pact of reciprocity between Malai and Timorese. In particular, they spoke bitterly about the abolition of the *finta* and its substitution in 1908 by a cash head tax. Mau Balen often portrayed Felix as opposed to taxation because it disrupted the reciprocity between "silent and speaking" beings; unlike tribute in kind, he said, the monetized tax precluded distributing a share to the birds and mice, and as a result the hungry creatures raided the fields and gardens, so that the harvest was diminished.[29] Resentment of taxation had many motivations.[30] The economic costs could be onerous for subsistence farmers, and taxation, which was collected on the basis of village residence rather than origin group, lacked the legitimacy of the tributary system it replaced. In Hohul and Raimaus traditions, the old tributary arrangements were ceremonial enactments of their hierarchical status; as such, people said, they had long been resented by the Aileun rulers; many people claimed the latter had somehow tricked the Portuguese into introducing taxation and accused them of skimming off profits.

It is difficult to separate anticolonial sentiments from the rumored rivalry between ritual authorities and political executives. During my first fieldwork, people often spoke of one Paulo Castro, a man from a Hohul branch house who they said had been accused of trying to "usurp the rule" (*hau ukun*) from Dom João of Aileu and had been exiled to Africa by the Portuguese. Castro, a minor civil servant, was literate (one of Hohul's few "educated people," as he was later described to me) and a collector of traditions, like me; his punishment was often cited as a reason why so many people feared to share traditional lore with me. It was only in 2001 that I began to piece together other elements of Castro's story. I was told that he had participated in a movement in which a young boy was presented as Felix's reincarnation, in what seems to have been as much a challenge to Hohul's spiritual preeminence as a rebellion against Aileun.[31] A number of people said they suspected that Castro had stolen sacred books from Hohul belonging to the original Felix. According to Mau Balen, who emphasized the diarchic rivalry with Aileun, Castro had acquired another book, one that, in a well-known narrative tradition, Dom Bau

Meta of Aileun had received from the Malaia and then stupidly lost to the Mambai ruler of Motain on the coast, thus making Motain superior to Aileun. Castro, said Mau Balen, had planned to use this book to usurp the position of the Aileun ruler, and he was arrested for that reason. But while it may well have been the local ruler who brought charges against him, Castro was actually implicated in a supralocal 1959 "conspiracy" against the Portuguese government; based in Dili, it had ties to Manatuto, Baucau, and Viqueque, and more tenuous ties to Aileu, Liquica, and Ermera (Gunter 2007: 31). The Portuguese caught wind of the plan and conducted mass arrests, which prematurely catalyzed the abortive "Viqueque rebellion" (Gunter 2007: 32). Castro was one of many Aileu people arrested on charges of participating in the putative conspiracy, although the extent of anyone's involvement in the interdistrict plot is uncertain.[32] In 2007, the representative of the Fretilin Central Committee in Aileu described Castro to me as having attempted to "unite Timor in order to liberate the people," but on the basis of a ritualistic "strategy" that was not adequate to the political task. Mau Bere's younger brother stressed that no "diplomacy" had been involved and lucidly articulated the mythological logic of the movement practice: Castro, he said, had reasoned that since his Hohul ancestors had brought the Malai to Timor, he could now send them away, and he had performed a ceremony to dispatch them.[33] Several members of Hohul were also arrested in 1959 and briefly exiled to Turiscai, including Leik Mau, who was the elderly head priest of Hohul when I first visited there in 1973. Small wonder that Hohul priests would repeatedly proclaim their respect for their Malai kin! Whatever else declarations of common ancestry and assertions of the complementarity between Timorese and Malaia may have been, they were ways of denying that the speaker harbored any subversive, anticolonial sentiments.

Occupation and Resistance

As it turned out, the Malaia announced their departure. After the "Carnation Revolution" of April 1974, word spread rapidly that the Portuguese would leave Timor in the near future. In Raimaus, where I was attending a house rebuilding ceremony, people formally assimilated the prospect to narratives of succession: their younger brothers, many people declared, had grown old and weary, they "descended and ascended with difficulty" (*du nor sai ba kode*) and so would have to "surrender the rule" (*sra ukun*). In the postoccupation period, people retrospectively described 2 May 1975, the day that Governor Lemos Pires announced the decolonization program, as the day when the outgoing Malai rulers had "bestowed liberty" on the Timorese people.[34] But a few months later, when the colonial administration abandoned the island during the civil fighting between UDT (Timorese Democratic Union) and Fretilin and then refused to return and resume the decolonization process, it seemed that they had prematurely abandoned their role as protectors of the community. It remained to be seen who would take it up.

Ironically, even before the invasion, there was a sense among Mambai that Indonesia was insufficiently foreign to substitute for the outgoing Portuguese rulers, and in my experience support for Apodeti was virtually nil in Aileu. Indonesian officials may well have hoped to cast their incursion as that of order-bringing stranger kings, but between the massive scale and violence of the invasion and Fretilin's success in coordinating local resistance, such claims had little credibility to East Timorese.[35] Nevertheless, retrospective accommodation was not precluded. In 2000, when describing to me their surrender to the occupiers in 1979, even people who represented themselves as staunchly pro-Fretilin at that time also told me that, had they only been treated fairly, they could have come to accept Indonesian rule in time. What precluded accommodation was the regime's unrelenting hostility and violence toward the population. I'm not sure at what point Mambai began representing Indonesians as descendants of Au Sa, the eldest brother who receives the tools of metalwork in the origin narrative, but by 2000, it was a widely used and wonderfully expressive trope. In Mambai symbolic schemes, a returning *elder* brother-ruler represents a categorical reversal, and to many people the representation conveyed the combination of material power and moral inferiority that they attributed to the Indonesian state. In contrast to Portuguese colonialism, as Mambai had represented it, Indonesian rule embodied sheer force without cosmological legitimacy.[36]

Many Timorese, Mambai included, portray the occupiers as a corruptive influence. It was understood that life under the occupation required duplicity, but individuals who visibly benefited from dealings with the Indonesians were morally suspect, and local political elites who flourished could be accused of "selling the people" (*sosa povu*). Ritual leaders could find themselves in a delicate situation. On the one hand, their authority seems to have been enhanced over the occupation in many regions; they were regularly consulted by Falantil forces to divine the outcomes of projected raids, and they were widely credited with mobilizing the spirit "lords of the land" (*rai nain* in Tetum) against the invaders (McWilliam 2011; Bovensiepen 2011). Many people told me that the alliance with the spirit world had helped the resistance to endure and triumph. On this logic, it was the task of indigenous ritual leaders to "put away the sharp and pointed things" and ritually "cool" the land after independence (though the multiple, competing claims to "center" status would have complicated any nationally unifying ritual performance). On the other hand, Indonesian government officials had also attempted to use indigenous ritual authorities for political ends, and in Aileu they seem to have displayed a disturbing interest in Hohul and Raimaus. When Hohul rebuilt Fad Maromak in the 1990s, the Bupati attended a key performance in which a water buffalo goes up into the house to be sacrificed.[37] When I first returned in 2000, I received numerous accounts of an event that took place during the charged period leading up to the referendum; on the orders of the Aileun ruler, who was pro-autonomy, the Raimaus priests had invited the Bupati to the origin village, dressed him in native cloths, and performed a ceremony of "brotherhood." Most people expressed the opinion that the priests had acted under compulsion, and they held the Aileun ruler at fault.[38] But the story was also widely cited as an index of how "the old-old ones" (*mai-mai*) had become improperly involved in *politika* under Indonesian rule. Inasmuch as the diarchic division had been aligned under Portuguese colonialism with the European distinction between "religion" and "politics," such involvement could be portrayed as an infelicitous mixing of separate spheres, and it had become common for people to admonish the priests for engaging in "*politika*"; I would note, however, that while such admonishments were usually met with denials, some priests proudly rejected the implied limitation on their authority, implicitly reaffirming a more expansive concept of the "political" and their own role as the legitimizers of power.

Durand argues (2004: 86) that a "gap" opened up over the occupation, which would be filled by the Catholic Church. As traditional political and ritual leaders alike were increasingly compromised, he suggests, the church came to combine the diarchic functions, taking on the active power of defending the people, while also representing "immobile authority, turned toward the interior." I find this suggestion provocative, if somewhat overstated. Traditional ritual leaders are still highly respected in Aileu and elsewhere, but few people felt that they could play a unifying role in the wake of the independence struggle, in part because they seemed internally divided. By contrast, the church had taken on the more inclusive position. The dramatic increase in conversions to Catholicism under Indonesian rule was motivated by more than the requirement to affiliate with one of the six religions recognized by the government under Pancasila; it also indexed a heightened sense of membership in the moral community of the Catholic Church.[39] There was a widespread sentiment that it was the clergy who had stood both with and for the people during the occupation, who had come down among them, shared in their suffering, and tried to protect them. During the transition, I found that expressions of respect for the church typically conveyed populist resentment of political elites, especially leaders of the new parties; many of these were returning diasporans who had not "suffered with the people" (*ba teurs nor povu*) but were self-interestedly "using the people's name" (*usa povu ni kalan*).

If Mambai were often disappointed by returning outsiders, they continued to nurture expectations of them. Even in the darkest days, there was comfort in the knowledge that José Ramos-Horta and other expatriate leaders who comprised the "Diplomatic Front" were serving as the "speaking voice" of the suffering people to the outside world. Sometimes, moreover, these hopes took enchanted form. Some followers of Felix may have tried to drive out the Portuguese, but the same mythological logic could be deployed to channel the protective power of the outside. In 1976, I was told, members of a movement associated with Felix had attempted to open the "mountain door" (*damata hoha*) to the Malai world, the Indonesians having blocked the northern "door of the sea" (*damata taisa*). Mau Balen was part of this movement, which I have written about elsewhere (Traube 2007), and so, in a sense, was I. Friends told me that the leaders displayed photographs of me and claimed to be able to contact me for help from the "great lands" (*rai tun*) across the sea. Some people said that movement leaders "exploited" (*esplora*) their followers and used my name for selfish gain. If so, the value of their represented relationship to me derived from the pact of reciprocity between Timorese and Malaia.

Within that much violated pact, Europeans remain beholden to those left behind even after returning to their own lands. This idea underwrites an interest in returns that is much wider than the Felix movements. Over the occupation, Mambai and other East Timorese came to see independence as theirs to earn, at the cost of immense suffering. But throughout the struggle, people also continued to believe that they have a moral claim on the outside world, not as rights-bearing members of an abstract humanity but as faithful partners in an exchange relationship that continues to evolve.

Acknowledgments

This chapter is based on research pursued in Aileu between 1973 and 1974 (supported by grants from the National Science Foundation and the National Institute of Health). I first returned to Aileu in October 2000 for approximately nine months of fieldwork; this work was supported by grants from the Wenner Gren Foundation and Wesleyan University. With the help of a summer research grant from the National Endowment for the Humanities, I returned for another two months of fieldwork in 2002; in July 2007, I visited several Mambai districts, including Aileu, as an election observer for the Carter Center. I thank, in particular, all the people of Hohul and Raimaus who have instructed me over the years, as well as the household of Era Bisa, which first received me and welcomed me back. An earlier version of this chapter was presented at UCLA to the "Culture, Power and Social Change" study group; I am especially grateful to Sherry Ortner for her suggestions.

Elizabeth G. Traube is professor of anthropology at Wesleyan University (USA). She began her research with Mambai-speaking people of Aileu when Timor-Leste was still under Portuguese rule and has returned to Aileu several times since renewing her research there in 2000. She is the author of *Cosmology and Social Life: Ritual Exchange among the Mambai of East Timor* (1986) and coeditor (with Andrew McWilliam) of *Land and Life in Timor-Leste: Ethnographic Essays* (2011). Recent publications have focused on Mambai perspectives on the legacy of resistance and the independence struggle.

Notes

1. By 2000, the term *kaladi* was primarily used in Aileu, as it was elsewhere, in opposition to *firaku*, to connote a purportedly regional distinction between "westerners" and "easterners" that was regarded as an obstacle to national unity. Although I was not specifically tracking usage of the term *kaladi* during my first fieldwork, my memory is that it was primarily used by educated Timorese in Dili as a label for the upland population, and that when Aileu Mambai occasionally used it as a self-representation, it was to contrast themselves to the coastal townspeople rather than to easterners. This impression is consistent with Douglas Kammen's argument for its origins in the term *callades* (or *caladas*) which appears in eighteenth-century Portuguese sources as a label for rebellious upland

peoples, and which seems to have been adapted from Malay *keladis*, "eaters of yams," reflecting a common pattern in which rice-cultivating lowland peoples refer to highlanders by the foods they produced (Kammen 2010: 248–49).

2. To Europeans, as Margaret Wiener (1995: 40) astutely observes, "spirituality" connoted piety and unworldliness, but taking the term more literally, as involvement with spirits, is closer to the Balinese conception of royal power that she explores.

3. Oral traditions that I collected also represent Aileu as having supported the Portuguese against Manufahi.

4. In Obeyesekere's view, emphasis on cultural categories makes indigenous peoples appear incapable of what he calls "practical rationality," which he defines as a universal mode of thought that allows individuals to think beyond inherited conceptual resources. Sahlins (perhaps unjustly) has assimilated Obeyesekere's concept to bourgeois rationalism, and charges him accordingly with universalizing Western norms (1995).

5. On the importance of regalia in Southeast Asian political life, see Errington (1989) and Wiener (1995).

6. The Dutch used gold staffs of office to construct the office of *raja* (Hoskins 1997: 56).

7. It is in many respects strikingly similar to Maori cosmogony.

8. Among the significant motifs I am glossing over is an identification of the flag with a menstrual cloth, stained red by "dead blood"; Loer Sa is said to have spied on his menstruating mother (or sister); he is represented as "wet mouth/bloody cheek" (*kuku tita /fau lara*), a reference to the menstrual blood that drops onto his face. Sahlins (1985: 79) observes that power, conceived of as an extrinsic force, is often associated with transgressive acts, such as murder or incest, or other acts that negate kinship behavior.

9. Hierarchical relations among origin villages associated with the delegation of regalia constitute what Mambai call "the old kingdom" or "kingdom of long ago" (*reinu akin* or *'reinu antiku*), as distinguished from the "new" territorially based administrative organization of nucleated villages (*suku*) established by the colonial government over the early twentieth century. The "old kingdom" is materialized on ritual occasions, most dramatically when the ritual centers rebuild their cult houses.

10. According to Hohul and Raimaus people, these relations were formerly enacted in tributary arrangements, in which the peoples of the interior sent agricultural produce to the Malaia on the coast and the coastal ruler of Motain sent reciprocal prestations of coastal products up to the interior.

11. Diarchic ideologies and patterns of politico-ritual governance, a feature of many Austronesian societies, are widely distributed across the island of Timor; ideas of a distinction between an active, masculine power and a more passive, often symbolically feminine, yet in many ways fundamental authority find expression in a great variety of forms, including origin

narratives, material structures, and ideal models of the polity; detailed accounts of such formations include Cunningham (1965), Schulte Nordholt (1971), Renard-Clamagirand (1982), Freidberg (1989), Traube (1986), McWilliam (2002), Hicks (2004), and Therik (2004).

12. On the stranger king theme as an expression of diarchy, see Sahlins (1985, 2000), Fox (1995), Siikala (2006), Henley (2002), McWilliam (2011).

13. On Timor, the retuning outsider is often a younger brother; see, for instance, Hicks (1999) on the connection between divine kingship and the figure of the younger brother in Tetum myth.

14. Sahlins has analyzed Polynesian versions of this pattern (1985); what he characterizes as the main pattern of Fijian kingship involves displacements and reversals: people of the land, displaced by a stranger king, take on the role of war king, while the stranger king and his descendants become the preeminent sacerdotal king. A notable departure from this pattern was the Fijian kingdom of Bau, where Sahlins says the war king was elevated over the ritual king (2000). According to Sahlins, the reversal of hierarchy is matched by a similar reversal in the traditions of the founding of the polity: elsewhere in Fiji, the war kings are descended from the original peoples of the land, who take on this role after the stranger kings usurp their ritual role. By contrast, in Bau, the (present) ritual kings were the original rulers, and two dynasties of war kings arrived subsequently (from the interior rather than from overseas) and usurped them as war kings (2000: 411n30).

15. In Southeast Asian conceptions of kingship such relative stillness would be an index of superior status (see Anderson 1972, Errington 1989).

16. Barnes (2011: 30) describes a similar theme among Naueti people of Viqueque: the Darlari elders represent the highest ritual authority within a domain claim that their ancestors once held both ritual and jural power; but later they delegate active duties to other houses and "retreat into darkness"; Barnes observes that Darlari presented this "retreat" as a conscious decision intended to keep the secrets of the land away from "outsiders"—the colonial authorities and the Catholic Church; in a footnote, she adds that Darlari portray the represented "retreat" as a source of strength rather than a sign of weakness or loss of power (Barnes 2011: 30n22).

17. When Hohul rebuilds its origin houses, the pole is also ceremonially replaced. On one such occasion, according to Hohul people, the Aileun chiefs demanded that the new pole be erected in their origin village rather than in Hohul, but the tree trunk that had been cut down became so heavy that no one could lift it, until the Aileun withdrew their claim and permitted it to be brought to Hohul; then it immediately became light. See Traube 2011.

18. The fundamental opposition between (active) power and (passive) authority that defines the idealized diarchic poles is also recursively rep-

licated at multiple levels; thus, within ritual centers like Hohul and Raimaus, houses are symbolically differentiated as "outer" and "inner"; the "outer" houses are sometimes represented as mediating between the origin village and the outside world; or, as in this case, they represent the place within the spiritual center where disputes relating to ritual matters are settled, whereas the older, inner houses are oriented exclusively toward the silent, spirit powers of the cosmos; the mistrust of Felix comes from the representatives of executive power within Hohul.

19. The Jesuits founded a college there in 1898.

20. *Fad-kreda* (or *uma-kreda* in Tetum) is the term for a Christian church, literally a house of worship.

21. In their version, the second priest died from flea bites.

22. Ritual authorities also claim titles, and some include Portuguese objects among their sacred heirlooms.

23. According to Durand's estimate, in 1882, only 1 percent of Mambai (210 out of 21,400) had converted (2004: 54).

24. The Canossians, one of the three orders that replaced the Dominicans after World War II, played a major role in the education of girls (Durand 2004: 95).

25. In a journal I kept during my first fieldwork, a passage I no longer recall writing reports that Mau Balen had told me Felix wanted to meet with me in Dili; I seem to have responded with indifference, tinged with indignation, apparently feeling that someone was trying to con me, and I rather smugly refused the invitation. "*Conforme Menina*" (As you wish), Mau Balen quietly replied.

26. Critics portray the commodified character of such transactions as in tension with both Christianity and indigenous practice; God (Maromak), they would say, doesn't demand chickens; and while traditional cult life certainly involves material obligations, there are, in principle, no mechanisms of enforcement other than symbolic capital; thus, ritual authorities emphasize that they cannot compel people to bring gifts or even to attend ritual events; in practice, considerable effort is invested in mobilizing moral sanctions, but speakers rhetorically emphasize the voluntary character of participation: those who recognize "their old mother and old father" are said to respond to the call, snatching up whatever they have, and bringing it to the origin village.

27. Citing Duarte, both Pélissier (1996: 118n185) and Durand (2004: 57) portray Hohul as the center of a syncretic sectarian movement inspired by Felix; I think this greatly exaggerates the heterodox character of Hohul's ritual practice.

28. According to Roque (2015: 80), witchcraft trials were seen as an especially "barbarous" custom that Portuguese colonial administrators were instructed in principle to avoid; yet, they were also told that told that even the executions of accused witches might have to be tolerated, as part of the strategy of adapting to and embracing Timorese "manners."

29. On one of my post-occupation visits, Mau Balen once told me that Felix had brought the "Japanese War" (the Second World War) in order to "drive out" (*fda*) the Malaia because the latter had inflated the costs of the head tax.

30. Pélissier (1996: 233) calls the move from the *finta* to a head tax "explosive"; according to Gunn (2001: 7), it was a primary motivation for the two major Manufahi revolts/rebellions against the Portuguese; Aileu executive chiefs were among the "loyal allies" in both campaigns, but there were also reports that several villages aided the rebels (Pélissier 1996: 193–94).

31. I now assume that Mau Balen was referring to this boy when he described Felix as taking the shape of a young boy named Mau Bere.

32. According to Duarte, who describes Aileu as the main area of influence of Hoho-hulo, Castro had planned a revolt against the Portuguese as part of the wider conspiracy.

33. Duarte notes that a decade or so prior to these events, Hohul had represented itself as the "doorway" by which Portugal sent its troops to Timor. This door literally swings two ways.

34. The plan proposed the formation of a transitional government and an elected consultative Assembly that would prepare for the election of a constitutional Assembly in 1976; it was the first time the Portuguese government officially recognized the right of the East Timorese people to independence (Durand 2001: 107).

35. The primary intended audience for the so-called Balibo Declaration was probably the international community; nevertheless, it resonates with Southeast Asian traditions of outer-island rulers seeking aid from Majapahit; given that the Indonesians had anticipated a brief military campaign (Anderson 1998), they may also have been laying the groundwork for legitimation of their rule.

36. Mau Bere's brother once contrasted the violent Indonesian intervention with the arrival of UNAMET (United Nations Mission in East Timor) and UNTAET (United Nations Transitional Administration in East Timor), observing, somewhat tongue-in-cheek, that the Malaia had once again brought peace and order.

37. Mau Bere's brother had a roll of undeveloped photographs he had taken at the event; I got them developed for him. There were several shots of the buffalo ceremony, and the Bupati was among the onlookers.

38. After the referendum, he had gone to West Timor (apparently voluntarily) and did not return until two years later.

39. This is how the proportion of Catholics in East Timor went from 30 percent in the mid-1970s to 80 percent in 1980, to more than 90 percent in 1990 (Durand 2004: 94).

References

Almeida, A. 1965. *O Povo Mambai: Contribuicão para o Estudo do Povo do Grupo Linguístico Mambai-Timor*. Lisbon: Instituto Superior de Ciências Sociais e Política Ultramarina.

Anderson, B. 1972. "The Idea of Power in Javanese Culture." In *Culture and Politics in Indonesia*, edited by C. Holt, B. Anderson, and J. Siegel, 1–69. Ithaca, NY: Cornell University Press.

———. 1998. "Gravel in Jakarta's Shoes." In *The Spectre of Comparisons: Nationalism, Southeast Asia and the World*, 131–38. New York: Verso.

Barnes, S. 2011. "Origins, Precedence and Social Order in the Domain of *Ina Ama Beli Darlari*." In *Land and Life in Timor-Leste: Ethnographic Essays*, edited by A. R. McWilliam and E. G. Traube, 23–46. Canberra: ANU Press.

Bovensiepen, J. 2011. "Opening and Closing the Land: Land and Power in the Idate Highlands." In *Land and Life in Timor-Leste: Ethnographic Essays*, edited by A. R. McWilliam and E. G. Traube, 47–60. Canberra: ANU Press.

Cunningham, C. E. 1965. "Order and Change in an Atoni Diarchy." *Southwestern Journal of Anthropology* 21: 359–82.

Duarte, J. B. 1987/88. "O fenómeno dos movimentos nativistas." *Garcia de Orta, Série de Antropobiologia* 5(1–2): 41–52.

Durand, F. 2001. "Timor Lorosa'e 1930–2001: Partis politiques et processus électoraux à hauts risques." *Aséanie* 8: 103–26.

———. 2004. *Catholicisme et Protestantisme dans l'Île de Timor: 1556–2003*. Toulouse and Bangkok: Editions Arkuiris-IRASEC.

Errington, S. 1989. *Meaning and Power in a Southeast Asian Realm*. Princeton, NJ: Princeton University Press.

Fox, J. J. 1995. "Installing the Outsider Inside: The Exploration of an Epistemic Austronesian Cultural Theme and Its Social Significance," revised draft. Paper presented at the first Conference of the European Association for Southeast Asian Studies: Local Transformations and Common Heritage in Southeast Asia, 29 June–1 July, Leiden University, Netherlands.

Freidberg, C. 1989. "Social Relations of Territorial Management in Light of Bunaq Farming Rituals." In C. Barraud and J. D. M. Platenkamp (eds.), "Ritual and Socio-cosmic Order in Eastern Indonesian Societies," *Bijdragen tot de Taal-, Land- en Volkenkunde* 145(4): 548–62.

Gose, P. 2008. *Invaders as Ancestors: On the Intercultural Making and Unmaking of Spanish Colonialism in the Andes*. Toronto: University of Toronto Press.

Guha, R. 1997. *Dominance without Hegemony: History and Power in Colonial India*. Cambridge, MA: Harvard University Press.

———. 1983. *Elementary Aspects of Peasant Insurgency in Colonial India*. Delhi: Oxford.

Gunn, G. 1999. *Timor Loro Sae: 500 Years*. Macau: Livros do Oriente.

———. 2001. "The Five Hundred Year Timorese *Funu*." In *Bitter Flowers, Sweet Flowers: East Timor, Indonesia, and the World Community*, R. Tanter, M. Selden, and S. R. Shalom, 3–14. New York: Rowman & Littlefield Publishers.

Gunter, J. 2007. "Communal Violence in Viqueque and the 'Charged' History of '59." *Asia Pacific Journal of Anthropology* 8(1): 27–41.

Henley, D. 2002. *Jealousy and Justice: The Indigenous Roots of Colonial Rule in Northern Sulawesi.* Amsterdam: VU University Press.

Hicks, D. 1999. "Divine Kings and Younger Brothers on Timor." In *Structuralism's Transformations: Order and revision in Malaysian Societies: Papers written in honor of Clark E. Cunningham*, Program for Southeast Asian Studies Monograph Series, edited by L. V. Aragon and S. D. Russell, 95–113. Tempe: Arizona State University.

———. 2004. *Tetum Ghosts and Kin: Fertility and Gender in East Timor.* 2nd ed. Long Grove, IL: Waveland.

———. 2007. "Younger Brother and Fishing Hook on Timor: Reassessing Mauss on Hierarchy and Divinity." *Journal of the Royal Anthropological Institute* 13: 39–56.

Hoskins, J. 1997. *The Play of Time: Kodi Perspectives on Calendars, History and Exchange.* 2nd ed. Berkeley: University of California Press.

Kammen, D. 2010, "Subordinating Timor: Central Authority and the Origins of Communal Identities in East Timor." *Bijdragen tot de Taal-, Land- en Volkenkunde* 166(2–3): 244–69.

Lamana, G. 2008. *Domination without Dominance: Inca-Spanish Encounters in Early Colonial Peru.* Durham, NC: Duke University Press.

McWilliam, A. R. 1999. "Development Technologies and the Classification of Strangers in West Timor." In *Structuralism's Transformations: Order and revision in Malaysian Societies: Papers written in honor of Clark E. Cunningham*, Program for Southeast Asian Studies Monograph Series, edited by L. V. Aragon and S. D. Russell, 377–402. Tempe: Arizona State University.

———. 2002, *Paths of Origin, Gates of Life: A Study of Place and Precedence in Southwest Timor.* Leiden: KITLV Press.

———. 2011. "Fataluku Living Landscapes." In *Land and Life in Timor-Leste*, edited by A. R. McWilliam and E.G. Traube, 61–86. Canberra: ANU Press.

Molnar, A. 2011. "Darlau: Origins and Their Significance in Atsabe Kemak Identity." In *Land and Life in Timor-Leste*, edited by A. R. McWilliam and E. G. Traube, 87–115. Canberra: ANU Press.

Obeyesekere, G. 1992. *The Apotheosis of Captain Cook: European Mythmaking in the Pacific.* Princeton, NJ: Princeton University Press.

Pélissier, R. 1996. *Timor en Guerre: Le Crocodile et les Portugais (1847–1913).* Orgeval: Pélissier.

Renard-Clamagirand, B. 1982. *Marobo: Une Société Ema de Timor.* Langues et Civilisation de L'Asie du Sud-Est et du Monde Insulindien 12, Paris.

Roque, R. 2010. *Headhunting and Colonialism: Anthropology and the Circulation of Human Skulls in the Portuguese Empire, 1870–1930.* New York: Palgrave Macmillan.

―――. 2015. "Mimetic Governmentality and the Administration of Justice in Colonial East Timor, c. 1860–1910." *Comparative Studies in Society and History* 57(1): 67–97.

Roque, R., and K. Wagner (eds.). 2012. *Engaging Colonial Knowledge: Reading European Archives in World History.* Basingstoke: Palgrave Macmillan.

Sahlins, M. 1985. *Islands of History.* Chicago: University of Chicago Press.

―――. 1995. *How "Natives" Think: About Captain Cook, for Example.* Chicago: University of Chicago Press.

―――. 2000. "The Discovery of the True Savage." In *Culture in Practice: Selected Essays,* 353–413. New York: Zone Books.

Schrempp, G. 1992. *Magical Arrows: The Maori, the Greeks, and the Folklore of the Universe.* Madison: University of Wisconsin Press.

Schulte Nordholt, H. G. 1971. *The Political System of the Atoni of Timor.* The Hague. Nijhoff.

Siikala, J. 2006. "The Elder and the Younger: Foreign and Autochthonous Origin and Hierarchy in the Cook Islands." In *Origins, Ancestry and Alliance: Explorations in Austronesian Ethnography,* edited by J. J. Fox and C. Sather, 43–56. Canberra: ANU Press.

Therik, T. 2004. *Wehali, the Female Land: Traditions of a Timorese Ritual Centre.* Canberra: Department of Anthropology, Research School of Pacific and Asian Studies, the Australian National University, in association with Pandanus Books.

Traube, E. G. 1986. *Cosmology and Social Life: Ritual Exchange among the Mambai of East Timor.* Chicago: University of Chicago Press.

―――. 1989. "Obligations to the Source." In *The Attraction of Opposites: Thought and Society in a Dualistic Mode,* edited by D. Maybury-Lewis and U. Almagor, 321–44. Ann Arbor: University of Michigan Press.

―――. 1995. "Mambai Perspectives on Colonialism and Decolonization." In *East Timor at the Crossroads: The Forging of a Nation,* edited by P. Carey and G. C. Bentley, 42–55. London: Social Science Research Council.

―――. 2007. "Unpaid Wages: Local Narratives and the Imagination of the Nation." *Asia Pacific Journal of Anthropology* 8(1): 9–25.

―――. 2011. "Planting the Flag." In *Land and Life in Timor-Leste,* edited by A. McWilliam and E. G. Traube, 117–40. Canberra: ANU Press.

Wiener, M. 1995. *Visible and Invisible Realms: Power, Magic and Colonial Conquest in Bali.* Chicago: University of Chicago Press.

Chapter 2

THE ENIGMAS OF TIMORESE HISTORY AND MANIPULATIONS OF MYTHICAL NARRATIVES BY LOCAL SOCIETIES

THE EXAMPLE OF BUNAQ-LANGUAGE POPULATIONS

Claudine Friedberg

Bunaq-speaking populations provide a good subject for confronting colonial archives with history as recounted by the Timorese themselves. These populations are located on both sides of the border between Timor-Leste and Indonesia. As Schapper has shown (2011b), they took part in the establishment of that border, which was only stabilized in 1914 with the Hague treaty between Portugal and the Netherlands.

Bunaq is the only non-Austronesian language spoken in central Timor, whereas populations speaking other non-Austronesian languages are found in eastern Timor. As Schapper reminds us, Austronesian languages nevertheless influenced Bunaq vocabulary and syntax. Borrowed terms concern status, particularly that of men, and ritual vocabulary.

"Bunaq-speaking populations" is a more accurate characterization than "speakers of Bunaq." Indeed, oral literature and ways of reciting it vary from one group to another. The same can be said about social organization and ritual practices.

I carried out my research in the villages of upper Lamaknen on the Indonesian side. There, Louis Berthe (in 1958–59 and 1966) and I (between 1969 and 1973)[1] collected narratives from several *lal gomo* (masters of the word), keepers of oral traditions. According to these narratives, the ancestors of the inhabitants of these villages came from the east, the part of the island that was under Portuguese rule at the time of the research. It is difficult to interpret ancestors' itineraries, or *bei gua*,[2] "ancestor's footprints," particularly the ones collected by Louis Berthe. People of Lamaknen trace their ancestors' paths according to three lineages from which they claim to descend, but it is impossible to establish correspondences between what happens to one lineage and what happens to another.

The events occurring at the beginning of these mythical narratives have etiological and cosmogonic meaning;[3] they take on a political sense as they recount the origins of status relations among the protagonists. The first event with political meaning is the reunion of the Great Ancestors, the primordial ancestors of the three lineages, in a place called Mali-ama Kan-wa,[4] which is impossible to locate geographically. The Great Ancestors of two lineages (Luta and Sibiri) arrive there directly from the Upperworld (where they are all supposed to originate), whereas those of the third lineage (Oburo) are said to use boats and arrive by maritime ways.

The Great Ancestors of each lineage then continue their own voyage, and their descendants gather once more in a place called Turul tuk Siol wa, where they meet other lineages before dispersing again. Informants used to locate this place in Portuguese territory, approximately in the region Schapper (2011a) considered the area from which the Bunaq language spread.[5]

However, there is no reason to assume that the members of the different lineages who gathered there were all Bunaq speakers. It cannot even be asserted that all the figures whom the inhabitants of upper Lamaknen consider their ancestors spoke Bunaq. Rather, Bunaq could have been the language of the autochthonous population, which was no doubt more numerous, and whose chiefs claimed to have superior tokens of power to those of the newcomers. In the narratives, it is said that these objects are wrapped. The ancestors of the three Lamaknen lineages then go to the kingdom of Wehali to fetch termites, the presence of which reveals the contents of the packages to be sandalwood. At this moment, the ancestors present their own tokens of power, which prove to be more prestigious. The contest leads to a great feast, to which all the neighbors are invited.

These "contests for rule" with local leaders are occasions to present valuable objects, which are supposed to justify claims to status. They are reiterated several times during the travels of the ancestors of the three lineages. Every time a contest occurs, these ancestors succeed in showing their higher status. The nature of the objects is rarely made clear. In Turul tuk Siol wa they are simply designated by the Austronesian expression *ukur naran*, translated by Berthe in the *Bei Gua* as "heritage" or "wealth." Considering that they are now too numerous to be kept together in one place, the ancestors once more split up in order to settle down, find wives, and found households, which are the basis of society. At this point in the narrative, events take place in localities on one side or the other of the current border between Timor-Leste and Indonesia. It is not always easy to be precise, given that the new place of settlement is often given the same name as the place of origin. To this we must add that the *bei gua* are difficult to interpret, in that they are told in a formal poetic language characterized by paired metaphorical expressions.

As for the narratives with etiological value, there is every chance that they are amalgams of traditions with different origins. But the same could be true for the itineraries of those whom the Bunaq of upper Lamaknen consider their ancestors.

The Journey of Luta and the Separation between "the Cold Path" and "the Hot Path"

The journey of Luta raises the most issues. The Great Ancestor sets off for the "World Below" (*pan moal muk moal*, "sky below, earth below") with his sister Tiq Liurai, whose name refers to Venus, the evening star. From this point, they leave on a boat they have built. On the way, the brother and sister commit incest, and the male children resulting from their union in turn commit incest with their mother, leading to numerous children who all have Mugi Dato Malae as their second name.[6]

One can imagine that these events are a metaphorical description of interisland voyages whose direction is difficult to interpret. Is the "Underworld" the sunset point where Venus disappears every evening? In that case, the ancestors would later return toward the east, where Venus appears in the morning under the name Bi Bel, "the star of the wind." Or, is the "Underworld" related to the "low wind," an allusion to navigation paths following the wind bringing the monsoon from west to east? In other words, was the journey headed for the east from the beginning?

The children born from the incestuous unions scatter to various destinations. The text then relates the path of four of them who again set off by boat. The boat runs aground, stuck in the mud of a mangrove. They leave once more on a new boat, stopping at several places (one of which is called Sina Mutin Malaka, "White Malaka China") and finally arrive at Kolobilaq Kabanasaq on the south coast of Timor.

After wandering through consecutive landscapes of *Borassus, Corypha* palms, and jujube trees, they stop, build a shelter, and prepare a field. As the preparations for the harvest are narrated, it seems to be a rice field. After the harvest, they go with *en mila*, "their people," to look for sandalwood and young bees. They load these products onto their boat and go overseas to Sina Mutin Malaka, where they present them to the local leaders, who express their thanks by giving them wives. They return with their wives to Kabanasaq Kolobilaq, where they leave their boat and go back home, to a place supposedly in Timor. They have offspring with these first wives, but they journey forth again in search of other wives, with whom they have many more children as they continue traveling. Every place they stop, they contract alliances with the leaders of the indigenous inhabitants. They settle in Luta dato Zapata, which is inhabited, and establish a rice field before setting off again in search of new wives. Finally, the primordial ancestors die, and it is the children they had with their last wives who arrive in Turul tuk Siol wa.

Few of the place names enumerated during the journey of Luta's ancestors are geographically identifiable, even when we can suppose that they are in Timor, and even less so in the case of maritime voyages. However, it is clear that the place called Sina mutin Malaka is associated with the sandalwood trade, even if we cannot know which Malaka is referred to. Malaka on the Malaysian peninsula? Malaka in Sulawesi? What is important is the role played by this place in the myth of origin of the Tetun kingdom of Wehali in south-central Timor; it is the represented origin place of the founder of Wehali, also called "the new Malaka."

To interpret the itinerary of the ancestors of Luta, we have to take several elements into account:

- First, the motif that the ancestors of Luta cultivate rice gives the impression that it was they who introduced rice to Timor; but this is contradicted by the itinerary of the Sibiri ancestors (recited after that of Luta in the text collected by Louis Berthe), on which the myth of the origin of seeds—which is in fact the myth of the origin of rice—unfolds. This myth is constructed on a generic model for the region. It is said that seeds come from a dead body, and this narrative plays an essential role in agrarian rituals at Abis.

- Second, in lower Lamaknen (particularly in Gewal) preeminence is accorded to the descendants of Luta after a common pattern in Timor, and elsewhere in the region, hierarchical predominance is given to those who come from outside.

According to information collected by Berthe in Gewal, two groups of ancestors are distinguished there: those whose first adventures are located around Mali ama Kan wa (thus establishing a certain confusion between the itineraries of the Oburo and Sibiri lineages), and those who are alternately called the ancestors of Luta or of Sina Mutin Malaka, who set off from the "high wind" of Sia wa Mugi wa and pass through Pan Lubu and Sina Mutin Malaka. Yet according to masters of the word living in Abis, the ways mythical texts are recited at Gewal and Abis are drastically different. Unlike Gewal, where they are not distinguished, texts in Abis are divided into *bei gua* related to coolness (*huruk gie*, "cool belong"), the side of life and fertility, and *tete tiep* connected to heat (*tinoq gie*, "hot belong"), the side of fighting, danger, and death. This division occurs from the moment of the descent from the Upperworld of the two primordial brother-sister couples. They separate and share out the inheritance and tokens of power they receive from their parents (*die eme hot die ama hul*, "their mother sun and father moon").

The primordial couples, parents of the Great Ancestors of the three lineages, Oburo, Luta, and Sibiri, whose itineraries constitute the *bei gua*, receive among other attributes *pana getel mone goron*, "the roots of women and the leaves of men" (i.e. the life of human beings), wealth (*ukur naran*), and tokens of power (*dato bul loro bul*).

Those whose adventures belong to *tinoq gie*, or *tigi ho* ("the blood that drips"), also get wealth and tokens of power in addition to weapons—in particular, the sabre and the spear. They give birth, by committing incest, to numerous children who all have as their second name Liurai Karisaen. The eldest is named Leki Liurai Leki Karisaen, and the youngest Suri Liurai Suri Karisaen. They become chiefs respectively of Likosaen and Wehali. Later, a war breaks out between the two after an act of deception by the latter against the former.

But various events take place before that.

At first, all the brothers go hunting together, but they argue over the sharing of the meat and split up. Leki leaves for Likosaen Lorosaen, taking away the attributes of a warrior. His brothers scatter to different places. One of them takes scales and weights with him and goes to Sina Mutin Malaka.

Finally, Suri Liurai, the youngest, and two of his brothers, Ikun and Bolan, go to Lubu dato Salaer, also called Pan Lubu Muk Lubu, "sky of Lubu, earth of Lubu." There they find only water and swamp plants. They go back to the Upperworld and ask their parents for help. Their parents give them a goat and a buffalo to get rid of the plants, and then a boat to drive back the water. They go looking for trees and stones (*hotel o hul*) to construct their dwelling. At this point, to help them populate their realm, their parents give them seven balls of mud, one of which turns into a man who multiplies immediately, and so constitutes their people.

Suri Liurai sends some of his men to Suai on the south coast of Timor, while he himself travels to various places (mostly difficult to locate geographically) where repeated conflicts and fights take place. Among these places are Suai Uma-hatus, Liurai Liwai Wehali, Likosaen Lorosaen, and Likosaen Railor.

Suri Liurai meets his brother Leki Liurai after a hunting party, and they decide to exchange wives. But Suri Liurai tries to trick his elder brother by sending him a servant disguised as a chief's wife, and the attempted deception triggers the war between Likosaen and Wehali. Does the conflict correspond to a historical reality, or is it a symbolic transposition of a competition for the recognition of suzerainty over territories and local chiefdoms? Is it a reflection of the rivalry between Portugal and the Netherlands?

The location of Wehali is known, although the extent of the territory over which it exerted its sovereignty is uncertain, but locating Likosaen raises problems. Several researchers seem to agree that it can be identified with the district of Liquiçá on the north coast, not far from Dili, but no one in Bunaq country seems to know Liquiçá. Depending on the place and the person speaking, they say they belong to Likosaen or Wehali, which appear to be regarded as complementary domains rather than as enemies; of the two, Wehali is always superior. According to ethnographer Brigitte Renard-Clamagirand,[7] for the Kemak of Marobo to "make Likosaen Wehali" means to make war—that is, to divide into two entities in order to go headhunting.

In 1970, when I researched in Bunaq territory in Portuguese Timor, people in Ai Asa told me that the ancestors of hierarchically superior households had come from the south, more specifically from Suai, and that they had chased the original inhabitants of the region—who were Bunaq—toward the west. At the same time, they said they belonged to a Likosaen warrior, and therefore male, household, inferior to a female Wehali. In Domon Siwe, informers said that

Suri Liurai and Leki Liurai came together to bring tokens of power to local chiefs. In Lamaknen, several ruling houses are supposed to have obtained tokens of power when fighting a war for Suri Liurai, in places difficult to locate geographically.

From all this we can draw out a recognition of a certain sovereignty of Wehali over this central region of Timor, with different inferences on the local political organizations and practices. This is doubtless what explains the colonial powers' perplexity about the relations of local chiefdoms to one another. Data collected also converge in attributing superiority either to nobles who came from the south or to tokens of power given by the Wehali (which are therefore also from the south). Activities of Luta's ancestors, as establishing rice-growing and sandalwood trade, and their itinerary including several maritime voyages, contrast with those of the other lineages' ancestors. Their gathering at Mali ama Kan wa seems all the more likely to be a political construction, not the reflection of an improbable historical reality.

One cannot help but be struck by the account of the adventures and itinerary of the "hot path" ancestors. They settle in a place evoking the Luwu kingdom in Sulawesi and the island of Salayar, where a full-blown creation of the world is accounted with its surfacing from the waters. Yet, one can find a different version at the beginning of the *bei gua*. Most startling is the account of the creation of human beings from mud. Their essence differs drastically from that of the ancestors, who originated in the Upperworld, "children of the sun and moon." Another point has to be added about the itinerary of Luta's ancestors. Several times in the narrative, it is pointed out that harvesting rice and collecting sandalwood was the task of people named *en* and *mila* (terms that Berthe translated as "people" and "slaves"[8] throughout the *Bei Gua*).

There is clearly confusion in the *bei gua* as they are recited in Gewal. Luta's itinerary seems to merge into the one attributed to ancestors of the "hot path" and declaimed by the upper Lamaknen masters of the word. This confusion is unacceptable for the latter. I once witnessed an outburst of anger on a visit with several Lamaknen masters of the word, who followed the Gewal tradition: after hearing the Luta version of the *bei gua*, which mixes the two paths, hot and cold, one man started to stamp out a war dance on the porch of the house where we were welcomed.

The choice to separate texts about cold path from those related to hot path, and to make all the Great Ancestors of the three lineages gather in one place, appears to be an affirmation of the common identity of the ancestors: they all came from the sky, they are all children of the Lord Sun and the Lord Moon (*Naqi hot gol Naqi hul gol*). Above all, they have nothing to do with the human beings made from the mud of Pan Lubu. But these textual manipulations do not preclude that the hierarchical status of a house depends on the tokens of power they possess.

The Mau Ipi Guloq Episode and the "Orange Wives"

A mythical episode that takes place on the journey of Oburo's ancestors, long after their departure from Mali ama Kan wa, also allows the Bunaq of upper Lamaknen to affirm their origin. It illustrates the common theme of a conflict between elder and younger brothers. This subject is widespread in the area and has been analyzed by Hicks (2007) through various versions, including a Bunaq version as recounted in the *Bei Gua*. Hicks interprets these texts as representations of humanity's relations with the divine.

For our demonstration, this aspect is of lesser importance. We focus on the epilogue of this mythical sequence in which the younger brother, Mau ipi guloq (Mau Rice-tail), who has triumphed over his elder brother, finds himself rich with four wives after his brother's death. Two of the wives were his brother's, who had refused to share them with him—this was the reason for their conflict. In addition, he receives two more wives from the chief of the "World Below." With the first two, Mau ipi guloq has numerous children, who are said to have spread into various regions of Timor, but whom the Bunaq of upper Lamaknen do not recognize as their ancestors. The first two wives are metamorphosed wild pigs, which came to eat the produce of the garden cultivated by the two brothers; marrying "boar wives" is a metaphor for a marriage with native women. Bunaq people claim to be descendants of the elder brother's wives and consider themselves immigrants, whose ancestors chased away (or killed?) all the original inhabitants of the land. In fact, inhabitants of Abis say that there was no marriage with any native women.

But what do the two women given by the chief of the World Below and also named "seed of the sea" (*besi meti gie bin mo gie*) represent for the people who consider themselves to be their descendants? Mau ipi guloq gets these wives in *pan moal muk moal*, "sky below, earth below," where the land's chief, a black bird (*bai guzu guzu bai hawen*), takes refuge after being injured. This bird, a crow according to informants, had been pecking the backs of the hero's buffalo. Mau ipi guloq shoots it in the head with a dart from his blowpipe. The bird flees with the dart in its head and returns to its domain, "World Below." This is the place where Mau ipi guloq, carried on the tail of another bird, finds it; there he sees the local population lamenting because the one they call *nei nomo nei nemel*, "our master, our genitor," is wounded in the head. Realizing that his dart had wounded the bird, Mau ipi guloq offers to heal it by removing the dart and applying unguents to the wound. Once healed, the chief of the World Below asks Mau ipi guloq what he wants as a reward. Refusing all kinds of wealth, he requests two ripe fruits from the top of a tree. The two fruits turn into women on the way home. According to the *lal gomo*, these fruits are oranges, or rather some sort of citrus with large fruit.

What is this "World Below," source of the "orange wives," who are also known as "seed of the sea"? The same *lal gomo* declared that it is not at all the same "World Below"[9] found at the beginning of the Luta lineage's journey, but the plains of Timor's north coast. It is the place where crows are found; they only migrate to the mountains for a few months each year. Should we therefore conclude that these brides are supposed to come from across the sea as, no doubt, citrus trees did too?

Once again we face a manipulation of the texts aimed at affirming a prestigious filiation; while in this case, descent passes through women, the common theme is the valorizing of what comes from outside.

The superiority of what comes from outside is a common theme in the region: it finds expression in the myth of the stranger king[10] as manifested, for example, in the origin narrative of Wehali. And yet we must note that the attitude of the Bunaq in Abis on this subject is ambiguous, as they refuse any superiority deriving from men who arrived via the south coast; they only accept this superiority when it is associated with women coming from the north coast.

The Nature of Tokens of Power and Their Transmission: The Two Forms of Marriage

Actually, the very construction of hierarchical relations is constantly called into question. On what criteria is hierarchy established? As we have already seen, claims to status are based on the possession of particular objects.

In the words of the *Bei Gua*, these objects were inherited from the primordial ancestors, who in turn received them from their own parents, "their mother sun and father moon." It is specified that the male ancestors of the inhabitants of upper Lamaknen take these objects with them throughout their wanderings. Every recitation deals more or less with the same enumeration:[11]

- *die dato bul die loro bul*, "the foundation of their title of chief, the foundation of their title of king";
- *die ukur gemel die naran gemel*, "the great and abundant wealth," which is also sometimes designated by the expression *ukur ginil ginil naran gewen gewen; die taka por die luhan por, die segen por die bulot por*, terms indicating the sacred objects of each household.

As a reminder, the competition over sacred tokens that took place at the gathering of Turul tuk Siol wa was an occasion for the ancestors to assert the power and prestige of their heirlooms without specifying their precise nature.

The last part of the narrative follows that gathering and deals with the foundation of houses in Henes, a village neighboring Abis. At this point, the account focuses principally on genealogical relationships, narrating successive marriages and listing the children born from those marriages.[12] The type of marriage at issue here is *sul suliq*, "the spear and the sabre"; the woman and her descendants enter the household of the husband, where they become part of a specific *dil*, designated by the name of the household from which she originates. This *dil* is different from her husband's *dil*. From this type of marriage derive the *malu ai*, marital alliances between "givers and takers of women," which constitute the framework of relationships between households. In fact, while the household is the basis of Bunaq society, in Lamaknen this unit is constituted by an association of fragments of matrilineages or *dil*. In the village of Abis, where I undertook a genealogical survey, I was given the list of *dil*, from two to six in number, along with their members for each household.

However, there is another form of marriage called *ton terel* (which Berthe translates as "the sharing of goods produced in common"), in which the woman and her descendants continue to belong to her household, whereas the husband remains a member of his own. This form of marriage requires a matrimonial compensation paid by the husband's family to the bride's family. By contrast, *sul suliq* marriage calls for contributions made by the whole *malu ai* network of the bride and groom.

Ton terel marriage enables the perpetuation of different *dil* within the household. In principle, no mention of this type of marriage is made in the Bei Gua. In the most common case of *ton terel* marriages, I was also provided with the household to which the husbands belonged. This shows the extent to which memory of filiation is alive—important for avoiding incest (marriage to a sister's descendants is forbidden). But more interesting is the memory of the transmission of goods linked to status. They remain the property of a *dil* rather than of all the members of a household, as we shall see later. At the time of my research, *dil* were usually perpetuated through *ton terel* marriages. *Sul suliq* marriages were rare. Nonetheless, there are two *dil* from a house that in principle cannot disappear: those of the founders, the *malu panu gomo* and *malu mone gomo*, "guardian provider of the woman" and "guardian provider of the man," to which the keepers of the house's sacred objects obligatorily belong.

In the text collected by Louis Berthe, *sul suliq* marriage is characterized by specific botanic metaphors, as when the bride leaves her house: *sasa o sulol pili o paqe*, "sucker and cuttings, pick and untie." From here on, she is represented as a sprout "transplanted" to another house. Repeatedly in the text it is said that the bride only agrees to leave her origin house if she is given part of its sacred heirlooms, including, in particular circumstances, those materializing her status in the hierarchy, which are associated with ritual prerogatives, such as the right to receive a specific bone during the ceremonial sharing of meat of domestic animals, or during ritual hunts. For example, in verse 7291 of the *Bei Gua*, two women from the royal house of Henes ask for and receive the right to the thigh as a dowry, a privilege of royal status. Yet Louis Berthe specifies in a note on verse 7303 that this gift involves no loss of status for the donor house.

This was set differently in Abis, a village of inferior status to Henes and under the lordship of Lakmaras, where the chief is entitled to a shoulder blade. In the village's foundation narratives, this right shifts with a woman, the daughter of the founders of the local chief's house. She marries a newcomer, and they found a house together; then she marries again with another newcomer and they found another house, a house which still held the position of chief at the time of my research. In both marriages, this woman took the right to the shoulder blade with her.

The question of the legitimacy of tokens of power held by a house thus appears very ambiguous. Inherited in principle from primordial ancestors who came down from the sky, they could also have been acquired along the journey, given by Wehali, passed on by men or by women; and yet, all this tells us nothing about their concrete nature.

What was evident in my fieldwork experience was the importance of respecting each person's hierarchical status. I witnessed this many times. For instance, in lower Lamaknen, during a ritual hunt, we had to wait for the participants to decide who should receive a particular bone traditionally presented to status superiors, as they did not accept the legitimacy of the leader chosen by the administration. During their deliberations, the game hung on a tree rotting in the sun for hours.

On the Portuguese side, I was sorely tested at Oe Lequ. Once the elders (gathered by the colonially appointed chief) had put forward the traditional social organization, they offered me the betel paraphernalia and asked, once I had used it, if I knew to whom I should give it next. Fortunately, I understood the principle of rank and held it out to the person who was at the top of the traditional hierarchy. On the other hand, in Mutul (where relations with the chief appointed by the administration were very tense), it was only after we had ridden some distance from the village on our horses that local informants agreed to give me the details of the distribution of meat from the hunt, and thus the legitimate hierarchical organization.

However, hierarchical relationships are played out at the intervillage as well as the intravillage levels and involve relations between different chiefs.

The Last Frontier Conflict between Bunaq before the Hague Treaty

Until the 1914 treaty, there were enclaves in the mountains of central Timor that belonged alternately to Portugal and to the Netherlands. They were attached to one lordship or another according to their position and role in local conflicts. Before the treaty, Mautacar belonged to the Netherlands and Lakmaras to Portugal. The two colonial powers quarreled over a third territory inhabited by the Tahakae population. According to the descendants of certain Tahakae noble houses, whom I met in Atambua, they lived on the slopes of Mount Lakan—located on the territory of Dirun—and spoke Tetun. This is corroborated by the Tetun name of the administrative center in Kecamatan (district) Lamaknen: Weluli, meaning "holy water," which is found on their ancient territory.

The Bunaq of Lamaknen say that the last war before the Hague treaty was caused by a conflict within the house Deu Gubul, the lord of Lakmaras. For the colonial authorities, who were largely unaware of the social organization of Timorese societies, and in particular of the diarchic distribution of power in many of them, these local conflicts were incomprehensible. In Lamaknen, the village hierarchy included a female lord (*Bein pana*) or a female chief (*dato pana*), according to the village's rank in the territorial hierarchy, and a male lord (*Bein mone*) or a male chief (*dato mone*). Men occupy both functions. The first is superior to the second and looks after the village's internal affairs; the second deals with external relations and, for this reason, was more involved in colonial administrative affairs than the first. There were also war chiefs and heralds whose job was to speak for the chiefs; the proliferation of offices led to great confusion for the two colonial powers, who often did not know the status of the person to whom they were speaking.

Further complicating the situation, the doubling of functions is also found within the lords' households. In the house of a *Bein pana* there is a distinction between the one who is responsible for the house's external relations and possesses "broad or extended power" (*oe nolaq*) and the one who holds "narrow or restricted power" (*oe til*) within the house, where he is the ritual chief and superior to the other. What makes the situation even more complicated is that each of these functions is linked to the possession of certain objects that are not the collective property of the house but, as we have just seen, of a particular *dil*. Men do exercise the functions, but only based on objects passed on by women within a *dil* enabling those functions.

In the Deu Gubul house, the *Bein pana* of Lakmaras, there were two sets of descendants (*dil*) who both possessed the title of *oe nolaq*. When the possessor of one of these titles died, the other wanted to take both for himself. The offended allies immediately ran off to Lamaknen, taking no account of borders, to fight for their rights. The two colonial powers understood nothing of the reasons for the conflict but were convinced that they had to solve the border problem as quickly as possible by getting rid of the enclaves. Several Lamaknen nobles were killed in this conflict. Their memory was still alive over thirty years later when, taking advantage of the problems caused by the Second World War, Bunaq and Lamaknen went off to kill the inhabitants of Bunaq villages on the Portuguese side.

I do not know if the same spirit of revenge was perpetuated under cover of the fighting that accompanied the Indonesian occupation of Portuguese Timor from 1975 to 1999. When I returned to Lamaknen in 1998, the traditional village of Abis had been burned down, along with the holy wood that protected it; and the hill it was built on had partly collapsed, attacked by erosion.

Conclusion

Through our exploration of the genealogical myths of the inhabitants of upper Lamaknen, which are supposed to recount the itinerary of their ancestors, we have seen how difficult it is to reconstitute historical reality. Nevertheless, our analysis has made it possible to highlight how these texts are used to justify hierarchical relationships and political constructions. Rather than giving us information on the history of Bunaq-speaking populations, these texts give us a glimpse of turbulent relationships between neighbors and perpetual disputes over status, based on claims to possession of objects, which remain hidden in the secrecy of houses. Persons placed at the top of the hierarchy, whose function is ritual, only expressed their will through functionaries responsible for communication with the outside. In these conditions the colonial and postcolonial administrations could play on these multiple ambiguities, choosing individuals as interlocutors and chiefs who were favorable to them.

Our brief exposé of the internal organization of Bunaq houses, with the continued separated identity of each *dil* and the possibility of using two types of marriage to regenerate the group (as Berthe had already pointed out, 1961) allows us to explain the capacities for expansion of this population speaking a non-Austronesian language while surrounded on all sides by speakers of Austronesian languages. Even if those languages influenced the Bunaq language, as Schapper has shown, the demographic weight of the Bunaq speakers, their cultural convictions, and their collective sense of themselves as different enabled their language to endure.

As the Kemak say, when your child marries a Bunaq, you lose all around: boys will be offered a *ton terel* marriage, in which the children will belong to the wife's house; girls will be given a *sul suliq* marriage and become part of the husband's house, along with the children.

It nonetheless remains true that the east-to-west journey of Bunaq and Lamaknen ancestors (attested by the fact that a house's wife-givers of origin in my enquiries were usually located on the Portuguese side) was no doubt due as much to a refusal to accept a superior hierarchical authority between Timorese populations as to a conflict with Portuguese colonial authorities. We could, however, wonder about the case that was presented to me as the most recent displacement: that of nobles who settled in the village of Henes, who were said to have left their territory next to the border on the Portuguese side but whose subjects stayed where they were. This would mean that there is mobility for nobles, who are always anxious to preserve their hierarchical superiority (founded on transportable objects), but permanence for ruled populations whose culture is inscribed in a territory.

Claudine Friedberg (1933–2018) was a distinguished ethnologist and botanist. In her late years she was a Professeur Honoraire at the Muséum Nationale d'Histoire naturelle de Paris, to which she was affiliated since 1956. She was also director of the research team on "Appropriation and Socialization of Nature" at CNRS, France. Her research drew on her training in ethnology and botany to focus on the relations between people and plants and on folk classifications. She was a world-renowned scholar on the ethnobotany of Southeast Asia, having conducted fieldwork in Peru, Indonesia, and, notably, in Timor, where she worked among the Bunaq people with her husband, the late Louis Berthe (1927–68), between 1962 and 1973. Professor Friedberg's extensive list of publications includes *Le savoir botanique des Bunaq* (1990) and the collection of Bunaq oral literature, *Comment fut tranchée la liane celeste* (1978).

Notes

1. These mythical accounts were collected during fieldwork founded by the Centre National pour la Recherche Scientifique (CNRS) regarding the first mission of Louis Berthe. His second fieldwork, carried out in 1966, was financed jointly by the CNRS and the Junta de Investigações do Ultramar. I undertook my fieldwork in 1969–70 with the support of these two institutions. The following missions were founded by the CNRS and the Muséum national d'Histoire naturelle.
2. It refers to mythical accounts collected by Louis Berthe during his first fieldwork. They constitute the corpus on which his linguistic thesis is based. I published his manuscript, *Bei Gua: itinéraire des ancêtres, mythes bunaq de Timor* (Paris: CNRS, 1972). It focuses on the mythical accounts without the study of the language and syntax. In my text, I refer to this text by using capital letters.
3. I discussed these peculiar aspects elsewhere, see Friedberg 1973 and 1980.
4. According to the versification system built upon two hemistiches and customary to the region (see Fox 1974), toponyms are double without the possibility of knowing if they are related to one or two different places. This versification system is applied to the three lineage names from which the Bunaq of Lamaknen consider themselves descendants. For simplicity and clarity, I use only one term, as my Bunaq interlocu-

tors used to do. Indeed, these lineages bear places names, all situated in Timor-Leste where the Great Ancestors passed for a more or less lengthy period. The Oburo lineage is called "Oburo Marobo" after the name of two hills in nearby Bobonaro. The complete expression for Luta is "Luta dato Zapata," a place situated between Lamaknen and the south coast. For Sibiri, "Sibiri Kailau" is a name given to Sibuni Hol Zemal, where the Sibiri Great Ancestor made a stage on the Lakus slopes. "Sibiri Kailau" is also the name given to a stone altar, which is given to the Oburo Great Ancestors.

5. It has to be specified that in numerous villages from Timor Leste, inhabitants consider themselves as autochthonous (see Sousa 2010).
6. The same versification system in two hemistiches is applied to people's names. However, it often occurs that the names of two persons are associated in one verse.
7. Clamagirand, personal communication with author.
8. Formerly, there were slaves in Lamaknen. Some of them may have been prisoners of war, and others were sold to settle debts. There were no longer slaves when I conducted my fieldwork. But, during a house feast, I met a family originating from Atambua, who complained that their parents had been sold as slaves.
9. In the *Bei Gua*, the expression *pan moal muk moal* is mentioned several times and refers to different mythical events. It is impossible to establish links between them and actual places referred to by the term "below."
10. See the special issue of *Indonesia and the Malay World* 36(105) (2008) on this topic.
11. These enumerations made in Bunaq include Austronesian terms.
12. However, the narration can include episodes of which etiological content may be difficult to interpret.

References

Berthe, L. 1961. "Le Mariage par Achat et la Captation des Gendres dans une Société Semi-Féodale: les Buna' de Timor Central." *L'Homme* 1(3): 5–31.

———. 1972. *Bei Gua: itinéraire des ancêtres, mythes bunaq de Timor*. Paris: CNRS.

Fox, J. J. 1974, "Our Ancestors Spoke in Pairs: Rotinese Views of Language, Dialect, and Code." In *Explorations in the Ethnography of Speaking*, edited by R. Bauman and J. Sherzer, 65–85. Cambridge: Cambridge University Press.

Friedberg, C. 1973. "Repérage et Découpage du Temps chez les Bunaq du Centre de Timor." *Archipel* 6: 119–46.

———. 1980. "Boiled Woman and Broiled Man: Myths and Agricultural Rituals of the Bunaq of Central Timor." In *The Flow of Life: Essays on Eastern Indonesia*, edited by J. J. Fox, 266–89. Cambridge, MA: Harvard University Press.

Hicks, D. 2007. "Younger Brother and Fishing Hook on Timor: Reassessing Mauss on Hierarchy and Divinity." *Journal of the Royal Anthropological Institute* (N.S.) 13: 39–56.

Schapper, A. 2011a. 'Finding Bunaq: The Homeland and Expansion of the Bunaq in Central Timor." in *Land and Life in Timor-Leste: Ethnographic Essays*, edited by A. McWilliam and E. Traube, 163–86. Canberra: ANU Press.

———. 2011b. "Crossing the Border: Historical and Linguistic Divides among the Bunaq in Central Timor." *Wacana* 13(1): 1–28.

Sousa, L. 2010. *An Tia: Partilha Ritual e Organização entre os Bunak de Lamak Hitu, Bobonaro, Timor Leste*. PhD diss. in anthropology—social and cultural anthropology. Lisbon: Universidade Aberta.

Chapter 3

THE DEATH OF THE *ARBIRU*

COLONIAL MYTHIC PRAXIS AND THE APOTHEOSIS OF OFFICER DUARTE

Ricardo Roque

This chapter explores colonial historicity at the juncture of Portuguese and Timorese understandings of the past. At the core of my inquiry is a tragic incident during the so-called "pacification campaigns" promoted by Governor Celestino da Silva in the late nineteenth century: the death of Portuguese *alferes* (sublieutenant) Francisco Duarte, known also by his Tetum name *Arbiru*, on 17 July 1899. In July that year, Duarte and his army were laying siege to the people of the Atabai kingdom, who refused to pay vassalage to Portugal and submit to the governor's authority. The Atabai people sought refuge inside the caves of Bui Kari, a rocky hill in the hinterland of Atabai, off the north coast of East Timor. From Bui Kari, men, women, children, and elderly fought fiercely against the invaders without giving up. On 17 July, in the course of this siege, Atabai warriors killed the Portuguese commander, Sublieutenant Duarte. His body was then retrieved by the Portuguese and taken to Dili to be buried in the Santa Cruz cemetery. What happened at the moment of his death; how, where, by whom, Duarte was killed; what happened afterward; and how the Timorese and, particularly, the Atabai people behaved after the officer fell dead became the stuff of legend.

Virtually until today, multiple and sometimes contradictory stories of military bravery, power, magic, conquest, resistance, and postcolonial nostalgia converge on the historical figure of the officer and, above all, on his dramatic disappearance during the campaign in Atabai. After the event and throughout the twentieth century, the death of Duarte, or the *Arbiru*, has been recounted recurrently in Timor and Portugal, becoming one powerful organizing theme in the narration of the Portuguese colonial presence in Timor-Leste. The historical making(s) of the *Arbiru* has likely been a plural and complex relational and intercultural process, in which Portuguese and Timorese agents and voices have been involved over time. In this chapter, I wish to focus on the ways through which this event became the object of a colonial type of mythic praxis that unfolded around stories and rituals about Duarte the *Arbiru* as an ancestral colonial hero. Yet I will also consider how the same event of the "death of the *Arbiru*" was articulated in East Timorese counternarratives. Since his death in 1899, an ensemble of Portuguese narratives, rituals and topographies took form within the colonial community, resulting in the consecration of Duarte as a major symbol of Portugal's modern imperial occupation. Portuguese practices and stories constructed the officer as a hero of colonial occupation, and these practices, I argue, articulated images and cultural materials of alleged Timorese origin. I focus particularly on the period from the 1950s to the 1970s. It was during these decades that the mythic narrative was institutionalized as a rite of colonial administration, in the formal ceremony of homage commonly designated as Feast of the *Arbiru*.[1] The feast was originally an initiative of the local colonial government. Created in 1959 and held possibly until 1974–75 at the site of Duarte's death at Bui Kari, the feast and the officer's memory also had metropolitan visibility. Images and footage of the Feast of the *Arbiru* were eventually disseminated in propaganda films (see Spiguel 1960); the officer's significance was repatriated, and a square in Lisbon (just like another street in Dili) bears his name until today.

This feast and the narratives, imageries, and procedures that informed its emergence and continuing performance provide the main empirical focus for this chapter. I am also interested in exploring how Portuguese engagements with the feast connect with Timorese cultural notions, and vice versa—to this end, then, the chapter involves both an ethnographic reading of Portuguese archival records and a fieldwork-based historiography of the death of the *Arbiru* at Bui Kari in 1899. In exploring the Feast of the *Arbiru* in the Portuguese archives and memories, I am interested in how colonial mythology is performed in narrative and ritual praxis, and how this performance entails the gathering of indigenous cultural materials and their effective inclusion in colonial constructs. My suggestion is that Portuguese stories of the *Arbiru* configured a relational mythology of conquest grounded on perceptions of colonial vulnerability that could not have been consolidated without the incorporation—although distorted and partial—of concrete indigenous cultural materials. Portuguese memories, rituals, and narrative representations of the officer's heroic death are revealing instances of colonial mythmaking as a practice dependent on interpretations of Timorese notions and historical understandings. As such, I will argue that the apotheosis of Francisco Duarte upon his death at Atabai in 1899 became a colonial myth of conquest that depended upon, and was productively fed by, knowledge praxis and anthropological speculations about indigenous meanings of colonial people and events. Yet I am interested also in tracing the connections between this colonial mythology further into Timorese cultural visions and counternarratives. Thus, complementarily to my reading of colonial mythology, I will bring forth field materials from Atabai concerning contemporary Timorese stories about *Arbiru's* death. These stories seem to articulate local visions of self-empowerment and freedom-fighting against Portuguese intrusion that, in counterpoint to the myth of conquest, might be read as a mythology of resistance. At Atabai, accounts of the officer's death are entailed in indigenous imageries of freedom/resistance that not only differ from but also interact (and at some points overlap) with Portuguese stories and ceremonial practices. My hypothesis is that such parallels, links, and contrasts between indigenous and European accounts suggest a relational form of colonial historicity characterized by difference and opposition, but also by reciprocal incorporation and cultural borrowings—one through which some sections and fragments of one another's variants could be ignored, but also used, distorted, amplified, or incorporated for distinct mythological ends.

Duarte's specific story of apotheosis evokes a wider trope in the history and anthropology of colonial encounters, most famously explored in the Sahlins-Obeyesekere dispute over the meaning of Captain Cook's death in Hawaii in 1779 (see Sahlins 1985, 1995; Obeyesekere 1992). Similarly, we can see in the Portuguese accounts the expression of a wider European "myth-model" of colonial conquest (see Obeyesekere 1992), founded upon the vision of the Portuguese officer as a superior and sacred-like figure to the indigenous people. A mythology of conquest did frame the Portuguese readings and interpretations of Timorese cultural materials about the Atabai events, and as such it can explain, to some degree, the partiality and limitations of colonial knowledge as regards indigenous incorporations of the Portuguese officer. However, contrary to Obeyesekere's arguments (1992), the fact that a European mythology of conquest is here at work does not preclude the possibility that the Timorese also incorporated the officer and his death on their own cultural terms, by means of magical, animistic, cosmological, or other correlate language and explanations. Moreover, another singularity perhaps of this Portuguese mythic praxis of colonial conquest in Timor, I argue, was that it expressed a sense of colonial vulnerability; it achieved ritual expression and symbolic strength as a historical result of perceived fragility of the Portuguese colonial establishment in the mid-twentieth century. Thus I take this European mythological practice seriously, in both its politics and its epistemic insights into indigenous conceptions. Portuguese inclusions of East Timorese meanings were politically as well as epistemologically significant. This requires attention to possible occlusions, biases, and exclusions that the colonial "myth of conquest" may have caused in the depiction of Timorese meanings—as well as vice versa, the possibility of Timorese mythologies of freedom having made use of colonial themes and obsessions. For, colonial narratives did refer to "real" Timorese stories; they did intersect with effective and pervasive indigenous cultural modes of incorporation of European (and other) strangers.

The integration of outsiders and strangers as ancestral figures of indigenous mythic significance has been an important trope in the anthropological literature of the Asia Pacific region, and even beyond. In what concerns Timor-Leste, this indigenous inclination to incorporate the Portuguese colonial outsiders through cosmological narratives as returning ancestors has been well-documented, as Elizabeth Traube originally demonstrated (1986) and again argues in her chapter to this volume. The case study explored in this chapter offers further material to reassess this trope. In another work I examined how the Portuguese administrators could include, and make sense of, Timorese incorporations of themselves through pragmatic theories, what I have called praxiologies (Roque 2010). Here, I would like to suggest that mythology could as well be a language through which the Portuguese articulated their position within Timorese cultural understandings, as they perceived them. Portuguese mythic narratives about colonial contact coexisted parallel to Timorese cultural inclusions—and, in a way, the former could not thrive without somehow claiming the inclusion of the latter. European myths and colonial perspectives, I argue, fed upon indigenous cultural materials. In the case explored in this chapter, myths of conquest and heroic apotheosis emerged as the idioms through which Timorese imaginaries of Francisco Duarte were to be included in Portuguese historical narratives.

I would like to argue in addition that an understanding of this colonial mythology requires an assessment (albeit tentative) of alternative

Timorese cultural conceptions of colonial history that such mythology ignores but with which it is also somehow entangled. To this end, the chapter follows the *Arbiru* story in the field, beyond the colonial archive, to reveal important sections of what colonial mythology ignored as well as some unexpected links of colonial legends to indigenous stories. I combine Portuguese archival records and publications with interviews that I conducted with former colonial officers and officials in Lisbon (who lived in Timor in the period 1950–75) and with fieldwork at Hatu Bui Kari and interviews with Timorese descendants of Atabai warriors. Accordingly, this case study also calls attention to the methodological productivity of crossing archival records with memories and oral history collected from both indigenous interlocutors and former European colonial agents.

The Feast of the *Arbiru*

In June 1969, the commander of the Cavalry Squadron no. 6 at Atsabe, Captain Norberto Lacerda Benigno, received a formal invitation from the Bobonaro Municipal Council to participate in the then commonly designated *Festa do Arbiru* (Feast of the *Arbiru*): "We are honoured," the invitation card read, "to invite Your Excellency to participate in a ceremony in homage to sublieutenant FRANCISCO DUARTE, the ARBIRU that will be held on the day 17 July, by 11 a.m., at HATO BUI CARI (Atabai)" (PVCMB 25 June 1969). Invitation cards like those received by Benigno—who twice participated in the ceremony, in 1969 and 1970—had wide circulation within the higher ranks of colonial administration. Military, administrative, and ecclesiastical authorities throughout the territory were thus summoned to suspend their routine duties and come, in dress uniform, to pay solemn tribute to the long-deceased officer at Hatu (Kemak term for rock) Bui Kari, deep in the Timorese hills. The ceremony brought the elite of the Portuguese colonial administration together with the Timorese traditional authorities of the Bobonaro district, *liurais* and *chefes de suco*, who came dressed in their customary ceremonial attire. Thus on that date, the secluded rocky hill of Bui Kari, located in Atabai's wild hinterland, became the epicenter of the colonial administration—the site of a ritual event that epitomized the Portuguese claims to have established a colonial empire, based on shared patriotic and Christian beliefs as well as on a Portuguese sense of their supremacy over the Timorese world.

Portuguese and Timorese authorities arrived at Bui Kari through a pathway in the bush made especially for the occasion (figure 3.1). In front of the imposing rock, the authorities stood up solemnly on a wooden stage. Companies of *moradores* (Timorese auxiliaries) provided ceremonial guard, with drum and flag. A Portuguese officer gave a ceremonial speech of patriotic praise. Opposite the hill, on a large open ground cleared of vegetation for the festivity, Timorese dances were performed; and afterward the cavalry squadrons came in imperiously on parade. Around the ceremonial site, surrounded by small arches of palm leaves, an East Timorese crowd watched the ceremony. The Portuguese national flag was hoisted; military horns sounded; there was a moment of silence; "the people, standing up, observed respectfully." In the climactic and closing moment, Portuguese military authorities, accompanied by Timorese young women, walked up to the rock to lay flowers on the commemorative stone that marked, so it was said, the "precise site of Arbiru's death" on the hillside of Bui Kari (Thomaz 1970a). "Then, the women would bring some flowers," Captain Benigno recalled in a conversation about the events in 2012, "and, afterwards, if my memory doesn't fail, the order to stand at attention would sound in respect to the dead" (figure 3.2). In an article published around the same time in the local newspaper *A Província de Timor* in 25 July 1970, army lieutenant Luís Filipe Thomaz (later to become one of the most highly regarded Portuguese

Figure 3.1. Timorese auxiliaries and Portuguese cavalry at Habu Bui Kari for the Feast of the *Arbiru*. Photo by Norberto Benigno.

Figure 3.2. Portuguese administrators laying flowers on the *Arbiru*'s memorial gravestone. Photo by Norberto Benigno.

Asianists and East Timor scholars to date) reported on the festivity he had witnessed, detailing the closing gestures of the ceremony:

> The official visitors walked the bamboo stairs up to the rocks, to lay a crown of flowers close to the place of Arbiru's death. From there they walked down to the caves where the rebels who had killed him were hiding. Then upon returning to the main ground the general parade followed—impeccable and showy parade, having as rough scenario the cliffs, the bush and the mountain. And with this the ceremony at the Bui Cari rocks ended. (Thomaz 1970a)

The Origins of the Portuguese "Cult of the Arbiru*"*

The ritual sequence of the ceremonies of 1969–70 replicated the main gestures of the original feast held at Bui Kari exactly one decade earlier, on 17 July 1959 (see AAVV 1961). The ceremony was established by Governor Filipe Themudo Barata as a rite promoted by the colonial state. In June 1959, Major Themudo Barata, a military engineer, arrived in Dili from Lisbon with his wife and five children to take up his appointment as governor of Timor. Very shortly after his arrival, he took the initiative to hold the grandiose ceremony. Barata's appointment to Timor came unexpectedly. Before he set foot on the island, he had little or no idea of Timor, let alone of the *Arbiru* legend (Barata 1998: 16–17).[2] Yet, in Timor he was quick to recognize the

fragility of the Portuguese situation in the colony and used the celebration of the officer's historical figure to administrative advantage.

Ideological, political, and pragmatic motivations led this governor
to create the ceremony as a response to a difficult political period.
Shortly before his arrival, the infamous "Viqueque rebellion" broke
out; in the absence of the governor (Barata was still on his way to
Timor when the revolt broke out), the interim government led the initial violent repression of the insurgency, continued by further impris-
onments and deportations.[3] The perception of growing anticolonial
and anti-Portuguese sentiment, pro-Indonesian integrationism, and
the conviction of an ongoing conspiracy on the part of Indonesia to
take over the country drew on and reinforced a sense of imminent
threat among the small and feebly armed Portuguese colonizing community. The year 1959 was a critical political moment; it was also a
momentous time in Portuguese mythological imagination of colonial
history. The political urgency to counter the perceived threats to Portuguese sovereignty after the Viqueque events seems to have propelled
a surplus in mythic praxis. Partly as an urge to suppress existing political dissension and prevent its further spreading, the governor decided
to project into the present a history of colonial supremacy and indigenous loyalty. Under these circumstances, Governor Barata decided to
take measures toward "restoring [Timorese] trust" in the Portuguese
authority, instilling feelings of respect and patriotism via the official
mythologizing of a pantheon of heroes and martyrs of Timor's recent
colonial history (Barata 1998: 101–3). Barata's celebratory policy,
moreover, echoed the nationalistic approach to imperial memory promoted by the fascist and imperial-nationalistic Estado Novo since its
establishment in 1933. Monuments, ceremonies, films, and publications celebrated the military officers of the occupation campaigns,
leading to the establishment of a literary pantheon of heroes and martyrs of colonial warfare. In Timor, Barata ordered the construction of
monuments together with the celebration of ceremonies for historical
individuals whose life-stories and—especially—death-stories stood as
ultimate symbols of the nerve of Portuguese colonization, and of the
extent of indigenous devotion and subordination to Portugal. Barata
decided to celebrate particular Timorese *liurais* and aristocrats—notably D. Aleixo de Corte Real and D. Jeremias de Luca—as heroic figures
of Portuguese colonization. Atrociously killed by the Japanese in the
Second World War, these noblemen had a loyalty to Portugal that was
meant to stand as evidence of "Timor as a sacred location of father-
land" (Barata 1963: 681). Simultaneously, Barata celebrated the Portuguese officer Francisco Duarte as the exemplary European mythic

hero of colonial conquest and power. In a context of perceived vulnerability, he pragmatically used the officer's story to political advantage,
turning the commemorations of the sixtieth anniversary of his death
into the launching pad for his patriotic policy. In his memoirs, published three decades later, Themudo Barata explained the rationale
behind his decision to institute the ritual tribute to the memory of
Sublieutenant Duarte:

> I took measures to remember and pay homage to Portuguese figures
> (metropolitan or Timorese indigenous) who, by their decision and cour-
> age, offered themselves to the peoples' consideration. The people despise
> the weak chiefs; they may fight the strong ones—but respect them. For
> this reason, the first solemn act that I celebrated after my arrival on
> Timor was the commemoration of the 60th anniversary of the death
> of the most legendary and bravest hero of the pacification campaigns:
> Sublieutenant Francisco Duarte, the "Arbiru." (Barata 1998: 101–3)

Weak chiefs are despised; strong chiefs are respected. Themudo
Barata possibly saw in Duarte's death the exemplary embodiment
of how, and why, Portuguese colonial authority could and should be
maintained in Timor—as a type of superior spiritual power that inspired Timorese "respect"; as a kind of charismatic energy that by
sheer demonstration of bravery could magically subject the Timorese
(see Roque 2010). Duarte, a reputed leading officer of hordes of wild
warriors, embodied this Portuguese claim to charismatic authority.
The bravery of his death was a model for subsequent generations—his
death and, above all, the mysterious, invisible potency that was said to
have emanated from his death in combat to the point of causing the
subjection and surrender of the rebels. It was as if, in this correspondence, the governor was projecting onto the Viqueque events in 1959
the vision of a handful of Portuguese heroically securing the sovereignty of Portugal against hordes of pro-Indonesian Timorese—just
as one single officer in 1899 had done against the rebels during the
Atabai siege.

The institution of the ceremony was a patriotically inspired gesture
that served clear political purposes. It came probably as a pragmatic
political decision in the context of an acutely perceived threat to Portuguese colonial sovereignty, further inspired by Barata's profound
imperialist-patriotic ethos and by his self-professed fascination with
the heroic contours of Duarte's death-story, as this circulated within
the colonial officialdom. "My father," Themudo Barata's son explained
to me in a conversation in 2013, "was a believer in the cult of the
Arbiru." Governor Barata may have been the institutor of the rite, but
his action was modeled on the initiative of preceding colonial officials

who had taken on the task of writing Duarte's heroic biography. In effect, the idea of celebrating the death of Duarte at Bui Kari in 1959 anteceded the arrival of this governor. Two dynamic Portuguese officials and amateur historians and journalists, Manuel Ferreira and Jaime Neves,[4] who had set out to create a heroic colonial historiography of Timor, passionately launched the idea. In the late 1950s, Ferreira and Neves were "collecting materials for the biographies of D. Jeremias do Amaral and Sublieutenant Francisco Duarte" (Neves 1960). According to Jaime Neves, then secretary of the Exchange Council, it was his friend Manuel Ferreira (deceased shortly after the first feast of 1959) who approached him "enthusiastically" with the idea of commemorating the sixtieth anniversary of Duarte's death at Atabai—and Neves took on the challenge (Neves 1960).

It was probably the stories he heard from his colleagues in Dili that convinced the governor of the significance of the *Arbiru*—a significance he saw contained in the officer's heroic death. Barata eventually grounded the official ceremonies upon a set of specific death-stories, entailing a specific mythic geography. In so doing, he was giving official weight to a body of narratives about the *Arbiru* that were already in circulation and accepted as truthful among the colonizers. From at least the 1930s, accounts circulated within the circles of Portuguese military and officialdom in Timor concerning the heroic passing of the *Arbiru* at Atabai. These accounts typically articulated two themes. The first referred to the valiant death of a warrior leader, the idea of a noble military death in combat; the second concerned the imagery of a death by magical means, the evocation of indigenous beliefs in the officer's sacredness and invulnerability, signaled by the possibility of his killing by magical weaponry. Yet a third theme was to emerge: the victorious death, the magical effects of the killing. I will start with the first theme.

A Heroic Death

"For the hero, more than birth, it is his death, spectacular or obscure but always conscious and generous emulation, which represents the safe principle of immortality," said Barata in his speech that closed the July 1959 commemorations. "His unperishable glory does not come from our applause but from the sublime substance of his sacrifice" (Barata 1961: 29). Duarte's heroic death appeared to the governor as well as to subsequent observers as an ideal-type, an exemplary model on which to ground Portuguese colonial agency and power. It meant glory and immortality; it symbolized Portuguese supremacy. "Arbiru has died; but he still lives" wrote Luís Thomaz in 1970. "He is alive as a symbol, and as an example. . . . For he walks ahead of us and shows us the way—and we shall follow him" (Thomaz 1970b: 17). In 1963, in an article published after his return to Portugal, Themudo Barata referred to the officer's "colossal" figure, emphasizing how the narrative of his death, martyrdom, and victory touched patriotic hearts and inspired him to solemnly commemorate Duarte as a mythic colonial hero at the Bui Kari site:

> Timor is a very special part of overseas Portugal. There were metropolitan heroes, it is certain, like that great Arbiru, who died on his feet on the Bui Cari rocks, and who, due to the colossal stature of his warrior soul and the beauty of his sacrifice, *achieved with his death a most surprising victory* which may seem paradoxical to those who do not understand that the true stature of a man is not a function of his body, his riches, his hierarchy—but of his soul. (Barata 1961: 680–81, my italics)

The motif of Duarte's death in combat at Atabai became the pillar of a colonial myth of conquest; it structured the establishment of the official ceremonies held since 1959 at Bui Kari. Indeed, the *Festa do Arbiru* translated into a ritual formula a set of colonial narratives about the Atabai campaign of 1899 centered on the theme of the officer's heroic death. For, it was not simply the warrior who was celebrated; it was the *place* and the *mode* of his death, *where* and *how* he died that formed the heart of the colonial myth. Notwithstanding his valiant life as a warrior, *Arbiru's* ultimate heroic feat, in other words, was the way he died, where he died, and what his death brought forth ("with his death he achieved a surprising victory"). The how and where were key to the story line of heroic death that fed into the official ritualization of the *Arbiru* legend; they were likewise central to the ritual sequence of the feast.

The Commemorative Stone

The colonial story of heroic death became inscribed on the landscape of Bui Kari, through the erection of a commemorative gravestone.[5] It is significant in this light that the place chosen for the ceremony and the stone was the Bui Kari bush site rather than the marble gravestone at the cemetery of Santa Cruz, in Dili, erected in 1899, where the officer was buried after his body was retrieved from Atabai soon after his death in battle in July 1899. The Bui Kari gravestone signals the importance of the place of death in the recounting of the colonial myth and, subsequently, in the ritual. The closing gesture of the laying of flowers on this commemorative stone, as seen above, is an indicator of the high symbolic and ritual significance of place. In effect, in the colonial accounts the place of death was a favorite theme, surrounded by a high level of topographical detail and narrative precision. For the Portuguese, Duarte did not die in an unknown place in the Bui Kari rock. The colonial recitations of the officer's apotheosis claimed that his death had taken place at a precise geographical location. Solemnly inaugurated on the first ceremonies of 17 July 1959, the stone—a rectangular stone handmade in the image of a grave by Portuguese craftsmen in Dili[6]—marked the *exact* location of Francisco Duarte's fatality, thus materially instantiating the claim to represent precisely what had happened. A caption of 1961 for an illustration of this gravestone describes it as, "Gravestone put on the place where 'Arbiru' died" (Neves 1961: 35; see also Barata 1998: 132). In the Portuguese accounts that inspired the ritual, Duarte was killed *there* while "on his feet," in combat, escalating the rough scarps of Bui Kari in a dramatic attempt to take over the rebels' position. Accordingly, the inscription on this stone—which to this date remains erected at the Bui Kari hill (figure 3.3)—reads:

> 17-7-1959. Homage from Timor. To Francisco Duarte "Arbiru" who on this stone died on his feet in combat, on the day 17-7-1899.

Figure 3.3. The colonial commemorative gravestone of the *Arbiru*. Photo by the author.

A mythic landscape was materialized in the monument erected by Governor Barata on the wild hillside of Bui Kari. The Portuguese historiographical claims for chronological as well as topographical accuracy of the myth culminated in this stone monument. Precision about the location of his death in combat stood as evidence of the truthfulness of the legend. The inscription of the colonial narrative on the materiality of stone functioned as an additional palpable fact in support of the truth-claims of the apotheosis of the officer. This insistence on exactly locating and naming the place of the *Arbiru* myth is remarkable also in the light of the indigenous significance attached, in Timor, to the mythic and poetic power of place and landscape (see Fox 2006; McWilliam and Traube 2011). The Portuguese naming and recapitulation of the death place of the mythic hero thus seems to emerge as a singular type of a colonial poetics of place and landscape—which, as we shall see, ran parallel to competing and intersecting indigenous histories and poetics of the "same" place and events.

The words on the stone are of further significance, in that they perform a similar mythological call to historiographical precision. It reveals also that such historiographical claims, moreover, are deliberately grounded on the fragmentary incorporation of indigenous words and cultural meanings—a process that I will pursue in the next sections of this chapter. The phrase *on this stone he died on his feet, in combat* is illustrative. The idea that the officer died an honorable death as a warrior is emphasized by the phrase *morreu de pé, em combate* (he died on his feet, in combat). Here, as in other colonial accounts, I believe we have an example of how the colonial mythology selectively absorbed, and obsessively fed upon, Timorese terms, images, words. The expression was possibly a literal translation from Kemak to Portuguese of an expression that could be found in indigenous cultural repertoire about these historical events. The Portuguese phrase *morreu de pé* is likely a translation of the last of the opening verses—*Bui Kari, Hatu Bui Kari / Arbiru mate ara lolo*—of a Kemak folk song (designated as "Kai Naba") that circulated about the events of the 1899 siege since an unknown date (the Kemak phrase *Arbiru mate are lolo* can be translated, into Portuguese, as *Arbiru morreu de pé*; or *Arbiru died on his feet*). It is symptomatic of the process of selective cannibalization and (ab)use of Timorese discourse, as it were, that no further verses from this folk song appear to make reference to *Arbiru* dying . . . *in combat*—a point to which we will return further below. Field data collected at Atabai in 2012 points to the existence of a longer folk song. I am thus led to believe that a fragment only of this folk song was used by the Portuguese creators of the feast, as well as by future disseminators of the Portuguese *Arbiru* mythology. In this light, the inscriptions on the gravestone along with the account of surrender (explored below) offer exemplary instances of the process of mythic substantiation that characterized the construction of the Portuguese colonial memories of the *Arbiru*—a process that seemed to function, to some extent, through partial and twisted inclusions of indigenous cultural discourses.

The Circuits of the Heroic Death-Story

It is difficult to trace the origins and routes of Duarte's heroic death-story in the archives. Yet it seems safe to assume that it grew locally within the Portuguese colonial community in Timor, possibly as a rumor that was slowly turned into an established and incontrovertible oral account over the years, perhaps even decades, after his death in 1899. In a widely cited report of 1897, his superior (also confessed admirer) during the pacification campaigns, Governor José Celestino da Silva, first launched Duarte's fame beyond Timor, verbosely praising his military bravery and heroism, his sacred-like aura of invincibility, and the name *Arbiru* for which he was known among the Timorese. However, in his many and lengthy writings to Lisbon, this governor was to remain silent about Duarte's death and apotheosis during the Atabai campaign (Silva 1897: 44–46). Indeed, as we will note below, he did not even communicate the simple fact of the officer's passing to Lisbon. It is only in the 1930s that we find the first literary references to Francisco Duarte's death-story. In 1939, as part of a series of pamphlets titled *Glories and Martyrdoms of Portuguese Colonization* (a typical example of Estado Novo historiographical propaganda), General Ferreira Martins dedicated one chapter to Duarte (there nicknamed as "Major Arebéro") and to his military feats in Timorese campaigns. About his death, however, the author had no information: "The late sublieutenant passed away, aged 35 years, on 17 July 1899," Ferreira Martins explained, "it not being possible for me, at the moment, to ascertain the causes of his premature death, about which the official documents I consulted in the archives are silent" (Martins 1939: 10). Francisco Duarte's detailed Individual Process (now held by the Military Historical Archives in Lisbon) does not provide information as to the historical circumstances of his death. On the front cover of Duarte's biographical record, only a short handwritten note mentions the date of his disappearance: "He passed away on 17 July 1899. Communication about his death was not received."[7] But for the Portuguese military in the colony there was little doubt: the officer died fighting at

Atabai. His tomb at the Santa Cruz Cemetery in Dili—probably made
for his burial by Governor Celestino in 1899—simply bears the epitaph: "Killed in combat at Atabai on the attack to the Bicari [sic] Rocks
on 17 July 1899."[8] Forty years later, undisputed stories circulated
locally about Duarte's apotheosis in combat. Such oral accounts compensated for absent archival information. Thus, in a footnote added
to the printed proofs of his text before publication, Ferreira Martins
corrected the above statement on the lack of data, with the following
observation:

> Later information, spontaneously and diligently provided by former
> military who served in Timor during the same period of military occu-
> pation of this colony, brought to my knowledge the fact that the brave
> sublieutenant Duarte had a sadly premature but glorious death, as it is
> proper for the heroes of his kind. He was killed in combat, on the 1899
> campaign against the rebel peoples of Cailaco and Atsabe, in that same
> colony to which he had consecrated the greatest efforts of his short life.
> (Martins 1939: 10n1)

In the 1930s, no record in Lisbon but the date of his passing survived. Yet in Timor, among colonial officialdom, Duarte's death was
actively remembered and profusely recounted in detail as a historical
event that took on the character of a mythic story of Portuguese colonial apotheosis. A fundamental component of this story (yet one still
unmentioned in Martins's above record) is the recurrent reference to
the officer as a godlike figure in Timorese legends and beliefs. The vision that Sublieutenant Duarte's persona was a magnet of indigenous
magic and superstition was a cornerstone of the Portuguese mythology. As such, the colonial cult of the *Arbiru* that came into emergence
in the 1950s was grounded on a set of alleged insights into the nature
and content of past and present indigenous beliefs and behaviors as
regards the officer.

First among these insights was the meaning attributed by Portuguese storytellers to the indigenous term *Arbiru*, by which the Timorese named the officer during (and after) his lifetime. According
to the Portuguese accounts, the Timorese commonly designated the
officer by the Tetum term *Arbiru* in order to signify the magical aura
of supernatural bravery, invincibility, and invulnerability that they
attributed to him as a warrior leader. The indigenous meanings entailed in this act of naming, however, are complex, and it is likely that
the colonial renderings of the term did not accurately convey the full
range of meanings that it can encompass. For instance, the set of
meanings attached to the Tetum term *Arbiru* include connotations of
wild, careless, and unruly behavior that seem never to have been con-

sidered in the Portuguese colonial accounts (see Gunter 2001; Roque, forthcoming). What now matters for my purpose here, though, is not the accuracy of the colonial interpretations, or the lack of it. What matters is how these colonial accounts were performed in relation to indigenous accounts and beliefs; how they seemed to draw their powers from epistemological claims of contact with, and effective understanding of, so-called Timorese "legends."

Colonial myth accounts of the *Arbiru* ultimately lived off the Portuguese belief in the reality of Timorese magical beliefs in the officer's supernatural powers. Yet, the Portuguese paradoxically struggled to put these same magical beliefs at bay, rejecting them as artifacts of Timorese imagination, devaluing them as mere fantasies that ultimately had no correspondence to historical reality. In other words: Timorese beliefs and legends about the officer really existed, but the claims these legends made about effective historical events were not "real." This can be followed in one of the most fascinating and recurrent themes of the apotheosis myth: the bullet.

The Denial of Timorese Bullet Magic

Over time, fragments of Timorese cultural discourse became selectively integrated into a diffuse realm of colonial stories about the death of Francisco Duarte as *Arbiru*, and as such they came to participate in its celebratory memories. Yet, in this process of contact and inclusion, colonial accounts also struggled to differentiate themselves from what they constructed as "Timorese legend." They excluded that which did not fit in the heroic framing of the events; they rejected that which could induce confusion between what they consider to be "fact" and what they thought was mere (Timorese) "fantasy." This movement of inclusion and denial was visible in the ways colonial storytellers managed the historical possibility of magical agencies having been the cause of the officer's death.

The recurrent allusion to the "bullet theme" in particular reveals the degree to which the colonial myth became deliberately dependent upon so-called Timorese "legends" and, especially, Timorese beliefs concerning the circulation of magic in weaponry and in warrior bodies. In East Timorese cultures, as in the wider region, warfare is a realm where invisible agencies, spiritual potencies, and magical forces meet, circulate, and act through warrior bodies, costumes, and weaponry. Weapons such as swords, rifles, spears, and bullets thus can become bearers and mediators of such potencies, to the extent that they may be seen to constitute agents in their own right (cf. Wiener 1995; Roque 2010). From the colonial period to the armed resistance against Indonesia, one may encounter varied instances of this magical imagery of war—the power attributed to bullets or the invulnerability attributed to certain warriors and/or their talismans (so-called *birus*) being one such prevalent trope. As regards the events of 1899 at Atabai, this culture of war magic became a powerful meeting ground of colonial and indigenous historical recollections. Francisco Duarte's presumed invulnerability to ordinary weapons, and the associated claims on how he met his end with a magical bullet, was to become a favorite of the colonial imagination of apotheosis.

How was he killed—*what* killed the officer? An ordinary bullet, some would say; a magical bullet, made of gold or silver, as Timorese believed; a deadly indigenous spear, some corrected. Reference to the bullet theme received official recognition in the first ceremony of 1959, yet it probably emerged from the outset of the colonial legend. In an obscure pamphlet of 1957 authored by Duarte's biographer, Manuel Ferreira, we read another explicit, though brief, reference. Referring to Francisco Duarte as one of the "martyrs" of the time of Celestino da Silva's governorship, Ferreira observed: "Sublieutenant Francisco Duarte, whom the natives called the *Arbiro*, that is, *the invincible man*, like no other existed. *Only a golden bullet could kill him, so legends said*" (Ferreira 1957: 9).[9] Two decades earlier, in 1938, Captain José Simões Martinho—a former army officer in Timor with two decades of experience and local knowledge—authored a historical piece on the military occupation of Timor, in which he praised the feats of Duarte as follows:

> Yes, because the sublieutenant Duarte, the major "Arbiru," dies also in the siege of Fatu-Bicar [Tetum expression for Hatu Bui Kari], in the Catubaba [*sic*] campaign, *hit by a bullet that the Timorese legend says is made of Gold, this people being convinced that such an illustrious officer could not be killed by an ordinary bullet.* (Martinho 1938: 212, my italics)

He was killed by a bullet (factual), which, according to Timorese accounts (fiction), was made of gold. Martinho's attribution of the legendary and magical aspects of the story to Timorese belief alone is exemplary of the officer's difficulty in managing boundaries between fact and fiction; between Portuguese and Timorese stories; between what they thought should pertain to a rational (European) account and what, instead, belonged to (Indigenous) fantasy alone. At the same time it shows that this gesture of denial and differentiation was a productive element of the colonial mythology. It therefore seemed as

if the realms of Timorese and Portuguese historical legend had come
into close relationship, intersecting to the point of becoming juxtaposed in some respects. And yet difference between historical "fact"
and indigenous "belief," as regards the mode of death, between what
were supposedly distinct historical epistemologies, was an artifact that
the colonial accounts equally attempted to articulate—a point exemplified here by the bullet trope.

The Portuguese negation of the validity of the magical cause of
Duarte's death could be articulated in varied, even contrasting, ways.
Officer Guilherme Alpoim Calvão, in an article published in a metropolitan newspaper around 1960, reported that Duarte was killed
by a bullet, without specifying *what* sort—thus simply omitting the
possibility of the bullet's magical action: "In June [*sic*] 1899, dies the
'Arbiru,' the bravest, in the heat of combat. When he led his men on
an assault of an enemy position, he was hit by a bullet that put him
down forever" (Calvão, n.d.). "It was even said [among the Timorese
people] that only a golden bullet could kill him . . .," Thomaz wrote
in 1970. Thomaz continued selectively rejecting the veracity of the
magical part of the death-story—the gold bullet: "A random bullet
lays him down forever. It was not made of gold, as popular belief demanded, but he died on his feet (*morreu de pé*), as the people stated"
(Thomaz 1970b: 17). The Timorese believed Duarte was killed by a
gold bullet; the Timorese believed he was standing up. However, only
part of these two so-called "popular beliefs" did the narrator accept to
be true: the "people's statement" legitimating the Portuguese vision
of a courageous death in combat. In 2012, Thomaz's contemporary,
Captain Benigno, recalled this subject in an interview. He similarly
rejected the theme of death by a "silver bullet" while remembering the
mutual Portuguese-Timorese significance of the *Arbiru*: "He had this
aura, on our side. . . . But the other guys, too [Timorese enemies] held
him in great respect! So much so that they said—this is a little bit uto-
pia, tradition—that he could only be killed by a bullet made of silver.
They said, it is clear that obviously he was not." The presence/absence
of the bullet theme is, therefore, revealing of how Timorese tropes
were selectively included in colonial lore, with a view (even if uninten-
tionally) to sustain and strengthen the colonial myth of apotheosis.

The incorporation of Timorese materials was critical to the colonial mythmaking; yet, a *total* incorporation was undesirable because
it could also pose a threat to the mythic claims to historical truth.
Portuguese faith in the existence of Timorese beliefs in bullet magic
was traversed by the mimetic threat to seeming to accept these beliefs
as their own. Portuguese storytellers were careful to attribute to the

Timorese Other the certainty of supernatural causes of death—as if fearing that, in reinstating the bullet spell as a historical fact, they could be seen to share in the substance of Timorese magical causality and, as such, undermine the historiographical validity of their own historical accounts. Thus the Portuguese rejected magic as a historical *cause* in the officer's death. Magic was denied as cause ... but it was accepted in colonial mythology as consequence, mediated by presumed Timorese beliefs in the magical cause of the officer's death in combat. Timorese ideas of Duarte's supernatural death should be dismissed; but Timorese practices in the aftermath of Duarte's death could be explained as virtually magical events in colonial narratives of the Atabai siege. In effect, one finds in the colonial mythology a distinctly *Portuguese* adherence to a magical explanation of the surrender of the resistance of Bui Kari. The magical effects of Duarte's heroic death were taken as a historical fact, to the extent that they corroborated a mythic vision of colonial power and conquest. Thus the stories of Duarte's apotheosis culminated with his own enemy's surrender and apology, with a Portuguese victory, the grand finale of the *Arbiru*.

Magical Surrender

> As soon as the rebels understood that they had killed him, they laid down their weapons and surrendered. They did not surrender to Portugal, they did not surrender to the Portuguese; they surrendered to that man.

Thus in 2013, Filipe Themudo Barata (Governor Barata's son) recalled in an interview the ending of the *Arbiru* story, as it had circulated in the early 1960s. This memory encapsulates the closing theme of the colonial imagination of the officer's death, so far mentioned only in passing: the virtually fantastic scene of the rebels' submission to the powers they perceived to be embodied in the officer, a submission expressed in a collective gesture of apologetic surrender in the aftermath of Duarte's fall in battle. In this account, the death of one single man brings about the submission of the otherwise indomitable rebels. Timorese enemies conceived of Francisco Duarte as a supernatural figure; therefore, they lamented his death, and to him, in the end, they gave up their arms. The reality of the supernatural is not excluded from this factual sequence of events. In contrast with the motif of the gold bullet, the surrender was something that had really happened. It emerged rhetorically as a virtually extraordinary effect

of virtually magical causes—the killing of *Arbiru* as a godlike figure
to the Timorese. Duarte's heroic death constituted a moment of colonial conquest activated by the fantastic release of a magic power of
surrender. Through the filter of the Portuguese belief in the Timorese
belief in the more-than-human condition of Duarte, colonial officials
took on the possibility of the supernatural as a historical fact that
revealed the force of heroic colonial power. Although still safe in their
mountain refuge in the rocks, the rebels nevertheless surrender to the
Portuguese at the moment they understand their terrible fault—the
transgressive killing of the mythic enemy they supposedly adored.
It is possible that Portuguese creative elaborations on Timorese guilt
built on fragments of Atabai folk imageries of *Arbiru*'s death as a fault
requiring reparation by means of expressions of regret and repentance, as seen below. Yet, significantly, the storyteller earlier stated
that he had never heard the narrative of surrender told by an indigenous Timorese. It was an account that circulated principally (if not
exclusively) within the community of Portuguese officialdom in the
early 1960s. This is suggestive, I believe, of the possibility that this
closing scene, with its emphasis on the magical connotations of Duarte's death, was largely a Portuguese construct.

The victorious closure of the story especially inspired the institution of the official homage to the *Arbiru* in 1959. This vision of a
"conquest by death" set in an otherworldly atmosphere particularly
impressed Governor Themudo Barata: "Mythical military figure," he
wrote in his memoirs referring to Duarte, "from whom the victorious
adversaries, after having killed him, beg forgiveness and surrender"
(Barata 1998: 102). Mythical figure he was *in Timorese eyes*. Even indigenous enemies idolized the officer. "The curious and bizarre thing
is," he added, "that Sublieutenant Duarte is killed. His armies have
been defeated. However, when his adversaries understand that they
have killed their enemy, who was also their idol, they stop fighting, and
subordinate themselves" (Barata 1998: 132). The original narration
of this legendary moment of conquest and surrender may have been
the account authored in 1959 by Duarte's enthusiastic biographer
and co-organizer of the official commemorations: the colonial official
Jaime Neves. On 17 July 1959, the date of the first Feast of the *Arbiru*, Neves gave a formal public lecture about the Atabai campaign
of 1899, with particular reference to the circumstances of *Arbiru*'s
death. Neves's lecture was presumably based on archival materials
and military reports in Timor, for which, however, he did not provide
bibliographical references. As such, it was presented in 1959 with
the authority of a truthful, historiographical narration of the actual

events, agents, and circumstances that led to the tragic end of Francisco Duarte at Bui Kari in 1899. Neves's speech received wider diffusion.[10] In his account, Neves described with nationalist verve the background of the punitive campaign against Atabai ordered by Governor Celestino; the fierce resistance of the Atabai peoples inside Bui Kari; the unsuccessful attacks of Portuguese auxiliary troops; the siege laid to the Atabai haven; the arrival of Sublieutenant Duarte on the scene; his decision to starve the besieged men, women, and children to death in the caves by cutting off their access to food and fresh water; and finally, the assault on Hatu Bui Kari, with Duarte at the forefront, leading the warriors, during which he was dramatically shot dead by random Atabai shooting, on top of the hill. Neves's lecture then concluded with an apocalyptical painting of the events that followed from the Bui Kari people's understanding of their fatal action:

> And when everyone, at the camp, was lamenting the loss of such an illustrious chief, there rises from Bui-cari a lugubrious song, terrifying, from the other world. One would say that the Bui-cari dead had been resuscitated. Men, women carrying their dead children in their arms, and semi-naked children, in a parade of mummies, mutilated, thirsty, their mouths open, ... just skin and bones, ulcerated legs, coming down from the stones and singing in choir: "Forgiveness Arbiru! Big man! Forgiveness! The evil is done! Forgiveness!"
> This was their unconditional mass surrender.
> Atabai redeemed themselves fully in this touching procession of misery; they self-punished in a supreme, sacred, evocation, begging forgiveness to Portugal. For them, "Arbiru" was a symbol of Portugal! (Neves 1961: 59)

Military surrender included a gesture of begging for forgiveness directed to the person of the officer. The idea was that the Timorese saw their action as a transgression, a misdeed, the breaking of some sort of quasi-sacred rule, precept, or prohibition concerning the person of the *Arbiru* as an incarnation of Portugal. Current evidence is still insufficient to ascertain whether or not this narrative of surrender corresponded to historical events, but it is certain that it did not conform to Atabai Timorese readings of this campaign. As in the case of the gravestone inscription, the theme of surrender seems to be a creative and transformative addition of colonial accounts that, nevertheless, builds upon a reference to "forgiveness" in an Atabai folk song. It is relevant in this regard that Jaime Neves does not claim that the specific fact of military *surrender* derives from indigenous meanings or "legend." Some ingredients of the colonial narrative of apotheosis, however, claimed to be explicitly grounded in indigenous lore regarding the event. From the late 1950s to the 1970s, colonial officials were to claim special anthropological insight into the collective memory of the people of Atabai of the siege in 1899, to support the veracity of this magic event of surrender. This "evidence" was presumably provided by fragments of the abovementioned Atabai folk song concerning the events of 1899—the same that had possibly provided the materials for the colonial imagination of an honorable death in combat, inscribed on the memorial stone. "His very enemies cried for his loss, and still today," wrote Thomaz in 1970, "the Atabai people, surrounding his death with legends, remember him in the verses of their songs" (Thomaz 1970b: 17). "In local tradition a song (which I collected) was preserved," stated Governor Themudo Barata in his memoirs, "in which the people are sorry for having killed 'the Arbiru,' repeating as a refrain that 'the evil is done'" (Barata 1998: 102; see also Junqueira 1987 [1964]). The attribution of this majestic collective gesture of guilt and repentance (allegedly followed by military surrender) was extrapolated from a few other Kemak verses from the opening sequence of the folk song: *Bui kari, Hatu Bui kari,* the song said, *Arbiru tau tuli lolo/ Beu beu sala kahi sai/ Au é dale tura kahi sai.* In 2000, Geoffrey Gunn, who collected the same opening verses (but apparently no more [Gunn, personal communication]) from an informant, Sr. António Luís Mota, in Dili, freely translated it from Kemak into English as follows: *Bui Cari rock Bui Cari/ Arbiru (the invincible) was gunned down/Bui Cari rock Bui Cari/ Arbiru lost his life/ All of a sudden the evil was done/ I meant to comfort him, but it was all over* (Gunn 2000: 245).

Colonial officials in 1959 and thereafter were quick to flag this section of the Atabai folk song—specifically *only* the above initial six verses out of a more extensive and less straightforward song—as further evidence of the fact that, even among the Atabai enemies who killed him, Duarte achieved, for generations to come, the status of *their* mythic hero. Atabai rebels felt guilty for killing their own god; for this reason they gave up their arms. Atabai words, gestures, and meanings appeared in the colonial accounts only as vehicles of the colonial mythology of the imperial hero, as cultural materials that could be read and interpreted solely on the terms of the Portuguese mythic framework. It is also possible, of course, as in other instances, that the indigenous informants intentionally omitted or occluded specific (perhaps seen as more important and truthful) words, meanings, and narrative themes in accounts to Portuguese. They may have kept for themselves the trunk, to use a common East Timorese image, revealing to the Portuguese no more than the tip of rather more complex and plural layered histories. In any case, in recognizing in Atabai memories little more than evidence of one heroic mythology of the *Arbiru*, the Portuguese circumvented the possibility of alternative (even oppositional) indigenous epistemologies and mythic praxis. I now shift focus from the archive to the field where I encountered such alternative stories.

Freedom at Hatu Bui Kari

We arrived at sunset in Atabai village on a hot day in August 2012.[11] We had come with the intention of visiting the Bui Kari rock and perhaps listening to some local stories about the Portuguese ceremonies concerning *Arbiru* once performed there. We knew we were not the first Portuguese *malae* to have come recently to Atabai with an interest in *Arbiru*. The *Arbiru* mythology and its Hatu Bui Kari topography remains a magnetic *topos* of Lusophone postcolonial nostalgia; since at least 2001, some Portuguese in Timor undertook excursions to Hatu Bui Kari, inspired by the colonial imaginary of *Arbiru* and the feast.[12] *Senhor* Alfredo Martins, a nurse at the local health post, had some rooms to let, and through the courteous intercession of a relative in Dili we were directed to his house. After settling in, we came to sit with Sr. Alfredo in the living room. Children played in the garden outside while his wife was doing the housework. I introduced myself and my companions and explained the reason for our presence. "We have come from Portugal and Dili to learn the story [*história*] of *Arbiru*," I said, "and we would like to write it down." Somewhat to our surprise (for we were entirely unaware of our host's lineage and his connection to the historical events), Sr. Alfredo was keen to respond. He expected our full attention. He spoke gravely about the death of the *Arbiru*, or, rather, as I soon realized, about the freedom Atabai people regained in killing him, during the siege of Bui Kari. The lives of his close kin from Hatu Bessi—a settlement in the vicinity of Hatu Bui Kari—were strongly linked to the terrible events of 1899. It was a story about his ancestors' bravery, astuteness, and heroic stubbornness in the face of violence and tragedy; it was *his* family story: "My father, José Leite," he began, "was born inside the cave on the day *Arbiru* was killed. On that same day we came out of the rock." He then explained the siege of 1899 to us as part of an expansionist attempt by the Portuguese to subdue the highlands—a conquest that was ultimately thwarted by Atabai resilience, the people's obstinate decision "never to surrender." "It was no war, *Arbiru* came with the intention of taming us [*amansar*]." "We" would rather die of hunger and thirst than submit to *Arbiru*, he continued:

The water had been cut off. They could not bear it any longer, with hunger, without food. Many people died; their bones are still in there. From inside Bui Kari they say, "We shall never surrender." They don't want to surrender, never. The Portuguese dominated the plains only. The mountains had not yet surrendered.

Placed in a precise historical time—the Portuguese conquest wars (the era of the so-called "pacification" campaigns)—Alfredo Martins's account presented the Bui Kari siege as an origin story of freedom and rejection of rule by outsiders. This account was emphatically punctuated with an explanation of the historical origins and meaning of the name given to the village or settlement of *Atabai*. "The people of Bui Kari rejected Portuguese presence," he said: "From this moment, from the siege, the name Atabai was born." In this folk etymology, Atabai—from Kemak *ata* ("slave") and *bai* ("are/have not")—was named in reference to the critical event of the siege; thereafter it stood for an untamed place where people are not slaves. Whether or not this is an accurate etymology, it is significant that the siege of Bui Kari and the death of the *Arbiru*, in other words, were foundational events in Atabai's history as a land of free people, never to be defeated by foreigners, never to be subjected to Portuguese (or any other external) rule.

Knowing the Portuguese archives, I was immediately struck by how this emphasis on Timorese independence contrasted with the accounts of Duarte's apotheosis and imperial glory. And yet some themes remained common, if only to reinforce the fact that their contents radically differed, as if such themes configured shared historiographical battlegrounds for contrasting claims to truth and power. The meticulously detailed circumstances of Duarte's death at Bui Kari—*the* nodal theme of Portuguese mythical storytelling, as seen earlier—was similarly central to Alfredo's account, only now the death motif took a rather distinct turn. Around such circumstances a number of important partial connections as well as open dissonances as regards the main tenets of colonial mythology are noticeable: the agents; the circumstances of killing; the place of death.

Not Slaves: An Origin Story of Atabai

The apotheosis of *Arbiru* gave way to the glory of the indigenous protagonists who defeated him and preserved Atabai's freedom. To begin, the officer's death was meaningful as a heroic *killing* revealing the cleverness, bravery, and ultimate victory of his Timorese opponents, rather than a heroic death that expressed the officer's military bravery and triumphant martyrdom. In Alfredo's account—which seems to resonate with a more widespread local story about the Bui Kari events associated with Hatu Bessi lineage—the story was also partly a celebration of the deeds of ancestors, a claim to autochthonous sovereignty against colonial rule, and a form of expressing a primordial attachment to land. Alfredo Martins told us that he was the grandson of one of the leading historical characters, who co-devised and was directly involved in the stratagem that led to the killing of *Arbiru* at Bui Kari in 1899. His grandfather was *Dato* Mau Mori, the old title of *dato* presumably standing as sign of his noble or high status. In highlighting his grandfather's role in the events, Alfredo explained in detail how his ancestor was able to draw *Arbiru* into a trap so that he could be shot and killed with a specially made weapon, a gold bullet:

> My grandfather, Mau Mori, met with Loko Mea, who was *Arbiru*'s Kemak interpreter and guide, and he arranged the following with him. Mau Mori said: "We never surrender," and Loko Mea responded, "Then I will tell *Arbiru* that you will surrender if he comes over and talks to you here." Loko Mea played this trick to catch the *Arbiru*. Mau Mori and Kapir Bia Banas[13] made a gold bullet. Loko Mea brought *Arbiru* to the rocks for the talk. When his body appeared from the chest up, they shot him down from a little door [*portinhola*] in a rock hole. The body of *Arbiru* was taken to Batugadé and then to Dili. Those who killed *Arbiru* became free. My grandfather always lived here until he died. They were never sent to prison. From the siege the name *Atabai* (meaning "not a slave") was born.

In 2003, historian Douglas Kammen collected an account congruent with the freedom narrative offered by Sr. Alfredo. "The people of Atabae," Kammen's interlocutor observed, "don't like being ordered and want to arrange their own affairs. The name Atabae comes from *Atan la bia*, meaning 'not a slave.'"[14] Kammen's notes are from a conversation with another elderly relative of one of the ancestral heroes of Bui Kari—possibly Kapir Bia Banas, since he claimed that "my father is the one who shot Arbiru. At close range," with "a rock [Indonesian *batu*] that had been burned/heated beforehand." Here, a stone, or a stone bullet, was used in the shot after undergoing a ritual transformation (see also a similar version in Pires 2015). Atabai-Atsabe alliances enabled the trick to bring *Arbiru* down, and this account made this point clear: "There were *adat* ties between Atabae and Atsabe. Ties even though they were in different *postos*." Thus, according to what seems to be a broadly shared account that circulates within lineages descending from the Bui Kari warriors, the killing of *Arbiru* was carefully planned; it resulted from a secret agreement, enabled by Timorese traditional alliances, between the head of the besieged people in the caves and *Arbiru*'s guide and interpreter, Beremau Loko Mea, a man from Atsabe. For Sr. Alfredo, it was his ancestor, Mau Mori, who led the people and negotiated the agreement; yet other local versions seem to circulate that instead elect Kapir Bia Banas as both the source of the deadly shot and the leader of the Atabai people in their refuge (see Pires 2015). In any case, it is agreed that Loko Mea sided with the Atabai people and played a double role: he led *Arbiru* into a trap where he was killed by a special gold bullet prepared by Mau Mori and Kapir Bia Banas—the "man who killed Arbiru." Loko Mea's trick depended on and reinforced the alliance between Atabai and Atsabe, which obligated them to provide mutual support—the sort of alliance that usually put the Portuguese administration under great stress, notably in times of war (Roque 2012). We reencounter the bullet magic theme as Timorese trope, a theme the Portuguese storytellers selectively integrated into the colonial mythology.

Most Portuguese depictions of Timorese stories omit the circumstance of truce talks, the figure of the emissary, as well as several other aspects of indigenous heroic lore. They portray the trickery as treachery; ignore a counternarrative of freedom; occlude the social alliances that enabled (and were reinforced by) the act of killing the *Arbiru*; and, most notably, obliterate the East Timorese historical protagonists of Atabai stories.[15] Still, shared elements can be identified. Reference to a truce having been made appear in one Portuguese account that precedes 1959—significantly, it says nothing about the exact mode and circumstances of Duarte's death. In 1948, prior to the consolidation of colonial mythology, Portuguese Captain José Simões Martinho wrote about *arbiru* and the Bui Kari events in an obscure newspaper article to the *Diário de Coimbra*. Rather than detailing the mode of death, he emphasized surrender talks, mediated by an "emissary" that led to Duarte's ill-fated meeting with the rebels (Martinho 1948: 3). Martinho saw Duarte as a Portuguese military hero, but he ended his brief note observing that a "shadow of mystery" surrounded "how" Duarte was killed. Yet Martinho's references to truce talks and a sudden shooting that left the Portuguese side perplexed virtually vanish, as we saw, from later Portuguese constructs of the *Arbiru* colonial myth. The figure of the emissary, however, may have not completely disappeared from Portuguese lore. In 2012, Captain Norberto Benigno, for instance, kept handwritten notes about the history of Duarte's death among his private papers, stating, "The Arbiru climbed the rocks to talk and on this occasion he was treacherously shot and killed in the back by his messenger." Absent from all Portuguese accounts of the events, nonetheless, are the Timorese protagonists.

"Kai Naba," a Kemak Folk Song

At a climactic point of his narrative Sr. Alfredo, by his own initiative, presented yet another, perhaps critical, piece in this historical composition. "There was even a song about this," he remarked, "a song named 'Kai Naba.'" And he then recited the verses of a Kemak song concerning the death of the *Arbiru* at Bui Kari. "This is a very old song"; it existed before the Portuguese began the *Arbiru* feast, Alfredo explained; it was a song he used to sing in primary school. Upon our request, he helped us write these verses down and translate them from Kemak into Tetum and Portuguese. *This* was the folk song to which, as seen earlier, Portuguese colonial officers recurrently referred as offering evidence of Timorese subordination to and respect and veneration for the sacred figure of Duarte, *Arbiru*. The song begins with a set of verses that can be translated into English as *Bui Kari, at Bui Kari Rock / Arbiru dies on his feet / Bui Kari, at Bui Kari Rock / Arbiru lost his life/ Now the fault is done / I want to speak, but cannot do it.* These six verses appear in Portuguese translations in support of the imperialist interpretation. Yet the full song contains much more. It goes on to praise the names and deeds of the three Bui Kari warriors—Loko Mea, Mau Mori, Bia Banas—and ends on an enigmatic moralizing reference to *Arbiru*:

> *Lokomea Bere Mau Lokomea*
> *Gleno returns to Atsabe*
> *Bia Banas Kapir Bia Banas*
> *He was the one who killed Arbiru*
>
> *Mau Mori Dato Mau Mori*
> *His people leave the cave*
> *He leaves the cave with his people*
>
> *Arbiru is a brave man*
> *But he forgot he had wife and children*[16]

In postindependence Timor-Leste, memories and accounts of past events of violence and war (including events of the Portuguese period) have turned into significant battlegrounds for political struggle between conflicting social groups, at both national and local levels (Molnar 2006; Bovensiepen 2017). Among the "political metaphors" that commonly frame East Timorese nationalist visions of the colonial past, as Douglas Kammen observes, the "master-slave" relationship stands out: the Portuguese colonizers are portrayed as oppressive "masters" who "enslaved" the East Timorese over centuries (Kammen 2003). In this sense, Sr. Alfredo's reading of the Bui Kari events as a kind of apotheosis of Atabai freedom fighting and liberation from a condition of "slavery" imminently to be imposed by the Portuguese echoes this postindependence imaginary. I asked Sr. Alfredo what, in his opinion, did this song principally convey. "Resistance" [*resistência*], he responded. In congruence with his memory of the Bui Kari siege, then, Alfredo reads the verses as carriers of a historical reality of "resistance" in the face of Portuguese colonialist intrusion. This retrospective anticolonial reading of the Bui Kari events possibly needs to be understood within a widespread Timorese *rezistencia* framework that gained traction in nationalist visions of independent Timor-Leste since 1999. It may also articulate political conflicts between local elites and lineages, which, however, I was unable to identify in my short stay. The local situation preceding the events of 1899 may have been more politically complex, as attested by documentary evidence of alliance through vassalage treaties established with the Portuguese government by Atabai leaders in at least 1895 (Boletim Oficial 1895). Specifically about Bui Kari events of 1899, however, the resistance viewpoint seems to be widely disseminated (cf. Pires 2015; Nascimento 2015; Buti 2012; CAMSTL 2015).

Yet I also asked what the first set of verses could specifically mean, and Sr. Alfredo added: "Repentance" [*arrependimento*]. "I wanted to speak, but I can't, suddenly this happened; I cannot speak, it already passed." The sense of a wrong action, requiring remorse and repentance, an ancestral fault committed by killing the officer paradoxically accompanies the poetic celebration of his death. Surely any attempt to interpret the song and its intelligent play of words and ambivalences is necessarily circumstantial, provisional, and tentative. Although Sr. Alfredo said nothing (and perhaps I did not ask insistently enough) about the closing two verses, the song culminates with what I read as a powerful social critique of *Arbiru*, preceded by an acknowledgment of his bravery. It is possible that Francisco Duarte was married to a woman in Timor; some Portuguese accounts mention his wife as playing an active part in colonial battles (Martinho 1948: 3; Fonseca 2003: 13). A "brave man" *Arbiru* was indeed, the song ends, but "he forgot he had wife and children": *Arbiru* was neglectful of social ties and disregarded proper norms—he forgot obligations to his close kin. I would note that, as mentioned above, the term *arbiru* in East Timorese usage connotes excess and carelessness as regards established norms. Hence the song's moral lesson: after all, he was a social being, he was human, like any other—his death comes as a reminder of what comes upon someone who forgets the bonds of his own humanity. Ultimately, then, it was *Arbiru*'s own excesses that caused his tragic death.

Through verse one could learn about Atabai's achievement of freedom; the oddly mixed, ambivalent attitude of regret and triumph; and finally a kind of veiled moral lesson, a critical message to *Arbiru* and, one may add, to the Portuguese invaders in general. This was a folk song, however, a condensed story that accordingly implied a specific type of dance and musical performance. Alfredo made this clear. "Kai Naba" was danced and sung by men and women: "It is a big group. Men and women in a circle. Men sing a verse, and then women respond with another." Most importantly for my analysis, Alfredo suggested that in the past this song was performed as part of a specific ritual celebration—during the "feasts" held on 17 July, the date *Arbiru* was killed and Atabai regained freedom: "They sang it on those times when there was feast." Data collected by Douglas Kammen suggest the historical possibility of "Kai Naba" being associated with a specifically *Timorese* commemoration of Bui Kari victory and of the disappearance of *Arbiru*—a man feared for his violence. Kammen's informant recalled in 2003, "Every year on July 17 we [the Atabai people] commemorate Arbiru's death. Every year five water buffalo are sacrificed." This explicit reference to "July 17" as a special date celebrated with buffalo sacrifices indicates that the Bui Kari events of 1899 were a special ritual occasion on Timorese cultural terms. The performance of "Kai Naba" by Atabai men and women was then possibly one moment of a wider ritual sequence in which Atabai's glorious engagement with colonial conquerors was recalled, celebrated, and reenacted. One wonders how these Timorese performances related to the Portuguese ceremonies instituted in 1959. Portuguese documentation bears little trace of any such Timorese popular practices. However, it may occasionally mention Timorese dancing and feasting occurring either simultaneously (sometimes as an integral part of the Portuguese official program) or alongside, in parallel to, or after the official ceremonies sponsored by the government—as when allusions are made to Timorese feasting that continued all night after formal functions ended at Bui Kari (see Thomaz 1970b).

Importantly, the song "Kai Naba" stood out as one of the dances performed on occasion of the Feast of the *Arbiru* before a colonial audience presided over by the Portuguese governor and his entourage of officials, army officers, missionaries, and Timorese authorities. "Still today [circa 1964] when the ceremonies of homage to Arbiru take place," wrote officer Junqueira, "the people of Atabai sing in Kemak the following song, which they say was first performed by the rebels, on the death place [of Arbiru], a few hours after its occurrence" (Junqueira 1987 [1964]: 20). At Atabai, in 2012, I showed Sr. Alfredo Martins a short video on my laptop of the colonial ceremonies made in 1970.[17] There is a brief filmed scene of Timorese men and women performing a circle dance for the Portuguese authorities on the ceremonial ground of Bui Kari, in front of the memorial stone erected in 1959 (see also the cover image of this volume). Sr. Alfredo immediately recognized it as a "Kai Naba" performance. At least between 1959 and 1974, then, "Kai Naba," perhaps originally performed for internal Timorese consumption, was incorporated into the colonial ceremonials of the Feast of the *Arbiru*. According to Atabai conceptions, "Kai Naba" conveyed an implicitly subversive and anticolonial celebration of autochthonous sovereignty. The Portuguese seemed unaware of these meanings and understood the song as yet another expression of the Timorese belief in and submission to the sacred powers of the Portuguese officer. This overlap thus contained a potential for conflict; or, as Sr. Urbano Martins (Alfredo's relative) also remembered, the feast caused "controversy" because the "Portuguese celebrate *Arbiru* as hero." In a similar vein, in a later conversation in Portugal in 2018, Francisco Soares, a grandson of Kapir Bia Banas, evoked this potential for political subversion entailed in the Atabai versions of the death of *Arbiru*. Soares told me that his family's story concerning Kapir Bia Banas as killer of the *Arbiru* was kept as a "secret" (*segredo*) from the Portuguese in the 1960s, because those were "times of the PIDE," the political police that operated in Portugal and its colonies during the Estado Novo regime.

Notwithstanding this tension, the song was possibly one of the highlights of the feast, upon which opposed Timorese and Portuguese stories ambivalently converged. While Atabai people sang and danced their celebration of freedom and resistance (and perhaps also regret), the Portuguese officialdom assimilated the Timorese dance to visions of imperial glory, as an indigenous amplification of the colonial myth of imperial apotheosis. Both sides came together in a seemingly equivocal occasion in which opposite historicities coexisted in connection, and yet became parasitic on one another. It is also, but perhaps not simply, an instance of "parallel" or "different perspectives" on the past (Bovensiepen, this volume). It is a case of different historicities connected in interaction. Portuguese colonials condescended to the Timorese legends and imaginaries they appropriated into a mythology of conquest. Yet Timorese performances of Atabai freedom stories during the feast reveal that the mythic praxis of indigenous resistance also fed upon the pomposity of the Portuguese ceremony. From this perspective, the Feast of the *Arbiru* configured a singular social form

that crossed Timorese and Portuguese colonial historicities. Two opposite mythic story lines—a myth of conquest and a myth of resistance—partially intersected and interacted, in the process reciprocally
appropriating bits and fragments of each other for their respective
projects of self-empowerment. Thus, at the crossroads of the feast, to
paraphrase freely Sahlins's observation on the Maori, Timorese storytellers as well as the Portuguese officials behave like "cunning mythol-
ogists, who are able to select from the supple body of traditions those
most appropriate to the satisfaction of their current interests, as they
conceive them" (Sahlins 1985: 55).

A final note concerns the ways the Timorese and colonial mythologies intersected through simultaneously concurrent and contradictory inscriptions into landscape. For the "Kai Naba" song, just like the
colonial stories, also cannot be dissociated from the place of Hatu Bui
Kari. As we saw, the colonial myth of Duarte's apotheosis was entailed
in a material and ritual realm in which certain stories implied certain
topography. Similarly, the indigenous myth of Atabai is entailed in a
specific version of the landscape of Bui Kari. Indeed, as I realized also
in my field visit in 2012, the Atabai memory of the death of the *Arbiru*
seems to have materialized in an equally ambivalent spatial topography (figure 3.4). At Bui Kari, two death places for *Arbiru* can be identified. Alongside the commemorative stone built by the Portuguese
authorities in 1959, the East Timorese now indicate an indigenous

Figure 3.4.   Stone upon which the *Arbiru* fell dead, according to Timorese
lore at Atabai. Photo by the author.

counterpart: there is a another death place elsewhere at Hatu Bui Kari, the actual stone upon which, according to Atabai lore, *Arbiru* fell down after being shot by Kapir Bia Banas on 17 July 1899.

Conclusion

This chapter has explored how Portuguese outsiders could insert themselves into Timorese cultural orders by means of mythic praxis and, even, ritual and magical frameworks. In parallel, it has explored how Timorese insiders could articulate colonial conquest through distinct, and yet connected, indigenous historicities of resistance. The rise of the feast of the *Arbiru* as colonial cult in the 1950s, I suggested, was to some extent a gauge of European colonial vulnerability. Originating in a historical situation of perceived colonial fragility, colonial mythmaking with regard to Duarte, so-called *Arbiru*, rested upon insights into Atabai viewpoints, about which sorts of anthropological and historical data were collected, read, and conveyed with a view (albeit, perhaps, sometimes unintentional) to reinforce and legitimize a colonial myth of conquest. The colonial cult of the Arbiru—a fantasy of power and a celebration of colonial supremacy that paradoxically rested upon a sense of vulnerability—thus entailed claims of ethnographic authority over its perceived indigenous cultural foundations. By these means the Portuguese produced their own colonial mythology of Timorese incorporations of themselves—and, ultimately, fabricated their own forms of magical explanation of history.

In proceedings of the feast of the *Arbiru* and its associated narratives, the Portuguese created the vision of a consensual mythology, one that united Portuguese and Timorese, conquerors and their enemies, into one imagined community connected by a mythic story of apotheosis, which ultimately communicated Portuguese superiority. I have articulated archival records and writings with oral history collected from former Portuguese colonials and from Timorese descendants of the Bui Kari warriors. I have suggested that we can move beyond this consensual imagination by considering seemingly alternative indigenous narratives, topographies, and heroes that have come into emergence alongside the colonial myth over time. Drawing on field materials from Atabai, I suggested the death of the *Arbiru* on 17 July 1899 is recounted and commemorated in Timorese stories in ways in many respects parallel or even opposed to the Portuguese versions. Yet, I also argued, the Portuguese and Timorese attachments to the death of the *Arbiru*, connected by that common chronotopia, seem to form a paradoxical and perhaps enigmatic entangled colonial historicity.

In resuming today the reading of East Timorese cultural materials and memories of the *Arbiru* at Atabai, we are confronted with the powerful presence of an assemblage of local stories and places that interfere with the colonial myth of conquest by means of another no less mythological idiom of resistance and freedom. The Kemak song "Kai Naba" stands as an example of the ambivalences of political opposition and cultural exchange that could be established between the conquest and the resistance mythic praxis. Since 1959, "Kai Naba" performances at the colonial feast emphasized an equivocal and yet mutually meaningful celebration of opposite versions of colonial historicity. Parallel mythologies of conquest and freedom prospered around connected ritual and narrative reenactments of one same moment, as if two contradictory versions of the past benefited from a relation of ambivalent overlap with mutual losses and mutual benefits—a particular modality, perhaps, of what I have elsewhere characterized as mutual parasitism (Roque 2010: 34–39). In this case, a double colonial historicity emerged. Contrasting truth and power claims about the colonial past gained independent strength from the ambiguities and distortions of their relative overlaps. The very materials on which their difference was grounded served to strengthen their interdependence around one chronotopia—"the death of the *Arbiru*" on 17 July 1899. It may be that the creative effervescence of the historical trope of *Arbiru* cannot be reduced to a Portuguese/Timorese-Atabai dichotomy, and other stories around *Arbiru* can be identified. In any case, it is certain the historical anthropology of the death of the *Arbiru* and its relational mythologies is not yet finished. This chapter, I believe, touched but the historical tip of the dark rocks of Bui Kari.

Acknowledgments

Research for this essay was funded by FCT, Fundação para a Ciência e Tecnologia, Portugal (grant references HC/0089/2009 and PTDC/ HAR- HIS/28577/2017). Fieldwork in Timor in 2012 was also supported by Fundação Oriente and by an Australian Research Council Postdoctoral Fellowship (FL 110100243). For generously sharing their memories and stories about *Arbiru*, my gratitude to Alfredo Martins, Urbano Martins, Aristides, and Luís Gonzaga (Atabai); Norberto Benigno (Carcavelos), Filipe Themudo Barata (Lisbon), and Francisco Soares (Porto). For companionship and exchanges, I thank Gonçalo

Antunes, Judith Bovensiepen, Luís Costa, Janet Gunter, Douglas Kammen, Sabina da Fonseca, Vicente Paulino, Lúcio Sousa, and João Tolentino. Lúcio and Vicente gave me invaluable support and insights
in translating Tetum materials and, especially, the "Kai Naba" song.
Chris Ballard encouraged me to integrate the Atabai field materials
in spite of my obvious difficulty in deciphering their complexities; his
critiques led me to reinvent this chapter substantially. I thank finally
Elizabeth Traube for constant intellectual inspiration and insightful
comments on an earlier version of this chapter.

Ricardo Roque is research fellow at the Institute of Social Sciences of
the University of Lisbon (Instituto de Ciências Sociais da Universidade
de Lisboa) and currently an honorary associate in the Department of
History of the University of Sydney. He works on the history and anthropology of human sciences, colonialism, and cross-cultural contact in the Portuguese-speaking world. He has published extensively
on the colonial history of Timor-Leste. Current research interests include the comparative history of twentieth-century racial sciences
and the theory and ethnography of colonial archives and biological
collections. He is the author of *Headhunting and Colonialism* (2010),
and coeditor (with K. Wagner) of *Engaging Colonial Knowledge* (2012)
and (with W. Anderson and R. Ventura Santos) of *Luso-tropicalism and
Its Discontents* (2019).

Notes

1. Later on, the Indonesian administration apparently acknowledged the
   existence of Francisco Duarte as a former Portuguese hero, but the ceremony was discontinued after 1975 (see Gunn 2000: 245–46).
2. The governor's son, homonymous Filipe Themudo Barata (then aged
   eleven), recalls thus the moment his appointment to Timor was communicated to the family: "One day my father came home and he said, 'We
   are going to Timor.' He didn't even know where Timor was located. We
   all went looking for it on a map" (Barata, 2013, interview).
3. See Barata 1998. But on the history and memories of this event, cf.
   Gunter 2007; Chamberlain 2009.
4. Manuel Ferreira wrote extensively in the main colonial periodicals in
   the 1940s–50s; he authored an article series on the greatest "figures" or
   "heroes of Timor." Jaime Neves was also a prolific local news writer; he
   was a founding member of Portuguese Timor's first newspaper *A Voz de
   Timor* and of the first radio service in Dili (see Barata 1998: 45; Paulino
   2011).

5. At some point after this date (1959), perhaps by order of a subsequent governor, another monument to the memory of *Arbiru* was erected at Maliana, where it still survives. According to Lúcio Sousa (personal email 9 November 2013) some people in the region of Maliana recall feasting performed around the Maliana monument in the Portuguese past. I have so far been unable to ascertain the origins of this monument and the rites that may have been associated with its existence.

6. The gravestone was fabricated by the company Miragaia; José Sequeira carved the inscription (Neves 1960).

7. Processo individual F. Duarte, AHM. Therefore, apparently Governor Celestino da Silva never formally informed Lisbon about the death of his favourite officer. The handwritten note on his archival record was possibly added years after his death, possibly as interest in his life story increased.

8. The full epitaph reads (my translation): "Here lies FRANCISCO DUARTE, Second-lieutenant of the Army of Portugal, on commission in Timor, killed in combat at Atabai on the attack to the Bicari Rocks [*Pedras de Bicari*] on 17 July 1899."

9. The later phrase only is my italics.

10. It was reproduced in Lisbon, in the popular newspaper *Diário Popular*, and also as a chapter in the volume *Figuras Portuguesas de Timor*, a 1961 publication sponsored by the Dili government to mark the recent creation of the various heroic monuments and ceremonies.

11. My companions were Gonçalo Antunes, Sabina da Fonseca, Vicente Paulino, and Lúcio Sousa. Conversations with Sr. Alfredo Martins were in Portuguese and Tetum.

12. In 2001, Rui Brito da Fonseca, a former official in "Portuguese Timor," renovated and repainted the memorial stone as part of a project for restoration of Portuguese monuments in Timor paid for by the Comissariado para o Apoio a Timor Leste (CATTL) (Fonseca 2003). In 2005 Fonseca returned to Bui Kari to organize a small reenactment of the former Portuguese *Arbiru* ceremony (Fonseca, personal email 2 March 2017). At least another group of Portuguese expats in Timor visited Bui Kari to pay homage to Francisco Duarte's memory in 2006 (Manel 2006). These returns perhaps explain why Sr. Alfredo Martins in 2012 remembers one "relative" of *Arbiru* coming to pay homage at Bui Kari.

13. Kemak: "Bia Banas"; Tetum: "Bia Manas" can mean literally "hot water."

14. I am grateful to Douglas Kammen for generously sharing his notes from interviews at Atabai on 30 May 2003. Kammen cannot confirm the identity of his Timorese interlocutor in 2003 (an uncle of Francisco Soares, then his colleague at UNTL) but it seems he was affiliated (or claimed to be affiliated) with the lineage of Kapir Bia Banas, one of the Bui Kari heroes.

15. One rare instance of reference to the names of Timorese killers of *Arbiru* in a Portuguese text is Junqueira (1987 [1964]: 19), who wrote: "'Arbiru' would find his death with a bullet shot by a certain CAPIR, from the village of ILESSO (Atabai)."

16. My English version is based on Tetum and Portuguese translations kindly arranged by Sr. Alfredo and Vicente Paulino at Atabai. In the Kemak original:

> *Lokomea Bere Mau Lokomea*
> *Glelu hali te Atsabe*
> *Bia Banas Kapir Bia Banas*
> *Tau tuli Arbiru lolo*
>
> *Mau Mori Dato Mau Mori*
> *No no povu, samai dia moron*
> *Samai no povu, dia moron*
>
> *Arbiru mane sia soi*
> *Mi ligo bali hen no anan*

17. I thank João Tolentino for access to a copy of this short 16-millimeter film (without sound) that was presumably made in 1970 and is part of the Portuguese Television (RTP) archives.

References

Archival Sources

PVCMB, Presidente e Vogais da Comissão Municipal de Bobonaro, Convite para a Festa do Arbiru, 25 June 1969. Private archives of Norberto Lacerda Benigno.

Processo Individual de Alferes Francisco Duarte, Lisboa, AHM (Arquivo Histórico Militar), Processos Individuais, Caixa 1052.

Calvão, G. A. N.d. "Homens do Ultramar. III." Newspaper cutting, Lisbon, private archives of J. Celestino Silva's relatives, Colonel José Carlos Montalvão.

Films

Spiguel, M. (director). 1960. *Timor Português*. Bucelas: ANIM, Cinemateca Portuguesa.

CAMSTL-Centro Audiovisual Max Stahl Timor-Leste. 2015. *Igreja Coragem. Parte III*. Facebook video, retrieved 14 February 2019 from https://www.facebook.com/audiovisualarchivetimorleste/videos/86924819 3245322/.

Published Sources

AAVV. 1961. *Figuras Portuguesas de Timor: Homenagem a Celestino da Silva*. Dili: Imprensa Nacional.

Barata, F. T. 1961. "Palavras proferidas na sessão solene de encerramento do 60º aniversário da morte de Francisco Duarte, 'O Arbiru,' Dili, 20 de

Julho de 1959." In *Figuras Portuguesas de Timor: Homenagem a Celestino da Silva*, AAVV, 29–30. Dili: Imprensa Nacional.

———. 1963. "Timor, Esse Desconhecido." *Estudos Políticos e Sociais* 1(3): 659–84.

———. 1998. *Timor Contemporâneo: Da primeira ameaça indonésia ao nascer de uma nação*. Lisboa: Equilíbrio Editorial.

Boletim Oficial do Governo da Província de Macau e Timor. 1895. "Tratado de Vassalagem." 24 August 1895: 359–60.

Bovensiepen, J. 2017. "Entanglements of Power, Kinship and Time in Laclubar." In *Fieldwork in Timor-Leste: Understanding Social Change through Practice*, edited by M. Nygaard-Christensen and A. Bexley, 144–68. Copenhagen: NIAS Press.

Buti, B. 2012. "Menvelusuri Daerah Potensi Wisata di Sub-Distrik Atabae." Atabae Ana Unidade, retrieved 7 June 2017 from http://atabae-ana .blogspot.pt/2012/02/menyelusuri-daerah-potensi-wisata-di_21.html.

Chamberlain, E. 2009. *Rebellion, Defeat and Exile: The 1959 Uprising in East Timor*. Point Lonsdale: Ernest Chamberlain.

Duarte, T. 1931. *O Rei de Timor*. Lisbon: A. M. Pereira.

Ferreira, M. 1957. *Timor: sua terra, sua gente e sua história. Conferência pronunciada por Manuel Ferreira, [em Dili] na Sede da Juventude Evangélica Portuguesa em 28 de Março de 1957*. S/I. S/L [Lisboa].

Fonseca, R. B. 2003. *Monumentos Portugueses em Timor-Leste*. Porto: Crocodilo Azul.

Fox, J. J. (ed.). 2006. *The Poetic Power of Place: Comparative Perspectives on Austronesian Ideas of Locality*. Canberra: ANU Press.

Gunn, G. 2000. *New World Hegemony in the Malay World*. Lawrenceville, NJ: The Red Sea Press.

Gunter, J. 2007. "Communal Violence in Viqueque and the 'Charged' History of '59." *Asia Pacific Journal of Anthropology* 8(1): 27–41.

———. 2011. "Arbiru." Return to Rai Ketak, retrieved 24 August 2014 from http://raiketak.wordpress.com/2011/04/04/Arbiru/.

Junqueira, J. B. 1987 [1964]. "O Arbiru." *Independência—Revista de Cultura Lusíada* 5: 19–23.

Kammen, D. 2003. "Master-Slave, Traitor-Nationalist, Opportunist-Oppressed: Political Metaphors in East Timor." *Indonesia* 76: 69–86.

Manel. 2006. "O Major Arbiru em Atabai." Hau hakarak ba uma!, retrieved 7 June 2017 from http://timor-mais-eu.blogspot.pt/2006/09/o-major-Arbiru.html.

Martinho, J. S. 1938. *Os Portugueses no Oriente: Elementos para a História da Ocupação de Timor*. Lisboa: Sociedade Nacional de Tipografia.

———. 1943. *Timor: Quatro Séculos de Colonização Portuguesa*. Porto: Progredior.

———. 1948. "O Arbírù." *Diário de Coimbra*, 27 January 1948, p. 3.

Martins, L. A. F. 1939. "O Major Arébéro." In *Glórias e Martírios da Colonização Portuguesa (III)*, 5–10. Lisboa: Colecção Pelo Império.

McWilliam, A., and E. G. Traube (eds.). 2011. *Land and Life in Timor-Leste: Ethnographic Essays*. Canberra: ANU Press.

Molnar, A. K. 2006. "'Died in the Service of Portugal': Legitimacy of Authority and Dynamics of Group Identity among the Atsabe Kemak." *Journal of Southeast Asian Studies* 37(2): 335–55.

do Nascimento, J. 2015. "Revolusaun Arbiru." Bagian Sejarah Timor Leste Yang Terlupakan, retrieved 7 June 2017 from http://nascimentojoao .blogspot.pt/2015/01/.

Neves, J. 1960. "Nas Pedras de Bui-cari foi solenemente recordada a morte heróica em combate do Alferes Francisco Duarte (o ARBIRU)." *A Voz de Timor*, no. 404 (July): 1.

———. 1961. "Conferência proferida na sessão solene no 60° aniversário da morte de Francisco Duarte, o 'Arbiru.'" In *Figuras Portuguesas de Timor: Homenagem a Celestino da Silva*, AAVV, 33–60. Dili: Imprensa Nacional.

Obeyesekere, G. 1992. *The Apotheosis of Captain Cook: European Mythmaking in the Pacific*. Princeton, NJ: Princeton University Press.

de Oliveira, L. 1949. *Timor na História de Portugal*, vol. 1. Lisboa: AGC.

Paulino, V. 2011. "Manuel Ferreira." In *History and Anthropology of "Portuguese Timor," 1850–1975*, edited by Ricardo Roque. *An Online Dictionary of Biographies*, retrieved 21 August 2014 from http://www.historyan thropologytimor.org.

Pires, R. 2015. "Rezisténsia Povu Atabai Kontra Kolonialista Portuges." Timor Actuál, retrieved 6 June 2017 from http://kota-baba.blogspot .pt/2015/12/rezistensia-povu-atabai-kontra.html.

Roque, R. 2010. *Headhunting and Colonialism: Anthropology and the Circulation of Human Skulls in the Portuguese Empire 1870–1930*. New York: Palgrave Macmillan.

———. 2012. "Marriage Traps: Colonial Interactions with Indigenous Marriage Ties in East Timor." In *Racism and Ethnic Relations in the Portuguese-Speaking World*, edited by F. Bethencourt and A. Pearce, 203–25. New York: Oxford University Press.

———. Forthcoming. "The Name of the Wild Man: Colonial *Arbiru* in East Timor." In *Swearing and Cursing: Contexts and Practices in a Critical Linguistic Perspective*, edited by N. Nassenstein and A. Storch. Berlin and Boston: De Gruyter.

Sahlins, M. 1985. *Islands of History*. Chicago: University of Chicago Press.

———. 1995. *How "Natives" Think: About Captain Cook, for Example*. Chicago: University of Chicago Press.

da Silva, J. C. 1897. *Relatório das Operações de Guerra no Districto Autonomo de Timor no Anno de 1896*. Lisbon: Imprensa Nacional.

Thomaz, L. [L. T.]. 1970a. "Festas do Arbiru em Atabai." *A Província de Timor*, 25 July 1970, s.p.

———. 1970b. "O Arbiru." *A Província de Timor*, 25 July 1970, 17–18.

Traube, E. G. 1986. *Cosmology and Social Life: Ritual Exchange among the Mambai of East Timor*. Chicago: University of Chicago Press.

Wiener, M. J. 1995. *Visible and Invisible Realms: Power, Magic and Colonial Conquest in Bali*. Chicago: University of Chicago Press.

Chapter 4

PACIFICATION AND REBELLION IN THE HIGHLANDS OF PORTUGUESE TIMOR

Judith Bovensiepen

> Towards the interior of the island in fertile mountain soil and among escarpments, lies the little *reino* of Funar. . . . The ungrateful turf makes only for bad pastures, which is why the natives use it to raise buffalo. In the smoother slopes of better soil, they plant corn that they live off. This sad people possessed nothing else, beyond their buffalo herds, a couple of hundred head, whose rearing had taken years. They thought they were rich, the poor devils, because they didn't need neighbours. (Zola 1909: 27)

At the beginning of the twentieth century, the Portuguese colonial army launched two military operations against the *reino* (kingdom) of Funar, which is surrounded by steep mountains. According to Zola (1909), the Portuguese colonial military attacked Funar in 1905 and again in 1907 under the pretext of putting down a rebellion. In reality, Zola argues, the attacks were aimed at stealing the highlanders' plentiful buffalo herds. The attacks by the colonial army eventually led to the total destruction and administrative division of the *reino* of Funar.

Today, Funar is a *suco* (village) located in the central highlands of the municipality of Manatuto. Its remote and once inaccessible mountain location may well be what prevented the Portuguese colonial military from penetrating this region effectively until the beginning of the twentieth century.[1] The attack on Funar in 1907 was not the last time the area was subject to an annihilating attack. During the conflict between the political parties UDT (União Democrática Timorense) and Fretilin (Frente Revolucionária de Timor-Leste Independente) in 1974, Funar was entirely destroyed, and all of its inhabitants were forcibly resettled during the first years of the Indonesian invasion in the late 1970s. Highlanders only started to return to their ancestral lands in the late 1990s.

Nowadays, Funar villagers again raise buffalo herds and plant corn in the soil on the steep mountains. Yet, many talk about the Portuguese colonial period as a time of plenty and power—especially when contrasted with the Indonesian occupation or with the years of poverty immediately after Timor-Leste regained independence. During my doctoral fieldwork (2005–7), "the Portuguese time" was described as a period when the *reino* of Funar was large and powerful—with a reach almost to Dili. Significantly, highlanders stressed that Funar was independent from neighboring domains in Laclubar (esp. Orlalan and Manelima)—echoing Zola's description of how the highlanders' pride derived from the fact that "they did not need any neighbours." Some went so far as saying that Funar was as "big" or influential as the *reino* of Samoro (located in present-day Soibada), which developed allegiances with the Portuguese colonial powers early on and appears in the earliest Portuguese list of kingdoms from 1702. "In the past, we ruled over all of them" (*ulukliu, ami ukun hotu*), I was told by a member of Funar's traditional "ruling" house (*liurai*).[2]

In my first interviews with elders in Funar, I asked them directly about the supposed revolt against Portuguese colonial rule, but they quickly denied any such occurrence.[3] With the exception of one research participant who had spent several decades living outside of Timor-Leste, and who insisted that Funar's inhabitants were known for being "rebellious," no one there mentioned their ancestors' having rebelled against the Portuguese, nor did they mention an attack by the colonial army against this domain.

This chapter explores different representations of the past in both Portuguese sources and the historical narratives of Funar villagers in the present. Whereas archival resources indicate that the people of Funar were subject to two military campaigns at the beginning of the twentieth century, many adults I spoke to in Funar talked about the Portuguese time in terms of wealth and success, when the rule of the *reino* extended well beyond its current boundaries. How can we explain the difference in accounts: the local representation of this period as the pinnacle of Funar's power and wealth and this particular account from the Portuguese archives that points to its violent subjugation by the colonial forces?

Representations of the Past

> However counterintuitive it may seem, I would argue . . . that history
> the historian creates is in fact fundamentally different from the history
> people make. No matter how much of the original, experienced past
> historians choose or are able to build into their narratives, what they
> end up with will, in specific and identifiable ways, be different from the
> past. This is so, moreover, despite the fact that the process of narrativ-
> ization in which the historian engages is not, in my view, intrinsically
> different from the process of narrativization in which the direct experi-
> ence of the past engages. (Cohen 1997: 3–4)

In his book *History in Three Keys: The Boxers as Event, Experience, and
Myth*, Paul A. Cohen (1997) describes the Boxer Rebellion in China
from three different epistemological perspectives. In the first part, he
analyzes the Boxer Uprising of 1899–1901 as an event, i.e. as it has
been reconstructed by historians. In the second part, he tries to explore
the experience of the participants by analyzing the rebellion through a
number of social phenomena connected to it in local representations,
such as drought and spirit possession. And finally, Cohen analyzes the
Boxer Rebellion as a myth that has been ideologically appropriated by
the New Culture movement. Cohen's argument is that one should not
privilege any one of these different historical epistemologies.

As in the Boxer Rebellion, different epistemologies are also at stake
in the written and oral accounts of the encounter between Funar's
ancestors and the Portuguese. Zola's account of the two wars of Funar mentions a man called Jeronymo. This name also appears in oral
narratives told in Funar concerning the encounter between "foreigners" (*malae*) and Funar's ancestors. In the local narrative, Jeronymo
is a foreigner who tries to betray the people of Funar by claiming that
the king of Funar looks like a beast (*animal*). To settle the dispute, the
king of Funar sends his son to meet the Portuguese administrator in
Dili. The administrator finds the son so incredibly beautiful that he
decides that Funar should be independent. The story ends by casting
the people of Funar as the winners of the dispute. This stands in sharp
contrast to Zola's account of the encounter between Funar villagers
and Jeronymo, which describes the total destruction and division of
Funar.[4]

One of the questions I want to explore in this chapter is, how can
we understand the discrepancy between these different, even opposed,
accounts? Why is it that the local narrative that involves Jeronymo is
a story of victory, whereas this singular Portuguese account emphasizes the violence and barbarity of the colonial army's attack, which

ended with the destruction and defeat of Funar? The accounts cannot be put into Cohen's clear-cut categories: event, experience, and myth. There is an element of all three in both accounts. Rather than treating Zola's account as "history" (because it is a written source) and Funar's account as "myth" or "experience," I treat them *both* as historical and anthropological sources. It is not the aim of this chapter to discuss debates about using oral traditions as historical sources (see Vansina 1985). Yet, I follow the basic premise that once past experiences have been narrativized, they persist as a *representation* of the past and have political significance in the present—"recalling is not the same as re-membering" (Bloch 1998: 118).

Before discussing the two accounts, I want to stress that there are several obvious interpretations to avoid, or at least to complicate. First, one could say that the Timorese account is simply a deliberate *mis*representation of the facts. Funar was destroyed at the beginning of the twentieth century, but today villagers recount the story as a victory, because that allows them to deal with the traumatic events of war and colonization. They are, so to speak, in a state of false consciousness where they describe a disempowering situation as an empowering one. This approach is insufficient because it assumes that the Portuguese narrative is the "true" or "rational" account, whereas the highlanders are somehow deceived about the true facts of history.

Another way of explaining the discrepancy between the accounts would be to say that the Timorese narrative of the colonial encounter embodies people's resistance to the colonizers' constructions of reality. By narrating the colonial encounter in positive terms, people are asserting their agency. Although there may be some truth in this interpretation, I think taking this argument too far would lead to an idealization of people's ability to resist in situations where they faced drastic colonial oppression. Rather than favor one account as truthful or factual, I want to explore what we can learn from "crossing" the two accounts, since they both concern the encounters between indigenous highlanders and members of the Portuguese colonial military.

The Wars of Funar: Zola's Account

The quote at the start of this chapter is an extract from António Pádua Correia's (1909) powerful pamphlet, *Quatorze Annos de Timor*. Correia used the the pseudonym "Zola" because the pamphlet presents a damning critique of the brutal reign of Celestino da Silva, who was governor of Timor from 1894 to 1908, and who pushed for the "pacification" and ever-greater control of the mountain interior in the eastern part of the island of Timor, which gave rise to numerous revolts among affected domains. Zola uses the destruction of Funar as the prime example for Celestino's barbaric rule. The colonial government justified the violent attack on grounds that the inhabitants of this *reino* had staged a revolt against Portuguese rule (*indigena rebelde* [Zola 1909: 27]), when in actual fact, it served the purpose of self-enrichment.

Zola's *Quatorze Annos de Timor* was published in 1909. Zola was a journalist and a doctor who specialized in tropical medicine and worked in the military, stationed in Macau, Timor, and Mozambique. Interestingly, he was not only a republican who criticized the colonial government but also a freemason. It is important to understand his account in the context of the tensions between monarchists and republicans in Portugal at the turn of the nineteenth century. Zola's antimonarchist account was written when the monarchy was truly under threat: King D. Carlos had been assassinated the year before the publication of *Quatorze Annos de Timor*, in a climate of growing antimonarchist sentiments, which eventually led to the establishment of the First Portuguese Republic in 1910. As I will discuss in more detail later, Zola's account is an expression of antimonarchism as well as a commentary on "pacification" campaigns in Timor-Leste more generally.

Zola's description of the "little *reino* of Funar" (1909: 27), situated in the deepest mountain interior, is reminiscent of James Scott's (2009) suggestion that highlanders of "Zomia" (in mainland Southeast Asia), who lived outside of state control, were originally lowlanders who sought to escape state centralization.[5] Accordingly, highlanders are not left behind in time or are remnants of the past, but are instead state-evaders who cherish their autonomy. This idea of highlanders as state-evaders can also be found in some of the colonial discourse on highland regions, which create an image of these regions as home to "the most hostile, untamed and savage peoples" that were "strategically chosen . . . as sites to escape" (Roque 2012: 265). These representations were part of a colonial "science" of race that reinforced certain stereotypes of "black races in the mountains," which were particularly untamed and threatened colonial authority. Zola describes the inhabitants of Funar somewhat pejoratively as a "sad people" who "possessed nothing else beyond their buffalo herds, a couple of hundred head, whose rearing had taken years. They thought they were rich, the poor devils, because they did not need neighbours" (Zola 1909: 27). Despite the condescending tone, this seems to be a more romantic version of the stereotype of rebellious and untamed highlanders, who were proud of their wealth and political autonomy.

Zola then describes a military commander named Captain Manuel das Neves, who found out that there were large buffalo herds in Funar. When das Neves proposed to buy them, the owners refused. Hence in 1905, Manuel das Neves, together with Celestino da Silva, the governor of Portuguese Timor at the time, resolved to steal the buffalo. They declared the people of Funar to be "disloyal rebels" (Zola 1909: 28). Then they prepared their attack. However, because of the steep mountains that surround Funar, the expedition was almost impossible. For this reason, Manuel das Neves ordered the construction of footpaths to Funar.

He assembled eight hundred *moradores* (soldiers, mostly Timorese)[6] and launched a full-scale attack. Zola sarcastically comments that "a pure and simple robbery would have disappointed the boastful warriors," so they went out in mobile columns to burn huts and "decapitate men, women and children" (Zola 1909: 28). Zola's account emphasizes the brutality with which the people of Funar were killed when their remote hideouts were found. It tragically describes how the highlanders threw themselves into a ravine when they were attacked.

> The attack erupted from afar. The volleys of fire got closer, and as the shooting decimated the pitiful, they would throw themselves into the only gorge open to them. There the killing continued in abundance. The troops ran them through at point-blank range, finishing off their lives with machetes. They took their heads, for their triumph. The rebelliousness was vanquished; the kingdom of Funar, a cemetery. Among the torsos on the ground rotting in the sun were the elderly, women and children. Superb victory! (Zola 1909: 28)

The cynicism of this account reveals Zola's deep hostility toward Celestino da Silva. After the theft, the buffalo were reported "lost," and Zola suspects that Celestino da Silva took them into his private possession. The *reino* of Funar was divided among the three neighboring "kingdoms." The largest part of Funar was handed over to the "Chief of Manatuto," called Jeronymo. (Manatuto is a coastal town north of Funar.)[7]

Zola describes how the inhabitants of Funar had to suffer from the misdeeds of Jeronymo. He demanded large fines from the local population, used his position to take advantage of women, and was known for committing robberies and indecencies. When people complained about Jeronymo's misbehavior, the Portuguese colonial military carried out another attack against Funar in 1907. However, when the military arrived in Funar this time, the villagers had abandoned their settlements. They had fled to the most impenetrable mountain peaks (Zola 1909: 30). Based on a report written by an accompanying doctor (perhaps Zola himself), Zola describes how three hundred troops searched and scorched the mountains. The ending of this war remains unclear. Although many inhabitants managed to hide, the doctor reports with shock how the troops returned with the heads of young children and an old man.

From this gruesome report, we learn that there were two wars in Funar, one in 1905, another in 1907. As a result, Funar was divided among its neighbors. The account does not tell us which neighbors, but considering that Jeronymo is said to have been from Laclo, Funar may have been integrated into the administration of Laclo. Both wars were justified by the accusation that the people of Funar had rebelled. Both included large-scale killings and the theft of buffalo by the colonial army. It is noteworthy that the account reveals how difficult it was for the Portuguese military to penetrate this remote highland area, and it implies that Funar was not under direct control of the colonial government until the turn of the nineteenth century. But Zola's account must also be understood in its own cultural and political context.

Zola's account is not necessarily representative of the colonial scholarship on Timor; it was written for a specific political purpose.[8] Celestino da Silva was antirepublican, an avowed monarchist, and well connected to King D. Carlos I (Roque 2010: 93). Zola was a republican intent on discrediting the governor, and his account was part of a controversy about Celestino da Silva's governorship. Da Silva's republican enemies accused him of having "pollut[ed] contact with different forms of indigenous barbarity," e.g. by taking part in rituals surrounding severed heads (Roque 2010: 94). Da Silva led twenty-two "pacification campaigns" in Portuguese Timor, and these were carried out with virtually no regular troops, just "indigenous irregulars" (Roque 2010: 29). Zola's description of the colonial violence committed against Funar was very much part of the antimonarchist critique, since it stressed the barbarity of da Silva's mission, portraying it as disruptive of "good" or civilizing colonial empires.

In his analysis of colonial appropriations and representations of indigenous practices, Ricardo Roque argues that Celestino da Silva was the target of political attacks inside and outside of Timor. Charges were leveled against him in the 1890s; the critiques grew in the 1900s and eventually led to legal action against him (Roque 2010: 93–94). Celestino da Silva was accused not just of "barbarity" but also of robbery. He did not respond to the charges raised against him in 1906–8, but earlier, in 1897, he did respond to the charge that he was leading the pacification campaigns for personal gains by saying that in Timor it was the customary right of a chief to appropriate the spoils of war and that he would not have been able to recruit Timorese soldiers had it not been for the promise of booty (Roque 2010: 95).

Therefore, while the highlanders' alleged theft of buffalo from their neighbors was used to justify the colonial attack on Funar, the governor justified his theft of Funar's buffalo as a recruitment strategy of indigenous warriors. However, Zola's claim that Celestino da Silva stole Funar's buffalo herds also formed part of a more general attempt to discredit da Silva's governorship. Similarly, the violence Zola attributed to the colonial army, including the claims that "complaints of victims are impossible because they are killed" (1909: 26–27), must be understood in context. It is possible that Zola exaggerated the violence of the campaigns against Funar to a degree, for political effect.

Téofilo Duarte, himself a former governor of Portuguese Timor and staunch supporter of Celestino da Silva, tried to rescue the latter's reputation by making him the main protagonist in his novel *The King of Timor*, the king here referring to Governor da Silva. Duarte tries to defend "the great governor" and his reputation against the "futile gossip and criticism in the government offices of Lisbon" (Duarte 1931: iii). The novel contains several chapters that are fictitious renderings of "the war of Funar," as well as an imagined love affair between Celestino da Silva and the "queen of Maubara." In some ways this novel may be understood as a response to the attack on Celestino da Silva by Zola, as it reclaims Celestino's rule as a "civilizing mission," eliminating the accusations of "barbarism" against the colonial regime by projecting it onto the indigenous realm through lavish descriptions of "blood rituals" that supposedly took place in Funar (Duarte 1931, chapter 8).

The various ways in which the campaigns in Funar were interpreted and portrayed by these colonial documents tells us less about the historical events themselves and more about the political climate in Portugal at the beginning of the twentieth century. Representations of "Funar" and "the war on Funar" became the battleground for disagreements among republicans and monarchists who used it to defend or critique the actions of Celestino da Silva and his particular colonial approach, which consisted of recruiting Timorese warriors as soldiers to fight neighboring domains. Whereas Duarte portrayed these events as one of Celestino da Silva's victorious and heroic achievements, Zola accused Celestino da Silva of leading the campaigns for his personal gain and of being complicit in what was commonly seen as the barbarism of local practices surrounding warfare.

Funar's Victory: The Tale of Avô Masuan

During my first fieldwork (2005–7), several villagers from Funar described the encounter with the Portuguese and with a man called Jeronymo (also described as a *malae*, "foreigner"). People seemed to enjoy recounting and listening to this story because it is also a story about indigenous superiority. This narrative also has its political bias, since it was recounted largely by members of the elite and seems to have been used to emphasize the preeminence and power of the *liurai* of Funar. It was told to me in various versions. I will only recount elements that the different versions seem to have in common:

> In the past, a man from Laclo named Jeronymo (or "Jeroni") tried to deceive (*bosok*) the people of Funar. The members of the ruling house *Bereliurai* are not allowed to eat eel. So Jeronymo caught an eel and put it into the bottom of a bamboo container, which he filled with palm liquor. Then he invited Avô Masuan, the guardian of the *ada lulik* ("sacred house"/ house of spiritual potency) to drink the palm liquor. With great foresight, Avô Masuan sent others to drink the palm liquor. When they had finished, the eel jumped out of the bamboo container. People were very angry, because it is forbidden (*lulik*) for members of that house to eat eel. Therefore, they chased Jeronymo away from Funar.
>
> In retaliation, Jeronymo went to Dili and told lies about Avô Masuan. Jeronymo said to the Portuguese *Administrador* that the ruler of Funar had body hair like a monkey, horns like a buffalo, and a navel so huge you could put a golden plate inside it. [Other versions say that he drinks palm liquor through his huge navel.] In response to these accusations, the *Administrador* in Dili asked for the son of Avô Masuan to be sent to Dili. The son was called José do Espírito Santo.
>
> When José arrived in Dili, the *Administrador* said: "Ohhh! But he is so *handsome* (*bonito*). His face is so white, like the face of a *malae*. If his father has horns like a buffalo, why does he not have any? If his father has body hair like a monkey, why does he not have it? He looks so good he must be a *liurai!*" Hence the *malae* gave a scepter to José do Espírito Santo in order to govern Funar [the scepter shows that he has the right to rule]. Jeronymo had failed to trick the people of Funar through his false reports. Funar won and no longer had to receive orders.

This story recounts the establishment of a direct relationship between the *liurai* of Funar and the *malae* in Dili. It also recounts the transformation of the relationship between Funar and its neighbors Laclo and Manatuto. The coastal polities Laclo and Manatuto were among the earliest to demonstrate "loyalty" to the Portuguese state, siding with the white governors in the early eighteenth century. In the middle of the nineteenth century, they renewed their "terms of vassalage" with Dili on a regular basis and thereby developed a degree of supralocal authority over smaller polities in the interior. It seems that this narrative refers to the process whereby Funar's elite developed a more direct relationship with the Portuguese, one that was no longer mediated by Laclo or Manatuto.

Not belonging to Funar, Jeronymo, either from Laclo or Manatuto, is described as a *malae*, even though he might have been Timorese or *mestiço*. In Funar, government officials from the coastal towns, even if they are indigenous Timorese, are often referred to as *malae*. In this account, physical appearance is mentioned as a factor that legitimizes rule, namely looking more like a white foreigner. José do Espírito Santos is praised by the administrator in Dili for looking beautiful and white. His white skin is juxtaposed with the animalistic features that Jeronymo attributes to José's father. One way of interpreting this would be to say that the distinction between the animal-like depiction of local people and the beauty of the foreign represents an internalization of racist colonial stereotypes. It may also be a variation of the widespread identification in Southeast Asia of whiteness with high status (see e.g. Geertz 1976), similar to the Javanese opposition between *alus* (refined and cultivated) and *kasar* (coarse and crude). The opposition between José's beauty and the coarseness of Avô Masuan's bestial appearance may have been drawn on already existing indigenous hierarchies of skin color that were reinforced and reshaped by colonial racial ideologies.

Several other themes in this account resonate with well-known Southeast Asian leitmotifs, such as the idea that an adversary employed trickery to bring someone to violate their food prohibitions or that a contest took place between different groups that led to one of them winning and hence gaining political power. Given that eel are *lulik*, sacred and forbidden, violating a prohibition on their consumption would certainly lower one's status. Narratives about contests of rule are often said to involve trickery, yet just as Avô Masuan already anticipates the deceit, those subject to attempted trickery can often see through this. Moreover, the attack is motivated by the theft of buffalo, which, as an embodiment of fertility, are extremely significant for exchanges between different house groups, which strengthen the status of these groups and the alliances between them. These well-known motifs are employed to represent specific historical interactions, so that Jeronymo, apparently a midlevel colonial administrator, is cast as would-be rival of the Funar rulers.

Every time a narrator recounted Jeronymo's claim that Avô Masuan looks like an animal, the audience in attendance burst out with laughter. One explanation for this might be that people are embarrassed by such an accusation. The trickery involved in these contest narratives about the exploits of the ancestors is also commonly a source of laughter. Yet, there is also a clear moral dimension because the story demonstrates that Funar's inhabitants are in fact competent rulers. The story may express a sense of consternation over those who suggest the contrary. Rather than being passive objects of colonial conquest, as in Zola's account, the local narrative represents Funar's rulers as active agents who manage to overcome foreign attempts to deprive them of their autonomy and position of authority. In that sense, the story could also be interpreted as a subversion of racist colonial representation of local inhabitants as being incapable of ruling themselves.

The Transformation of Indigenous Hierarchies

In Timor, like in other places in Southeast Asia, indigenous power is perceived to be divided into spiritual/ritual and political/jural domains. This diarchic structure is frequently connected to other "binary" or "complementary oppositions" (Errington 1990: 18) that characterize the social and ritual organization. Diarchic patterns are certainly evident in Funar, where power is split into political power (*ukun*) and spiritual potency (*lulik*). This particular understanding of power and its misrecognition is also at the heart of the claim that Avô Masuan looks like a beast. Avô Masuan was the guardian of the *ada lulik*. This significance is not recognized by the Portuguese, who define power in terms of "rule" and thus give a "scepter" (a sign of political power) to his son.

People might be laughing when they hear this story because the Portuguese administrator does not understand that spiritual potency is ultimately superior to political power. Hence when Jeronymo accuses Avô Masuan of being ugly and beastly, he does not recognize his immense strengths in the rirual realm (or if he does, he may be belittling what was once a component of power, which under indirect rule may have become an unnecessary vestige). Jeronymo claims that Avô Masuan has horns like a buffalo. Buffalo are not invaluable exchange items, but these horns could be alluding to the powerful adornment that traditional authorities wear on their heads in Timor (called *kaibauk*). Golden plates (*belak mean*), which potentially fit into

Avô Masuan's navel, are also signs of potency and status. Similarly, in this region of Timor, the navel stands for spiritual centrality—it represents the origins of humankind; Avô Masuan's large navel may therefore not be an ugly feature that shows him as a beast but a sign of his enormous spiritual authority.

Moreover, the opposition between Avô Masuan's beastly appearance and his son's beauty resonates with similar representations in Timor-Leste of spiritual authorities as "stupid and ignorant," coarse and badly dressed, opposed to the sharp-sighted and alert political rulers who are associated with education and learning (e.g. Traube 1986: 55–56). The idea that spiritual authorities harbor enormous powers or are the "true" holders of authority despite this appearance and their inward orientation plays on widespread regional variations of the stranger king paradigm, whereby the autochthonous population is thought to retain ritual responsibilities while the "outsiders" gain political office.

In the account from Funar, the Portuguese gave political power (the scepter) to the son of Avô Masuan. By doing so, they inadvertently united political power and spiritual potency—which were previously separated in two different houses—in the same named house, called Manekaoli. Even though the giving of a scepter implies a relationship of dependency on the Portuguese who "gave" political rule to Funar, this act also strengthened the position of Avô Masuan's house (Manekaoli) and thus transformed the indigenous hierarchy. This act of unifying political and spiritual authority is not unique to Funar, yet more commonly we find accounts that suggest political and spiritual power have the same origin but became separated when one group (or younger brother) had contact with outside power (e.g. Barnes 2011).

From one perspective, one may even say that the Portuguese made a "mistake" because they gave political power to the house that bears spiritual authority. From another perspective, this unification of both kinds of power in one house was legitimate, since José do Espírito Santo is the *younger* son of Avô Masuan (see figure 4.1), and this fits into the widespread Austronesian pattern whereby power is split between an older and a younger brother. The appointment hence remains within the indigenous logic, whereby the older brother is the bearer of ritual authority and the younger brother represents political power.

The transformation of indigenous hierarchies is expressed in terms of the unification and bifurcation of named house groups. Af-

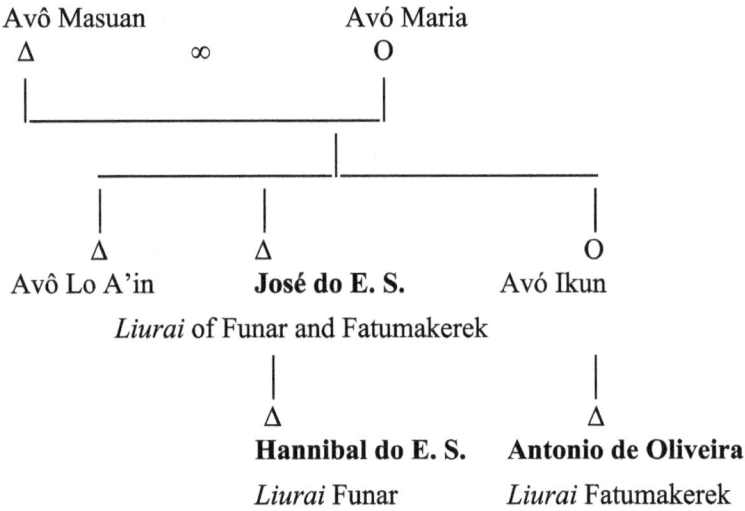

Figure 4.1. Simplified family tree of *Liurai* José do Espírito Santo. Created by the author.

ter independence, there was a general tendency in Funar to separate political and spiritual power into two different houses, so that they would no longer be contained within the same house. This led to a situation where a number of different origin houses claimed to possess both, a house of ritual authority and a house of political power, whereas previously they considered themselves to be independent (Bovensiepen 2014b). The relationships between diarchic elements are by no means fixed, but they can be reshaped through different historical events (see also Nygaard-Christensen 2012). Political and spiritual domains can be transformed into the other—even though the spiritual component tends to precede and encompass the political component.

After Timor-Leste regained independence, the traditional hierarchies in Funar were contested, and there have been conflicts between different house groups over ownership of the right to "rule"—expressed as the ownership of a "scepter" (see Bovensiepen 2014b). These conflicts over the identity and legitimacy of the "traditional rulers" can in part be traced back to the establishment of indirect rule by the Portuguese. The appointment of José do Espírito Santo was probably made after Funar was destroyed and divided the second time, putting into place a new *liurai* who was perhaps more loyal to the Portuguese.

Finally, Zola's account ends in a defeat, because it measures victory only in terms of political power and does not take into account the significance of indigenous spiritual potency. Hence, the discrepancy between the two types of accounts arises from differential understandings of what constitutes power. Nevertheless, both narratives are necessary to understand the transformations of the political organization that were put into place through the colonial intervention, and it also illustrates both the physical and the symbolic violence that was committed against highlanders by the colonial military.

Unofficial Accounts

> Beyond verbal narratives there are at least some and perhaps many evocations of the past in the most mundane actions. (Bloch 1998: 110)

Tracking through the forest near Funar in late 2006 on the way to a cornfield, the small group of people I was with stopped as a man in his thirties suddenly pointed to a forested area in the distant valley and said, "That is the "place of Jeronymo" (*Jeronymo-Ba*)![9] Over there Jeronymo came with his men from Laclo." He imitated holding a gun and shooting. "There is a large stone, where the people of Funar shot Jeronymo and his men." Astonished by this statement, as no one had ever mentioned a violent conflict between Funar and Jeronymo, I asked my companion to take me to the stone. But he maintained that the slope was too steep for me and refused to take me there. Knowledge about the past can be expressed in everyday situations, prompted by the geographic context, and it is thus quite different from that of official historical narratives (cf. Bloch 1998: 107).

In the evening around the fire, I asked a woman in her eighties, who was the daughter of José do Espírito Santo, about the war at *Jeronymo-Ba*. She was resolute that there had been no such war and that there had never been any fighting between the people of Funar and Jeronymo. A relative interrupted her, stating that the place is not called *Jeronymo-Ba* but *Rii-Hatu* (literally the "pillar-stone"). He then went on to tell me the "official" account discussed earlier about Jeronymo's false accusations (*lia falsu*) against Avô Masuan. Very few people I spoke to spoke about violence in relation to Jeronymo. Moreover, the conflict was never mentioned without my prompting, and it was only when I happened to pass by the place that the variant was spontaneously offered.

Another day I heard a group of men who were sitting around smoking use the word *nona*. Since I did not understand it, I asked about its meaning. The men laughed and no one wanted to tell me what the word meant. Then one of them said, "It is a woman like the one Jeroni had." I asked, "A wife? Jeronymo's wife?" Everyone laughed and explained that a *nona* refers to a woman that a man has without marriage, i.e. a concubine (the term is also Tetum for "young woman"). On a different occasion, one female research participant claimed that Avô Masuan "gave" a woman named Bii Koon from his named house (the *liurai*) to Jeronymo to marry, but this claim was contested by most other women I spoke to about it.

There are clearly various different accounts and points of view about the role of Jeronymo. Not all the adults living in Funar today have the same knowledge or are willing to share what they know. While there are clearly rumors about Jeronymo that extend beyond the official version, they are not told in public and are not readily disclosed to a nosy foreigner. Vansina (1985: 6) stresses the importance of taking hearsay and rumors seriously as forms of historical knowledge. Once an interpretation of historical events becomes commonly accepted, he argues, the information survives to the next generation and can become part of the oral tradition. The problem with hearsay about Jeronymo is that it is not part of the widely shared narratives told about the past, which made them harder for me to access.

The mode in which unofficial accounts of the past were revealed differs radically from the way official narratives were expressed. Specific "secrets" were always conveyed more privately, in small groups of two or three people and with an emphasis on how this information should not be shared (Bovensiepen 2014a). The reason for secrecy might be because the gossip and hearsay about Jeronymo contain the potential to challenge the official representations of the past. As I noted before, there is no mention in any of the accounts of the violent destruction of Funar by the colonial army in 1905. Acknowledging these events might also mean challenging the position of local power-holders who benefited from the establishment of indirect rule.

A significant amount of time had elapsed between my fieldwork in 2005–7 and the wars in 1905/7. This means that none of my interlocutors in Funar were alive during the "rebellion" of Funar. I cannot say how the 1905 and 1907 wars were remembered by those who lived through them; instead, I have sought to explore how collective violence may be refracted in local discourse. Of course, we can never say for sure whether knowledge of the presumably violent encounter between the Portuguese colonial army, its Timorese auxiliaries, and villagers in Funar in 1905/7 has been passed on or not. But in the material I gathered, direct references to the defeat are absent.

The official oral narrative about Jeronymo is relatively stable; it is recounted publicly and used by members of the *liurai* to assert their position of authority, status, and right to leadership. However, less formalized accounts about Jeronymo coexist and undermine the narrative of Funar's victory and success over Laclo. While ethnographic research on political organization helps us to understand misrepresentations in the colonial archive, Zola's account is useful for understanding what has been omitted from Funar's public narratives and how to interpret some of the stories that were told to me in private.

In the oral narratives I was told during fieldwork, there is another connection to Zola's description of the wars in Funar. It is an account about how the house that initially represented political power lost its power to the house of spiritual potency. It centers on a man called Don João da Cruz, part of the house Manehiak, the "younger brother" of Funar's *liurai* Manekaoli (to which José do Espírito Santo belonged). According to this account, Don João da Cruz of Manehiak was the holder of the "scepter," and therefore the political authority in Funar, but lost his position through trickery.

> One day a foreigner (*malae*) named Manuel (or *Manu Wer* in some accounts) came to visit Funar. He asked João da Cruz whether he wanted to have half a chicken or a whole chicken. Da Cruz replied he just wanted half a chicken. So the *reino* of Funar was divided up.

Although this account does not explicitly mention a conflict, it may indirectly refer to the first "war of Funar" in 1905 described by Zola, since the *malae* named "Manuel" could refer to Captain Manuel das Neves from Zola's account.[10] When this story was recounted, narrators often laughed with a sense of embarrassment—maybe because they were embarrassed about the division of Funar, or maybe even because they were aware that there must be more to this story.

There were other stories about Don João da Cruz told to me in confidence by people who were not members of the *liurai* house. I was told not to repeat them to other villagers in Funar, as this could create conflict. According to these accounts, Don João da Cruz of the house Manehiak was the "guardian of the scepter" in Funar with political responsibilities. The house Manekaoli, to which Avô Masuan and José do Espírito Santo belonged, was the house of spiritual potency (*ada lulin*). I was told that the Portuguese had imprisoned Don João da Cruz and sent him to the island of Ataúro. Members of the *lulik* house Manekaoli then gained political power.

There are numerous rumors about the relationship between the two houses Manekaoli and Manehiak. Publicly, people stress the common origin of the two houses and their friendly relations as elder and younger brothers. When I asked about Don João da Cruz and José do Espírito Santo (and who ruled first), the answers were usually evasive, and discussions were brought to an end by statements such as, "Both of them ruled both" (*Sira hotu ukun hotu*, Tetum). But these narratives of cooperation were undercut by secret accusations and lingering conflicts.

Even though today Manekaoli is recognized as the *liurai* house, there were rumors at the beginning of my fieldwork that the descendants of Don João da Cruz still have his scepter, which they keep hidden somewhere. The rumored existence of the secret scepter indicates that its guardians still have a right to rule (*ukun*). Some even said that members of the house Manekaoli tried to kill the rulers of Manehiak, who then fled to another house called Bamatak. Bamatak killed a goat and showed the blood to Manekaoli, saying that they had killed Manehiak's ruler on Manekaoli's behalf. But instead, Bamatak's members accepted the people of Manehiak on their land and hid them from Manekaoli, who then became the *liurai*.

The narrative of victory and success of the ruling houses was further challenged by another incident. During my fieldwork, a grandson of José do Espírito Santo's sister, Avó Ikun (see figure 4.1.) visited from abroad and suggested that members of the ruling house (Manekaoli) had African ancestry. He remembered from his childhood that his grandmother Avó Ikun was black. When an elder recounted the tale of José do Espírito Santo's encounter with the Portuguese *Administrador* in front of this man, he kept on interrupting, arguing that "José cannot have been white because his sister [Avó Ikun] was black! She was African!" The surrounding men looked embarrassed; they did not want to contradict someone they respected. They agreed that she was very dark but maintained that her brother José was white.

The matter remains unresolved. The Portuguese army regularly employed soldiers from the African colonies in Timor, so the suggestion was not implausible. In neighboring village Fatumakerek (which was later governed by Avó Ikun's son), there were rumors that a black foreigner (*malae metan*), a Portuguese administrator, was once stationed there and that he had several concubines (*nona*) among the local women; however none of them ever bore him children, I was told; this may refer to Jeronymo, but this was never said explicitly. This is one of the many mysteries about these past events that may remain unsolved.

Conclusion

I started this chapter questioning the different representations of the encounter between the Portuguese military and the ancestors of Funar. By bringing together the diverse sources, both from the colonial archives in Portugal and from the field in Timor-Leste, it is possible to try to piece together some aspects of the events in the past. Given the sensitivity of these issues, this necessarily remains incomplete—and my reconstruction is one of several possible interpretations.

Funar probably remained comparatively independent from direct Portuguese control until the early twentieth century. Until the "wars" of Funar, relations with the Portuguese seem to have been mediated by neighboring domains Manatuto and Laclo, which were allied with the Portuguese colonial administration much earlier. In 1905, under the rule of Celestino de Silva and under the command of Captain Manuel das Neves, the Portuguese military and its Timorese allies attacked Funar and imprisoned its political leader—"the guardian of political power" (Don João da Cruz) in Ataúro. Jeronymo, who may have been a *mestiço* from Laclo or simply a Timorese with an official function, was then sent as an administrator to the region. Jeronymo behaved in a way that offended people—expressed by the rumors about his mistresses (*nona*), accounts about his womanizing and the fact that he is described as having broken an essential taboo against the consumption of eel. The highlanders' discontent with the new administrative structures may well have fueled a second attack in 1907 as described by Zola. Since Jeronymo was from Laclo and the colonial military drew their troops largely from neighboring domains, Funar's inhabitants saw this as an attack by their neighbors, even though this attack is only expressed metaphorically in the oral traditions in terms of Jeronymo's trickery.

Funar was then divided, possibly ceasing to exist as a political unit recognized by the Portuguese until a new political representative was put into place. Unwilling to appoint a member of João da Cruz's house as local chief, the Portuguese colonial administrator appointed the son of the spiritual authority (José do Espírito Santo). Hence, for Avô Masuan's house, this new appointment was indeed a victory, since both spiritual and political authority, which had been previously split, came to be united in the same house. This would explain why the story of Jeronymo is told as a story of victory, whereas Zola's account tells us about the destruction of Funar. The annihilation of Funar meant a victory for some.[11]

Persistent rumors and fragmented observations present alternatives to the public narratives about colonial times and undermine the official accounts of victory and triumph associated with the colonial encounters. Many of the political power struggles in Funar today are indirectly related to some of these past events and their interpretation in the present. Significantly, unlike Zola's interpretation, the "two wars" of Funar are rarely recounted in local accounts today in terms of the opposition between Timorese and colonial powers. Instead Portuguese intervention in local affairs is understood in terms of the transformation of local power relations: either in terms of the conflicts between Funar and their neighbors, like Laclo (cf. Muller 1997), or in terms of the power struggles between different named houses.

The suggestion that history is written by the winners has become a cliché. Yet it is clear that the account of Jeronymo and José do Espírito Santo strengthens the position of the *liurai*. Nevertheless, competing and unofficial accounts have survived, and they continue to pose a challenge to the authority of Funar's *liurai* today.

Acknowledgments

Special thanks go to the research participants from Funar and Laclubar for their invaluable support. I would also like to thank Douglas Kammen, Ricardo Roque, Christopher Shepherd, and Janet Gunter for their helpful advice on the Portuguese archival material. Janet Gunter, Frederico Balbi Amatto, and Oriana Brás have provided fantastic help with the translation of the Portuguese documents, and thanks go to Ricardo Roque, Elizabeth Traube, and Susana Viegas for their astute comments on a previous draft of this chapter. An earlier version was published in Portuguese in *Timor-Leste: Colonialismo, Descolonização, Lusutopia* (Porto: Edições Afrontamento, 2016). I would like to thank the editor Rui Graça Feijó for permitting re-use of the material. Archival research was supported by a postdoctoral fellowship from the Musée du quai Branly in Paris.

Judith Bovensiepen is a social anthropologist at the University of Kent. She has written several articles on changing relations of place, kinship, and power in the years after Timor-Leste regained independence. She has also been doing research on religious transformations and on the politics of resource extraction in the country. Her most recent publications include *The Land of Gold: Post-Conflict Recovery and Cultural Revival in Independent Timor-Leste* (2015) and *The Promise of Prosperity: Visions of the Future in Timor-Leste* (2018).

Notes

1. Zola describes the *reino* of Funar as independent from Portuguese rule at the beginning of twentieth century, yet it seems that some relations between Funar and the colonial power existed long before that. Loureiro (1935: 235) includes Funar in a list of the *reinos* that were in a dependent relationship with Portugal in 1815, listing D. Esperança dos Santos Pinto as *coronela* of Funar. Funar only occasionally reappears in the Portuguese records of the twentieth century (see Belo 2011: 187; da França 1897: 244–45; Pélissier 1996: 61).
2. Inhabitants I interviewed from Samoro and Laclubar rejected these suppositions and suggested that the inhabitants of Funar are self-important (*halo aan*). Zola's account seems to support the claim of Funar's independence, even though I found no evidence that Funar had any administrative reach over neighboring domains—it might, however, have had a ritually significant role that neighbors paid respect to.
3. The only revolt they mentioned is the famous rebellion in Manufahi in 1911/12, where inhabitants from Funar/ Laclubar say that they collaborated with Portugal to put down the rebellion.
4. Interestingly, in her descriptions of prophetic movements in the Mambai-speaking area around Aileu, Traube (2007: 16) also describes accounts about a man whose name she transcribed as "Seronimo" or "Seroni" (or "Seroniku").
5. Zomia refers to the Southeast Asian mainland massif, containing about one hundred million people of diverse religious and ethnic background, covering an area about the size of Europe (*zo* meaning "remote" and *mi* meaning "people" in several related Tibeto-Burman languages). James Scott (2009) popularized this term when he suggested that it is one of the last remaining regions of the world whose inhabitants had not become part of nation-states.
6. Roque (2010: xiii) describes *moradores* as special companies of indigenous irregulars established by the Portuguese in the eighteenth century.
7. There is different information as to how Funar is divided up. According to Celestino da Silva (1905), from 1906 onward, the land of Funar was divided among Samoro, Turiscai, and Laclubar, for which these jurisdictions had to pay additional tax.
8. In Celestino da Silva's extensive correspondence and reports to Lisbon, now held at the Arquivo Histórico Ultramarino in Lisbon, no reference to the Funar war of 1905 is made. This may be because the governor decided not to report on this particular war in his correspondence to

Lisbon, or it simply may be that documentation about it did not survive in the colonial records (Roque, personal communication). Celestino da Silva does however mention "operations against the rebels of Funar" in the *Boletim Oficial*, where he names the grounds for the attack as the rebellious nature of Funar inhabitants, who are represented as disobedient, without proper authority, refusing to cultivate their land "running about and stealing buffalo from their neighbouring kingdoms" (Silva 1905: 65ff.).

9. *Ba* also means hamlet, settlement, or place.
10. There are a number people in Funar today who carry the surname "das Neves."
11. In order to avoid the concentration of power—or to control the territory better—power was later divided up among José do Espírito Santo's son Hanibal do Espírito Santo, who ruled Funar, and José's sister's son, António de Oliveira, who governed Fatumakerek (see figure 4.1; see also Belo 2011: 187).

References

Barnes, S. 2011. "Origins, Precedence and Social Order in the Domain of Ina Ama Beli Darlari." In *Land and Life in Timor-Leste Ethnographic Essays*, edited by A. McWilliam and E. G. Traube, 23–46. Canberra: ANU Press.

Belo, C. F. X. 2011. *Os Antigos Reinos de Timor-Leste (Reys de Lorosay e Reys de Lorothoba, Coronéis e Datos)*. Baucau: Tipografia Diocesana Baucau.

Bloch, M. 1998. *How We Think They Think: Anthropological Approaches to Cognition, Memory, and Literacy*. Oxford: Westview Press.

Bovensiepen, J. 2014a. "Words of the Ancestors: Disembodied Knowledge and Secrecy in East Timor." *Journal of the Royal Anthropological Institute* 20(1): 56–73.

———. 2014b. "Installing the Insider 'Outside': House-Reconstruction and the Transformation of Binary Ideologies in Independent Timor–Leste." *American Ethnologist* 41(2): 290–304.

BPMT. 1871. *Boletim da Província de Macau e Timor* XVII, no. 50 (11 December).

Cohen, P. A. 1997. *History in Three Keys: The Boxers as Event, Experience, and Myth*. New York: Colombia University Press.

Correia, A. P. 1934. *Gentio de Timor*. Lisbon: Ed. Autor.

Duarte, T. 1931. *O Rei de Timor*. Lisbon: Parceria António Maria Pereira.

Errington, S. 1990. "Recasting Sex, Gender, and Power: A Theoretical and Regional Overview." In *Power and Difference: Gender in Island Southeast Asia*, edited by J. M. Atkinson and S. Errington, 1–58. Stanford, CA: Stanford University Press.

da França, B. 1897. *Macau e os Seus Habitantes: Relações com Timor*. Lisbon: Imprensa Nacional.

Geertz, C. 1976. *The Religion of Java*. Chicago: University of Chicago Press.

Hägerdal, H. 2012. *Lords of the Land, Lords of the Sea: Conflict and Adaptation in Early Colonial Timor, 1600–1800*. Leiden: KITLV Press.

Loureiro, M. J. G. 1835. *Memórias dos Estabelecimentos Portugezes a Leste do Cabo da Boa Esperança*. Lisbon: Typographia de Filippe Nery.

de Matos, A. T. 1974. *Timor Português: 1515–1769; Contribuição para a sua História*. Lisbon: Faculdade de Letras da Universidade de Lisboa/Instituto Histórico Infante D. Henrique.

Muller, J. C. 1997. "'Merci à vous, les Blancs, de Nous Avoir libérés!' Le cas des Dìì de l'Adamaoua (Nord-Cameroun)." *Terrain* 28: 59–72.

Nygaard-Christensen, M. 2012. "The Rebel and the Diplomat: Revolutionary Spirits, Sacred Legitimation and Democracy in Timor–Leste." In *Varieties of Secularism in Southeast Asia: Anthropological Explorations of Religion, Politics and the Spiritual*, edited by N. Bubandt and M. van Beek, 209–29. London: Routledge.

Pélissier, R. 1996. *Timor en Guerre: Le Crocodile et les Portugais (1847–1913)*. Orgeval: Ed. Pélissier.

Roque, R. 2010. *Headhunting and Colonialism: Anthropology and the Circulation of Human Skulls in the Portuguese Empire, 1870–1930*. New York: Palgrave Macmillan.

———. 2012. "Mountains and Black Races: Anthropology's Heterotopias in Colonial East Timor." *Journal of Pacific History* 47(3): 263–82.

Scott, J. C. 2009. *The Art of Not Being Governed: An Anarchist History of Upland Southeast Asia*. New Haven, CT: Yale University Press.

da Silva, J. C. 1905. Boletim Official do Districto Automo de Timor (BODAT), 1 April 1905, no. 15, Boletins Officiais de Timor, retrieved 22 February 2015 from http://btimor.iict.pt.

Traube, E. G. 1986. *Cosmology and Social Life: Ritual Exchange among Mambai of East Timor*. Chicago: Chicago University Press.

———. 2007. "Unpaid Wages: Local Narratives and the Imagination of the Nation." *Asia Pacific Journal of Anthropology* 8(1): 9–25.

Vansina, J. 1985. *Oral Tradition as History*. Oxford: James Currey.

Zola [alias for António Pádua Correia. 1909. *Quatorze Annos de Timor*. 1ᵉ. Série. Dili.

PART II

Following Objects

Chapter 5

CATHOLIC *LULIKS* OR TIMORESE RELICS?

MISSIONARY ANTHROPOLOGY, DESTRUCTION, AND SELF-DESTRUCTION (CA. 1910–74)

Frederico Delgado Rosa

Introduction: "Fear and Orgies"

In 1931, the difficult historical reconstruction of the precolonial cultural setting—and in particular of native religion—in East Timor received an astonishing solution. The then–mission superior, Father Abílio Fernandes, confronted this colossal challenge in a chapter of his small, 125-page book, *Esboço histórico e do estado atual das Missões de Timor* (*Historical Outline and Current State of the Missions in Timor*), titled "Primitive State of the Natives upon the Arrival of the Missionaries" (in the middle of the sixteenth century). Although the landing in question actually occurred in western Timor, we can say that Friar Antonio Taveiro played a symbolic role as the first Portuguese missionary to arrive in Timor, and the chapter's entire argument is addressed to the eastern half of the island that subsequently became a Portuguese colony. More significant is Father Fernandes's admission that he didn't know of the existence of any surviving accounts from that time: "It would be interesting if Father Taveiro had left us with an accurate description of the state in which he found the peoples of Timor. I'm not aware of any works in this field" (Fernandes 1931: 15). It was precisely due to this heuristic obstacle that the author imposed a conjectural alternative, which he considered to be an obvious solution and which is "too obvious" to us:

We can, however, reconstruct this primitive state quite accurately, if
we accept, as the prevailing currency of this former period, acts of savagery that are still secretly practised in kingdoms located far from Dili
and especially in kingdoms where the missionary's evangelizing work
has been least felt. That's what I will try to outline to the reader who is
unaware of the customs and habits of this people. (Fernandes 1931: 15)

The cultural unity of the Timorese people was thereby announced,
in contrast to the recognized linguistic diversity that posed so many
impediments to the missionaries' work. More than the classificatory
obsession often associated with colonialism, this overarching construction of the "Timorese people," sometimes even of its *Volksgeist*, or
alma (soul) in good Portuguese, was in fact a recurrent feature of the
anthropological reflections made by the multiple agents of late imperialism in East Timor. If there were differences from region to region,
particularly in terms of religion, they were viewed as variations on a
theme, effects of a pervasive process of cultural diffusion, associated
with the endemic wars between different kingdoms and the simulta-
neous capture of women and children.

In a word, the missionary's solution seems to be a perfect target
of the current widespread criticism of the attempts to reconstitute
the precolonial worlds, considered as a form of essentialism that dis-
seminates "nostalgic ideologies of cultural continuity, difference and
authenticity" (Tagliacozzo and Wilford 2009: 17). As a matter of fact,
our reading of Catholic "anthropology" will appear to be more complex than this. To start with, there was nothing nostalgic in Father
Fernandes's description of the pre-European past of the Timorese people. On the contrary, the locals were simply, in his words, "people be-
having like animals," first and foremost because of the "promiscuity
of the sexes," "quasi-nudity," "pornographic language," and "truly
infernal nocturnal dances" (Fernandes 1931: 18, 40).

It therefore isn't difficult to predict what he had to say about the
religion of the East Timorese people: "They didn't have any religion
in the strict sense of the term." What he actually meant by this was
that "all their religiosity boiled down to a fear of spirits," in particular
the fear of the dead, since they lacked the moral component that only
Christianity could bring. Although they worshipped their ancestors,
they carried out sacrifices motivated by fear of the deceased's malev-
olent intrusions into the world of the living. This was done in order to
placate them rather than as a show of love of their lost relatives. The
higher the social status of the deceased, the greater the number of animals that needed to be sacrificed; thus, the funeral was transformed
into a "filthy orgy." And in order to complete his dubious historical

reconstruction, the twentieth-century missionary subordinated other components of the Timorese religion to an omnipresent fear of the dead, while introducing in the meantime some Tetum vocabulary:

> The sense of terror they held in relation to the spirits was the source of the respect with which they guarded and stored any object manip-ulated by their ancestors, especially the machete, the spear, the vessel used to ground betel nuts, the bamboo where they stored their betel palm and lime, their bed, etc., etc. All these objects are stored in a spe-cial house, *uma lulik* (sacred house), . . . where only one man, the *makai lulik* (a kind of priest) could enter. That was where they carried out their sacrifices. (Ibid: 22)

In the light of Father Fernandes's book, so striking in its ethno-centrism, we ask, what is ultimately the place of missionaries in the context of Portuguese colonial anthropology in East Timor in the twentieth century? To what extent were the Christian colonial and the "pagan" precolonial realities dissociated or related within the Catholic discourse? Considering diversity within the church, even the some-times contrasting sensibilities between its agents, this chapter does not aim to isolate a single missionary worldview but definitely looks for recurrent ideological traits that may be mobilized in that broad context by different actors in different combinations, whether in reli-gious or in diocesan clergy. This is the main question we address in this chapter.[1] We are interested in the missionaries' own categories—with their correlative evangelizing actions—and we are willing to view such literature as a contribution to the enduring anthropological dilemma of religious interaction in colonial settings, a dilemma that obviously transcends East Timor. It nonetheless concerns this context in very specific ways, not least because of the antiquity of the Portuguese presence. We will therefore focus on the historical interpenetration of the two realms, based on the Catholic missions' archive.[2] We must ultimately realize whether or not Father Fernandes's pejorative gaze—according to which everything, *in illo tempore*, boiled down to "fear and orgies"—was simply the radical case of a more general trend (ibid: 23). But our true challenge lies in the Catholic Church's outright rebuttal (more than rejection) of any form of syncretism resulting from the long-term interaction between Christianity and "Timorese religion."

Ignoto Deo: Missiology and Ethnology in East Timor

The winds of missiology, i.e. the science of the missions, of which eth-nology was an important branch, had a troubled arrival in Portugal, and therefore in East Timor. In the 1930s, much of the Portuguese clergy proved to be highly wary of the theories of the (Catholic) missiologists who, without having conducted any fieldwork and without knowing the particularities of the local peoples, defined principles and methods that were designed to enable missionaries to get closer to local customs, as if to suggest that knowledge of such customs had been superficial up until that point. In the *Ecclesiastical Bulletin of the Diocese of Macao*, the missiologists were practically accused of being anticolonialists, if not "Bolsheviks," at least those of a certain wing ("Observações a um missiólogo" 1932). The problem was that missiology, which at an international level organized a wide array of different conferences and university courses, exhibitions, and publications, was sponsored by none other than Pope Pius XI, who was known as "the missionary Pope" (Capela 1934: 853),[3] and necessitated a more pacific reaction to the movement. "We don't encompass within this designation the orders and directives from Rome," wrote Father Jaime Goulart (who subsequently became the bishop of Dili) in a 1932 editorial on the subject of "the missiological call from the office" (Goulart 1932: 109).

Even the bishop of Macao, Costa Nunes, traveled to Europe in 1933 with the deliberate purpose of meeting with "some of the most authoritative propagandists of modern missiological ideas" in order to be able to "discard current pre-conceived ideas" (Goulart 1933: 366). After returning to Macau, he published an article in the diocesan bulletin designed to help the local missionaries embrace the new trend. The idea furthermore was to bring into the modern age the oldest tradition of evangelization of the church, which had been advocated by Saint Paul when he took the Unknown God for the theme of his sermon at the altar of the Athenians: "Therefore, the One whom you worship without knowing, Him I proclaim to you" (Acts 17:23). The twentieth-century missionary should now do the same, with the aid of ethnology: "In the first place, study the religion of the people to be evangelised, because you will undoubtedly find many points of contact between this religion and Christianity, given that there are always certain moral principles and beliefs shared between all religions" (Nunes 1934: 462).

Although general in scope, the bishop's article, signed with the initials CN, established a strong link with the history of Timor, which was marked by missionary episodes that were extremely aggressive when it came to dealing with the native religion:

> Religion has always been, for all peoples, the final stronghold, where the most delicate feelings of spiritual life are concentrated. A direct as-

sault on this stronghold and, even worse, the use of weapons that hurt people, is likely to cause revolt, and will pose a tremendous hindrance to spreading the Gospel. The missionary who begins his life of ministry by hurting the religious feelings of the people that he aims to evangelize, will soon find that all the doors to preaching the Gospel are closed to him. The situation will be even more serious if he has the impudence to perform any disrespectful or violent act against, for example, the idols, pagodas or sacred objects of the pagans. (Nunes 1934: 461)

In his position as the superior of the missions in Timor, Father Fernandes was nonetheless undoubtedly responsible, in this same period, for a rather unmissiological policy of systematic destruction of some of the most tangible elements of the "Timorese religion," in particular the well-known relics of the dead and other *lulik* objects preserved in the sacred houses. While boasting that he had captured "a veritable arsenal" of spears and machetes among "various trinkets," the priest went so far as to equate this missionary method with the "pacification" project of Portuguese colonialism:

In Timor, to convert one of the natives is to dispossess him of all the warlike instruments inherited from his elders, he must hand them over as a *sine qua non* pre-requisite in order to be baptised, since for him they constitute grounds for practising acts of idolatry. In this manner, a converted kingdom is a disarmed kingdom . . . (Fernandes 1931: 102)

In vogue during the missionary revival of the final years of the Portuguese monarchy, this practice had faded away with the decay of the missions during the First Republic (1910–26)—which we will discuss later—but was effectively resumed on a larger scale during the dictatorship era (from 1926 onward), without the words of Bishop Costa Nunes having exactly reversed this trend. In fact, the missionaries who adopted this policy told him everything in the letters sent to Macao.

Salvaging and Destroying the "Cult of the *Luliks*"

It was in this context, highly complex in terms of religious doctrine and ambiguous in practice, that a missionary, whose explicitly ethnographic writings would make a major difference, landed in Timor in September 1932. Father Ezequiel Pascoal was neither the only person nor the first to produce such texts, but he was undoubtedly the most persistent practitioner. He certainly embraced the idea that the missionary should not convert people without studying them in the process. From the missiological perspective, this meant seeking God in the native religion and accepting that it was possible to find Him—capitalized, it should be understood—lost somewhere within an intricate web of pagan representations. Following a degenerationist model, Father Pascoal would reach the conclusion that the Timorese Supreme Being, Maromak (with his equivalents in various regions), had been eclipsed by a multitude of spiritual beings that were more involved in the pettiness of everyday human life. There had been a "degeneration" from relative transcendence to immanence and from a primitive monotheism to animism. The "cult of the *luliks*," as he termed it, was then considered to be the core of the Timorese religious experience.

With respect to the word *lulik*[4]—implicitly including its equivalent terms in other Timorese languages—he reached the conclusion that it had a double meaning. As a qualifying term, in the broadest sense, it meant "venerable" or "intangible"; but he was quite certain that it also served as a noun, used to designate a large number of spiritual entities of the alleged native religion, thus revealing the concept's fluid contours. "Strictly speaking," he said, "it means beings whose definition is difficult to pin down, wherein the Timorese people themselves don't know what they are." They were believed to be invisible, essentially independent from the material locations or objects "that, for whatever reason, represented them, incarnated them, or would preferably host them."[5] If there were *lulik* trees, rocks, fountains, groves, or lands, it was because these sites were "mansions" of the spirits, even though the spirits always ended up being confused within the indigenous psychology of this material expression (Pascoal 1949a: 13). We are therefore faced with a reading that, far from systematizing or structuring the native religious representations, subsumed them into a main category that was far too broad. Though need was sometimes felt to differentiate the so-called *luliks* from one another, such attempts had little theoretical or ethnographic consistency.[6]

More importantly to us, Father Pascoal also suggested that the relics of ancestors, such as gold and silver moons, swords, and machetes, were possible manifestations of the alleged *lulik* spirits. Other documents written by him in the 1930s conveyed the argument that there was a main *lulik* in each sacred house and that the other objects deposited there, although sacred, were subsidiary to this spirit (Pascoal 1937: 848). In this sense, the names of specific *luliks*, inside or outside sacred houses, were often referred to by Pascoal and other missionaries, who also did not hesitate to classify them using substantives. Be that as it may, many other Catholic missionaries viewed the *luliks* as inseparable from the objects that the Timorese stored in their sacred houses. More than mere material expressions of native cults, these objects were considered to be sufficient proof of the basic materiality of this native kind of worship, in contrast to the high symbolism of the Catholic objects.[7] This perspective may be considered a hallmark of missionary thought and action in East Timor.[8]

As a consequence, there was evident rivalry between the church and the *uma lulik*, each with their tangible contents. It is therefore no wonder that the sacred houses were identified as "temples" of Timorese religion in general, somewhat at the expense of their special association with ancient ruling families or with aristocratic leadership positions in the village, or *suco*: "The *luliks* have their temples." Hence the ritual specialist who took care of them was also designated by Father Pascoal as a "heathen hierophant." Occupying "almost always the centre of the village," and distinguished "to a considerable extent" from profane homes, these "temples" conserved the aforementioned relics and other *luliks* and hosted many of the rituals intended to protect men against the potentially maleficent actions of this multifaceted category of spirits, parallel to the dead (Pascoal 1949a: 13, 15).

This brings us to the crux of the "cult of the *luliks*," according to Father Pascoal. These were "dark, vengeful, arbitrary" beings in terms of their intervention in the lives of the "Timorese pagan":

> They constitute his ongoing obsession. The idea of the *lulik* pervades his life in a paradoxical manner, inaccessible to the European mentality. The *luliks* are a shadow that haunts him and at the same time, a form of defence that shelters him. They are a nightmare that haunts him but also a pretext for his biggest orgies. . . . From the foregoing it is easy to deduce that the cult of the *luliks* has nothing to do with love or affection. Fear is the only motivating force[9] that guides all relations with these strange beings who control the fate of the Timorese pagan. (Pascoal 1949a: 13, 14)

Fear and orgies, once again. It therefore wasn't in this "cult," which in his eyes was practically devoid of deism and morality, that Father Pascoal found points of contact with Christianity. On the contrary, he even stated that "the *luliks* are one of strongest bonds holding these people to the yoke of the devil" (Pascoal 1936: 283). He therefore attempted to destroy it, in a deliberate and committed manner, as revealed in his letters to the bishop, especially in the 1930s during his early years of activity. One of the key concepts of the missionary endeavors, in this sense, was exhortation. This allegedly involved persuading converts, with a strategic focus on the "chiefs," to surrender or destroy on their own initiative the relics that had been worshiped by their grandparents, thus proving their new faith by deeds and not

by words alone.[10] The seized items, in defiance of or at least thereby
undermining the influence of the *lulik na'in*, were burned in "auto de
fé"–style ceremonies near the church, or, in more extreme cases, the
sacred houses were incinerated with their contents kept inside. There
was resistance from many Timorese people, but, according to the missionary record, they were slowly overcome and finally succumbed to
the persistence of exhortation, precisely, which would situate this dia-
lectic at an intermediate psychological level—somewhere between the
native "consciousness" and "unconsciousness" of the missionary colonization—referred to by John and Jean Comaroff. (1992: 259) There
are accounts of people who were reluctant to hand over their sacred
items, as well as some evidence of deliberate desacralization of sacred
houses, possibly to conceal them (Pascoal 1936: 283; De Almeida
1937: 750–51; Parada 1937: 593–97; Correia 1935: 60–61).

As an alternative to the seizure of these familiar, movable *luliks*,
the missionaries, "based on an understanding with the authorities,"
also took the initiative to attack, in particular through the erection of
wooden crosses or by creating niches for other Catholic imagery, the
traditional religious meaning of certain rocks and other *luliks* located
outside the villages, or in any case, outside the sacred houses (Correia
1935: 62).[11] Although there are several significant examples, two reports written by Father Ezequiel Pascoal are sufficient for the purposes
of illustration. The first concerns the role of the Canossian nuns in the
"profoundly superstitious" village of Obruto:

> They urged the locals to fulfil their religious duties, but explained that
> they could only do it sincerely if they surrendered their *luliks*. They
> responded to that request, by stating that they didn't have any *luliks*.
> One of the nuns, dismayed at this refusal, was sitting in the shade of
> a tree, lamenting the blindness of that people. . . . The locals noted her
> sadness. They fetched a table and prepared to bring her some food.
> The nun told them that she wasn't there in order to eat. That she only
> wanted them to convert to Christianity and surrender their *luliks*. (Pas-
> coal 1936: 283)

This anecdote reinforces the idea that, via so-called exhortation,
the main issue at stake was a mechanism of psychological coercion:
"This time her request took effect. A few moments later she was
handed a *lulik*, a yellow metal plate and some swords. On that same
day they also surrendered a *lulik* snake—a stick measuring over one
metre in length that had some red rags tied to it . . ." (Pascoal 1936:
283; see also De Almeida 1937: 750–51; Parada 1937).

In the second example, the missionary reports a "reasonable collection of *luliks*" that he himself made in 1935 during his visits to

Lacló, a missionary station that reported to Manatuto. This action took place in three phases. First, he identified a sacred house via its "special form," and, suspecting that "the main *lulik* of the kingdom" was located inside, he almost succumbed to the temptation to act in breach of the local penalties: "I thought of entering the house and dethroning the *lulik*" (Pascoal 1937: 847). But he restrained this rather unmissiological impulse, which gave way to a second stage of fruitless dialogue:

> It seemed to me that without a certain preparation that would favourably influence their mood, it wouldn't be prudent to assume such an attitude. I simply talked with the guard of the *lulik*—a frail old man, bent over by the weight of so many years, and who, like almost all persons entrusted with this task, had very long hair, like that used by the women. The old man greeted me at the door of the house, as if to stop me entering, but with extreme gentleness. . . . He responded with a sarcastic laugh, that sounded like that of the devil himself, to the advice I gave him, in an attempt to dissuade him of the value of the *luliks* and I recommended that he prepared for his own death, that would not be long in coming, and would only be a good death if it were Christian. The old man died soon afterwards, in the darkness of the superstitions that surrounded him. (Pascoal 1937: 848)

In a third stage, the destructive action was finally perpetrated, but not in an immediate fashion, because it always involved local agents who legitimated the process from the missionary standpoint, if only due to their mere presence:

> Only the other day, due, it could be said, to a coincidence, I was given the opportunity to dethrone this *lulik*. The elders accompanied me. We removed everything—a multitude of things covered in dust and smoke, that had absolutely no value other than that which the natives attributed to them as a *lulik*. The *lulik* itself, was an object made of gold, in a crescent shape. . . . A bonfire was lit next to the Chapel to burn all these items, including two drums that before being used as *luliks* had been voices that summoned the warlike residents of Laclo to battle. (Pascoal 1937: 848)

These "ethnographic" accounts are even poignant, at times, because they make it possible to visualize the annihilation of objects that were affectively linked to the memories, and the lives, of the deceased relatives of the Timorese converts, such as a piece of cloth in which a grandmother "demonstrated her skill in the art of embroidery" or a tooth that "must have also belonged to her" (Pascoal 1937: 848). But that's not the only reason why it's possible to define this missionary activity as a form of violence. The issue at stake was also self-destruction. Let us see why.

Mutilated Images: Archaeology of
an Impossible Syncretism

For missionaries, the *lulik* objects were a purely native reality, which had nothing to do with Christianity—in either spiritual or historical terms. But even in supposedly hidden locales it was possible to encounter unlikely traces of Catholic influence from previous eras. The missionary history of Timor was seen as a cycle of withdrawals and returns. In the light of the huge scale and vicissitudes of the Portuguese colonial archive, historical doubts still subsist today concerning the extent of the debility of the missions, at least up until 1834. This is obviously not the place to attempt a comprehensive historical overview of the missionary presence in East Timor. But one thing is certain: the failure of more than three hundred years of attempts at evangelization was fully admitted in the twentieth century. The nostalgic idea of splendorous though short-lived moments in the past, with large *cristandades* (Catholic, or Christianized, communities)[12] in bygone eras, was recurrent among late-imperialism missionaries due to the fact that some or all religious orders had been dispossessed, for political, anticlerical reasons, and subjected to repeated involuntary withdrawals from the island (actually from the metropolis and all her colonies), namely, in 1759, 1834, and 1910.

Bishop Costa Nunes felt that a definitive resurgence of the *cristandades* would only be possible in Timor—a "resurrection," as was often metaphorically stated—if these become gradually independent of the priests sent from the metropolis (Nunes 1923: 705). Even if cyclical, the shortage of missionaries on the island had to be resolved once and for all through the overdue creation of a local clergy. "This is what would evangelize the locals, just as the European clergy evangelized Europe." Such an idea wasn't his own—it had been suggested by the Vatican, given that there were "more than one billion pagans to convert, and only about thirteen thousand missionaries" in the world. Influenced by the missiological thinking of the time, he even wrote in the diocesan bulletin that a native missionary had certain qualities that placed him above the European missionary, due to his knowledge of the language, the "uses and customs," the "mentality and tastes" of his countrymen (Nunes 1935a: 611, 612, 613; 1935b). This new trend was revolutionary, together with the advent of the dictatorship in Portugal in 1926, which from the outset favored the activity of the missions and restored their political dignity.[13]

Ignorant of the full story of their predecessors, the twentieth-century missionaries harbored doubts, for example, concerning the missions undertaken in the kingdom of Bobonaro before 1908, wherein the prevailing idea was that the kingdom's people were possibly the most "savage" people in Timor. It was only after several years of intensive work in the early 1920s that a missionary finally heard of a native tradition that two missions had actually existed in the region many years before—one in the Tetum plain of Rai-Mea and the other further west, in Suai. He extended his research into these two sites, and the results were amazing. Among the local *lulik* objects, several Catholic items were encountered, the most spectacular of which was a wooden statue of Our Lady of the Rosary, which had been mutilated. In a letter to his bishop, the missionary wrote in this regard:

> This does not mean that the peoples who preserved the objects of worship for so long, had also kept the religious faith of their ancestors. They possessed religious objects of the old missions, on the basis of the custom that all locals had to save everything that belonged to their ancestors, even if a simple letter of no importance. With the passage of time, these people once again fell back into paganism, becoming as superstitious as the people where no mission had ever occurred and can currently be found in this state. (Cardoso 1923: 50)

There was, for example, a Portuguese letter, written in 1790, which was read by the priest and allowed him to conclude that the missions in Rai Mea and Suai were already extinct at the end of the eighteenth century. It is extraordinary that such documents, potentially invaluable for the reconstruction of the Catholic presence in Timor in previous centuries, were valued and preserved more by the non-Christian Timorese locals than by the Catholic missionaries, who disparaged not only their historical significance but above all their religious significance, which was considered to be virtually nil. From the perspective of the church, any vestiges of the true faith had simply disappeared. First and foremost, in the case of holy statues, Catholic doctrine did not consider that they had an intrinsic and enduring sacred status. Unlike an "idolatrous" cult, their meaning was strictly and explicitly symbolic and therefore inseparable from the faith of the believers (Gibbons 1925: 108–15). If this faith disappeared, as it had indeed disappeared among the wayward descendants of the former believers, the objects became stripped of their original value. We can therefore follow the argument that the image of Our Lady of the Rosary, for example, had indeed degenerated into a native *lulik*, from a doctrinal viewpoint.

The ironic aspect of this story is that for the Timorese "heathens," these objects of Portuguese origin were still sacred—or more precisely, they were *lulik*. As an integral part of a cult of the ancestors, rather than of a "cult of the *luliks*," they had remained inside a sacred house for an indefinite period of time, but certainly for many years—otherwise the fragile paper items, such as the abovementioned letter, would have disintegrated completely. We are clearly faced by a case of "archaeology of colonialism" (Lyons and Papadopoulos 2002). And we are tempted to suspect or imagine that there would be some form of historical continuity, although subject to transformations, in the mystical attitude of these communities in relation to their own Catholic heritage. Even if they were unaware of the respective Christian meanings, they would probably be aware of a Portuguese connection,[14] since the objects in question were presented to the priest when he began his on-site research. The phenomena of indigenization of Catholic objects was, however, rejected by the church, even if those objects were the unforeseen historical result of an ancient and stronger missionary influence. Father Pascoal reported one such case:

> I remember, in this regard, from a visit that I made, a few years ago, to the top of a hill, a short distance from the current chapel of Caju-Laram in the civil district of Viqueque. They told me that friars had formerly lived there. They said that they could show me the place where a chapel had existed whose statues were kept in a hut that had been erected there. I went. I wanted to see the statues. I entered the hut and the dark compartment where they kept them. In a kind of oratory, amongst the various dirty, half eaten away, *lulik* objects, I saw the statues. (Pascoal 1949a: 13)

It is tempting to ask whether, in the twentieth century, the profound respect of the Timorese people in relation to their ancestors and relics could have been otherwise or more effectively exploited by the missionaries. Knowing that there was a possibility of finding Catholic "vestiges"[15] within the sacred houses, there might have been a chance to "evoke" and "recover" a "lost religion"—that of Catholicism—which could be presented as the true faith of the locals' ancestors. But the missionaries decidedly chose the opposite path—to cut the historic also the spiritual bridge between the two domains. Thus, it is not surprising that, in his article on "The Cult of the *Luliks*" Father Ezequiel Pascoal showed indifference to the Catholic or Portuguese origin of these peculiar objects while blaming the natives for their loss of meaning:

> Parts of crockery, batons, flags, even a lamp from the tabernacle, a candlestick, a statue, can be a *lulik*. Once they have fallen into the possession of the locals, due to a war or for any other reason, they will be stored with utmost veneration, and with the passage of time, they will be purely and simply considered a *lulik*. (Pascoal 1949a: 13)

We suggest that this option corresponded to a form of violence, not only to the Timorese people but to the missionaries themselves. It should be stressed that the theological explanations concerning the symbolic meaning of the Catholic statues did not exhaust their power over believers, whether peasants in a rustic village in Portugal or educated priests. Even if transformed into a "pagan" object, the statue of Our Lady of the Rosary was still a potential object of Catholic worship. Ultimately, we may admit that the missionaries, whether consciously or unconsciously, tended to project their own faith in the Mother of God onto the wooden statue and thus restore its religious value. If this was the case, it would be unthinkable to burn it in the same manner as any other *lulik* object. The same could be said, *mutatis mutandis*, of the Portuguese flags, dating back to the period of the monarchy, that were encountered sporadically among the relics handed down from the Timorese ancestors in different parts of the island.

And yet the indiscriminate incineration of sacred houses could affect materials of Christian origins. However detailed the historians' efforts to reconstruct the four centuries of missionary presence on the island (for example, Durand 2004), the assumption that there were Catholic objects inside the Timorese sacred houses is no more hypothetical from a historical perspective than to assume that there was exclusively native content. We prefer to keep the dates of this history open, because in a certain way we are dealing with (let alone creating) a legend; in any case, this chapter is intended to be an anthropological essay more than a historical reconstruction. The inadvertent destruction of traditional Timorese objects and spaces thus had a hidden dimension—the destruction of a material and spiritual heritage related, if not to the converts, at least to the Portuguese missionaries from previous eras.

The attitude of the missionaries in relation to indigenous appropriation of Catholic paraphernalia, simply viewed as a form of adulteration, was related to the very essence of Catholicism, as a universal orthodoxy that could solely be sanctioned by priests. Whenever a *cristandade* was left abandoned, it was necessarily condemned from the missionary perspective, not only because its members and descendants would not be able to reproduce the Gospel in an adequate manner but also and especially because of the lost sacraments, in particular the communion, associated to confession. The issue at stake wasn't the mere outward manifestation of faith by the converts but above all the continued redemption of their sins. Furthermore, without the control and guidance of the priest, the "psychological fickleness" of the Timorese locals would prevail, according to current phraseology.[16] Only via the continued presence and perseverance of the missionaries, as they said themselves, would it be possible to eventually eradicate the parallel influence of "superstition." Surrounded by "heathens," the native Christians would otherwise inevitably succumb to "paganism." "Without the priest, the Timorese local will soon abandon the God of Abraham" (Fernandes 1931: 35). Despite its rather disorganized appearance, the native religion was therefore portrayed as if personified at the expense of historical actors and was finally judged to be very powerful, capable of transforming *saints* into *luliks*. But we have still to consider an exceptional case—in which this process of transformation was never completed, whether from the perspective of Catholicism or that of the native religion.

The Case of "Amo-Deus Coronel Santo António"

One of the most prominent Catholic *luliks* in Timor was the statue of a saint that the church was forced to restore as a Catholic icon, to the extent that its indigenization was never completed. In fact, it never lost its Portuguese name, or its notoriously Christian framework. In the early 1930s, Father Ezequiel Pascoal began to chart the history of this small statue of "Amo-Deus Coronel Santo António," as it was called by the people of Manatuto, in a mixture of military and divine honor that followed the old Portuguese tradition of "lyrical Christianity" (Freyre 1986; Pascoal 1938: 459).[17] He collected oral traditions and consulted historical documents stored in the archive of his mission at this time, that of Manatuto, which culminated in an article written in five parts. This text, published between 1949 and 1950, was like an exercise in historical anthropology *avant la lettre*, in which the missionary found himself confronted with the most difficult intellectual question in matters of the religion of the Timorese and their relations with Catholic influence: "Were they bad Christians? Were they Heathens?" (Pascoal 1949–50: 217). This is the question that he posed in relation to the *moradores*[18] of Manatuto and the other followers of "Amo-Deus Coronel Santo António," who, during the head-hunting period, refused to set off for war without first placing a pebble or grain of corn at the statue's feet, "mingled with several authentically pagan rites" (Pascoal 1938: 459). Indeed, they would only be ready to cut off the heads of their enemies if they bore on their foreheads the mark of the guardian of the "great *lulik*" Hato-Neno. The "hierophant" would chew the areca and betel placed next to the statue and remove the "red and disgusting" mixture from his mouth, which he then used to mark the warriors (Pascoal 1949–50: 219).

This was a delicate case, an exception that proved the rule that Catholic statues had been transformed into pure *luliks* as a result of abandonment by the church. Despite having been kept in a chapel under clerical tutelage during the eighteenth century, at which time it was used to preside over processions and other initiatives, the saint's statue ended up, certainly during the decadence of the missionary movement in the nineteenth century, in a sacred house that had been especially dedicated to him, associated with the *liurai* of Manatuto. In the 1930s, during the time of Father Pascoal, this unclassifiable temple no longer existed, but the statue of Lord-God Colonel Saint Anthony remained in the hands of the widow of the last chief, a woman who, as a Catholic, kept the statue in a corner of the former royal residence that had been transformed into a *"sui generis* chapel." It continued to attract many proselytes of this hybrid devotion, a devotion that the author categorized as lying "outside the spirit and laws of the Church." In 1933, at the time of a new pastoral visit to Timor, Bishop Costa Nunes decided "that the venerated statue of the people of Manatuto should return to the local church, where it would be worshipped, excluding any heathen worshippers" (Pascoal 1949–50: 84). Having witnessed this entire phase himself, Father Pascoal reported that the widow and her second husband heeded the bishop's ruling "without the slightest reluctance": "The next day, in addition to Saint Anthony, they ordered that a case should be delivered to the mission, filled with crumbling and shapeless statues, that had been brought in the first ships that had transported the founding friars of the oldest *cristandades*, together with dismantled crucifixes, faded and torn paintings and even a skull" (1949–50: 84).

It may be assumed that these Portuguese bones underpinned the status of a Catholic relic, given that, at the beginning of his article, the author incautiously reported that until 1937 the statue of "Amo-Deus Coronel Santo António" had been accompanied by the skull of an eighteenth-century friar that, according to local legend, worked miracles in the name of the great saint—in particular it preached to mice and birds to spare the rice fields. Faced by such a complex context, Father Pascoal observed that the ancient guardians of the statue had even invested themselves simultaneously "as pagan and Christian priests." And it was with "fond memories" of these times that an entourage of the "staunchest worshippers of the *lulik*" went to the mission in Manatuto and requested that the statue be returned to the house of the *liurai*, which of course was denied, since only the Pope could revoke the bishop's order (Pascoal 1949–50: 84).[19] Father Ezequiel Pascoal went even further in his admission that this old cult of indigenous appropriation, although it could never be recognized by the Catholic Church, was nonetheless a "symbiotic reality of a spiritual character." Actually, he only used this specific expression later, influenced by the theses of Gilberto Freyre and perhaps also by the Second Vatican Council (Pascoal 1967: 28). But the idea already existed in an embryonic form, in the following words:

> I must admit that the Lisbon saint[20] competed, like no-one else, to ensure that the spears and machetes of the warriors of Manatuto were, in times of crisis, one of the strongest pillars of the Portuguese sovereignty of this remote outpost. The deep devotion to Saint Anthony . . ., although deformed, transforming him into a god and a magical charm, will always be one of the unmistakable features of our passage through this land. (Pascoal 1949–50: 85)

Conclusion

The debate about the place of missionaries in anthropology is already very old, either as objects or subjects of observation (Stipe et al. 1980). In the present case, we're faced by a decidedly antisyncretic ideology, which is susceptible to analysis via historical anthropology (Stewart and Shaw 1994; Axel 2002). Despite the missiological challenge that was issued to them by their bishop in the 1930s—to seek possible points of contact between Christianity and the native religion—the Portuguese missionaries prolonged an inverse logic during the dictatorship era.[21] At the same time, we should concede that the missionary viewpoint engendered a certain kind of knowledge. One thing is certain: the contribution of Catholic priests to the anthropological archive of East Timor goes well beyond the recording of ethnographic data in the strict sense of the term and may also be appraised in terms of its intellectual reach. This is not to deny the political implications of the missionary record but to explore its other meanings. Catholic anthropology had limits that were difficult to surpass, dictated by the presumption of the inferiority of local rites and beliefs; but from our point of view, it was nonetheless an *anthropology*, conveying, in its own manner, a possible anthropological reading of the complex Timorese reality, particularly in terms of the appropriation of the material or immaterial traces of Christianity.

The Portuguese clergy in East Timor recognized that the historical result of such processes, more often than not, was an absolute form of indigenization, up to the point of eschewing Catholic items encountered in native sacred houses. The reports on the seizure or physical destruction of *lulik* objects by missionaries constitute a fundamental part of this vision, based as it was on a persistent moral dichotomy between the two interacting religious systems. Hence, in their *Weltan-schauung*, the missionaries assumed the setbacks of four centuries of evangelization. We even suggested the idea of self-destruction associated with the manner in which the Catholic clergy neglected these ancient heritages. The missionaries didn't attempt to salvage the old statues, since in their view they had already been spiritually destroyed. If there were several layers of destruction, effective or imaginary, it is because there were also several layers of religiosity. And if, by chance and exceptionally, a statue that had been lost to the sacred houses still preserved a modicum of Christian meaning, the same logic imposed itself through a rescue operation in the opposite direction, restoring the object to the bosom of the church, as happened in the case of the statue of Saint Anthony of Manatuto.

We may conclude that Father Fernandes's idea of seeking the remote past in the remotest parts of the island was purely rhetorical, not only because the idea of remoteness was relative but because in practice the missionaries were enabled, through their perspective of things, to find authenticity or Timorese religious ancestry anywhere, and, namely, in kingdoms where the missionaries' evangelizing work had been felt more or less strongly. In short, the problem of the centuries-old interaction between "Timorese religion" and Christianity was resolved through its negation. The native representations were systematically linked to a precolonial universe. I have thus suggested that the missionaries developed an extreme, albeit *legitimate*, mode of precolonial studies in a colonial context, precisely because they admitted the endurance, the powerful resistance of native religion to the intrusion of Christian things and ideas, in the sense that the former was able to subvert and even *destroy*, not physically but spiritually, the original meaning of Catholic sacred objects.

Partly in accordance with the missionary perspective, it may then be accepted that East Timor was the setting of recurrent selective appropriations of Catholic items that were integrated within (and therefore preserved) predominantly native religious patterns. In spite of the lack of consensus within the anthropology of religion concerning the limitations and potentials of the concept of syncretism, the concept in this specific case may not be pertinent indeed. On the other hand, the appropriations I have discussed here do not exhaust the diversity of interactions and resulting hybridizations. In the context of the Portuguese missionary setbacks in East Timor, they were certainly variable in time and space. Other conceptual alternatives, such as selective acculturation or selective inculturation, vernacular translation or dual religious participation, may be considered in assessing the religious history of Timor. In one way or another, this chapter may perhaps enlarge our classifications of "indigenous encounters with missionary Christianity" (Lindenfeld and Richardson 2012). Nonetheless, I prefer to leave open its theoretical inferences. Following D. Lindenfeld and M. Richardson's words in their *Beyond Conversion and Syncretism*, "Our terminological arabesques ultimately point to the lack of finality of any such conceptual schemes, and to the endless creativity that culture-mixing exhibits" (Ibid.: 20).

In addition, a further dimension should be considered in the missionary interpretations of the phenomena of indigenous appropriations. This dimension concerns theology rather than anthropology. In other words, Catholic discourse represents half of the historical equation (native perspectives representing the other half, obviously). As such, it must be considered in the evaluation of the actual sense of native religious phenomena of Christian influence. In any case, there is much more at stake in the missionary record than the reconstitution of the precolonial past. For sure, this reconstitution was undoubtedly based on the assumption of the conservatism of the local society and of the continuity of certain age-old traditions, even those that had supposedly been eradicated under Portuguese rule. But that was just one side of the coin. The other was Catholicism itself, not apart from but at the core of indigenous history.

Acknowledgments

Research for this essay was funded by FCT, Fundação para a Ciência e Tecnologia (grant reference HC/0089/2009).

Frederico Delgado Rosa is assistant professor at the Department of Anthropology of NOVA University (Lisbon) and researcher on the history of anthropology at CRIA NOVA FCSH and LAHIC/IIAC-CNRS. His publications include *L'Âge d'or du totémisme* (2003); and *Elsdon Best, l'ethnographe immémorial* (2018). He is the codirector (with Christine Laurière) of *BEROSE—International Encyclopaedia of the Histories of Anthropology* (berose.fr), and co-convenor (with Han F. Vermeulen) of the History of Anthropology Network of the European Association of Social Anthropologists (EASA). He presently works on several pre-Malinowskian ethnographers of the period ca. 1870–1922.

Notes

1. In spite of some illustrations, we do not aim at demonstrating in definite who made use of that recurring trait, and how and when they did it.
2. Necessarily, via a fragmented view of the missionary archive. The missions' local collections were destroyed during the Second World War, and neither that of the Diocese of Macau nor those of the seminaries in the metropolis is currently available to be consulted. Therefore, the documents selected for publication assume an unprecedented representativeness, in particular those that appeared in the diocesan bulletin, which were written by the missionaries in Timor (see Pascoal 1949: 31). Interestingly, one of the bulletin's editorials explicitly assumed this function of preservation, rescuing newcomers from "the thousand difficulties that are always encountered by lovers of historical bric-à-brac, when having to scour through archives" ("Mais um ano . . ." 1929; see Bickers and Rosemary 1996.)
3. Missionaries in Timor had even been urged to contribute not only with "native objects" but with compilations of "uses and customs" for the ethnography and ethnology pavilions of the Universal Missionary Exhibition, inaugurated in the Vatican in December 1924 (Nunes 1924). The list of items that was sent was reproduced in the church newsletter ("Lista dos Artigos" 1925).
4. Sometimes spelled *lúlic* or *lúlique* in the Portuguese records.
5. Two decades later, Ezequiel Pascoal would refine this definition as follows: "*lulik*—Any object or place where, for any reason, the natives believe that one or more spirits inhabit or that are closely related to those spirits. Only certain individuals, which they call *na'i lulik*, may touch these objects or enter these places. Therefore *lulik* also means intangible, forbidden, sacred. *Luliks* are also these same spirits, considered vaguely, without any connection to any object or place" (Pascoal 1967: 9).
6. The use of the term "totemism" perfectly illustrates this point, not so much by the anachronism of the circulation of ideas from the nineteenth century (usually derived from secondhand dissemination of an outdated text by James Frazer on this topic) but because the concept reached the missionary circuit (and the colonial circuit) in its most inconsequential action, i.e. the most generic, of sacred, animal species that were the object of taboos (see Ferreira 1953: 249; Rosa 2003).
7. In short, *lulik* objects were perceived as "fetishes," as material objects that had become "confused" with the spiritual beings they signified, reinforcing an overvaluation of the material at the expense of the spiritual. For Catholics, of course, the condemnation of pagan "fetishes" was always a delicate issue, requiring the distinction between "false idols" and (true) signs of the true God. Protestants could be more uncompromising in their condemnation of materiality (see Keane 2007).
8. The missionaries were, of course, probably projecting their own references onto the Timorese religious landscape. David Hicks even suspects

that the Portuguese priests had influenced those "educated Timorese Catholics" who insisted that the "*luliks*" were the objects of worship, although, he says, "this is not the case" (Hicks 2004: 26).

9. This was a widely held assumption among Christian missionaries vis-à-vis pagan belief: having (mis)attributed agency to a host of *invisible* spiritual beings, the reasoning went, pagans lived in fear of the beings they had imagined; in order to influence the invisible beings, they turned to the material objects that stood for them, in the process confusing the material "fetish" with the immaterial beings.

10. This seems reminiscent of the emphasis in early Christianity on public recognition of oneself as a Christian.

11. We may see this as an effort to appropriate the indigenous beliefs/symbols by absorbing them into Christian ones, i.e., a form of symbolic warfare. The concept of "mimesis" might therefore be pertinent here. In any case, the Christians were seeking to desacralize the Other while claiming to be the true embodiments of sacred power.

12. This Portuguese word, literally the plural of Christendom, had the sense of Catholic communities.

13. The process triggered by Costa Nunes culminated in the first seminar for local clergy on the eve of the Second World War and the creation of the diocese of Dili in 1940. The Japanese invasion of the island caused a further departure of the Portuguese clergy (as would happen one last time in 1975, following the Indonesian occupation), but the bishop's pioneering vision to a certain extent was proven by history (see Pascoal 1949).

14. Or, in any case, a foreign origin. We should note that many sacra were in fact imported objects believed to have come from far away centers of power. From this perspective, Christian objects took their place alongside other foreign goods.

15. Whether or not the objects were in fact "vestiges" of any significant Christianization seems to be the issue.

16. The mere possession of relics could not be perceived by the priests as a declaration of faith.

17. Lyrical Christianity, as Gilberto Freyre coined it, may be defined as a peculiarly Portuguese form of religiosity based on the acceptable intimacy between sacred liturgy and profane manifestations, particularly in terms of the folk sensibility on matters such as virility and sexuality, family life, gluttony, etc.

18. Timorese irregulars at the service of the Portuguese colonial army.

19. During the Japanese occupation, the "Amo-Deus Coronel Santo António" was hidden by the people, but after the war it was returned to the church.

20. Better known as Saint Anthony of Padua, this Franciscan doctor of church was born in Lisbon in 1195.

21. Alternatively, but with exactly the same result, we can say that the degenerationist perspective was taken too far, i.e., in the case of Timor it was considered to be practically impossible to find God, whose decadence

had been completed well before, under the emporium of an age-old animism that was in full force upon the arrival of the first missionaries.

References

Axel, B. K. (ed.). 2002. *From the Margins: Historical Anthropology and Its Futures*. Durham, NC: Duke University Press.

Bickers, R., and R. Seton (eds.). 1996. *Missionary Encounters: Sources and Issues*. London: Curzon Press.

Capela, J. 1934. "Necessidade de despertar vocações." *Boletim Eclesiástico da Diocese de Macau* 361: 853–62.

Cardoso, G. A. 1923. Letter to the Bishop of Macau. *Boletim Eclesiástico da Diocese de Macau* 241: 50–52.

Comaroff, J., and J. Comaroff. 1992. *Ethnography and the Historical Imagination*. Boulder, CO: Westview Press.

Correia, A. P. 1935. *Gentio de Timor*. Lisboa: Lucas & Cia.

De Almeida, D. A. M. 1937. "Relatório da Missão de Manatuto e suas agregadas." *Boletim Eclesiástico da Diocese de Macau* 397: 749–60; 398: 830–39; 399: 890–95.

Durand, F. 2004. *Catholicisme et Protestantisme dans l'Ile de Timor 1556–2003: Construction d'une Identité Chrétienne et Engagement Politique Contemporain*. Toulouse: Editions Arkuiris; Bangkok: IRASEC.

Fernandes, A. J. 1931. *Esboço histórico e do estado atual das Missões de Timor e refutação dalgumas falsidades contra elas caluniosamente afirmadas por um ex-governador de Timor*. Macau: Tip.Mercantil.

Ferreira, M. 1953. "Díli: Apontamentos etnográficos." *Seara: Boletim Eclesiástico da Diocese de Díli* 5: 246–49.

Freyre, G. 1986. *The Masters and the Slaves: A Study in the Development of Brazilian Civilization*. Berkeley: University of California Press.

Gibbons, C. 1925. "O Culto das Santas Imagens" ["The Cult of the Holy Images"]. *Boletim Eclesiástico da Diocese de Macau* 266–67: 108–15.

Goulart, J. 1932. "Editorial: Missões e Missiologia." *Boletim Eclesiástico da Diocese de Macau* 341: 108–10.

———. 1933. Letter to Father Neves. *Boletim Eclesiástico da Diocese de Macau* 356: 366–68

Hicks, D. 2004. *Tetum Ghosts and Kin: Fertility and Gender in East Timor*. Long Grove, IL: Waveland Press.

Keane, W. 2007. *Christian Moderns: Freedom and Fetish in the Mission Encounter*. Berkeley: University of California Press.

Lindenfeld, D., and M. Richardson (eds.). 2012. *Beyond Conversion and Syncretism: Indigenous Encounters with Missionary Christianity, 1800–2000*. New York: Berghahn Books.

"Lista dos artigos." 1925. "Lista dos artigos enviados pelas Missões de Timor e da China para a Exposição Missionária Vaticana." *Boletim Eclesiástico da Diocese de Macau* 258–59: lxxxii–lxxv.

Lyons, C. L., and J. K. Papadopoulos (eds.). 2002. *The Archaeology of Colonialism*. Los Angeles: Getty Publications.

"Mais um ano. . . ." 1929. *Boletim Eclesiástico da Diocese de Macau* 304: 657.

Nunes, J. C. 1923. Circular Letter to the Superior of the Missions of Timor. *Boletim Eclesiástico da Diocese de Macau* 239: 704–9.

———. 1924. Circular Letter to the Superior of the Missions of Timor. *Boletim Eclesiástico da Diocese de Macau* 248: 500–501.

———. 1934. "O Ataque . . . (Notas missionárias)." *Boletim Eclesiástico da Diocese de Macau* 369: 461–63.

———. 1935a. "Recrutamento de vocações indígenas (Notas missionárias)." *Boletim Eclesiástico da Diocese de Macau* 371: 611–15.

———. 1935b. "Catequistas (Notas missionárias)." *Boletim Eclesiástico da Diocese de Macau* 372: 701–4; 373: 775–78; 374: 874–76.

"Observações a um missiólogo." 1932. *Boletim Eclesiástico da Diocese de Macau* 342: 189–92.

Parada, N. 1937. Letter to the Bishop of Macau. *Boletim Eclesiástico da Diocese de Macau* 395: 593–97.

Pascoal, E. 1936. Letter to the Bishop of Macau. *Boletim Eclesiástico da Diocese de Macau* 391: 280–85.

———. 1937. Letter to the Bishop of Macau. *Boletim Eclesiástico da Diocese de Macau* 398: 847–50.

———. 1938. "Visita Pastoral de S. Excia. Rvma. às Missões de Timor." *Boletim Eclesiástico da Diocese de Macau* 406: 426–70.

———. 1949a. "O Culto dos "Lúlic." *Seara: Boletim eclesiástico da Diocese de Díli* 1: 12–15.

———. 1949b "Dezoito anos de intensa actividade—1924 a 1942." *Seara: Boletim eclesiástico da Diocese de Díli* 2: 29–31.

———. 1949–50. "Amo-Deus Coronel Santo António." *Seara: Boletim eclesiástico da Diocese de Díli* 6: 135–36; 7: 154–57; 9: 217–19; 11: 257–59; 5–6: 83–86.

———. 1967. *A Alma de Timor vista na sua fantasia*. Braga: Barbosa & Xavier.

Rosa, F. D. 2003. *L'Age d'or du totémisme: Histoire d'un débat anthropologique (1887–1929)*. Paris: Éditions du CNRS, Maison des Sciences de l'Homme.

Stewart, C., and R. Shaw (eds.). 1994. *Syncretism/Anti-syncretism: The Politics of Religious Synthesis*. New York: Routledge.

Stipe, C., et al. 1980. "Anthropologists versus Missionaries: The Influence of Presuppositions [and Comments and Reply]." *Current Anthropology* 21: 165–79.

Tagliacozzo, E., and A. Wilford (eds.). 2009. *Clio/Anthropos: Exploring the Boundaries between History and Anthropology*. Stanford, CA: Stanford University Press.

Chapter 6

FUNERARY POSTS AND CHRISTIAN CROSSES

FATALUKU COHABITATIONS WITH CATHOLIC MISSIONARIES AFTER WORLD WAR II

Susana de Matos Viegas and Rui Graça Feijó

One day, in the village of Laiara, located in the easternmost Timorese district of Lautem, where the Fataluku speakers reside, we entered a house, built on high wooden pillars; behind it were the graves of several of its deceased residents, which we later visited. We had come to talk with a group of six men about Nari, a locality situated on a nearby plateau six hundred meters above sea level.[1] All those men were patrilineal descendants of the central figure in a book authored by the Salesian missionary José Bernardino Rodrigues. In that book, Father Rodrigues describes his relationships with Fataluku speakers in Lautem between 1947 and 1957, referring specifically to his personal relationship with a man named Perekoro, whom he called "the king of Nari."

At that time, Perekoro lived together with his wife and several of his unmarried children up in the plateau of Nari. In our conversation, which took place in July 2014 in Laiara, near the district main town of Lospalos, diverse interpretations were offered of Perekoro's life, as well as different views on the site of Nari in present times. These descendants of Perekoro made clear to us that Nari remains a site of belonging for them and their kinsmen. Among other indications, they talked about frequent visits to Nari in order to perform propitiatory and protective rituals around the graves of their ancestors (*calu ho papu*), a type of relationship with former dwelling places that has been described for other areas in Lautem (see McWilliam 2006: 258)

In our conversation, the six men also offered their perspective on how the missionary came to know Perekoro. From their point of view, he was attracted by the magnificence of Perekoro, as he heard for the first time the echo of his deep voice—"Oh, oh, oh . . .!"—when he was calling pigs to come and eat. Normally, Perekoro's call would only be heard in the vicinity of his house, but on that particular occasion it echoed far away, miles from where he stood, reaching the mission at Fuiloro (Lautem). From this fact, they told us, the Salesian missionary realized that Perekoro must be a brave, strong, and powerful man, and so he hastened to meet him. As one of the men from Laiara told us,

> When he arrived, Father Rodrigues was not capable of making himself understood. It was the call [of the old king of Nari] that brought the two men together. Father Rodrigues used to go and spend the night with the old man, eating roasted sweet potatoes and grilled corn accompanied by *tuaka*[2] and having long talks with him. (Laiara, July 2014)[3]

Implicit in this conversation with descendants of Perekoro is the argument that we shall be developing in this chapter. In spite of the enormous power and authority bestowed upon the missionaries in the colonial period, which will be taken into consideration in this chapter, we will argue that ambivalence and tension also characterized the relations between the missionaries and the local leaders.

While Timorese opposition to the Portuguese administrative and military regimes is increasingly acknowledged (e.g. Pélissier 1996, Roque 2010, Kammen 2015, Leach 2017), the particular ways in which Timorese from different regions experienced and negotiated these colonial forces at distinct periods in time still require attention. By exploring a specific narrative of an interpersonal tie between Father Rodrigues and the "king of Nari," this chapter contributes to a wider discussion of negotiations between missionaries and Timorese in the colonial period and the sociocultural questions they raise.

Since the early sixteenth century, missionaries in both the Portuguese part of the territory and what would later become the Dutch part had invested in converting local chieftains, who received the title of "king" (cf. Durand 2004: 36, 46). Nevertheless, as this chapter demonstrates with reference to the Fataluku speaking region, they also had to negotiate with the indigenous people, specifically about certain "customary" practices. In elucidating Fataluku responses to missionaries in a specific period—when the Catholic mission settled in the region, after World War II—we also consider how these negotiations contribute to rethinking the historical conditions for cultural resilience in present day Timor-Leste.

Crossing history and anthropology, we will consider the relationships between the missionary and the Timorese here as intercultural encounters that pertain to an "interconnected reality" (Roque and Wagner 2012: 19), or ways of maintaining "conversation" as Sweet put it when analysing Christian missions in the Americas (Sweet, 1994: 92). Exploring the crossing between colonial history and ethnographic knowledge based on contemporary empirical research (Roque and Wagner 2012: 12; see also Fausto 1998 [1992], Roque 2011: 2), we shall show that Salesian priests in the Fuiloro mission in the period under analysis were in a relatively fragile position when confronted with powerful local leaders.

To put in evidence this political configuration of intercultural relations, we focus an ethnographic and historical gaze on the entanglements between Fataluku funerary rituals and Christian practices embodied in the cohabitation of funerary posts hung with skulls of buffalos sacrificed in the mortuary ceremonies and Christian crosses placed on top of the graves. Graves are a crucial site among the Fataluku, where relationships to ancestors are perpetuated (McWilliam 2007, Viegas 2017). Social relationships marked by a strong ambivalence between asking for permission, as a manifestation of respect, and obeying will be considered as part of how Timorese from the Lautem region negotiated with the missionary's authority in that colonial period. In both cases, we shall explore the notion of cohabitation, highlighting a kind of coexistence marked by tensions, misfits, and equivocations that nevertheless may generate compatibilities in specific historical moments (cf. Pina-Cabral 2002, Viegas 2007, Viegas and Feijó 2017).

Historical and Ethnographic Background

The mission of Fuiloro was founded in 1947, only two years after the end of the Japanese occupation and the arrival of the Salesian priests in Timor-Leste. It is located 214 kilometers from Dili, and various Salesians hold that it has always had difficulties in entertaining relations with the locals. Father José Bernardino Rodrigues was a member of the original team of five missionaries to arrive in Lautem and establish the first fixed Catholic mission in Fuiloro. During our fieldwork in Lautem (in 2012, 2013, 2014, and 2016), we spoke with many former students educated in the mission's school (founded in the 1960s). We also spoke with Father João de Deus, a Salesian who was the founder of another mission (Fatumaca/Baucau) in 1965 and who spent ten months in Fuiloro in 1969, residing permanently in Timor-Leste for over fifty years. These conversations confirmed the view that in Fuiloro, as most likely in other cases in the territory, considerable negotiation was necessary in order for the missionaries to be able to settle in the region and develop some form of relationship with the locals. This was particularly clear when talking about mortuary practices and ancestor worship either in the past or in present day.

Funerary posts hung with buffalo skulls form what Fataluku call *cau* (buffalo heads). They are widely distributed across the landscape of the district of Lautem, the easternmost part of Timor-Leste. Their sculptural relevance, along with the hollow gaze of the buffalo and sometimes also horse and oxen skulls, which are pierced by a wooden post that often reaches five meters high above graves, catches the attention of foreigners and Timorese from other parts of the country alike (figure 6.1).

Figure 6.1. *Arapou cau* and a horse skull on the left (Assalaino). Photo by the authors.

When we initiated our field research back in 2012, interlocutors with whom we spoke offered us different opinions as to the reasons for the persistence of this funerary practice. Some stated that this practice was limited to those who had not converted to the Catholic faith, while others suggested that it could only be found in a restricted number of villages. Both considerations have a grain of truth. However, neither of them implies that these funerary practices are in the process of disappearing. In fact, they are widely disseminated across the territory, as the graves of Fataluku do not tend to be concentrated in one single, central location, as the notion of "cemetery" often implies. On the contrary, graves are often organized according to patrilineal segments, separated from present-day dwellings but corresponding to the location of former villages or houses of the same patrilineal branch. This type of place, called in Fataluku *lata matu* (old dwelling sites), concentrates many graves. In other cases, for a variety of historically complex reasons that lie beyond of the aim of this chapter, graves are located in the vicinity of houses.

Mortuary ceremonies and graves thus play a particularly important role in the lives of the Fataluku-speaking people inhabiting the Lautem region in Timor-Leste, reinforcing the centrality of the relations between the living and their ancestors (cf. Viegas 2017). The importance to social life of mortuary ceremonies and the worship of the ancestors has been well described by anthropologists who did fieldwork in different parts of Timor-Leste during the colonial period (e.g. Hicks 2004; Forman 1980; Traube 1980, 1986). In his monograph based on fieldwork carried out in the 1960s, David Hicks (2004) has shown that a multitude of social facts depend on the connection between the living and the diversified world of ancestors, and that funerals occupy a central role in the ceremonial life that sustains such connections, making the funerary ritual "the most complex of the Tetum rituals" (Hicks 2004: 132). Elizabeth Traube describes similar ideas and discusses mortuary rituals that make up what she calls the "spectacular ceremonial complex" of the Mambai (Traube 1986: 228). While different in many respects, both Traube's and Hicks's monographs suggest the complex relation between dying and living as critical to understanding social life. The sequences of mortuary ceremonies extending over many years are the specific object of Traube's ethnographic analysis of the Mambai (cf. 1980; 1986: 200–35), while Forman's (1980) detailed ethnographic analysis of mortuary practices among the Makassae is particularly useful for a comparative reflection on the case of the closely related Fataluku. For the contemporary period, Grenfell (2012, 2015) has showed the enduring centrality of burials and mortuary ceremonies and the caring for the dead for the whole country.

In the specific Fataluku context, references to ancestors and their associated rituals are underlined by Andrew McWilliam, who has worked in the region for over a decade (McWilliam 2006: 258; 2008: 232; 2011a; 2011b). McWilliam explicitly places the subject of ancestor worship in the context of the debate on customary resilience in Timor-Leste:

> Despite the high levels of avowed Catholicism and the depredations of Indonesian rule of Lautem for many years, indigenous religious belief and ritual practice remains fundamentally important in Fataluku social life. Close attention to ancestral obligations and fear of the consequences of their neglect condition the rhythm of social life and link domestic rituals with the sacred landscape of ancestral origins across the region. (McWilliam 2006: 258)

In the mid-1960s, Francisco de Azevedo Gomes lived for two years in a military mission in the region of Lautem very close to Fuiloro (cf. Viegas 2011). His monograph on Fataluku social life devotes some attention to the low degree of conversion to Catholicism among the native inhabitants of the region, underlining the significance of the relationship of the Fataluku to the ancestors:

> The efforts at conversion by the missionaries have so far borne little fruit among the Fataluku. Many of those who have taken baptism and attend services in church remain intimately connected to their past. The largest obstacle to the acceptance of Christianity resides, according to them, in the irreparable loss of conviviality with the beyond and the ancestors they never forget. (Gomes 1972a: 40)

Nowadays, resilience of customary practices in Lautem and specifically of connections with the ancestors has been widely acknowledged. In the first comprehensive analysis of the situation of Timor-Leste after the Referendum of 30 August 1999, James Fox called one's attention precisely to the resilience and persistence of Timorese cultural traditions and their role in enabling local groups to both resist and assimilate various external influences (and not only the Indonesian invaders) (Fox 2000: 4; 2011: 255).

In Timor-Leste, at various moments, the colonial state attempted an explicit intervention in funerary practices, as, for example, in the levying of fines on those who did not bury their dead within a short time span defined in the regulations (Figueiredo 2004: 107). Efforts to control funerary practices resulted both from the formal colonial administration and from the missionaries' activities. The period under scrutiny in this chapter (1947–57) saw a new and more intensive missionary investment in many different regions in Timor-Leste, influenced by three important political trends: (1) the end of the Japanese occupation and the difficult start of a new life after the period of extreme violence perpetrated by the occupiers (Figueiredo 2003: 522–25; Gunter 2015); (2) the renewal of Portuguese colonial domination (Figueiredo 2011a); (3) the reinstatement of missionaries in the territory following their withdrawal in the first decades of the twentieth century as a result of the policies of the Portuguese First Republic (1910–26), which installed a secular state separated from the church. In 1935, the dictator António de Oliveira Salazar reestablished the power of the church and officially delegated the "Christianization and civilization of the non-assimilated populations to the Catholic Church" (Figueiredo 2003: 559–63; Durand 2004: 64, 67). Finally, the renewed strength of the church after World War II in Timor-Leste was also enforced by its separation from Macao, with the creation of a diocese in Dili under Bishop Jaime Garcia Goulart—a clergyman born in the Azores—who had an important role in fostering a rapprochement between the church and the natives (Durand 2004: 67).

In Lautem, up to the mid-twentieth century, there were no Catholics, let alone any mission (Durand 2004: 50).[4] Only a few Fataluku speakers (a dozen or so) were converted (Rodrigues 1962: 47; Bouza 2012: 53). Those few were mainly former students returning from missions located far away from Lautem—in Soibada and Dili (Rodrigues 1962: 48). Even if missionaries had visited Lautem before World War II and the ravages suffered at the hands of the Japanese, it was only in 1947 that a Catholic mission was physically established in the region.[5] The conditions under which the first five missionaries (including Father Rodrigues) who founded the Salesian Fuiloro mission lived and established contact with natives were generally described as precarious.[6] Moreover, at that time the local people spoke only Fataluku. At first, the priests thought of teaching them Portuguese while at the same time learning Fataluku (Bouza 2012: 53). However, as former Fataluku students of the mission and missionaries we interviewed assured us, most missionaries never learned any Fataluku.

The plateau of Nari is located midway between the Fuiloro mission and Laiara and adjacent villages where former inhabitants of Nari live nowadays. Forced resettlement from Nari plateau to this area of Laiara (where we met the king of Nari's descendants in 2014) must have occurred in the first decade of the twentieth century, during Celestino da Silva's governorship.[7] However, in 1947 Father Rodrigues testifies to the existence of material vestiges of previous dwellings in Nari—dry water fountains, old vegetable gardens surrounded by stone fences, and even a special place where the skulls of enemies were kept as trophies (described as a reminiscence of the time when headhunting was widely practiced). More importantly, Father Rodrigues attests to the presence in Nari of a noncompliant individual—the king of Nari and his family. Rodrigues never mentions, however, a crucial historical fact we have been able to identify: that the mission was established in the region just as the Portuguese colonial administration was implementing a final phase of forced resettlement. The resettlement policy is described in local colonial administrative reports from Lautem, which were only made accessible for public consultation by the National Archives of Timor-Leste in Dili in 2016. A report from the local colonial administration of Lautem in 1947 dedicated to "works under consideration and in the process of implementation" explicitly mentions, "Indigenous villages have been erected in places chosen by their local chieftains" (*Relatório* 1947: 2). In the 1948 report, a section dedicated to "indigenous villages" (*aldeamentos indígenas*, settlements or villages made by the colonial government for native people) observes that "almost all villages in this administrative area were concluded with buildings that are of the local type only built with better quality." The rationale given for this policy stresses the benefits derived from "increasingly easier surveillance over the indigenous peoples performed by gentile authorities and consequently by the [Portuguese] authorities" (*Relatório* 1948: 4).

In a very short piece titled "Nari," Francisco de Azevedo Gomes (1972b) remarks that during the Japanese occupation in World War II, Nari had been a refuge for the population of the region:

> Fearful of the invaders, some villagers, with their herds and other belongings, sought refuge in Nari because of the difficult access. . . . Once the Japanese had left, those villagers abandoned their poor and fragile huts that had been erected upon the ruins of the old settlement and returned to their typical houses. (Gomes 1972a: 68)[8]

Nari's history is therefore closely associated with its status as a secluded and sacred place, but also as a site of resistance to colonial power. First, this results from the difficult access to the plateau, without a permanent road or even footpath: "a plateau on top of a steep mountain, with cliffs looking like lime blades, in the centre of the Fataluku world: it takes a few good hours of painful trekking" (Gomes 1972a: 66; Rodrigues, 1962: 40, 272). As Gomes has observed in the 1970s, in Nari "death is sovereign . . ., gigantic graves, fallen houses, vegetable gardens abandoned, old *eteuruá* (sacred symbols) eaten away by time" mark the spirituality of the landscape (Gomes

1972a: 66). In our days, places like this one, located on top of valleys or plateaus, remain religious sites (McWilliam 2006: 258, 261; Viegas forthcoming).

After the independence of Timor-Leste (2002) and the reestablishment of freedom of movement, some former inhabitants of Nari went back up to the plateau, not only to be close to their ancestors' graves but also to tend their vegetable gardens. One of the descendants of the king—locally known as "Justino, the grandson of the king of Nari"—who was acknowledged as responsible for all things pertaining to Nari, explained to us in 2013 how peaceful it was for him to sleep up there, in his hideout located next to the graves of his father and grandfather.[9] He told us how he would often venture along the winding path even during the rainy season and would go and stay alone with his deceased relatives in the plateau, searching for this spiritual peacefulness. Father Rodrigues was thus right to acknowledge the importance of Nari as a sacred place for some of the inhabitants of Lautem and the strength of the king of Nari as a man of spiritual power.

Materialized Cohabitations

The level of intimacy that Father Rodrigues's text reveals in his relationship with the king of Nari can be explained not only in terms of the challenge that the former felt to convert a noble man, independent from the colonial regime, but also because of the close proximity between himself and one of the king's sons, Telukoro, who was baptized and became his best "informant." Through Telukoro's testimony, he transcribes detailed descriptions of funerals performed in the past, and the son himself became a mediator in baptizing his father and making sure that when he died he would have a Christian cross put upon his grave.

With its emphasis on the relationships between the missionary, the king, and his son, the book reflects a particular narrative structure supported in reports of different interpretations from the priest and the natives about specific events. In this it diverges from the vast majority of sources kept in the colonial archives about death and funerary practices in Timor-Leste, which are positivist descriptions of native customs and beliefs (e.g. Andrade 1920; Sylvan 1963). Father Rodrigues describes funerals and various related events combining the testimony of the king and the way in which he himself witnessed or became aware of those events.[10] In the description of a funeral that Father Rodrigues witnessed—the funeral of the grandson of Perekoro

Figure 6.2. *Arapou cau* and a Christian cross at a grave in Lautem. Photo by the authors.

who had been baptized—the missionary explains condescendingly that the king, saddened by the sudden disappearance of his grandchild, ordered the slaughter of an animal so that "the souls of relatives could come towards his grandchild and receive him ... given that, although he was a Christian, he still belonged to the family" (Rodrigues, 1962: 155). When the king was about to die, Father Rodrigues thought his main fear would be "the idea of separation from his relatives in the afterworld" (Rodrigues 1962: 106). In the same vein, he explains that when the king's grandson was baptized, the king insisted that "even going to Church he should never forget his family's *teis*" (Rodrigues 1962: 197). The Fataluku term *tei* has often been translated as "sacred," but as used in this sentence it refers to observances associated with ancestors.[11] In the face of the king's wish to sacrifice animals at his own funeral, Father Rodrigues argues that this would only meet the goal of honoring "the ancestors" and would not substitute for the Christian cross (Rodrigues 1962: 271). In the end, however, he acknowledges that both the erection of a cross and the sacrifice of animals did occur at the king's funeral ceremony:

> On the third day of the month of January, the time of death finally arrived for the old man. He called his sons, ordered them to open a grave not far away from the graves of his own parents and grandparents, and since he was already a Christian, told the children to go up to the missionary and ask for his permission to slaughter five buffaloes. He also mentioned he wished a cross to be erected on his grave. (Rodrigues 1962: 274)

Father Rodrigues thus asserts that he gave his permission for the slaughtering of buffalos "under the condition that sacrifices are not made." Further on, however, he describes the sacrificial destiny the buffalos had during the funeral ceremonies. As we have witnessed in our fieldwork, buffalo heads are hung from trees in order to dry up before being moved to the gravesite (figure 6.3).

Figure 6.3. Buffalo skulls hanging on a tree before being transported to the grave. Photo by the authors.

Father Rodrigues says that in 1957, when the funeral of the king of Nari took place, he immediately noticed upon arriving in Nari "buffalo heads hanging from trees," but he explicitly denied the possibility of these being sacrificial buffalos, explaining instead that they belonged to animals that the deceased's family had used to put up a feast for their visitors (Rodrigues 1962: 274–75). He also expresses his satisfaction that the same family recited the *Pater Nostrum* before taking "the last patriarch and king of Nari" away to the grave, where they erected a cross symbolizing the conversion of the king to the Christian faith (Rodrigues 1962: 275).

Different, though compatible with this missionary's perspective on the king and his family's funerary practices, is the king and his relatives' perspective on the Catholic orientations expressed by the missionary. First, the association between the cross and the funerary posts was present in the king's demand that five buffalos had to be slaughtered and a cross be erected next to his grave. The juxtaposition of the two symbols, the post and the cross, reveals a story of coexistence. The king's own vision of his baptism, implicit in the description of the long effort that the missionary had to make to convince the king to be baptized, attests to this coexistence. Only at the end of the missionary's stay in Fuiloro did the king ask to be baptized, in 1957, when he was about to die.

Father Rodrigues recounts that one day a son of the king came to the mission lodgings and reported that the king himself asked for the missionary to visit Nari because he "was sick and wished to be baptised" (Rodrigues 1962: 272). Father Rodrigues says he did not set out at once, because going all the way up to Nari required complex preparations. However, a few days later, a new message arrived, saying that the ruler's health had deteriorated, and the king requested Father Rodrigues to visit Nari in order that he be baptized. Only then, Father Rodrigues writes, did he set out for Nari. Contrary to his expectations, however, Father Rodrigues, upon arrival in Nari, found the king "in a very cheerful mood" (Rodrigues 1962: 273). Moreover, the king received him as if he had not requested his presence. When Father Rodrigues explained that he had come in response to the king's request and alluded to his intention to be baptized, the king retorted that "assuming it was a kind of medicine, he would request baptism if ever he fell ill again" (Rodrigues 1962: 273).

Christian doctrine has long insisted on the curative properties of baptism. But from the perspective of the king of Nari a different reading of the idea of healing properties is possible, which in turn conveys a Fataluku notion of personhood and its connections to proper name giving. This is the conclusion to be drawn from the information in-scribed in other parts of the same book, as well as from ethnographic work on the subject (cf. Gomes 1972a; Viegas 2011: 7; Valentim 2014). Father Rodrigues states that, while attempting to convince the king to be baptized, he spoke with him about the new name he should acquire afterward. This association between baptism and the acquisition of a new name had already been mentioned several times in the book, as had the relationships between names and personhood among the Fataluku.[12] Anthropologists (e.g. Gomes 1972a: 71, 109–12, 168, 178–80; McWilliam 2008) have observed that Fataluku associate a person's names with conditions of sickness and health. Thus, illness may indicate that a spiritual part of the person has been imprisoned outside his body, posing the danger that it will not be able to return to the body. A curative practice, in the case of children or youths, consists precisely in changing their names, as Rodrigues ac-knowledges: "Apart from other medicines that I have mentioned, they also revert to changing the sick person's name," thereby "fooling" the spirit who wishes to imprison the soul. That spirit, hearing a new name, "believes the person not to be the same one, and lets that per-son go" (Rodrigues 1962: 103–4). When the victim is a young boy, it is usually the maternal uncle who offers a new name "in order to cure him" (Rodrigues 1962: 103; Gomes 1972a: 180).

Father Rodrigues's ambition was to baptize the king and convince him to have a cross laid against his grave by persuading him that bap-tism would be a way to achieve a successful voyage to the afterworld as conceptualized in Christian eschatology: "Bear in mind that you shall die, that you have one soul, one single soul, and that baptism may open you the doors of Paradise in order for you to join the Almighty" (Rodrigues 1962: 233) However, the long dialogue that transpired between him and the king suggests that the latter may have envisaged baptism as a performative act of bestowing a new name that might possibly cure his illness. For that reason, he was keen to call upon the priest when he felt sick, but the sense of urgency declined once he felt recovered.

We commonly heard in Lautem (even from people who were avowed Catholic converts) that *arapou cau* and wooden crosses are "the same": "Those buffalo heads represent or are the same thing as the cross that the priests have brought." This does not mean they are identical or translated into each other. It means, we argue, that Chris-tian and indigenous attitudes to death and personhood have been made compatible in order to cohabit. Both Catholic priests and Fata-luku preserve their own ideas about the meaning of these objects. For the priests, the post could be replaced by the cross, but, if that were not possible, then the post could be seen as a symbolic device to mark and strengthen family ties; for the Fataluku, the cross, like the post, is a mediator between worlds and helps the deceased to travel and meet their ancestors. No translation is made. Neither replaces the other.

Missionary Authority in the Colonial Context (1947–57)

Coexisting side by side, without necessarily generating any sort of hybridization, posts and crosses on the graves are not only an index of cultural processes—they must also be considered in the context of the political and social power relationships between missionaries and Timorese in this particular colonial period. The compromise between missionaries and the colonial administration is a preliminary condition explicitly acknowledged by Rodrigues.[13] In the preface of the book, Father Rodrigues affirms his pledge toward the "Lusiad Empire" and his complicity with colonial government (Rodrigues 1962: 9). The action he developed and describes in the book clearly expresses, however, the limits of his own power, and at the same time it points to the idea already established that in many instances "in Timor-Leste colonial mechanisms were actually appropriated by the natives' strategies of power" (Roque 2011: 9).

Evidence suggests that Portuguese missionaries could take part in the destruction of local sacred objects deemed *lulik* during the colonial period (Hicks 2008; Rosa, this volume). However, at least in the specific regional context and during the historical period under examination here, the destruction of religious objects in Lautem was not effective (cf. Viegas 2017).[14] In his book, Rodrigues refers to it only once, apropos some *helura* objects he came across. In a single paragraph, he claims he was once called by the locals "to come and burn the *teis* of a village where everybody was already Christian" (Rodrigues 1962: 158). His words about *helura*, however, indicate an equivocation. He mentions that when he became aware of the specific name *helura*, he concluded that he had been in contact with such objects for a long time without knowing what they were, "believing them to be *ex-votos* offered to the *teis*" (Rodrigues 1962: 158). This is because the objects had been mostly brought by Timorese who he considered had converted to Catholicism in order to be blessed: "A widow who had baptized her daughter brought me some earrings to be blessed. When I asked what that was, she said: '*Helura*, sir'" (Rodrigues 1962: 158–59). In fact, in the Fataluku-Portuguese dictionary compiled by Father Nacher, which is greatly indebted to information gathered in the 1950s by Father Rodrigues and by Brother Ribeiro, *helura* is translated as "familiar *tei* (idol); a sacred object; religious image, corresponding to the Tetum *lulik*" (Nacher 2012: 167). However, our field research indicates that the destruction of *helura*, where it took place, may have constituted a rite of separation, resolving dubious situations regarding the true ownership of the objects in question, which is still an issue in some families in Lautem.

According to Maria Olimpia Lameiras-Campagnolo, *helura* are, among the Fataluku, objects that materialize the ancestors who were killed in war (Lameiras-Campagnolo 1975: 55). Our interlocutors told us that *helura* are objects received by a family as compensation for the murder of one of its members. As such, objects of this kind should not circulate indiscriminately, possibly passing through the "wrong" hands, that is, among those who may not have legitimate rights of possession. We heard different versions of situations where a person wanted to get rid of such objects. Improper handling of them might cause harm to their possessors. In this vein, the priest's destruction of these specific objects may have been a kind of rite of separation that could solve ambivalent situations. For Fataluku-speaking people, *helura* were objects with ambivalent meaning that were dangerous if they fell into the wrong hands. For the missionaries, who perceived them under a wide category of the "native sacred" (*tei/lulik*), these objects were not "true" *sacra* but belonged rather to the category of the fetish. Destroying them was a sign of the missionaries' success in eradicating false beliefs held by the natives, thus bringing them into the true religion. However, as shown earlier, success of the missionaries was in this case misleading, if seen from the Fatalukus' point of view. For them, delivering *helura* to the priests was in some cases a way of getting rid of dangerous objects. Of course, regarding the temporal limitation of the data we are using here, we suspect that relationships allowing for equivocal compatibilities between the priests and the natives were only possible in this particular period and region. As is well established by now, the influence of the central colonial administration over local authorities in Lautem was only extended slowly over the twentieth century (Feijó 2016a, 2016b). Even then, the colonial rulers had to deal with native hierarchical structures.

As we have already showed, Father Rodrigues's book often refers to situations in which the missionary turned a blind eye to the customary practices of the king's family. Simultaneously, the king's attempts to limit the influence of the missionary are also implicit in the book's descriptions of events. For instance, when Father Rodrigues describes the announcement of the death of the king's grandson, he claims that word was given to the king that the funeral could not be performed in the customary manner "because the missionary does not want (it)," but that the king had retorted, "Let the missionary stay at home and allow us to bury our dead the way we want" (Rodrigues 1962: 150). At the same time, the king was very worried because the missionaries "were teaching things he could not at all agree with" (Rodrigues 1962: 128–29).

All through the book we find episodes where the king is able to maintain his authority. In many instances, the king "asks for permission" (*pede licença*) from the missionary to perform certain practices, namely those he suspects are not favorably viewed by the missionary. In this regard, a detailed description of events surrounding a marriage is particularly illuminating. The account of the occasion starts with the description of a visit Father Rodrigues received from the father and other relatives of a girl, who was a student of his in religious education, to "ask for permission" for her to marry one of the king's sons. The priest reports that he received the visitors in the mission with politeness and calm and explained to them that marriage was not possible under the circumstances, given that the groom had not been baptized. Father Rodrigues subsequently states that he was utterly convinced he had settled the matter and that his prohibition would be obeyed. Later on, however, much to his surprise and dismay, he learned that the girl had married the king's son. The contours of the process are described thus: the prohibition he had imposed generated heated protests from both families, including the king, who is supposed to have reacted with these words: "Let the missionary stay home in Fuiloro and allow us to marry our children the way we know how." The bride's father's sister asked, "Why don't we go ahead with the marriage without letting the missionary know about it?" Acting upon this suggestion, which pleased the king, they conducted the process in "the utmost secrecy in order for the missionary not to see and, once again, ruin their plans" (Rodrigues, 1962: 141).

In the description of the sequence of events in the book, the strength of the native hierarchy is apparent. The idea of formally "asking for permission" often appears, thus, not less in the case of the king himself, more as a gesture of respect than as a real solicitation of consent. When the king asked for permission, he was simply showing proper deference, not the possibility of actually submitting to an order. The missionary in some cases took such expressions as real requests for authorization to perform certain acts or customary practices. In other cases, the missionary himself entered into negotiations between respect and obedience. This happened, for instance, in the case of the funeral of the king's grandson, which was partly witnessed and ritually assisted by the missionary. Father Rodrigues acknowledges his own limits in forcing the natives to obey him. He mentions, for instance, that he attempted to block the way to have material goods—like rice or personal objects—offered to the deceased, "because the soul does not need such things" (Rodrigues 1962: 153). But a woman intervened in these terms:

> – "Poor little thing (*coitadinho*)! . . . If he is hungry, what will he eat? . . ."
> And others joined in:
> – "How will he be protected against cold?
> – "How can he appear before his relatives barehanded? . . ."
> (Rodrigues 1962: 153)

In reality, Rodrigues adds, "taking advantage of the fact that I was chatting with his father—and maybe he was talking to me with this purpose in mind—they brought to the grave a coin, a bit of cloth, boiled rice, tobacco and other little things" (Rodrigues 1962: 154). The missionary describes his own attitude as a tacit acknowledgment of the limits of his position of authority by claiming, "I pretended not to see what was happening, as the family and most of its relatives were pagans, and I did not wish, in a situation like this one, to hurt their feelings" (Rodrigues 1962: 154).

Asking for permission (*pedir licença*) may have thus been considered by the king, in many instances, as an act of respect and not a request for authorization—a notion consistent with the Timorese ideology of hierarchy. From the missionary point of view, they were at first sight actual pleas for authorization, whereas for local leaders the missionaries' presence entailed dealing with a colonial authority that called for an extension of the native system of respect and deference to another ruler.

Conclusion

The present essay departs from postcolonial approaches that look at colonial administrators and missionaries as entities with unquestionable power, underestimating, as Pina-Cabral puts it, that "colonial encounters, violent as they may have been, were inscribed in local visions of the world, opening a path, with the passing of time, to new negotiations of self-respect and self-determination" (Pina-Cabral 2010: 11). In this vein, our argument is also consistent with what Sahlins (1981) called "structures of conjunction" highlighted for the Timorese territory by Elizabeth Traube's interpretation of the integration of foreigners into native worldviews, where the Timorese "have not passively submitted to colonial domination" exactly because "they have endeavoured actively and creatively to make sense of their colonial situation by drawing upon pre-existing symbolic categories" (Traube 1986: 52).

We have shown that, in the period during which the mission of Fuiloro was being established in Lautem, new and contingent cohabitations have been raised, where negotiations and tensions emerged both at the level of the meaning of material icons pertaining to indigenous religious life—the funerary post hung with sacrificed buffalo skulls—and Christian icons, such as the Christian cross. On the one hand, natives preserved the significance of the funerary post as a way of helping the deceased to join the other dead relatives, while the priests upheld the significance of the Christian cross as a means for the deceased to attain eternal salvation. On the other hand, the priest considered the posts and buffalo sacrifices as part of native family life, thus making them compatible with Christian social values, while natives considered the cross another spiritually charged device that could facilitate the journey of the deceased to meet his ancestors. This is what inscribes these relationships in a scheme of equivocal compatibilities.

The recognition that misunderstandings and equivocations are important elements in intercultural confrontations is not new, of course. Janet Hoskins for instance, when analyzing how Protestant and Catholic missionaries approached the Sumbanese, acknowledges that "when the dialogue began, each side saw the encounter in fundamentally different ways" (1997: 275–76). Likewise, we argued that parallel coexistence describes tense relationships between different religious worldviews, aligning ourselves with similar current views on the subject in Timor-Leste (e.g. Carey 2003; Loch 2009; Grenfell 2012; Boarccaech 2013). Among these, Loch (2009, 2011) underlines that the people he met in Baucau present themselves not as hybrid subjects; they instead assume an "omnipresent coexistence" of different practices—Catholic and traditional. He specifically observes that this omnipresent coexistence of tradition, modernity, and Catholicism is mirrored in the fact that "modern constructed graveyards may be decorated by traditional buffalo horns and topped by a Catholic cross," just as a postconflict reconciliation ceremony supported by the United Nations could be organized according to modern, international patterns, at the same time as it practically consisted of chewing betel nuts in a traditional manner for reconciling actors, accompanied by Catholic praying (Loch 2009: 97). Castro (2012) argues that syncretism is not the best way to conceptualize "religious" historicity in

Timor-Leste. Rather, "it would be better understood as the appropriation of elements strange to one given belief's system by another one, transposing its meaning" (Castro, 2012: 90). Alessandro Boarccaech similarly argues with ethnographic support that the identification of the Humaili of Atauro with Catholicism should be envisaged, specifically in the case of relationships with ancestors, as "practices and beliefs" that are placed "side by side" (Boarccaech, 2013: 188–90, 218). As Grenfell asserts, even if Catholic and customary funerary rites are often ritually combined, "the two worlds that are being brought together should be treated as non-syncretic and as answering to distinct sets of beliefs" (Grenfell 2015: 25).

In sum, the argument developed here highlights that contemporary forms of social and cultural life, namely those related to the sacrifice of buffalos and the relationships of the living to ancestors by hanging buffalo skulls on the funerary posts, may be viewed as long-lasting cohabitations of different kinds. The tension between respect and obedience in colonial order is central to understand how this cohabitation becomes possible. These cohabitations, namely between Fataluku funerary posts and Christian crosses—placed side by side, not replacing one another—should then be considered as historical meaningful facts in contemporary discussions on customary resilience in Timor-Leste. By paying attention to dynamics of ambiguous and ambivalent conjugation between Timorese practices and those of the missionaries between 1945 and 1957, this chapter contributes to historicizing contemporary ethnography, allowing us to consider resilience and the maintenance of customary practices regarding funerals as part of a long-term historical process where politics, as well as contextualized social and cultural interactions, installed structures of cohabitation. The post and the cross can be seen as an index of that structure, where foreign worldviews are partially integrated but also kept side by side, in parallel, contributing to one among many multilayered complexities of sociocultural life in contemporary Timor-Leste.

Acknowledgments

The final version of this chapter benefited from comments on former draft versions from various colleagues and friends. We thank João de Pina-Cabral and David Hicks for their comments on a first Portuguese version authored by Viegas in May 2014. Subsequent fieldwork periods in Lautem helped to address many of the issues that were still fragile by then. For that fieldwork research, we are most indebted to

Justino Valentim (*in memoriam*), dearest friend who, without knowing, was already seriously ill when he came with us to visit the descendants of the king of Nari in Laiara in 2014. Justino Valentim sadly died in November 2014. We also thank the family of the king of Nari, several former students of the Fuiloro mission, and two Salesian missionaries whom we interviewed. Archival research in Dili in 2016 was only possible through the generous encouragement and support of Dionisio Babo Soares, the minister in charge of the National Archive, the solicitous disposition of its director, and the concourse of the technical adviser Dra Cristina Prata. We are especially thankful for the input and various suggestions given by both organizers of this book Ricardo Roque and Elizabeth Traube on a second English version of the original article. These were crucial to the final revision of the argument. None of our generous readers are of course responsible for any of the fragilities of this essay.

Susana de Matos Viegas is an anthropologist and a research fellow at the Institute of Social Sciences of the University of Lisbon. She conducted fieldwork in Brazil (a total of eighteen months in 1997–1998 and 2004–2005) and Timor-Leste (a total of eight months in 2012) with research grants from the National Ministry of Science (Portugal), Brazilian Ministry of Science (PRONEX), and Brazilian Ministry of Justice (FUNAI). Her research focuses on the study of personhood, kinship, place and territorial belonging, indigenous transformations, and historicity both among Amerindian Peoples of Lowland South America and since 2012 also among the Fataluku-speaking people in Timor-Leste. Recent publications include the edited volume (with Rui Graça Feijó) *Transformations in Independent Timor-Leste: Dynamics of Social and Cultural Cohabitations* (2017).

Rui Graça Feijó (DPhil Oxford, 1984) is a researcher at the Centre for Social Studies—CES/University of Coimbra, and integrated researcher at the Institute for Contemporary History—IHC/Nova University of Lisbon. He has taught at the University of Porto, Portuguese Open University, the Catholic University, and the National University of Timor-Leste. Over the last fifteen years, his interest in East Timorese society, culture, and politics has been a dominant part of his academic life. He has published widely on naming practices, the politics of the nation, and the significance of death and associated cultural practices in Timor-Leste. He is also interested in photography. He is the author of *Dynamics of Democracy in Independent Timor-Leste* (2016), editor of

Timor-Leste: Colonialismo, Descolonização, Lusutopia (2016), and coeditor (with Susana de Matos Viegas) of *Transformations in Independent Timor-Leste* (2017).

Notes

1. This chapter results from a research project carried out in Timor-Leste, supported by the Portuguese agency for science and technology, Fundação para a Ciência e Tecnologia, and titled "Co-habitations: Dynamics of Power in Lautem (Timor-Leste)" (FCT-PTDC/CS-ANT/118150/2010). We have completed eight months of fieldwork in Lautem, split in four periods in 2012, 2013, 2014, and 2016.
2. A kind of palm wine.
3. The conversation took place in Fataluku, and it was mediated by direct translation provided by Justino Valentim. A more detailed translation was provided later by Sabina Fonseca based on tape records of the interview.
4. According to different sources, some "itinerant missionaries" had toured the country in 1918 and settled in Iliomar, more than two hours on horseback from Fuiloro. However, those priests, fearful of the bellicose attitude of the locals, soon abandoned the region, prophesying, "These are evil and wild people, and they will be the last to come under Christianity" (Rodrigues 1962: 50; Bouza 2012: 53).
5. The mission of Fuiloro is not yet included in a chart dated 1949 and quoted by Alexandre Fernandes (2014: 24).
6. Father Alfonso Nacher, who arrived in 1955, wrote that even by then "the missionaries lived in poverty and in bad conditions, as rats ran all over the place at night, and when the rain came they had to protect their beds with umbrellas" (Nacher 1975 in Bouza 2012: 53). They settled in an abandoned Japanese military barrack, having converted some of the military tools, such as tanks, into agrarian machinery; they also used these tools as piping and for transportation (cf. Nacher 1975 in Bouza 2012: 162; see also Gunter 2015).
7. Governor Celestino da Silva is known in Lautem by his nickname Savarika (scorpio), and his tenure (1894–1908) is identified as a period during which resettlements were frequent and the territorial reordering of the region very expressive, including bringing mountainous people down to the plains. We have been able to acknowledge several such trajectories, which McWilliam also describes for the Tutuala *suku*, reporting that the village of Vero was moved from the Vero river valley in the Paicao Mountain, where a village existed before the time of Governor Celestino da Silva, to the foot of the mountain (McWilliam 2006: 263–66; 2012: 160).
8. In fieldwork carried out in this region after 2012, we have been able to confirm this information through a reconstruction of family histories with a special emphasis on territorial dislocations.

9. In 2013 we met Justino, who promised to lead us to Nari if ever we returned outside the rainy season. In 2016 we returned to Lautem to discover he had passed away a few weeks after our departure. We tried to enlist the support of his descendants to plan a trip up to Nari, and that was the context for our meeting with the six men of Laiara. However, after a lengthy debate, they decided the conditions were not met for them to authorize our venture. For this reason, we could not experience the trail up to Nari and visit the location.

10. One full chapter of the book is about a specific funeral that must have happened in the nineteenth century and is a relevant historical document. It also helps to understand how missionaries were capable of acknowledging the religious atmosphere surrounding Fataluku funerary rituals; they mention the funerary posts as a "staircase," which is deemed to facilitate the journey of the deceased to the world of his ancestors (see Rodrigues 1962: 170). The literal figuration of the staircase and the idea that the buffalo skulls and their enchainment indicate the ascension of the deceased so that he may join his previously gone relatives is very important to the contemporary narratives and is a key ethnographic comparative issue to be taken into account on the journeys of the afterlife in many different contexts in Timor-Leste (e.g. Traube 1980, 1986: 201; Hicks 2004; Bovensiepen 2014a; Sousa 2010: 213; Viegas 2013; Viegas and Feijó 2018).

11. This issue on *tei* and *lulik* would warrant detailed analysis that is beyond the scope of this chapter. However, see Pannell (2006) Hicks (2008) and Bovensiepen (2014b).

12. On Timorese naming practices and "Christian" and "Portuguese" names, see Feijó (2008).

13. See also Roque (2012) on the importance of looking more closely to the relationship between missionaries and the colonial administration in Timor.

14. In this light, we have to consider Frederico Rosa's (2012) approach to the role and the practices of the Fuiloro missionaries among the Fataluku as thinly grounded, stemming from the basic ethnographic error of assuming there were native Fataluku "sacred houses" in Lautem, which the literature, namely Lameiras-Campagnolo (1972), shows to be a mistaken assumption.

References

Archival Sources

Arquivo Nacional de Timor-Leste (ANTL) Dili.

Relatório das obras em estudo e execução na area desta circumscrição durante o período de um de Janeiro a trinta de Setembro do corrente ano. Colónia de Timor. Circumscrição administrativa de Lautem. 4 October 1947. Signed by Olimpio Augusto Gonçalves. ANTL, Administração Portuguesa em Timor. Concelho de Lautem. IP. 23-33 (1939–1975; Box No 894).

Relatório referente ao ano de 1948. Apresentado pelo administrador designado Domingos Mendes Gomes e Cunha. ANTL, Administração Portuguesa em Timor. Concelho de Lautem. IP. 23-33 (1939–1975; Box No 894).

Published Sources

de Andrade, J. J. 1920. "O funeral." *Boletim do Governo Eclesiástico da Diocese de Macau* 200: 288–91.

Boarccaech, A. 2013. *A diferença entre os iguais.* São Paulo: Porto de Ideias.

Bovensiepen, J. 2014a. "Paying for the Dead: On the Politics of Death in Independent Timor-Leste." *Asia Pacific Journal of Anthropology* 15(2): 103–22.

———. 2014b. "Lulik: Taboo, Animism, or Transgressive Sacred? An Exploration of Identity, Morality, and Power in Timor-Leste." *Oceania* 84(2): 121–37.

Bouza, E. L. 2012. "Oleu pitine." In *Léxico Fataluku-Português (P. Alfonso Nácher 1905–1999),* edited by A. F. Castro and E. L. Bouza, 40–77. Díli: Gráfica Pátria.

Carey, P. 2003. "Third-World Colonialism, the *Gerasaun Foun,* and the Birth of a New Nation: Indonesia through East Timor Eyes, 1975–99." *Indonesia* 76: 23–67.

Castro, A. F. 2012. "A Religião em Timor-Leste a partir de uma Perspectiva Histórico-Antropológica." In *Léxico Fataluku-Português (P. Alfonso Nácher 1905–1999),* edited by A. F. Castro and E. L. Bouza, 79–118. Díli: Gráfica Pátria.

Durand, F. 2004. *Catholicisme et Protestantisme dans l'Ile de Timor 1556–2003: Construction d'une Identité Chrétienne et Engagement Politique Contemporain.* Toulouse: Editions Arkuiris/Bangkok: IRASEC.

Fausto, C. 1998 [1992]. "Fragmentos de história e cultura tupinambá: da etnologia como instrumento crítico de conhecimento etno-histórico." In *História dos índios no Brasil,* edited by M. C. da Cunha, 381–96. São Paulo: Companhia das Letras.

Feijó, R. G. 2008. "Língua, nome e identidade numa situação de plurilinguismo concorrencial: o caso de Timor-Leste." *Etnográfica* 12(1): 143–72.

———. 2016a. *Timor-Leste: Colonialismo, Descolonização, Lusutopia.* Porto: Afrontamento

———. 2016b. *The Birth of a Democratic Nation: Dynamics of Democracy in Timor-Leste, 1999–2012.* Amsterdam: Amsterdam University Press.

Fernandes, A. 2014. "Em searas do Timor Português: um estudo sobre as práticas de mediação da Diocese de Díli no período colonial (1949–1973)." Master's thesis, University of Brasilia, Brazil.

Figueiredo, F. 2003. "Timor (1910–1955)." In *História dos Portugueses no Extremo Oriente: Macau e Timor no Período Republicano,* edited by A.H. Oliveira Marques, 519–70. Lisboa: Fundação Oriente.

———. 2004. "Timor: A presença portuguesa (1769–1945)." PhD thesis in history, Universidade do Porto, Porto.

———. 2011a. "Timor na viragem do século XIX para o século XX: tipo de colonização e seus agentes." In *Timor: Missões Científicas e Antropologia Colonial. Actas do Colóquio.* Lisboa: IICT/ICS-UL, edited by V. R. Marques, A. C. Roque, and R. Roque, digital edition [DVD], retrieved April 2014 from http://www.historyanthropologytimor.org/wp-content/uploads/2012—01/08—FIGUEIREDO_FA.pdf.

———. 2011b. *Timor: A Presença Portuguesa (1769–1945).* Lisboa: Centro de Estudos Históricos, Universidade Nova de Lisboa.

Forman, S. 1980. "Descent, Alliance and Exchange Ideology among the Makassae of East Timor." In *The Flow of Life: Essays on Eastern Indonesia,* edited by J. Fox, 152–77. Cambridge, MA: Harvard University Press.

Fox, J. J. 2000. "Tracing the Path, Recounting the Past: Historical Perspectives on Timor." In *Out of the Ashes: Destruction and Reconstruction of East Timor,* edited by J. J. Fox and Dionisio Babo Soares, 1–29. Adelaide: Crawford House Publishing and C. Hurst & Co.

———. 2011. "The Articulation of Tradition in Timor-Leste." In *Land and Life in Timor-Leste: Ethnographic Essays,* edited by A. McWilliam and E. G. Traube, 241–57. Camberra: ANU Press.

Gomes, F. A. 1972a. *Os Fataluku.* Graduation dissertation. Lisboa: Instituto Superior de Ciências Sociais e Políticas Ultramarinas.

———. 1972b. "Nari." *Geographica* 8(31): 64–74.

Grenfell, D. 2012. "Remembering the Dead from the Customary to the Modern in Timor-Leste." Edited by D. Grenfell (guest editor). *Local-Global: Identity, Security, Community: Traversing Customary Community and Modern Nation-Formation in Timor-Leste* 11: 86–108.

———. 2015. "Of Time and History: The Dead of War, Memory and the National Imaginary in Timor-Leste." *Communication, Politics & Culture* 48(3): 16–28.

Gunter, J. 2015. "Os mortos inquietos e o Império despido. A II Guerra Mundial e as suas consequências em Timor-Leste." In *Timor-Leste: Colonialismo, Descolonização, Lusutopia,* edited by R. G. Feijó, 63–74. Porto: Afrontamento.

Hicks, D. 2004 [1976]. *Tetum Ghosts and Kin: Fertility and Gender in East Timor.* Long Grove, IL: Waveland Press.

———. 2008. "Afterword: Glimpses of Alternatives—the Uma Lulik of East Timor." *Social Analysis* 52(1): 166–80.

Hoskins, J. 1993. *The Play of Time: Kodi Perspectives on Calendars, History, and Exchange.* Berkeley: University of California Press.

Kammen, D. 2015. *Three Centuries of Conflict in East Timor.* New Brunswick, NJ: Rutgers University Press.

Lameiras-Campagnolo, M. O. 1975. *L'habitation des Fatuluku de Lórehe (Timor Portugais).* Paris: Thèse de doctorat de 3ème cycle; Université René Descartes, Sorbonne.

Leach, M. 2017. *Nation-Building and National Identity in Timor-Leste.* New York: Routledge.

Loch, A. 2009. "Nation Building at the Village Level: First the House, Then the Church and Finally a Modern State." In *East-Timor: How to Build a New Nation in Southeast Asia in the 21st Century?*, edited by C. Cabasset-Semedo and F. Durand, 95–104. Bangkok: IRASEC.

Loch, A., and V. Prueller. 2011. "Dealing with Conflicts after the Conflict: European and Indigenous Approaches to Conflict Transformation in East Timor." *Conflict Resolution Quarterly* 28(3): 315–29.

McWilliam, A. 2006. "Fataluku Forest Tenures and the Conis Santana National Park." In *Sharing the Earth, Dividing the Land: Land and Territory in the Austronesian World*, edited by T. Reuter, 253–75. Canberra: ANU Press.

———. 2008. "Fataluku Healing and Cultural Resilience in East Timor." *Ethnos* 73(2): 217–40.

———. 2011a. "Exchange and Resilience in Timor-Leste." *Journal of the Royal Anthropological Institute* 17: 745–63.

———. 2011b. "Fataluku Living Landscapes." In *Land and Life in Timor-Leste: Ethnographic Essays*, edited by A. McWilliam and E. G. Traube, 61–86. Canberra: ANU Press.

———. 2012. "The Unsettling Histories of Ponta Leste." *Property and Social Resilience in Times of Conflict: Land, Custom and Law in East Timor*, edited by D. Fitzpatrick, A. McWilliam, and S. Barnes. Farnham and Burlington: Ashgate: 149–76.

Nacher, A. 2012. "Léxico fataluku-português." In *Léxico Fataluku-Português (P. Alfonso Nácher 1905–1999)*, edited by A. F. Castro and E. L. Bouza, 121–201. Dili: Gráfica Pátria.

Pannell, S. 2006. "Welcome to the Hotel Tutuala: Fataluku Accounts of Going Places in an Immobile World." *Asia Pacific Journal of Anthropology* 7(3): 203–19.

Pélissier, R. 1996. *Timor en guerre: le crocodile et les portugais, 1847–1913*. Orgeval: Ed. Pélissier.

de Pina-Cabral, J. 2002. "Equivocal Compatibilities: Person, Culture and Emotion." *Between China and Europe: Person, Culture and Emotion in Macao*, 105–25. London: Continuum.

———. 2010. "Lusotopia como ecumene." *Revista Brasileira de Ciências Sociais* 25(74): 5–20.

Rodrigues, J. B. 1962. *O Rei de Nári: Histórias, Lendas, Tradições de Timor e Episódios da Vida Missionária*. Lisboa: Agência Geral do Ultramar.

Roque, R. 2010. *Headhunting and Colonialism: Anthropology and the Circulation of Human Skulls in the Portuguese Empire 1870–1930*. New York: Palgrave Macmillan.

———. 2011. "Os Portugueses e os reinos de Timor no século XIX." *Oriente* 20: 91–110.

———. 2012. "Marriage Traps: Colonial Interactions with Indigenous Marriage Ties in East Timor." In *Racism and Ethnic Relations in the Portuguese-Speaking Countries*, edited by F. Bettencourt and A. Pearce, 203–25. London: British Academy.

Roque, R., and K. A. Wagner. 2012. "Introduction: Engaging Colonial Knowledge." In *Engaging Colonial Knowledge: Reading European Archives in World History*, edited by R. Roque and K. Wagner. New York, Palgrave Macmillan: 1–32.

Rosa, F. D. 2012. "Uruvatju e Tjiapu: Genealogias Invisíveis da Etnografia Missionária em Timor-Leste." In *Léxico Fataluku-Português (P. Alfonso Nácher 1905–1999)*, edited by A. F. Castro and E. L. Bouza, 11–40. Díli: Gráfica Pátria.

Sahlins, M. 1981. *Historical Metaphors and Mythical Realities*. Ann Arbor: University of Michigan Press.

de Sousa, L. M. G. 2010. *An tia: partilha ritual e organização social entre os Bunak de Lamak Hitu, Bobonaro, Timor-Leste*. PhD diss., Universidade Aberta, Lisboa.

Sylvan, F. 1963. "Como Vive, Morre e Ressuscita o Povo de Timor." In *Actas do Congresso Internacional de Etnografia Promovido pela Câmara Municipal de Santo Tirso*. Vol. 4: *Colóquio de Etnografia Comparada*, 281–85. Santo Tirso: Câmara Municipal de Santo Tirso.

Sweet, D. G. 1994. "Reflections on the Ibero-American Frontier Mission as an Institution in Native American History." In *Where Cultures Meet: Frontiers in Latin American History*, edited by D. Weber and J. M. Rausch, 87–98. Wilmington, DE: SR Books.

Traube, E. G. 1980. "Affines and the Dead: Mambai Rituals of Alliance." *Bijdragen tot de Taal-, Land- en Volkenkunde* 136(1): 90–115.

———. 1986. *Cosmology and Social Life: Ritual Exchange among the Mambai of East Timor*. Chicago: University of Chicago Press.

Valentim, J. "Cailoru." 2014. "Ema Nian naran tuir kultura Fataluku." *Timor Lorosa'e Nippon culture center (TNCC) Pamfletu*. Typescript. Edisaun Jullu 2014.

Viegas, S. de M. 2007. *Terra Calada: os Tupinambá na Mata Atlântica do Sul da Bahia*. Rio de Janeiro & Coimbra: 7Letras/Almedina.

———. 2011. "Três etnografias nas décadas de 1960–1970: os Fataluku." In *Timor: Missões Científicas e Antropologia Colonial*, edited by V. R. Marques, A. C. Roque, and R. Roque. Actas do Colóquio. Lisboa: IICT/ICS-UL, digital edition [DVD].

———. 2017. "*Arapou Cau*: A convivência com os antepassados entre os Fataluku (Timor-Leste)." *Revista Oriente* 25: 28–46.

———. Forthcoming. "Paths to Infinity: Ancestorship, Origin Narratives and Differentiation." In *Routledge Handbook of Contemporary East Timor*, edited by A. McWilliam and M. Leach. New York. Routledge.

Viegas, S. de M., and R. G. Feijó. 2018. "Moving the Dead and Building the Nation: Martyrs in Timor-Leste." In *Death on the Move: Managing Narratives, Silences and Constraints in a Trans-national Perspective*, edited by P. J. Havik, J. Mapril, and C. Saraiva, 245–62. Newcastle upon Tyne: Cambridge Scholars Publishing.

Viegas, S. de M., and R. G. Feijó (eds.). 2017. *Transformations in Independent Timor-Leste: Dynamics of Social and Cultural Cohabitations*. New York: Routledge.

Chapter 7

THE STONES OF AFALOICAI

COLONIAL ARCHAEOLOGY AND
THE AUTHORITY OF ANCIENT OBJECTS

Ricardo Roque and Lúcio Sousa

This chapter explores archaeological knowledge, scientific author-ity, and indigenous power at the crossroads of colonial interactions mediated by East Timorese ancestral objects—ancient stones in par-ticular. It concentrates on a singular event in the colonial past: the exhibition to the Portuguese of ancient sacred heritage from the house of Soko Lai Mau Besi of Afaloicai by their authorized indige-nous keepers. On 30 September 1957, a small group of East Timorese men from a secluded hamlet some miles away arrived ceremoniously at the Baguia *Posto* to meet with the administrator Victor Santa and his guest, Portuguese anthropologist António de Almeida. They had walked for several hours from their mountain village, Bui Bela Ne' La, carefully carrying a set of objects deemed *lulik*, a complex Timorese concept that conveyed the high sacredness, danger, spiritual agencies, and ritual powers with which the objects were endowed. On that day, Almeida (1960: 129–30) later recalled, "it was possible to examine and photograph several objects used in certain ritual ceremonies by *Makai Liliki*, in the role of priest or beneficent wizard [*feiticeiro ben-fazejo*] . . . and by the *Cabo* or assistant [*ajudante*] (*Asúrate* . . .) which the two brought on purpose from Afalicai (or Afaloikai—*Afa* = stone, *Loikai* = name of the men who died there) a hamlet [*povoação*] at the distance of 15 kms, where it was impossible for me to go." These two men, according to Almeida's notes, were named Loi Rubi, "former *suco* chief of Afaloikai [*sic*],"[1] who (according to Almeida) held the function of *Asurate*, and Rui Boro, holder of the title of *Makai Lilik* and who Almeida considered to be the main ritual officer (Almeida 1960: 130).[2] Both men—who Almeida also treated, by analogy with Catholic liturgical roles, as *sacerdotes* or *padres* (priests)—held important indigenous ritual functions associated with the material things that they had brought to display to the Portuguese (figure 7.1).

This chapter traces the history of this event, to reveal how distinct forms of authority—scientific, colonial, and indigenous—were mutually invested in, and extracted from, Timorese displays of *lulik* objects to Portuguese colonial officers and anthropologists. It asks how transits, occlusions, and manipulations of power and knowledge come into being through the mediation of objects in the past, and also how, in the present, such transits may recur through mediation of photographic archives, associated stories, and narrative recollections of those same past objects and events. Back home, based on interviews

Figure 7.1. The ritual authorities of Bui Bela Ne' La at Bagula in 1957. Photo by Victor Santa. IICT Photography Collection, INV. ULISBOA-IICT-MAT26662. Reproduced by kind permission of the authorities of MUHNAC/ ULisboa.

he conducted and direct inspection of *lulik* stones on that occasion, Almeida published an archaeological article in which he classified the "prehistoric past" of the East Timorese of the Matebian region as "Neolithic." Yet, beyond these archaeological speculations, we argue, the field encounter itself became a theater for the performance of contrasting kinds of symbolic power. Through contact with sacred objects, the Portuguese scientist envisaged archaeological authority and the creation of an ethnogenic narrative about Timor's prehistoric past. Conversely, the Timorese foresaw in that momentous—though unusual—display of sacred objects to foreigners an exemplary instantiation of the alternative and higher authority of the ritual powers of Afaloicai. Indigenous ceremonial subordination to the Portuguese authority coexisted with assertions of superior insider powers and knowledge, simultaneously revealed to and hidden from the colonial outsiders. In local Timorese conceptions, we argue, the stones displayed to Almeida, alongside flags and guns, were deemed not simply *lulik* but also regalia of rule, designated as *rota*—that is, powerful tokens of ritual and sociopolitical authority that structured both the inner fertility of land and the order of social status and ruling hierarchies within the realm. Accordingly, with regard to the objects' special condition in the event, it was not just sacred prohibition they expressed; it was also a kind of sociopolitical potency contained in their quality as an assemblage of companion *rotas*.

We returned to Baguia, Afaloicai, and Bui Bela Ne' La in 2012 and 2013 to explore the objects, their indigenous stories, and their colonial traces.[3] Inspired by a wealth of stimulating scholarship on (colonial) photo-elicitation (e.g. Bell 2006; Geismar and Herle 2010; Buckley 2014), we followed the track left to us by Almeida's published photographs (1960) and by his ethnographic record held today in the Portuguese archives. The latter worked as a methodological device to elicit conversations about the past and encourage our interlocutors to offer their own understandings of the past colonial encounter, and about the objects and their historical paths before, during, and after 1957. Thus crossing archival research in Portugal and fieldwork in East Timor, the chapter offers an analytical narrative of the Portuguese-Timorese mutual and contrasting assertions, appropriations, and misrecognitions of knowledge and power through the mediation of contact with ancient stones.

The chapter begins with an exploration of the 1957 encounter based on António de Almeida's paper records. We first show how Almeida's interests in prehistoric and ethnogenic archaeology, as well as his involvement in the networks and authority of Portuguese colonial administration, precipitated the encounter at Baguia. The display of sacred objects to the self-styled archaeologist occurred as a colonial ceremonial interaction, framed within obligations acknowledged as customary by the Timorese to pay respect in the presence of Portuguese government officials. Almeida used his complicity with the colonial administration to extract "archaeological evidence" that allowed him to build up a capital of scientific authority on the prehistory of Timor. Based on purely morphological analysis, he would classify the stones as "Neolithic" migrant materials from outside Timor. Yet Almeida's work was also a singular, and somewhat eccentric, blend of archaeology and ethnography. His ethnographic record emphasized the functional nature of the stones in agricultural rites. Timorese agency in the encounter, however, explains Almeida's failed attempts at obtaining knowledge about the historical past and origins of the stones, and at acquiring the objects themselves. Finally, the chapter confronts Almeida's speculations on the foreign origins of the stones with contemporary Timorese oral accounts about the ancient stones' identities and paths that concern their past and present significance as autochthonous tokens of power. Conceived of as *rotas*, the (now, apparently, missing) stones of Afaloicai are understood as agents of hierarchizing authority that was bestowed upon Bui Bela Ne' La, Afaloicai by the Timorese realm of Luca. The stones apparently embodied the potency of an insider kind of power whose origins were, nevertheless, external to Afaloicai but internal to Timor. During our field visits, we were confronted with vivid recollections of the ancient objects and of the Timorese protagonists of 1957 as holders of power and authority. We realized, however, that the stones of Afaloicai were no longer in the possession of their owners. They were lost in the waves of violence that wiped out the houses of Bui Bela Ne' La in 1959 and 1975. Lost, missing, still wandering, or perhaps just invisible, however, their hidden agencies seem very much alive in East Timorese stories and in local attachments to photos and memories of the encounter of 1957.

The Prehistoric Archaeology of Timorese *Lulik* Objects

"Afaloicai 15 km from Baguia," he wrote by hand in his "Prehistory" (*Pré-história*) field notebook, "there is a *lulik* house with several things" (Almeida 1957). In late September 1957, Portuguese physical anthropologist António de Almeida—an influential figure of the Estado Novo colonial sciences and by then the all-powerful director of the Center of Overseas Ethnology Studies—made a change in his itinerary to visit the administrative post of Baguia on the foot-hill of Mount Matebian. The official purpose of Almeida's field trip, sponsored by the center and approved by the Portuguese minister of overseas, was to collect fresh blood samples in order to determine the distribution, across different East Timorese "ethnic groups," of the "Rh blood-group type"—at the time widely considered to be a critical racial marker. The trip was presented as a follow-up to his first (much larger and opulent) fieldwork trip, as leader of the "Timor Anthro-pological Mission" of 1953–54. Almeida collected large numbers of blood-group samples with the support of the local colonial admin-istration. However, he did not come to Baguia to measure and take blood from Timorese bodies. He came with the intention of examining some objects of archaeological interest—a set of *lulik* stones, in partic-ular, that the Portuguese suspected were "prehistoric." At Baguia, in other words, Almeida envisioned a meeting with Timor's Stone Age. He aimed at expanding his archaeological inquiries into the deep hu-man past of "Portuguese Timor" into the mysterious possessions of Timorese sacred houses. Indeed as Almeida (1960) later explained in the overtly archaeological paper that resulted from this trip—titled *Contribuição para o Estudo do Neolítico de Timor Português* (Contribution to the Study of the Neolithic in Portuguese Timor), originally read before the Lisbon Academy of Sciences in 1959 and published in the society's memoirs in the following year—his journey to Baguia had a clear and prearranged objective: the observation of stone artifacts as archaeological evidence.

Surveying the Prehistoric Past of "Portuguese Timor"

Almeida prefigured his encounter with *lulik* objects, still in ritual use and charged with powerful vernacular meanings, as an archae-ological inquiry into the ancient prehistoric past. In the early and mid-twentieth century, similar ideas concerning the persistence of the prehistoric past into the present, as revealed by the continuing use of stone tools by contemporary indigenous people, were common among colonial archaeologists working on Indonesia (Bloembergen and Eickhoff 2015). They also bear the mark of the temporal poli-tics of anthropological discourse (Fabian 1983). Specifically in the context of Almeida's type of colonial race science, "archaeology in general, and specially prehistory" was understood (also in the wake of nineteenth-century understandings of "prehistoric archaeology and anthropology" as a connected disciplinary whole) as complementary to physical anthropological studies about "native tribes." Archaeology provided, in the words of Almeida's mentor, the Portuguese physical anthropologist António Mendes Correia, "irreplaceable ground for the knowledge of the ethnic origins and evolution of peoples, and is an important element in the evaluation of the role of the latter in humankind" (Correia 1941). Archaeology was also not negligible in the Portuguese scholars' anxiety to attain visibility in international scientific circles (Poloni 2012, 2017). The first decades of the twentieth century, following the discoveries of early evidence of *Homo erectus* at Java in the 1890s, were times of enthusiasm in the archaeological study of island Southeast Asia. There was rising interest in stone tools and human fossil finds that would allow for either a more nuanced view of ancient humanity's geographical distribution or an even deeper historical horizon of human time in the region. Human remains and chipped stones, in particular, were important materials in this knowledge quest; accordingly, they were crucial to the making of scholarly authority as regards the prehistoric past of the Indonesian archipelago. In what concerned East Timor, archaeological scholarship by the 1950s was signaled by the pioneering work of Swiss anthropologists Alfred Bühler and Fritz Sarasin based on excavations at—precisely— the hilly outskirts of Baguia. In 1935, Alfred Bühler excavated one cave site near Baguia, on the slopes of Mount Matebian, and there he found solid evidence of ancient human occupation at the lowest stratigraphical levels: pottery, stone tools, bones of domestic animals. In the resulting works, in collaboration with Sarasin in 1936, the authors argued for the existence in East Timor of a "Neolithic culture" introduced by ancient Papuan and Melanesian settlers, of whom the present-day peoples of Matebian were the descendants. Bühler and Sarasin established that the earliest human settlement on the island dated from the Neolithic period, but they found no evidence of earlier human presence.

Portuguese anthropologists in Timor in the 1950s were aware of this international debate and seemed eager to leave their mark. In this context, chipped stones had become critical materials upon which to ground ambitious claims for scientific authority concerning the deep prehistoric past of East Timor. From the Timor Anthropological Mission headed by Almeida, Mendes Correia also expected evidence for his hypothesis concerning the deep ethnogenic antiquity of Timor Island as a primordial place of "anthropogenetic mutation," an independent origin center of human evolution (Correia 1944). Accordingly, stone artifacts were actively procured from the outset to bear proof of Correia's ethnogenic theories while also intervening in the international debate. In August 1953, in the company of Mendes Correia and Ruy Cinatti, Almeida collected a set of "lithic artifacts" on the surface of the Laga lagoon of Gasse-Liu (on the western coastal region opposite to the Matebian). In haste, Almeida declared in November that same year at the Pacific Sciences Congress in Manila that the stone tools were first evidence of the earliest known human occupation in Timor, dating back to the Upper Palaeolithic, and expressed hope "that further findings will deepen the knowledge [*sic*] here expressed" (Almeida 1954: 351). Going beyond Bühler and Sarasin, then, Almeida et al. advanced a new Palaeolithic classification of a previously unimagined antiquity for humans in East Timor. In 1953 at Manila, this hypothesis was received with curiosity, but principally with strong skepticism by the major archaeological authorities present at the meeting, such as Von Koenigswald, who never accepted the classificatory conclusions of the Portuguese even after he perused the lithic materials directly in Lisbon, decades later (Almeida 1954; Zbyszewski, Neto, and Castro-Almeida 1985–86: 24). In spite of international skepticism (except perhaps for the French archaeologist Henri Breuil) Almeida would never abandon his early hypothesis of a Paleolithic dating for human occupation in Timor (see Poloni 2012; Correia, Almeida, França 1956; Almeida and Zbyszewski 1967).

Although controversially classified as Paleolithic, Almeida's first findings of chipped stones at Laga promised him recognition in a scientific field in which, ultimately, he was no expert. He henceforth looked upon Laga and the surrounding area as a relevant "archaeological station" where further lithic discoveries were expected. In 1957 he went back for further "prospections," wandering on the Laga beaches; but he found nothing, no "exemplars" "characteristic of the High Palaeolithic, Mesolithic, Neolithic, or even Bronze and Iron Ages" (Almeida 1960: 128). His disappointment at Laga was compensated by news of "native" objects of interest awaiting his inspection in the interior, at Baguia—the already well-known location where, as mentioned above, Bühler and Sarasin had "discovered" East Timor's Neolithic Age. Indeed, Almeida understood his trip to Baguia—which he would refer to as the "Baguia station"—also as a *return* to an acknowledged archaeological location where he may have prefigured new discoveries that could match the Swiss.[4] But, surprisingly, in contrast with Bühler, his archaeological fieldwork at Baguia would involve neither ground prospections nor cave site excavations. He was a medical doctor and physical anthropologist by training, not a professional archaeologist. His field archaeology has been described as intuitive, chance-based, and unreliable by then-prevailing international stan-

dards.[5] Stone tools were gathered on the surface, open-ground excavations were left almost entirely to the judgment of unskilled workers
(he left excavation work entirely to his subordinate technicians and to
Timorese laborers). Such fieldwork offered little or no subsidiary evidence (geological, zoological, and so forth) that could help *dating*, with
some precision, the chronological age of the lithic artifacts—a critical
and sensitive issue in archaeological sciences. His fieldwork in Baguia,
however, stands out as particularly extravagant. To base speculations
on prehistory upon objects deemed ancient by the indigenous peoples was a questionable method that even his mentor, Mendes Correia
(1944: 134), criticized as unreliable and amateur. "Without any stra-
tigraphy and without indication of coexisting fauna or of the general
conditions of the find," Correia remarked, "they could well come from
an *uma lulic*, from a *pomali*, from a sacred ground, archive or museum
of the most unpredictable relics."[6]

Indifferent to such predictable methodological objections (never
acknowledged in his own writings), Almeida saw his study of *lulik*
heirlooms as a work of intrinsic archaeological worth. And yet Almeida's archaeology at Mount Matebian was based on interpersonal
encounters rather than excavations—it became effectively ethnographical. Almeida treated sacred objects in use in the Timorese colonial present as scientific evidence of human activity in the prehistoric
Timorese past. His represented encounter with "Timorese prehistory"
was grounded in a colonial ethnographic interaction with indigenous
authorities and their sacred possessions. We now turn our attention
to the kind of knowledge generated in this encounter and to how it
was entailed in the intercultural politics of colonial interactions in
East Timor.

Ethnographic Records in Colonial Encounters
with Ancestral Objects

Almeida's fieldwork was embedded in the institutional networks and
authority of the Portuguese colonial government in Timor. At Baguia, it was probably the head administrator of the Baguia Post, Victor
Santa, who orchestrated the encounter. Santa was one of Almeida's
favorite colonial men and field assistants in Timor. Almeida's notes
are not explicit about Santa's role, but he does acknowledge him as
author of the photographs of the sacred objects (Almeida 1976: 30).
Prior to the events, Santa was already acquainted with the value that
Almeida attributed to stones as prehistoric evidence. In November

1953, Santa had participated actively in the excavations in the search of Stone Age tools at the Laga lagoon. He then used his authority as post administrator of Laga to recruit natives as laboratory subjects and as laborers for the excavations. Similarly, in 1957 he used his administrator's authority to order the objects to be taken from the *lulik* house at Bui Bela Ne' La and brought to the Baguia administrative headquarters to be presented especially to the anthropologist. The archaeological encounter was thus a colonial interaction, at the core of which was a set of power-charged objects.

The encounter took place at the *Posto*, an old fortified building in the middle of Baguia town. The physical location (the local seat of Portuguese government), the social standing of the participants, and, finally, the fact that the encounter concerned the display of powerful indigenous sacred objects suggest that the interaction was invested with the sort of complex ceremonialism with which Timorese dealt with people, things, and situations that embodied higher intangible powers—including, ordinarily, Portuguese *malae* (foreigners) who represented the Dili government. In Timor, public colonial encounters between persons of status—often involving the display of *lulik* tokens of power in the presence of Portuguese representatives—were inherently ceremonial and thus inherently political (Roque 2010, 2012). The correct manifestation of authority through proper handling and visibility of things (and of their associated knowledge) was a paramount and delicate issue in these situations. Accordingly, the Baguia encounter can be understood as an event that participated in the type of codified ceremonial occasions mediated by the display of objects and insignia of power, through which power, status, and authority were customarily communicated, constituted, and regulated across the colonial divide. The anthropologist's ascendancy as regards the administrator, the administrator's position in the local chains of command that linked the Portuguese to the Timorese, and the general juxtaposition with outsider/colonial power help explain the Baguia encounter. The relative and partial imbrication of Timorese powers with the realm of Portuguese authority is critical to understanding the events that followed. Yet, although the occasion came as a response to a colonial command, indigenous agency was paramount. The mobility and display of the sacred objects depended heavily on the intentional cooperation of East Timorese ritual keepers, and this colonial interaction, as we will see, was likely prone to mutual manipulations. Importantly, then, this was an encounter in which the objects, not the persons, were the focus of attention. The visibility of objects and the transaction of knowledge about them was similarly part of this theatrical complex of authority. For, the Timorese keepers came with certain stories to tell about their powers.

We observed earlier that Almeida's prehistoric archaeology was also ethnographical. Indeed his field notes and the 1960 article contain a wealth of information about the ethnographic *present* of the same objects that Almeida, paradoxically, perceived to be but mere vestiges of a nebulous prehistoric Neolithic *past*.

Stone Stories

Almeida was impressed by the curatorial gestures of safekeeping and extreme care with which the two Timorese treated the objects in his presence. He took note of all objects presented, comprising the following materials:

> Two naturally or artificially polished stones, one rectilinear and the other angular; one stone ball with rough surface; one old Portuguese flag with the royal shield; two wooden statues, representing mother and child; one old flint stone rifle; two wood sticks; one sword; one stick with a horse mane; and two wood whistles. (1960: 130)

Almeida considered the ensemble under his eyes as a coherent "magic-religious apparatus" (*arsenal mágico-religioso*), a term that placed functional and instrumental emphasis on the ritualistic character of the objects. From another lens, social anthropologists since the 1960s have called attention to the great social, political, and symbolic importance of sacred possessions in Timorese societies. Ordinarily classified after the disseminated Tetum term *lulik* and usually kept out of sight in special places (so-called *lulik* houses), these ensembles are critical to social life, power, and identity across East Timor. Almeida, then, was in the presence of a lineage, house, or community's "ancestral legacy," imbued with certain special powers and spiritual potencies. The special treatment of the objects was a strong indicator of their value. The stones, the whistles, and the flag were kept inside palm leaf baskets, and the baskets were carried in tightly closed bags on a wooden tray (1960: 130). Almeida (1957) understood this care as a sign of the objects' sacred condition—the stones above all: "excessive care in handling the stone objects and putting them back into [rudimentary] baskets." "All these materials are blackened or falling apart," he remarked in the 1960 article, "the priest and the assistant touch, wrap up, and preserve the flag and the sculptures' dresses, as well as the stone objects, carefully in a large special house, *lulik*, sacred (known as *Sokolai Mau Bési*, the name of the female statue . . ." (1960:

130). In fact, Almeida's observations went beyond the list above; they included attention to the materiality of the items and to the social and cultural practices that surrounded them. Based on information given by his Timorese interlocutors, he took a number of notes concerning the ritual use and the social functions associated with the objects.

The fact that the objects were originally stored in a *lulik* house was the ultimate indicator of their special powers and sacred condition. Almeida was informed that similar caring procedures were employed in the mountain village, inside the sacred house. Almeida had been unable to travel to Afaloicai to see the house, allegedly due to the difficulties of travel and the distance from Baguia. From information received at Baguia, however, he made various extrapolations about the house's architecture and construction; rules of access—"Every person can enter it," he declared, "through a staircase, blocking the access to domestic animals"; contents, including objects not shown him at Baguia (a boy's wooden statue; a kitchen; a cooking pottery). Almeida may have interpreted the rules of access to the house too liberally. In other instances, his interpretations also ignored important dimensions. For example, in the published article, Almeida refers to Afaloicai alone as the exact location of the sacred house; however, as Almeida himself recorded in his field notes, Afaloicai was the "region," whereas the house was located in the hamlet of Bui Bela or Bui Bela Ne' La—a place name that never appears in his publications ("Afaloicai—region where the lulic house is located," his field notes mention: "place Bui Bela = slopes of Mount Mate Bian within 1 km straight" [Almeida 1957]). Almeida also presents Sokolai Mau Besi as *one* house named after the female statue. However, Almeida failed to understand the house was being presented to him as a male/female pair, and overall he did not grasp the genealogical and classificatory structures of complementary dualism that pervaded the "house system" (e.g. Traube 1986; Fox 1993) in which, as we will see later, the house and the objects themselves were entailed.[7] Nonetheless, his notes and publications offer interesting clues into Timorese understandings of both the encounter and the power-charged nature of the objects.

Although passages of Almeida's notes and writings refer to the ensemble and inform about distinct objects, it is clear that Almeida valued the stones to the detriment of other objects in exhibition—such as the national flag, an object he would in other instances overemphasize as a trace of successful colonization, a "sign" of Timorese submission to the Portuguese government (Almeida 1961: 38). Almeida's fixation on the stones, as we will see, let pass the fact that flag-and-stones constituted one interconnected assemblage of power-charged objects. Interestingly, then, in contrast with many Portuguese-authored colonial ethnographies (missionary accounts excluded), his record sheds light on objects associated with the Timorese spiritual and ritual realm as opposed to the jural and political spheres of action. Guided by his archaeological interests, he conducted his inquiries in order to obtain information specifically about the stones rather than, for instance, the flag, the scepter, or the rifle. His ethnographic report concentrates on describing the ritual powers of the four stone objects—the stone ball and the adzes—as agents in important fertility ceremonies held annually to propitiate and celebrate the rice and corn crops. Almeida's description in fact conforms to agricultural fertility rites known to have existed in different regions of East Timor in the 1960s–70s, which are still practiced today. The objects, Almeida described, were used by the *Makai Lilik* and his helper "in the ceremonies celebrated on occasion of the corn and rice crops," when meat from ritually killed pigs and chickens and cooked rice were "offered to the stone tools ["every object eats" he also writes], which are sprinkled with the victims' blood"; then, according to Almeida, the heavy stone ball was considered to be the first and foremost ritual item, followed by the other stone artifacts: "The first attentions go to the ball (*lórò*), the most revered," he noted; "the [stone] ball is the principal," because it avoided illness and promoted the abundance of crops and the fertility of buffalos and horses (Almeida 1960: 132; 1957).

Stone Secrets

Timorese officers described the ritual procedures and effects, but they gave him "no reason" for *why* the heavy ball was the principal object (Almeida 1957). The *how* but not the why: the ultimate *reason* for the stone ball's ritual primacy was not given. Certainly, this was a colonial situation in which the Portuguese administrator and anthropologist were in command and had the initiative in asking questions; the exchange unfolded, in fact, almost as a kind of police or medical interrogation. However, indigenous agency and control of transacted knowledge were also paramount in the encounter. Twice Almeida saw his wishes overtly denied—and he accepted it. First, Almeida's desire to acquire the stones was rejected. He wanted the stones to become scientific specimens in his archaeological collection of Timorese lithic artifacts. But, for his interlocutors, these were inalienable possessions. "I having proposed to them the acquisition of the [stones] for a very considerable amount, they refused, saying no amount of money would pay for their value"; Almeida regretfully respected this, supposedly on account of his interlocutors' deep attachment to the objects, "their dearest stone artefacts" (Almeida 1960: 133; see also Almeida 1976: 31). Similarly, fearing the "well understandable opposition of their guardians," Almeida refrained from requesting samples—"small fragments"—of the objects to be extracted for laboratory analysis (Almeida 1960: 134). The Timorese were careful to guard against the loss and alienation of the objects to the outsiders—and they succeeded. They were also careful not to disclose certain information about the objects' past. Thus, second, Almeida's desire for historical knowledge about the past and *origins* of the stones was not satisfied. This absence contrasts with the profusion of data he otherwise received about the stones' ritual functions and agencies, as well as the fact that the stones were under the control of the Timorese officers. This latter circumstance seems to suggest the Timorese shared knowledge about the powers of objects and about the exclusiveness of their own ritual authority. They reciprocated Almeida's interest with information that reinstated the powers they had come to make visible and manifest in the presence of the Portuguese authorities. In this light, Almeida's questions about the stones came as an opportunity to demonstrate the great powers of the Soko Lai Mau Besi house; in the indigenous viewpoint, possibly, the anthropologist's interrogations were an instance of the acquiescence of the Portuguese to the higher spiritual authority of the indigenous ritual leaders. But in relation to the origin stories of the stone objects, *no* information at all was disclosed, as if Almeida's questions were entering a zone of special secrecy, or potentially violating a prohibition.

Almeida was eager to transform indigenous historical accounts into ethnogenic elaborations on the Timorese prehistoric past, thus creating a type of archaeological narrative of origin. But he did not collect historical accounts about the stones. This was not because he lacked interest. Rather, his interlocutors' evasiveness explains the absence of indigenous stories about the objects' past. The heritage displayed at Baguia, we believe, probably combined ancestral objects whose qualities came from having belonged to actual genealogical ancestors and objects whose origins were associated with mythic entities. Almeida lists the names of the sword and gun, and refers in passing to the magic powers of the *kábora* (*pau com crina*) in warfare, for example (1960: 132). He also mentions the sword that "belonged to *Modokai*, individual of high prestige deceased long ago"; the rifle named "*Ai auku*"; "*bandera*," which "was the name given to bandeira [flag]"; and "*solokó* to the whistles which were inherited from *Sánu-Bóro*, great-great grandfather of the present priest." Finally, in Almeida's notes, the stone artifacts were simply named "*kádi* (stone)" (Almeida 1960: 132). Thus the sword, the flag, and the rifle were belongings inherited from named historical ancestors and had a story that could be revealed. In contrast, stones were presented as if they had no history. "Makai Liliki says he knows not, with truth or without it, the origins of his dearest stone artefacts . . .—neither does he know if they did or did not come from outside Portuguese Timor or Mount Mate Bian . . ." (Almeida 1960: 132–33). The *Makai Lilik* evaded Almeida's question; by claiming ignorance on that occasion, he avoided disclosure of special knowledge. The apparent secrecy about origin stories suggests the stones belonged to the mythical ancestral legacy, about which knowledge concerning either their past or their named identities could not be revealed to foreigners. "The origins of [the] most sacred object are a closely guarded secret," writes Susanna Barnes about ancestral legacies at Babulo; "Secrecy surrounding its origins is part of what sets this object apart and imbues it with spiritual potency" (Barnes 2017: 87). It seems that, similarly, at Baguia in 1957, the origin stories of Bui Bela's most sacred objects—the stones and above all the rounded stone—were secret knowledge, and keeping such knowledge from foreigner outsiders was an implicit demonstration of the objects' powers on that occasion. For this reason, we believe, the narratives of their ultimate origin may have been deliberately withheld.

The absence of stone stories was a limitation to the Portuguese anthropologist, who could otherwise use (and abuse) this type of indigenous knowledge to speculate about prehistoric origins. However, this limitation was not an impediment to producing an alternative archaeological narrative of origins. Almeida was denied acquisition of objects and access to certain knowledge of the past. Yet he was able to see, manipulate, photograph, and measure the sacred stones. He gained this special access perhaps on account not just of the colonial circumstances but also of his position as *malae* figure of authority to whom certain rules and prohibitions possibly did not apply on the occasion. From this contact, Almeida generated a kind of physical or morphological knowledge of the materiality of stones. Upon this knowledge he would articulate his archaeological conjectures.

The Invention of Neolithic Stones: The Morphological Record

In his 1960 article, Almeida described in detail the appearance of each stone and presented measurements. He saw what he took for vestiges of "magic-religious" use (dark and dirty stones) and handcrafting work visible on their surface. He observed, finally, that *one* stone adze in particular was "certainly of volcanic origin," and he added, "These types of rocks do not abound in Portuguese Timor, some of them are imported from more or less distant lands, as the natives confess" (1960: 135). From this Almeida concluded that such "black volcanic" stones belonged to a "Neolithic culture" that possibly was not autochthonous to the Matebian. It constituted an example of the "Neolithic migrations" in the wider archipelago, as it was argued by Dutch archaeologist Van Heekeren in his then-recent studies on Indonesian stone adzes (Van Heekeren 1957). All five lithic objects from Afaloicai did bear a resemblance, Almeida argued, to similar volcanic stone (adze) materials from Java and Borneo that the Dutch scholar had identified as "Neolithic." In conclusion, he hypothesized that the Baguia "tools had been imported, in more or less recent times, from territories elsewhere in Indonesia, where many have already been found" (Almeida 1960: 136). Hence the sacred stones of Afaloicai, central to the Timorese claims to *internal* sovereign power, were transformed into evidence of an *external* Neolithic culture of foreign Indonesian origins; and they became instrumental to the alternative ethnoarchaeological narrative of origins in the service of Almeida's thirst for scientific authority.

Almeida's "Neolithic stones" were meaningful in his attempt to strengthen and expand a certain racial and ethnogenetic narrative of Timor's deep human past. They did not offer credence to the Paleolithic thesis, but over the years they were instrumental to Almeida's continuing claims to speak on behalf of Timor's prehistoric past. In 1967, Almeida reinstated his morphological classification as definitive (Almeida and Zbyszewski 1967: 57). In the vein of his experience at Baguia, he remained on the lookout for further specimens of prehistoric stone artifacts, stored inside sacred houses elsewhere in "Portuguese Timor." In the late 1960s, for instance, he again used secondhand knowledge of certain ancient *lulik* at Balibó—the presumable existence of a stone knife in the *uma lulik* of Uro Luli, at Bazartete—to reinforce his earlier claims based on the Baguia artifacts (Almeida and Zbyszewski 1967: 65; Almeida 1976: 32). He would never doubt the quality and accuracy of his archaeological study; and throughout the years (lonely, save for his rare Portuguese acolytes), he counted his Baguia field encounters and conclusions as solid research in archaeology. In those later publications, the ethnographic data present in his first 1960 article—the house, the officers, the ritual—was gradually replaced by an archaeological narrative and a classificatory prehistoric past. By this point, Almeida had already created the origin story that his ethnography had denied him. By sheer force of his comparative morphology he could speak of migrant stones from Neolithic Indonesian cultures. Nevertheless, he continued to regret the gaps in his ethnographic record. Years later, in a 1967 paper jointly authored with the Russian geologist Georges Zbyszewski (then based in Portugal), Almeida speculated on the external genesis of the Afaloicai sacred artifacts as strangers to Baguia:

> The Neolithic instruments were not executed in the area because there was no raw material for them. If they were brought there from a foreign place, who brought them? Why were they introduced there? When did they come to the lands of Baguia and Balibó? Would they have been left there by accident? Would not such valuable pieces have been used for barter and brought there by strangers who exchanged them for salt, which was thought to be produced by supernatural agents? (Almeida and Zbyszewski 1967: 65)

Almeida's story emphasized the foreign origins of the stones; they were migrant objects, from outside Timor, made out of "Indonesian" rocks that were not native to the island—a remark that contrasts with Timorese notions of sacred stones as autochthonous Timorese entities, insider forces, and guardian spirits. But Almeida still had no response to his questions concerning where, when, how, and why the objects originated, and who originated them to appear at Afaloicai. He longed for further historical or ethnographic data that could enable him to retell an origin narrative for what he saw as migrant objects, outsider stones. Almeida's archaeological narrative bears contrast with the possibility that in 1957, regardless of their foreign geology, these objects had already been incorporated as potent autochthonous ancestral objects within insider claims to sovereignty and identity. Moreover, their external origins beyond the place of Bui Bela Ne' La (as bestowments of Luca authority) entitled them, as we will see, to enter the path of *lulik* indigenization as *rotas*.

Given, as we have seen, the secrecy that surrounded the origin stories of these materials, it was possible that Almeida's questions could never be answered. Or perhaps some stories could be told, we wondered back in 2012. What stories, if any, were accessible by outsiders about the people and sacred objects of Afaloicai, which Almeida encountered in 1957? Beyond Almeida's biased "prehistoric archaeology," could one revisit that early colonial encounter to illuminate the past and present significance of the ancestral materials? The following section is an experiment in the analysis of our fieldwork materials concerning the Afaloicai heritage as they were recounted to us through the intermediary of Almeida's texts and photos. The assertion of indigenous power and authority through the appropriate presentation of ancient *lulik* heirlooms—along dualistic oppositions: inside/outside; visibility/invisibility; mobility/immobility—remains a structuring story line of accounts of the colonial event, and of the objects themselves. Now mediated by the colonial photographic *images* of the objects rather than the objects themselves, stories of the authority and powers attributed to stones, and memories of the colonial encounters themselves, cross paths with stories of destruction, loss, and reconstruction.

Stones Are *Rotas*: Loss and the Powers of Soko Lai Mau Besi

> They are not here any more. Not these ones. In the past they were, but today they are no more. There must be other stones, but these have been thrown away; they disappeared in the middle of the grass or in the bush, and you cannot find them. When war began everyone was on the run. The stones were left inside the house. The houses were burned down. It is no longer possible to find them.

Thus our host at Baguia Guesthouse *Senhor* Martinho Meneses Amaral began his recollections about the ancient stones that figured in Almeida's publication. A former soldier in the Portuguese colonial army, he was by then already used to engaging with foreign researchers' inquiries about the local past.[8] Then aged seventy-five, he remained, in Janet Gunter's words, a "self-styled guardian of tradition of the hamlet of Oekilari" (Gunter 2010: 290), a status he claimed during our visit, presenting photos of himself holding the "authentic" Oekilari *rota* (named *rota san*), a long wooden scepter that had been bestowed on his ancestors by Soko Lai Mau Besi in a remote mythic past. We told him about the encounter at Baguia *Posto* between Almeida, Santa, and the Afaloicai ritual officers, while he inspected carefully our hard copies of photographs of stones, ancient objects, and the Timorese officers. Those were times of *ditadura* (dictatorship), he recalled, of power and rigid status differences: "We could not come near a *malae* at the time unless he summoned us." Martinho vaguely recalled António de Almeida from his days as a soldier in Dili, before 1975; he remembered seeing him from a distance, as a man in "large trousers," an old *malae* figure of authority whom he never approached. In contrast, he had clear recollections of the Timorese objects and people in the photos as biographically significant, at both personal and collective levels (cf. Hoskins 1998). He stared gravely at the images of the stones. To begin, these were lost objects—part of a sacred heritage now missing as a consequence of the waves of war and violence that, since 1957, affected the Matebian region. Martinho's immediate memories concerned stories of loss, either by sheer destruction by fire or by removal, dispersal, and disappearance (in the grass; in the bush; or, also, by theft or inappropriate removal, as we will see) as a consequence of imposed violence. The first event, still alive in local memory, was the so-called "Viqueque rebellion" of 1959: the last anti-Portuguese uprising that was followed by violent and devastating repression by the Portuguese colonial administration (see Gunter 2008a, 2008b). In this event, *liurai* Pedro Ximenes, the *suku* chief of Afaloicai Baguia, was murdered and beheaded near Bui Bela, where his grave still remains (Gunter 2008a: 63). The local sacred houses, including Soko Lai Mau Besi, were set on fire and destroyed.

According to Sr. Martinho and people at Bui Bela Ne' La, the mountain houses that stored the objects were first burned in the wars of 1959. It seems that the great majority of sacred objects was destroyed or went missing on this occasion. Narratives of loss of the Bui Bela heritage during the Viqueque rebellion already circulated in the 1960s. Almeida makes veiled reference to this circumstance in a later article in which he omits (deliberately or not) reference to the Portuguese part in the violence of the events (Sousa 2011). In 1974, he mentions having been "informed, years later [after 1957]" that the stones were "lost in a dreadful fire that completely destroyed the gentile temple" (Almeida 1976: 32). By 1962, the Soko Lai Mau Besi houses were reconstructed at Bui Bela. However, the Indonesian invasion of 1975 and the terror that, in 1979, swept through Mount Matebian—where thousands of East Timorese people and resistance fighters sought refuge, to be besieged and massacred in the tragic Indonesian assault on Matebian in 1979—again resulted in destruction of the houses and loss of their contents. It seems most of the stones were destroyed or lost earlier, in the 1959 fire, when the old flint gun by the name of *kilat antigu* was also stolen. Not until 2010 was the house pair physically restored in a ceremonial reconstruction of the Soko Lai Mau Besi houses at the mountain hamlet of Bui Bela Ne' La. Only one sacred stone was unanimously said to have survived the fires of 1959 and 1975, but it, too, as we will see, is considered to be a missing or wandering object (the stone adze named *kadi*; see figure 7.2). This layered violence disturbs the complex chronology of the object disappearances. Yet Sr. Martinho and our other interlocutors insisted on historical-biographical claims about how and when *each* specific named object was lost. Historiographical precision mattered because,

Figure 7.2.   Timorese stone artifacts and baskets in 1957. Photo by Victor Santa, 1957; originally published in Almeida 1960. IICT Photography Collection, INV. ULISBOA-IICT-MAT26669. Reproduced by kind permission of the authorities of MUHNAC/ULisboa.

we argue, biographies of such objects remain strongly connected to claims about house ascendancy and power in the area. It is significant that East Timorese oral accounts of the stones' powers and histories came in connection with non-nostalgic accounts of their loss—as if in recalling the objects' traditional strength, people could project forward into the present and future a past when sacred things were in their proper place. For the objects' photos elicited narratives of death and the loss or scattering of ancient objects; they were also accompanied by accounts of replacement ("There must be other stones," for instance, Martinho affirmed), survival, rebirth, and/or reconstruction. They elicited, above all, precise descriptions of how those specific ancient stones, the monarchic flag, the flint gun, and so forth, were intimately connected to the historical making of social order and to the past and present authority of people and lineages relative to one another.

As conversation continued around the photographs, Sr. Martinho provided a complex account of the rightful connection between the objects displayed in 1957, the house(s) to which they belonged, and the status and authority they upheld. This revealed how circuits of possession, preservation, and display of stones and other *lulik* objects were embedded in the historicity of social order; and the explanation of these circuits implied a form of historical narration. Looking at the photos, Sr. Martinho's attention (as well as that of other interlocutors at Oekilari and Bui Bela Ne' La) was drawn primarily to the Timorese people and objects. In contrast with his vague recollections of Almeida or the administrator, he had clear views of the Timorese objects' and the people's name and histories, as elements of present significance. He was quick to point out Soko Lai Mau Besi as the house/s to which the objects belonged. This, he explained, was a female-male pair: Soko Lai, the male house, and Mau Besi (or Liurai Mau Besi), the female house. For our interlocutors, the house Soko Lai Mau Besi and the locality of Bui Bela Ne' La remain today, as in the past, the critical ritual center (Gunter 2010: 282), the "place where one ought to return," as Sr. Martinho emphasized. He examined a copy of figure 7.1 and immediately recognized Rubi Boro as officer *Makai Lilik*, an affiliate to the house of Lahu Wo, and his companion Bada Ona, the *asurate*, from the house of Alata. (It must thus be noted here that Almeida misnamed the *asurate* Bada Ona and took him to be Loi Rubi, another historical character likely involved in the events, as we will soon see.) In addition to naming the persons, Sr. Martinho named the objects displayed to Almeida, emphasizing their condition as important tokens of power and social hierarchy. He highlighted the old musket, or flint gun, named *kilat antigu*; the Portuguese monarchic flag, named *bandera monarkia*; and the stones, *fatu kadi*. These were *all* significant objects that *together* belonged to the category of *rota*.

The notion of *rota* to refer to tokens of rule and regalia of office—absent in Almeida's notes, as is any connection between the stones and the sociopolitical hierarchy—was given to us as key to understanding the role played by the stone artifacts, in particular, as profoundly powerful ancient objects within Afaloicai society. This classification of stones as *rotas*, or as *rota lulik*, seems to follow a differentiation between stones as objects in the natural landscape and stones as humanly made artifacts, the latter associated especially with the condition of *rotas* as regalia of rule. Significantly, moreover, the conversation concentrated on the complementary authority of the ensemble of stones and the flag *bandera monarkia*. Both were *rotas*. Martinho disclosed names and told us stories, including stories that—although not rendered in poetic language—alluded to accounts of object-origins. The so-called prehistoric stones viewed by Almeida in 1957, in other words, were presented to us as *rotas* within historical narratives of the house-system and the local structures of indigenous authority.

Stones as Rotas *and the House System*

Anthropologist Janet Gunter (2008a, 2010) has observed the critical significance occupied by the notion of *rotas* as regalia of office in Timorese oral accounts of the establishment of political hierarchy and authority in the region of Afaloicai-Baguia in the late nineteenth- and early twentieth-century period. Based on Martinho Menezes's (among others') accounts,[9] Gunter suggests that, especially prior to the 1920s–30s, "the 'legitimacy' of these hierarchies was located in a mimetic appropriation of what were believed to be Portuguese symbols" (2010: 282), the monarchic flag, military ranks, and—in particular—the scepters (wooden staffs). In the past, scepters were distributed by the Portuguese government to Timorese "vassal" kingdoms as a way of expressing subordination to Portugal and empower indigenous *liurais* as "kings" to exercise authority legitimately in their own domains (Roque 2010: 40–69). Gunter equates "rota" with a specific object, the "scepter" (the *bastão* in colonial Portuguese documents, Roque 2010: 44; 2011), and she calls attention to how the circulation of scepters as *rotas*—either the "original," or "mother," scepter or its copies—became critical to the constitution of indigenous authority and hierarchy. Indigenous interest in absorbing foreign power through possession of foreign objects anteceded European arrival and, as Janet Hoskins (1997) observes (see also Traube, this volume), was reflected in the potency attributed to regalia of office; throughout the region, a variety of imported objects became inextricably entangled with local claims to rule. While such evidence suggests the category of regalia of rule originally encompassed a wide array of objects associated with sovereignty, the Europeans' practice of distribution of scepters and flags interfered with existing structures and may have partly displaced former traditional heirlooms with new symbols. Portuguese strategies of ceremonial power also became meaningful within these indigenous conceptions. Since the eighteenth century, and intensely at the turn of the twentieth century, the creation and circulation of *rota*-scepters and Portuguese flags became embedded in Timorese disputes between

elite lineages for superiority and independent ritual-political authority
and centrality. Such disputes often concerned complex local ties of
allegiance and opposition between minor and major "kingdoms" that
sometimes had less to do with the Portuguese colonizers than with
alternative regional claims for hegemonic ritual and political centrality. In the case of the Matebian and Viqueque regions, this is particularly important with regard to the lasting centrality of the domain or
"kingdom" of Luca that—although often in some sort of alliance with
the Portuguese—claimed alternative symbolic supremacy and maintained an independent galaxy of tributary polities in eastern Timor-
Leste, including in the domain of Afaloicai (see Gunter 2010; and on
Luca more widely, Barnes, Hägerdal, and Palmer 2017).

In this conception, *rotas* were foundational tokens of superior authority within the Afaloicai realm, which in the past had been in the
orbit of Luca and—perhaps also—Dili.[10] "Rota is special because it
comes from the forefathers. It is because of the rota that one has to
respect one another, one has to obey." Sr. Martinho connected the potency of *rotas* to the ritual centrality of Soko Lai Mau Besi and to Oekilari's subsidiary authority, within a complex local house system that
resonates with Gunter's prior inquiries. However, Timorese *rotas* in
the Portuguese times did not come exclusively in the form of staffs or
"scepters." Portuguese-origin scepters and flags, either the originals or
their copies, were not the only things that could take on such quality.
"Some are with *belak*; some are with scarf [*lenço*]; others with sword.
This is my *lulik* [the scepter] that I keep here to govern. You believe in
the *liurai*, you believe in the *rota*." Martinho's observations make clear
the close interdependence between the authority of *liurais* and the
authority of *rotas* and further suggest that, at Afaloicai at least, *rotas*
could take a wider array of physical or material forms—including
that of ancient stone artifacts. The *rotas* could be more discretionarily
constituted, out of a certain range of possible materialities; they could
be made with/from almost anything, so long as its empowerment respected the proper ritual procedures and the circuits of bestowment
of authority that emanated from Portugal and Luca to their galactic
realm. "Luca says and the *liurai* orders the preparation of the *rota*. It
is the *liurai* who orders the rota to be prepared with what he wants; it
can be stick [*pau*], it can be sword [*espada*] [and so forth]." Anything
the *régulo* declared, upon instruction from Luca, to be a *rota* became a
rota. This liberal understanding of the materiality of *rotas* perhaps explains why Martinho also declared the Bui Bela stones to be a certain
kind of *rota*. In thus defining the Bui Bela stones as objects that shared
the quality of being *rotas*, Martinho de Menezes's account expanded

significantly on the strictly "ritual" or spiritual agencies of the sacred stones to include in their agencies and powers also the potency to produce and structure a type of political authority over land and people. Therefore, although usually associated with the guardian spiritual custodianship of land and magical powers (so-called "ritual authority" in the strict sense), stones could also become politically charged tokens of rule and authority over the realm, especially in contexts, for example, of strong political dispute. "The *rota*," Gunter observes insightfully (2010: 290), "represented the interdependence of political and ritual power." In some historical instances, stones could be presented as *rotas* in opposition to scepters and flags as a means to oppose both Luca and the Portuguese networks. This possibility appears in examples in the oral record collected by Gunter in 2004. Gunter heard a story about a great battle between Ossucai'ua and a kingdom, Ossuroa, that owed tribute to Luca and the Portuguese at the turn of the century. The allegiance to a kind of insider *rota*-stone in this case became the basis for opposing Luca and making power claims that differed from and competed with *rota*-scepters: "Ossucai'ua refused to pay tribute to Luca, which was in a period of expansion. Instead of accepting a sceptre as a symbol of this tributary relationship, Ossucai'ua openly *declared its allegiance to the magical stones* (lita) *that embodied the guardian spirits of the land*. Luca and the Portuguese accused Ossucai'ua of practicing witchcraft and used this as a pretext to destroy the small kingdom" (Gunter 2010: 289, our emphasis).

The stones of Afaloicai thus shared some qualities with the Portuguese flag on account of their common category *rota*. Yet the stones viewed by Almeida had been *rotas* of a deeper, most ancient kind of internal indigenous power. The Portuguese flag and the stones were tokens of power whose origins were external to Afaloicai: they were either in Portugal, *monarkia*, or in Luca and its ruling houses. The two *rotas* formed a pair, the members of which were equally inalienable and unique to Soko Lai Mau Besi, and their possession had defined the house's high status and powers. "In ancient times they adored this," he said pointing to the objects on the photo, "as their *liurai*, their government. Only one *suku* possesses the flag, Soko Lai Mau Besi. This is the name of the house that received the *lulik*, but the *suku* name is Afaloicai." Stone and flag were both kept in the Soko Lai Mau Besi *lulik* houses. There, immobile and secluded, they played an essential role in establishing order and respect, and they were taken out of the houses only for ritual occasions and special events. They were a prerogative of the *liurai* or *régulo*, a tool of ruling power, a gauge of social hierarchy in the domain that ordered the superior status of upper classes as regards the commoners through relations of "respect." The historical origins of *rota* were thus associated with the historical origins of order and peace; consequently, the latter continued to be secured through relations of respect and awe toward the *liurai* and his/her *rota*: "In the old times," before *rotas* came, Gregório Menezes added later, "people would be captured randomly by anyone. The *rota* had to come so they would start fearing the *rota*."

In the past, stone and flag were ultimate bearers and guarantees of order and hierarchy. They ensured the social order and the unity of a realm in which, apparently, a double attachment to ancient Luca and (Portuguese) *monarkia* were paramount. Thus, in a recursive application of complementary dualism, the two object-worlds were distinguished as insider/outsider formations, hierarchized by relations of precedence. Flag and stone were presented as having distinct historical stories that stood for parallel but linked modes of authority. The internal division of regalia of office was conveyed by Martinho in the form of stories of circulation, or stories about two paths or routes: the path of the flag, and the path of the stone. This division presumed a first, primordial, stone route originating in the realm of Luca, representing a kind of external-insider authority source; and a second, the flag route originating in an outer circle of external-outsider authority, Portugal, or, rather, in *monarkia*—a term, as noted below, used by our interlocutors to indicate an older kind of Portuguese authority realm located in a historical time that preceded the 1910s.

Stone-*rotas* overlapped political and ritual power, and they had historical and sociosymbolic precedence over the flag. They also seemed to stand for a deeper, internal, autochthonous modality of power and authority. The stones were the true *lulik antigu*, or the *rota antigu*, the most ancient ones. They had been a gift bestowed to the ancestors of Soko Lai Mau Besi by the high authorities of the realm of Luca, in the past, the ancient times of the *régulos*—the *Zon* (*Don*). Their origins went back to times prior to the coming of the Portuguese and to tributary circuits disconnected from the Europeans. The stones were in the keeping of appointed custodians who only took them out of the house to perform the rituals of *sau batar*, the fertility rite of eating the first corn, including sacrifices and distribution of corn according to the local hierarchy. Yet, *bandera monarkia* remained strongly and more strictly associated with the manifestation of external jural powers. The flag, in Martinho de Menezes's words, was the "voice of the government." "The Portuguese flag," he said, "came when Portugal started governing here in Timor. Timor was discovered by a priest in Lifau, Oecussi." According to Sr. Martinho, the specific flag

Figure 7.3.   Sr. Martinho and Sr. Gregório Menezes examining photographs from 1957, at Oekilari in July 2012. Photo by Ricardo Roque.

bandera monarkia came originally from Oecussi; from Oecussi it went to Dili; from Dili to Laleia; from Laleia to Vemasse; from Vemasse to Soko Lai Mau Besi, sometime before 1910. By referring to the realm of *monarkia*, Sr. Martinho indicated a specific historical time that preceded Portuguese Republican rule in Timor: "Portugal still did not come, it was the monarchy that ruled." This split between "*monarkia*" and "Portugal" seems to indicate a time of Portuguese rule *before* the establishment of the Republican regime, the change of Portugal's flag colors in 1910 (a change that, according to some historical accounts, displeased a number of Timorese), which was followed by the Manufahi rebellion and a hardening of Portuguese effective administration in the highlands in the 1920s–30s (see Gunter 2010).

Memories of a Ceremonial Encounter

Sr. Martinho's accounts, in interaction with Almeida's photographs, oriented our focus toward the indigenous forms of authority and social hierarchy embedded in the objects, according to local conceptions. By following the path of the objects as *rotas* (rather than "Neolithic evidence") we were also able to retrieve at least some of their associated stories. Memories of loss and destruction seemed to supersede memories of Almeida and the Baguia encounter itself. In other instances, the circumstances of the encounter of 1957 were more vividly recalled as an extraordinary event of temporary removal and display of the sacred objects. For this reason, perhaps it left a mark in collective memory. At Oekilari we met with Gregório de Menezes, an elder brother of Sr. Martinho, who, in the latter's own words, knew more and had more to tell us about the past encounter. "Why did Almeida and the administrator want to see the objects? Why did the meeting at Baguia take place?" we asked him. His response implied that it was because the Portuguese wanted to see and recognize the *régulos*' power. Sr. Gregório recalled the story told him by old people about the event: "These people, the *régulos*, what do they have inside the House [the Portuguese asked]? People respect them because of this [the objects inside the house]. The *malae mutin* asked this: in the ancient times [*antigamente*] where did this come from? It came from Luca. But where did it come from in Luca?" And he continued, retelling for us part of the paths of the *rotas* stone and flag, their passage from Luca and their transfer from house to house, as Martinho had previously noted. Hence, Portuguese interest in the objects and their stories of origin back in the 1950s is now retrospectively understood as an acknowledgment of Timorese powers, thus totally ignoring Almeida and Santa's investment in the event as archaeological fieldwork. In hindsight (and, we believe, also back in 1957), the event was explained as a power-and-authority-charged occasion that indigenous officers ingeniously used to manipulate their own claims of the

Figure 7.4.   Sr. Agostinho Guterres and the reconstructed houses of Soko Lai Mau Besi in July 2013. Photo by Lúcio Sousa.

higher powers of Soko Lai Mau Besi before Portuguese and Timorese audiences past and present.

Command and authority feature centrally in the *katuas*, old *liurai* of Bui Bela, Agostinho Aparício Guterres's recollections of the 1957 event. Indeed, in our visit to Bui Bela Ne' La, Agostinho Guterres re-told the event with accuracy and offered reasons similar to Gregório de Menezes for why and how the encounter of 1957 occurred. "On that time," he narrated,

> he [Rui Boro] left, he took those things to Baguia, in the epoch of *suku* chief Luís, I think. They stayed there for two days. From here to Baguia they took three hours. Then they rested there for a while. With work for the Portuguese in the morning around 8 A.M. they [Portuguese] start asking questions.
>
> Afterwards they came back, they slept at Oekilari, and in the morn-ing they returned here [to Bui Bela]. The men of Oekilari [and] Uai Mata charged a little pig. They opened the door, they put [the things] inside; after [preparing] a roasted little pig and they ate it [laugh]. I knew them but they are dead now. . . . They [also] took with them my father, José, the oldest *suco* chief. Only they three [Rui Boro, Bada Ona, José] spoke. There was another one, along with Aleixo, from Osuna, what is his name? Manel . . .

Reference to the ritual killing and eating of pigs, both prior to the removal and upon the return of sacred objects to Bui Bela, reveals the careful procedures required to move the objects outside the house. A ritualized control of mobility of the objects was required. Guterres's brief account is revealing in several other aspects. It sheds further light on the identity of the Timorese participants in the 1957 event. Rui Boro and Bada Ona went to Baguia accompanied by a former *suku* chief named "José." The name of José (Zé) Loi Rubi appears in Gunter (2010: 294) as the name of an Afaloicai *liurai* that was removed from office by the Portuguese in the late 1920s for incompetence. The latter thus possibly corresponds to the person identified as "Loi Rubi" in Almeida's papers and whom Almeida mistook for the *asurate* Bada Ona. Guterres's memory of a certain "Manel" echoes Almeida's mention of a third man as "informant," Manuel da Costa Gusmão, or "Léki Dara, ex-chief of *povoação* of Laku Hu, *suco* of Osu Huna" (Almeida 1960: 130). Aleixo, however, never appears explicitly in Almeida's papers.

The sacrifice of pigs was fundamental to keep the powers and dangers of the *lulik* under control; they could appease their anger so that they would not unleash their terrible powers upon the living. If proper ritual procedures were adopted and the administrator's request followed, an exception could be made. But if such procedures and rules were not respected, terrible things could happen. The objects could not be brought out of the houses randomly. It was in this light that we were repeatedly told a story about the tragic destiny of the last surviving stone of Bui Bela Ne' La. As mentioned earlier, one of the ancient stones survived the fires of 1959. In 1975, when war broke out with the Indonesian army, a descendant of *Makai Lilik* Rui Boro took possession of the stone for himself and ran away with it, out of Bui Bela, leaving the hamlet never to return. It is said that he has gone mad while he wanders alone randomly with the stone. This brief story was presented as a historical event; it conveyed a moral lesson about the importance of leaving the *rota antigu* to rest in their proper place. It was also perhaps a reminder, a word of caution, to us, foreign outsiders on a visit, about the great dangers that could fall upon us if, like Almeida, we ever happened to use our rights to touch with our bare hands and see with our own eyes the potencies of Bui Bela's sacred stones.

Conclusion: The Double Bind of Authority

In this chapter we have followed stones and their stories across the field and the archive to reassess the encounter between an anthropologist, an administrator, and the ritual keepers of the ancient *lulik* objects of Soko Lai Mau Besi in 1957. This was a singular colonial event that, through the mediation of material objects, significantly short-circuited Portuguese and Timorese understandings of, and authority claims for, higher powers and knowledge. Because it concerned inalienable sacred possessions with relevant cultural meaning and current use, Almeida's prehistoric archaeology implied also a kind of ethnography of things; in his own way, Almeida's studies of the prehistoric past at Baguia configured a kind of crossing between archaeology and ethnography. Almeida's crossing was predicated on the use and abuse of Timorese knowledge and objects to generate scientific authority in archaeology, itself a kind of symbolic power in Bourdieu's terms (1991), expressed in a racialized ethnogenic narrative of the primitive "prehistoric Neolithic past." Sacred stones counted above as "evidence" on the terms of Almeida's ethnoarchaeological blend and led to classifying the stones as foreign objects of impossible geological autochthony. Almeida could not collect stories about the stones' origins and historical trajectories. As a consequence, therefore, his ethnographic record becomes less a register of his obsessive quest for the objects' ancient past than a register of the indigenous desire to make indigenous authority visible, legitimate, and recognized, through the exhibition of ancestral objects of power.

Recovering at least some of this indigenous historicity required a crossing between history and ethnography that foregrounded original indigenous cultural conceptions and imaginaries of the Timorese powers and autochthony of the lithic materials. Central to our argument was the interpretation of the colonial encounter as an entangled ceremonial occasion. The object exhibition at Baguia encapsulated complex relational transactions of power and authority mediated by sacred objects, on East Timorese terms. The Timorese who accompanied the objects were persons of rank that mediated higher powers. The audience—Almeida and the administrator—were persons of acknowledged authority in Portuguese colonial hierarchies; in the Timorese eyes too, they fell in the category of holders of high status and executives of jural command, embodying the outside-ruling powers with which the Portuguese colonial government was associated and to whom deference was customarily owed. The event therefore corresponded to an occasion regulated by the social norms and cultural conceptions that customarily surrounded the manifestation of power and status in Timorese-Portuguese colonial interactions. Almeida's archaeological field visit to Baguia, in other words, was primarily a type of ceremonial colonial encounter at the core of which was the enactment of authority.

This helps explain why sacred paraphernalia from a distant village were temporarily removed for display to the Portuguese in Baguia, without apparent disruption or break of social order. Moreover, the high status of both Portuguese and Timorese people and things in presence also indicate that this colonial situation could be configured as theater for making not only Portuguese but also Timorese authority manifest. The presentation to the Portuguese of certain sacred objects (such as the Portuguese flag) could be read as an assertion of connectedness, alliance, and/or symbolic subordination to the powers of Portugal and Dili. However, we also argued, the encounter itself can also be understood as a forum for the performance of a distinctive, and even alternative, type of indigenous power, imagined as older, deeper, and supreme. In her ethnographic work on the Naueti-speaking people of Babulo (where a considerable number of Afaloicai migrants currently inhabits), anthropologist Susana Barnes emphasizes that the authority and legitimacy of indigenous elders is, by their own admission, reliant "on acknowledgement and recognition of others. It is, ultimately, deeply relational and reflects the enduring dilemma between the need to share and the desire to control" (Barnes 2017: 89; see also Traube 1989). The interplay between hiding of/reclusion (in sacred houses) as well as the display of "ancestral legacy" by their keepers is, Barnes also observes, central to the relational process of production of authority that requires constant reenactment (see also Bovensiepen 2015). From this perspective, Timorese autonomy and even ascendancy, rather than mere submission, was at stake in the presentation of sacred objects to the Portuguese colonial administrator and anthropologist. In indigenous conceptions, making potent object-embodied authority ceremonially *visible* could represent a statement of independent and superior authority on its own right. The encounter, in other words, reads not simply as a sign of subordination to Portuguese colonial command but also as an event that implied indigenous claims to independent authority and control on Timorese terms.

In this light, Almeida's scientific desire to see, touch, and possess the ancestral legacy of Afaloicai could be interpreted as an outsider's gesture of recognition (or even) subordination to Bui Bela's powers. For the two Timorese men did not simply exhibit sacred objects to the Portuguese foreign authorities; they also came to assert their own forms of indigenous power—among which was the kind of autochthonous, insider form of power embodied in the stones- *rotas*. The special rights to access and visibility of Bui Bela *lulik* heritage that the Timorese granted to the Portuguese *malae* (whether missionaries or administrator or anthropologist) presupposed the Portuguese engagement in an act of recognition of the superior powers of Bui Bela. Thus the Timorese trick in which Almeida was caught. For, if it is true that the Timorese were caught by the abusive appropriations of the archaeologist, they were simultaneously subjecting the Portuguese outsiders to an imperative recognition of the higher powers of Bui Bela Ne' La. Thus the trap of mutual ignorance: a double bind of symbolic power within which both the Timorese and the Portuguese fell prey in 1957.

Just like Almeida, however, we are aware that many questions remain unanswered. We wonder why the connection of the stones to the notion of *rotas* never comes up in Almeida's ethnographic record; or, why was Almeida not told the stories about the paths of *rotas*? Perhaps it was because, in the context of the late 1950s, Timorese might fear that disclosing such knowledge could be received by the Portuguese as an act of insubordination or defiance of Portuguese authority. We wonder why, finally, stories of missing objects, missing *rotas*, were and still are essential for the hierarchies of Soko Lai Mau Besi at Afaloicai. If the ancient stones, *rota antigu*, are gone with the fires, how does the power of the Soko Lai Mau Besi continue, where does it remain materialized? People move and die, objects get lost, buildings are destroyed, but the houses and their inner powers remain. Perhaps for this reason the photographic images of the lost stones of Afaloicai that Almeida saw and touched continue to be such powerful magnets of indigenous colonial historicities.

Acknowledgments

Research for this essay was funded by FCT, Fundação para a Ciência e Tecnologia, Portugal (grant references HC/0089/2009 and PTDC/ HAR- HIS/28577/2017). Fieldwork in Timor in 2012-13 was also supported by Fundação Oriente and by an Australian Research Council Postdoctoral Fellowship (FL 110100243). In Timor we are grateful to Martinho de Menezes, Gregório de Menezes, Agostinho Guterres and our interlocutors at Bui Bela Ne' La for generously sharing their memories and experiences. Thanks are also due to Nuno Vasco Oliveira, Sabina da Fonseca, Vicente Paulino, and Gonçalo Antunes. Thanks to Fundação Oriente for hosting us at Dili. We thank Elizabeth G. Traube and Christopher Shepherd for comments and criticisms to an earlier version of this paper.

Ricardo Roque is research fellow at the Institute of Social Sciences of the University of Lisbon (Instituto de Ciências Sociais da Universidade de Lisboa) and currently an honorary associate in the Department of

History of the University of Sydney. He works on the history and anthropology of human sciences, colonialism, and cross-cultural contact in the Portuguese-speaking world. He has published extensively on the colonial history of Timor-Leste. Current research interests include the comparative history of twentieth-century racial sciences and the theory and ethnography of colonial archives and biological collections. He is the author of *Headhunting and Colonialism* (2010), and coeditor (with K. Wagner) of *Engaging Colonial Knowledge* (2012) and (with W. Anderson and R. Ventura Santos) of *Luso-tropicalism and Its Discontents* (2019).

Lúcio Sousa is an assistant professor in the Department of Social and Management Sciences at Universidade Aberta (UAb), Portugal, and he heads the Research Group on "Migrations and Cultural Diversities" at the Centre for Migration Studies and Intercultural Relations (CEMRI-UAb). He is also a research associate at the Traditional Literature Research Institute (IELT). He wrote his PhD thesis on ritual practice and social organization in a Bunak community in the Bobonaro district of Timor-Leste. Current research themes include rituals, symbolic practices, and mythology in Timor-Leste. He is the coeditor (with K. Silva) of *Ita Maun Alin . . . O livro do irmão mais novo: Afinidades antropológicas em torno de Timor-Leste* (2011).

Notes

1. Unless otherwise mentioned, hereafter we will use the term "Afaloicai" according to current Tetum orthography. Yet, as the just-quoted passages illustrate, the term appears in different orthographies in Almeida's papers (Afalikai, Afoloicai, Afaloicai, Afolikai, etc.). Today, in the administrative organization of Timor-Leste, Afaloicai is a *suco* of the subdivision of Uatocarbau within the Viqueque district, located in southeastern Timor. Afaloicai also is the name for other villages located in neighboring areas. This dissemination of the term is arguably related to origin stories of the old Afaloicai mountain kingdom and the mimetic circulation of *rotas*. Today's division of former Afaloicai into three *sucos*—Baguia, Uato Lari, and Uato Carabau—possibly connects to an equivalent tripartition of the original domain, eventually portrayed in myth as a departure of brothers from the center to create three new domains: Afaloicai-Uatolari, Afaloicai-Uatocarbau, and Afaloicai-Viqueque (Gunter 2008a: 62; 2010: 293, and later in this chapter).

2. However, as we shall see below, there is no mention in Almeida's writings of the name of Bada Ona, who contemporary interlocutors in East Timor

acknowledge as the actual *asurate* that followed Rui Boro to Baguia in 1957.

3. Both authors (accompanied by Gonçalo Antunes) conducted fieldwork at Baguia and Okilari in July 2012. Sousa alone went back in July 2013, and on this occasion he also visited Bui Bela.

4. Baguia preserved its attractiveness as a recurrent research site for other professional archaeologists. After Almeida's visit, Australian archaeologist Ian Glover in 1966 and Portuguese archaeologist Nuno Vasco Oliveira in 2004 returned to Baguia with the purpose of excavating further caves, in the wake (again) of Bühler and Sarasin (see Oliveira 2006).

5. Although not necessarily by national standards: by the 1950s–60s, Portuguese archaeology in the metropole could reveal similar methodological problems (Poloni 2017). Since the early 1960s, radiocarbon dating was already available for lithic technologies, but Almeida never used it. Almeida's field methods are considered unreliable by present-day archaeologists. Australian archaeologist Ian Glover, who conducted fieldwork in Portuguese Timor in the mid-1960s, offered a first sustained criticism of Almeida's research methods from the viewpoint of "modern" archaeology. Since 2000, critiques of the flaws of Almeida's archaeological practice have been put forward by a new wave of professional archaeologists working in Timor-Leste (Glover 1986; Oliveira 2006, 2011).

6. Comparable precautions concerning biases in indigenous conceptions of time were followed by more recent archaeological research at cave sites in Baguia: "As the local concept of time depth differs greatly from our own, many sites referred to as 'old' and 'sacred' by local people have only been so for the past 30 years" (Oliveira 2006: 90).

7. Even if another reading of his field notes could suggest a more complex dualistic identity. In his field notes: "Lulic house = Sokolai Mau Bési . . . Sokolai = female, woman. Mau Bési = statue [xx]."

8. Martinho has been a resident in Baguia since 1967, when he came to work as an official under the Portuguese administrator at Baguia Posto. There he married the daughter of Agostinho Freitas Cabral, a pro-Portuguese *liurai* who resisted Japanese occupation. Prior to our visit, Sr. Martinho's kindness and hospitality was already legendary. He had been a fieldwork interlocutor for anthropologist Janet Gunter and archaeologist Nuno Vasco Oliveira (through whose intercession we came to his acquaintance at Baguia). After our research in 2012–13, Martinho Amaral also collaborated with Joanna Barrkman in her experimental engagements with local East Timorese communities at Baguia concerning the archaeological collections of Swiss scholar Alfred Bühler (Barrkman 2017). This is a region of Makassae and Naueti speakers. Our conversations at Baguia, Oekilari, and Bui Bela were in Tetum; with Sr. Martinho, conversations also took place in Portuguese.

9. Gunter's other informant at Baguia was elder *liurai* Luís de Menezes (aged over ninety in 2012, and by then very debilitated) to whom we

were introduced with solemnity by Martinho de Menezes as the *liurai* "since the times of the Portuguese."

10. It must be noted that this understanding of the term may not be universal. Further East, Fataluku interlocutors talk about *rota* as being simultaneously a whip (*chicote*), a pathway (*caminho*), and a token of authority, thus associating it with the terrors of Portuguese punitive powers. We thank Susana de Matos Viegas for this information.

References

de Almeida, A. 1954. "Relatório—IV Congresso de Pré-história do Extremo Oriente." *Separata de Garcia de Orta* 2(3): 349–57.

———. 1957a. Field notebook Timor 1957 [ms.]. Lisboa: Arquivo IICT—Espólio Missões Antropológicas.

———. 1957b. António de Almeida to Presidente da Comissão Executiva da Junta de Investigações do Ultramar, 5 Junho 1957: In *Centro de Estudos de Etnologia do Ultramar*, vol. 1. Arquivo IICT/ULisboa.

———. 1960. "Contribuição para o estudo do Neolítico de Timor Português." *Memórias da Junta de Investigações do Ultramar*, 2ª série, 16 (1960): 127–39.

———. 1961. "Presenças culturais no Timor Português." *Estudos de Ciências Políticas e Sociais* 51: 25–40.

———. 1976. "Da Pré-História do Timor Português—Pinturas Rupestres." *Memórias da Academia das Ciências de Lisboa—Classe de Ciências*, tomo XIX Lisboa [comunicação apresentada em 1974], 1–47.

de Almeida, A, and G. Zbyszewski. 1967. "A Contribution to the Study of the Prehistory of Portuguese Timor—Lithic Industries." In *Archaeology at the 11th Pacific Science Congress*, edited by W. G. Solheim, 1:55–67. Honolulu: University of Hawaii.

Barnes, S. 2017. "The Re-assertion of Sacralised Authority in Post-occupation Uato-Lari." In *Transformations in Independent Timor-Leste: Dynamics of Social and Cultural Cohabitations*, edited by R. G. Feijó and S. M. Viegas, 79–93. London: Routledge.

Barnes, S., H. Hägerdal, and L. Palmer. 2017. "An East Timorese Domain Luca from Central and Peripheral Perspectives." *Bijdragen Tot de Taal-, Land- en Volkenkunde* 173(2–3): 325–355.

Barrkman, J. 2017. "Return to Baguia: An Ethnographic Museum Collection on the Edge of Living Memory." PhD thesis, Australian National University, Canberra.

Bell, J. 2006. "Losing the Forest but Not the Stories in the Trees: Contemporary Understandings of F. E. William's 1922 Photographs of the Purari Delta." *Journal of Pacific History* 41(2): 191–206.

Bloembergen, M., and M. Eickhoff. 2015. "The Colonial Archaeological Hero Reconsidered: Post-colonial Perspectives on the 'Discovery' of the Prehistoric Past of Indonesia." In *Historiographical Approaches to Past Ar-*

chaeological Research, edited by G. Eberhardt and F. Link, 133–64. Berlin: Edition Topoi.

Bourdieu, P. 1991. *Language and Symbolic Power*. Cambridge: Polity.

Bovensiepen, J. 2015. *The Land of Gold: Post-conflict Recovery and Cultural Revival in Independent Timor-Leste*. Ithaca, NY: Cornell University Press.

Bovensiepen, J., and F. D. Rosa. 2016. "Transformations of the Sacred in East Timor." *Comparative Studies in Society and History* 58(3): 664–93.

Buckley, L. 2014. "Photography and Photo-Elicitation after Colonialism." *Cultural Anthropology* 29(4): 720–43.

Correia, A. M. 1941. Plano de Estudos Antropológicos Coloniais, criado por indicação da Junta de Missões Geográficas e de Investigações Coloniais, 12 de Março de 1941. In Processo 150, IICT, Espólio das Missões Antropológicas.

Correia, A. M, A. de Almeida, and C. França. 1956. "Nouvelles stations lithiques du Timor Portugais et la prehistoire de l'Indonesie Orientale." Separata de Cronica do IV Congreso Internacional de Ciencias Prehistoricas e Protohistoricas, Madrid 1954. Zaragoza, pp. 295–300.

Fabian, J. 1983. *Time and the Other: How Anthropology Makes Its Object*. New York: Columbia University Press.

Fox, J. J. 1993. "Comparative Perspectives on Austronesian Houses: An Introductory Essay". In *Inside Austronesian Houses: Perspectives on Domestic Designs for Living*, edited by J. J. Fox, 1–28. Canberra: ANU Press.

Geismar, H., and A. Herle. 2010. *Moving Images: John Layard, Fieldwork and Photography on Malakula since 1914*. Honolulu: University of Hawaii Press.

Glover, I. 1986. *Archaeology in Eastern Timor, 1966–67*. Canberra: Department of Prehistory, the Australian National University, Terra Australis 11.

Gunter, J. 2008a. "Violence and 'Being in History' in East Timor: Local Articulations of Colonial Rebellion." Master's thesis, ISCTE-Instituto Universitário de Lisboa.

———. 2008b. "Communal Conflict in Viqueque and the 'Charged' History of '59." *Asia Pacific Journal of Anthropology* 8(1): 27–41.

———. 2010. "Kabita-Kakurai, de cada dia: Indigenous Hierarchies and the Portuguese in Timor." *Portuguese Literary and Cultural Studies* 17/18: 281–301.

Hoskins, J. 1997. *The Play of Time: Kodi Perspectives on Calendars, History and Exchange*. 2nd ed. Berkeley: University of California Press.

———. 1998. *Biographical Objects: How Things Tell the Story of People's Lives*. London: Routledge.

Oliveira, N. V. 2006. "Returning to East Timor: Prospects and Possibilities from an Archaeobotanical Project in the New Country." In *Uncovering Southeast Asia's Past: Selected Papers from the 10th International Conference of the European Association of Southeast Asian Archaeologists*, edited by E. A. Bacus, I. C. Glover, and V. C. Pigott, 88–97. Singapore: NUS.

———. 2008. "Vasco Subsistence Archaeobotany: Food Production and the Agricultural Transition in East Timor." ANU Digital Theses, Department of Archaeology and Natural History, Australian National University, Canberra.

———. 2011. "75 anos de investigações arqueológicas em Timor-Leste." In *Atas do Colóquio Timor: Missões Científicas e Antropologia Colonial*, edited by V. R. Marques, A. C. Roque, and R. Roque. Lisboa: IICT/ICS, http://www.historyanthropologytimor.org/wp-content/uploads/2012/04/23-OLIVEIRA_NV.pdf

Poloni, R. J. 2012. "Expedições Arqueológicas nos Territórios De Ultramar: Uma Visão da Ciência e da Sociedade Portuguesa do Período Colonial; Tese de doutorado." Universidade do Algarve, Setembro de 2012.

———. 2017. "A autoridade através dos vestígios: a arqueologia na Missão Antropológica de Timor, 1953." *Anuário Antropológico* 42(2):109–132.

Roque, R. 2010. *Headhunting and Colonialism: Anthropology and the Circulation of Human Skulls in the Portuguese Empire, 1870–1930*. New York: Palgrave Macmillan.

———. 2011. "José Celestino da Silva e o relatório sobre os *usos e costumes* de Timor." In *Atas do Colóquio Timor: Missões Científicas e Antropologia Colonial*, edited by V. R. Marques, Ana C. Roque, and R. Roque. Lisboa: IICT/ICS, http://www.historyanthropologytimor.org/wp-content/uploads/2012/01/10-ROQUE_R.pdf.

———. 2012. "The Colonial Command of Ceremonial Language: Etiquette and Custom-Imitation in Nineteenth Century East Timor." In *Portuguese and Luso-Asian Legacies in Southeast Asia, 1511–2011*, edited by L. Jarnagin, 2:67–87. Singapore: Institute of Southeast Asian Studies.

Sousa, L. 2011. "Objetos lulik, Neolítico e casas sagradas: um episódio de antropologia colonial em António de Almeida." In *Atas do Colóquio Timor: Missões Científicas e Antropologia Colonial*, edited by V. R. Marques, Ana C. Roque and R. Roque. Lisboa: IICT/ICS, http://www.historyanthropologytimor.org/wp-content/uploads/2012/01/18-SOUSA_L.pdf.

Traube, E. G. 1986. *Cosmology and Social Life: Ritual Exchange Among the Mambai of East Timor*. Chicago: University of Chicago Press.

———. 1989. "Obligations to the Source." In *The Attraction of Opposites*, edited by D. Maybury-Lewis and U. Almagor, 321–44. Ann Arbor: University of Michigan Press.

Van Heekeren, H. R. 1957. *The Stone Age of Indonesia*. Leiden: KLTV/Martinus Nijhoff.

Zbyszewski, G., M. C. Neto, and M. E. Castro-Almeida. 1985–86. "Note préliminaire sur le gisement paléolithique de Laga (Timor-Dili)." *Garcia de Orta Seria Antropobiologia*, Lisboa 4(1–2): 15–27.

PART III

Following Cultures through Archives

Chapter 8

CONTESTING COLONIALISMS, CONTESTING STORIES

EARLY INTRUSION IN EAST TIMOR THROUGH PORTUGUESE AND DUTCH EYES

Hans Hägerdal

Introduction

Colonial history is, and has always been, an ambiguous affair. In these days this may seem a platitude; the pertinent questions posed by post-colonial critics have obviously given the very term "colonial history" doubtful connotations. The modernization and impact-response theories so long fashionable when analyzing colonial processes are seen at best as insufficient and at worst as blatantly Eurocentric. However, there is another side of ambiguity that is not so easily resolved with the application of new methodological perspectives. This has to do with the sources that in the last instance inevitably form the basis of what academic scholars are trying to do. Of the vast areas that fell under European domination in the centuries after 1500, only parts had a written tradition. Most of the Americas, Africa, Australia, Oceania, and various tribal areas of Asia had not. Moreover, climatic factors, lack of resources for preservation, and political turbulence have taken a severe toll on what there was—one may recall the fate of the thousands of historical manuscripts in Timbuktu during the current Malian civil war.

Whether we like it or not, it remains that the written materials for periods of colonial domination were frequently produced in a Western or Western-derived context, even in areas with an advanced tradition of issuing records. For example, we have extensive records from the European trading companies in Asia but relatively little from the Chinese traders who plied the waters of East and Southeast Asia, a phenomenon easily explained by the companies' status as record-keeping organizations in contrast with the small-scale organizations of the Chinese (Blussé 1996: 148). It goes without saying that textual records are only part of the picture; areas with few or no indigenous written texts can be studied in other ways. The well-known studies in global history by Jared Diamond have shown what a combination of physiology, human geography, linguistics, anthropology, and archaeology can do to illuminate our understanding of the past (Diamond 1997). The nonliterate humans of the past can speak through a confluence of fine-tuned scientific methodologies. If we want to base our conclusions on concrete records of people, events, and circumstances, we are nevertheless confined to the tyranny of the colonial archive. There lies the ambiguity: the material represents a discourse of external domination, but we simply cannot do without it.

The present study deals with an almost archetypical example of the dilemmas described above, namely the Portuguese colonial intrusion in the eastern part of Timor in the seventeenth century. How did it come about, what were the consequences, and what are the imprints in the collective memory? The sparse documentation of the period up to the seventeenth century allows for a variety of interpretations here. This leads to interesting methodological queries of how to formulate a Timorese history of Timor, in other words a reaction against the colonial historiography of past generations of scholars. To put it simply, how do we approach an island from which no writings have been preserved outside the auspices of the colonial apparatus until far into the eighteenth century? One way to move forward is, I believe, to apply a critical triangulation of the categories of source material. We may think of Dutch and Portuguese texts in the first place, but oral tradition offers an interesting third opinion in spite of the methodological difficulties to assess it. In a nonliterate society, this was the normal means of conveying information and was accordingly institutionalized in local societies through oral recordkeepers (*makoan, lian na'in, mafefa*). While the narratives evidently change over time, a collation of the data from various parts of Timor yields interesting patterns that may be compared with archival, archaeological, and ethnological data.

In contrast to classical historical criticism, this is done not so much in order to establish a "definite" sequence of events. Alun Munslow, among many others, has argued that "the idea that history is ultimately determined by 'what happened' in the essentialist sense that it possesses its own given meaning, is giving way to a much more sophisticated engagement with the past" (Munslow 2003: 157). I do not want to press this point too far since there are after all sound methodologies that allow us to make approximations of chains of events. For a period with limited sources that involves a set of cultural encounters, I nevertheless find the implication of Munslow's discussion appealing: history may be seen as historiography, or in other words a written discourse about the past and its narratives. Here I wish to explore the contrasts between narratives; in other words, to find the divergences rather than confluences in the accounts and see how they work according to their own logic. Only then can we begin to destabilize colonial narratives and possibly replace them with a Timor-centered view of Timor with the help of nonarchival materials and the great strides made within Southeast Asian historical studies in the last three or four decades. Against this background, this chapter aims to take a fresh look at the published and unpublished sources and draw some tentative conclusions on the processes involved in the conquest phase of the seventeenth century.

The State of the Field

As highlighted by the bibliography of Timor by Kevin Sherlock, a maybe surprising amount has been written on Timor since the nineteenth century.[1] As a matter of fact, serious histories of both Dutch and Portuguese Timor were authored long before anything similar was done with many other countries of Southeast Asia. Taken together, this historiography constitutes a very substantial resource for the study of Timor's past since the sixteenth or seventeenth century.

Leaving aside for a moment the problem of a possible Eurocentric and nationalistic slant, the older texts suffer from some apparent shortcomings. The Portuguese publications before 1975 almost exclusively used sources and literature written in Portuguese, thereby missing the important body of Dutch writings entirely. Ethnographic literature was used very sparsely. Nor did they take the larger Southeast Asian context into account, but this is probably characteristic of the myopic way of writing the history of various countries in the region until the postwar period—it should be remembered that the first histories of Southeast Asia were only written by Brian Harrison and Daniel George Edward Hall in 1954 and 1955, respectively. As for the Dutch studies of their Timorese colony and its past, they basically suffered from the same problems in terms of language and contextualization. The prolific British scholar Charles Ralph Boxer had a good command of the seventeenth- and eighteenth-century sources in both Dutch and Portuguese. His works are full of good insights, but he only published a few brief sketches on early colonial Timor (1947, 1968). It was only in the 1970s that a few anthropologists tried to make sense of early Timorese history, namely the former colonial official Herman Schulte Nordholt (1971) and the Australian scholar James J. Fox (1977). Their works tried to establish historical trajectories based on a study of available sources seen against local culture and tradition and remain essential reading for anyone wishing to study the region. However, none of the authors had much to say about East Timor, and there was much spadework left to do with regard to the early sources.

Since the 1990s, studies of Timor have gained momentum, partly obviously as a consequence of the interest that the East Timor question evoked internationally. The final decolonization process in 1999–2002 was accompanied by some general histories of East Timor by authors such as Geoffrey Gunn (1999). On Timor itself the proliferation of texts was interestingly an affair for Indonesian West Timor rather than the fledgling republic in the east. The fall of Soeharto and the ensuing emphasis on decentralization and *muatan lokal* made way for a number of local studies, sometimes centered on the traditional kingdoms (such as Wadu et al. 2003, Widiyatmika 2007). These studies often yield interesting data not previously known to Western scholars, but are hampered by a lack of knowledge of Dutch and Portuguese (and sometimes English). On East Timor, the only major historical study to my knowledge is that of the Nobel Prize winner Bishop Belo on the traditional kingdoms of Timor (2011).

Some new directions that studies of colonial history might take have been envisaged by a couple of recent scholars. In his substantial thesis *De jacht op sandelhout* (The hunt for sandalwood, 2002), the Dutch historian Arend de Roever studies seventeenth-century Timor in the context of the economic links of maritime Asia that emerged under the influence of the Portuguese Estado da Índia and the Dutch East India Company, where the keyword was the trade in sandalwood. He shows how the phases of external domination on Timor were interconnected with the fluctuations in the supply and price of sandalwood, which in turn had to do with developments in other parts of Asia. De Roever does not study the indigenous societies in detail. This is done, on the other hand, by Ricardo Roque in *Headhunting and Colonialism* (2010), in which he analyzes the nature of Portuguese-Timorese relations in the mid-colonial period. Here he notes the atavistic features of Portuguese colonialism. A vassal system was established at an early stage; the numerous small domains in East Timor and their lords were termed kingdoms (*reinos*) and kings (*reis*) and were established by the governor in Dili via solemn oaths. This was not a one-sided affair but rather a case of mutual parasitism, to use a term by the philosopher Michel Serres. The marginal Portuguese presence on Timor, dismissed as weak and obsolete by many observers, was in fact embedded in a structure that was functional for the Timorese elites (or parts thereof). Roque does not detail the actual emergence of the system, however, since his study starts in about 1870.

Timor on the Eve of European Encroachment

During a few eventful decades in the fifteenth and sixteenth centuries, the Portuguese established enclaves of authority along the coasts of Africa, Asia, and South America at a rapid pace that has not failed to intrigue posterity. A second-rate European state with a population of well under a million managed to secure a foothold in a string of faraway places that partly remained in Portuguese hands until the second half of the twentieth century. This potentially heroic picture (which has indeed been propagandized as such in schools, textbooks, and monuments) has been greatly qualified in modern research. A relative lack of interest in maritime affairs among the Asian great powers at the time of the Portuguese arrival, rather than European technological superiority, might have been decisive for the rapid progress. But one also needs to look at the African or Asian side of the matter. The contact zones—the *fortalezas* and ports with their hinterlands—engendered strong cultural dynamics that created hybridity. While racial ideas were prevalent on the Iberian Peninsula since some time, intermarriage was never shunned as long as it did not contaminate religious unity. Catholicism and the trappings of European culture must have been attractive to certain groups of people, but presumably only if it could be successfully localized within prevalent values and customs. All over the far-flung Portuguese realm, people who had taken up Portuguese markers of identity would retain their Luso-African or Luso-Asian identity, even when their place of residence was lost to some other political power (Newitt 2005).

When we consider developments on Timor, this element of hybridity is important to keep in mind, as well as the formal and informal aspects of the Portuguese colonial realm. The Estado da Índia was established in the main centers of gravity such as Goa, Malacca, Macao, Ternate, and so on. However, there were areas where no effective central control could be exerted over the Portuguese merchants and adventurers who roamed Asian lands. To these belonged Flores and Timor and the islands nearby. After the capture of Malacca in 1511, the Portuguese settlers rapidly gained a rather detailed idea of the commercial geography of Southeast Asia, as testified by the works of Tomé Pires (ca. 1512–15) and Duarte Barbosa (ca. 1516). It is clear from these accounts that trading routes already connected Timor to the western part of maritime Southeast Asia, on which the Portuguese could profit. A trip from Malacca to Timor was already planned in 1514 and presumably got underway in 1515 (Hägerdal 2012: 17–21). At any rate, a letter from 1523 confirms that Portuguese merchants operated on Timor without the consent of the Estado da Índia, perhaps related to the establishment of a post in the Banda Islands in the same year (Newitt 2005: 122). By the 1550s, they had begun to stay over winter (the rainy season) on the well-protected northern coast of Solor, a small island to the north of Timor. Concurrently with this, the first missionary enterprise got underway in about 1556.

Very little is known about Timor from sixteenth-century published or unpublished texts. In spite of the interest in the sandalwood riches, conditions on the island are usually mentioned in passing. The most important texts are Antonio Pigafetta's narrative of the Magellan expedition, which visited the island in 1522, and the Malaccan geographer Manuel Godinho de Erédia's treatise *The Golden Chersonese*, which is usually dated between 1597 and 1600 (Pigafetta 1923: 234–37; Erédia 1997: 253–54). What we get are some details about local products and the import goods that the Timorese coveted, plus information on the various petty kingdoms, which varies greatly between the two sources. Further progress can be made through the application of archaeology and linguistics. Thus James Fox has studied the ritual language that is transmitted within Timorese groups and drawn conclusions about the change of edible plants from the pre-contact period to the period of direct or indirect Western influence. The introduction of maize as the principal crop some time before 1658 is presumed to have increased the resources of sustaining larger populations (Fox 1988, 1991). Increasingly secure scientific dating has given further relief to historical processes: for example, Peter Lape and later Sue O'Connor et al. have studied some of the hundreds of fortified settlements found on Timor and found that construction of several of them commenced in the immediate pre-contact period (fourteenth to sixteenth centuries), which evokes suggestions of profound societal changes. Joanna Barrkman has drawn attention to the early dates of some imported *patola* cloths, further highlighting the pre-European external contacts (Lape 2006; O'Connor et al. 2012; Barrkman 2009).

Portuguese Sources on the Conquest Phase

A few fundamental facts are well documented. The Dominican missionaries kept a fort on Solor since the 1560s from where Timor could be reached with relative ease. This fort was conquered by the Vereenigde Oost-Indische Compagnie (VOC) in 1613, after which the center of Portuguese activities moved to Larantuka on easternmost Flores. However, the limited official Portuguese presence in the Flores-Timor area meant that few sources from these quarters survived. There was no João de Barros or Diogo do Couto to chronicle the saga of the semi-isolated group of Portuguese on the islands. Fragments can be gleaned from scattered reports and letters, but the only narratives that pretend to chronicle the Portuguese establishment on Timor are a few texts written by the Dominicans, in the first place the *História de S. Domingos*, in which Timor is only described as part of the larger overseas missionary project (Santa Catharina 1866). In the scholarly literature, the Dominicans have a poor reputation as writers, being accused of exaggerations and downright sloppiness; they are often contrasted with the well-educated and perceptive Jesuits. Nevertheless, such condescending opinion might be too categorical: their ideas of arranging the past into a meaningful narrative were not the same as those of modern scholarship. Dutch archival sources have evoked more praise as "first class" due to their regularity and detail. From 1613 to 1657 the VOC had a representation on Solor, albeit with a few long interruptions, and from 1653 they were steadily established in Fort Concordia in Kupang on the Timorese mainland. Some of the pieces, in particular the *Dagregisters*, which give the annotations of the VOC commander from day to day, are far more detailed than anything produced by Portuguese writers. Relations with the Portuguese loom large in these seventeenth-century sources. Nevertheless the Dutch colonial archive has its setbacks too. No master narrative of the early Dutch exploits on Timor was ever produced, and we only have brief treatments in standard works such as Pieter van Dam's *Beschryvinge van het Ostindische Compagnie* and François Valentijn's *Oud en Nieuw Oost-Indiën*.

Under these circumstances, the material does not give an immediately clear image of when and how Portuguese commercial and missionary influences were transformed into political dependency. The lack of comprehensive sources makes the modern Portuguese historians concentrate on a few key events, largely culled from the *História de S. Domingos* (Santa Catharina 1866). The studies of Affonso de Castro (1867) and Humberto Leitão (1948) mention the propagation of Christianity among the kingdoms of West Timor in about the 1630s as a prerequisite to political domination. This is followed by a Makassarese seaborne invasion that ravages the Timorese coasts in 1641 and induces the rulers of Servião (part of West Timor) and Wehali (Central Timor) to become Muslims. The Islamic Sulawesi-centered Makassar Empire is at its height at this time and encompasses wide areas of northern and eastern Indonesia. The acute threat of an Islamized Timor triggers two Portuguese expeditions that assist the Lifau (Ambeno) and Mena kingdoms on the north coast and defeat Servião and Wehali in turn (Belo 2011: 12; cf. Fox 1982). The lord of Wehali is revered like an emperor by the other petty rulers on the island, implying as it seems that the Portuguese take over his role as suzerain; a letter from Goa from 1645 asserts that "the petty kings of Timor are not only friends but even vassals of His Majesty" (Belo 2011: 12). Somewhat later on, the Portuguese and their local allies inflict a number of devastating defeats on the Dutch rivals in 1655, 1656, and 1657. The scene is now set for the emergence of the two families Da Costa and Hornay, of mixed or non-European ancestry (so-called Black Portuguese or Topasses), who dominate politics on Timor until 1702 when finally a white governor arrives. However, neither the missionary sources nor the preserved letters and reports are explicit about East Timor itself. We just learn that the missionary-cum-politician Frei Manuel de Santo António establishes his spiritual authority in Viqueque in 1698–99 and manages to convert the rulers of Viqueque, Samoro, Luca, Fatuleteluli, Alas, and Manatuto—some kingdoms in the list being among the more important in East Timor (Leitão 1952: 10; Belo 2011: 13). The transition brings about their (temporary and symbolic) allegiance to the king of Portugal.

The focus of Portuguese interest on the western half is also illuminated by the few detailed maps of Timor that were made in the seventeenth century. Mapmaking involves not only a collation of geographical data but also the relation between power and knowledge, which is very clearly seen in the Timorese case. A map by Manuel Godinho de Erédia from 1613 gives thirty-one names of places on the north coast, ending with Bobonaro (Babonao). While this place is actually in the center, close to the present border to Indonesia, the map puts it close to the northeastern point of the island. In the south, twenty-three places are indicated up to Luca, which still leaves a large part of the southern coast unaccounted for (Durand 2006: 80–81). The map by Andre Pereira dos Reis from 1659 gives an even more pronounced west-centered perspective; on the north coast the easternmost name is Lusapuca (Nussepoko), some distance to the west of Dili, and on the south coast no names apart from Amabesi and Amarasi in the far west are provided (Durand 2006: 102–3). The very state of Portuguese geographical knowledge indicated most of East Timor as a *terra incognita*.

The VOC Records

It is typical of the fragmentary state of our knowledge of eastern Indonesia at the time that key events, such as the 1641–42 expeditions, are not spoken of in the VOC sources. It underscores the need to study the described sequences of events as historiography, as an engagement with the priorities and mentalities of the writers of texts. The VOC, being a profit-driven commercial company at the core (although it soon took up imperial-colonial features) produced reports and other documents with some regularity. But the aims of these reports were limited and based on the immediate needs of the central VOC organization. Such as they are, the documents mention Timor from the inception of VOC authority on Solor in 1613, and reports are issued regularly after the construction of Fort Concordia in 1653. The geographical position of Kupang means that much attention was devoted to the western part of the island while there was a relative lack of interest in East Timor. The sources mention a number of Atoni kingdoms as subjected to Portuguese authority or influence by the mid-seventeenth century: Ambeno, Amarasi, Amabi, Sonbai, Batumean, Amanuban. How this came about is not very clear. Even less clear is the early penetration of present-day Timor-Leste. A missive from January 1624 informs us that

> the Portuguese have been active in the last year, and have taken and occupied the harbours on the north coast of Timor before our people could do so, with four frigates. The north-eastern coast of Timor, where there is trade with beeswax, slaves and cicir [turtle-shell], was also occupied with eleven junks before the arrival of the yacht *Timor*. (Generale missiven 1960: 142)

The passage might suggest that the Portuguese began to regain their influence a decade after the loss of Solor, which at first threatened to wipe them out of eastern Indonesia. On the other hand, it is impossi-

ble to say what "occupied" means here—the establishment of actual
suzerainty through demonstrations of violence or just the securing of
peaceful relations? This may be compared with two other pieces from
1668–69 when the company, for once, harbored hopes of gaining
the East Timorese rajas as subordinate allies. The Portuguese leaders
in Lifau reacted angrily to the Dutch advances and asserted that the
places on East Timor's north coast, such as Ade (Vemasse), Manatuto,
and Lacló, had been tributaries under the king of Portugal "for more
than 60 years."[2] In a likewise animated letter to the Black Portuguese
leader, or *capitão mor*, Matheus da Costa, the Dutch *opperhoofd* of
Kupang questioned the Portuguese claims to Ade at the time. The letter referred to a previous statement by da Costa, who claimed to have
heard these things from the *capitão mor* Francisco Fernandes, who
died sometime after 1641 at a very advanced age and led the Portuguese community after their setback in 1613.[3] Taking the Portuguese
leaders at face value, this would imply a degree of suzerainty since the
early years of the seventeenth century. We shall come back to this.

The Dutch silence about the 1641–42 expeditions is remarkable
if their consequences were as far-reaching as the Dominican chron-
icles imply. The chances are that they were not. A continuous Portuguese suzerainty in the western and central parts of Timor is gainsaid
by some VOC pieces. In 1662 the Dutch received information from
their allies on Rote, close to Timor's western cape, about "the *negeri*
[land, settlement] Wehali that was once ravaged by the Portuguese,
who were however once again beaten by the inhabitants; item Cal-
isou, Tiris, Suai, Camenaça, Bouro, Bibiluto, Vessoro and Maccaky
[Viqueque?], all situated on the south-east side of Timor where the
Portuguese until this day have nothing to say and are kept out."[4]
Moreover, in about 1649 the Portuguese of Larantuka allied with
the resourceful kingdom of the interior of West Timor, Sonbai, which
violently attacked areas specifically stated to have been subjugated
in 1641–42. The Dutch perceived the threat of the Portuguese becoming masters of all Timor "under the guise of the Sonbai lord."[5] In
other words, the Portuguese realm in the Flores-Timor area stands out
as a contest state on par with many similar ones in Southeast Asia.
The lack of an administrative structure meant that the network of
political dependences had to be reinforced from time to time.

The VOC records are the more verbose about a series of events in
1668–70 that appear to have inaugurated the concrete Portuguese
grip on East Timor. By this time the company was securely established
in Kupang and also had a degree of control over the islands in the
vicinity of East Timor (Kisar, Wetar, Leti, etc.), which were monitored

by the VOC post on the Banda Islands. The Portuguese undertaking therefore evoked the worried and enraged attention of the Dutch officials (McWilliam 2007; Hägerdal 2007). In brief, the Dutch *opperhoofd* in Kupang sent a scouting expedition to the ports of northern East Timor in 1665 since there were slaves, beeswax, and turtle-shell to be purchased there. They found a politically fluid situation where both the Portuguese and the Makassarese of Sulawesi staked claims over the coastline up to Ade, modern Vemasse. Some of the domains entertained hope that Dutch interference would rid them of the Portuguese as well as the Makassarese. At the same time the Dutch noted that seaborne Portuguese expeditions bested coastal domains that did not follow their economic policy and traded with other sea powers. They already dominated Matayer (Motael by Dili?), Tibar, Nussepoko, Lanqueiro, and Fatuboro. Further to the west, Balibo, Batugade, Silawan, and Joanije (Jenilu?) had been destroyed by the Portuguese, who also wielded close influence in Assem and Mena in present-day Indonesia.

The Makassar Empire was broken by a concerted attack by the company and its local allies in 1667. The resulting Treaty of Bungaya reduced the immediate area of the realm to part of South Sulawesi, meaning that the formal ties to East Timor were severed. In the next year, the Dutch archival pieces relate a dramatic series of events. The Larantuka Portuguese, irritated that the VOC-affiliated raja of Kisar tried to purchase slaves on Timor, equipped a fleet of twelve crafts manned with White and Black Portuguese and some Makassarese seamen. After ravaging Kisar horribly, they were met by a VOC fleet at Leti and forced to yield their prisoners.[6] The Dutch proceeded to the north coast of East Timor where they swiftly made rudimentary contracts with the local rulers of Ade, Manatuto, Lacló, Waimaa, Hera, and Laivai in May–June 1668 (Corpus diplomaticum 1931: 394). The Portuguese in Lifau reacted furiously, in spite of Dutch warnings, and in turn sent a fleet along the coast in the fall of 1668. A number of Timorese settlements were destroyed, and numerous people were killed and taken prisoner.[7] The Dutch did absolutely nothing about this, although they later tried to use the contracts to "prove" that they had juridical rights to large parts of East Timor. The Portuguese expansion continued in the next few years. In 1670, it was reported that Matheus da Costa worsted Suai. In the same year, his seaborne musketeers rounded the eastern cape of Timor and proceeded to expand the Portuguese suzerainty to Tiris-Serin in present-day southwestern Timor-Leste.[8] Through a series of effective and brutal expeditions, the Portuguese leader António Hornay was able to confirm the conquests in 1673, 1675, 1677, 1686–87, and 1691–92, campaigns that even reached the inland areas.

Though the outlines are reasonably well documented in the VOC archival sources, this violent process may well be termed the unknown conquest of East Timor. Nothing coherent was published on the issue, and Portuguese sources only contain the barest hint of what must have been a chain of events of utmost importance for all involved.[9] Part of this is no doubt due to the differences in recordkeeping: Portuguese letters and reports were simply not preserved to the extent that Dutch items were. Although eastern Flores and Timor were the only remaining Portuguese possessions in Southeast Asia after 1641, important changes there were not even noted in Lisbon, Goa, and Macao.

What has been said so far highlights the traps of reconstructing early East Timorese history with the help of the extant archival record. A reconstruction from Portuguese materials will produce a significantly different story than a corresponding Dutch one. There are very few non-Portuguese or non-Dutch travel accounts from the seventeenth century that could otherwise have provided a third opinion. History stands out as a set of competing narratives that are each perfectly explicable from their own preconditions but are not easily subsumed into a synthesis. So how do we go further from here? I will suggest a few tentative ways to explore early colonial processes.

Indigenous Voices?

Contrary to the doubtful reputation that colonial records have in postcolonial writings, they do sometimes give a voice to the indigenous. This is actually part of the early colonial parcel: Western establishments in Africa and Asia were always dependent on local informants-cum-allies, and detailed administrative records contain a certain amount of statements by chiefs, commoners, and even slaves. This is also the case with early Timor, but only in the western part where the colonial administrations were centered until 1769 in the Portuguese case, and 1949 in the case of the Dutch. So, can we know anything about how the locals of East Timor experienced the obviously rather violent conquest phase?

The sheer detail of the Dutch reports and *dagregisters* sometimes hint at the consequences for the locals or even quote them. A VOC report relates the story of a visit of a Portuguese ship to Ade and Manatuto in September 1666 on the eve of the final conquest. On board were three Dutchmen who had been lent to the Portuguese in Lifau with an eye to improve commercial relations. They sailed to Ade and Manatuto in order to purchase an amount of beeswax. However, the crew had an encounter with locals on account of flying the Portuguese banner of the *quinas*, and were regarded as obvious enemies. People stood at the seashore with weapons in their hands and forbade the crew members to come ashore. They even refused to provide them with drinking water. Then the three Dutch sailors discovered a *princevlag*, that is, the Dutch tricolor. The three of them pointed out that they were Dutch subjects and that their ship was neither Portuguese nor Makassarese, but their own. When they had sworn an oath about this, the atmosphere changed in an instant. They were treated friendly and given drinking water, and were abundantly purveyed with refreshments. The Portuguese, on the other side, had to remain aboard the ship. As they talked to the locals, the chiefs asked if no ships were to be expected from the Dutch, which a captain from Kupang had promised in the year before. They claimed to be the enemies of the Portuguese as well as the Makassarese. Although they had been warned that they would be assaulted and killed by them for disobedience, they said that they very much longed for the Dutchmen to take possession of the land. They asked the Dutch persons to make this known, since they could not withstand their enemies more than a year still. The three Dutchmen promised to do this and later reported to the authorities in Banda.[10]

Scenes like this must obviously be taken with a grain of salt. The Dutch saw the Portuguese and Makassarese as rivals, although they were at formal peace with the former. The scene where the East Timorese chiefs express their longing for a Dutch overlord is presumably adapted to Dutch wishful thinking—it cannot be known if the Dutch were better liked than their opponents.[11] On the other hand, the setting is perfectly explicable. The small-scale nature of polities in this part of the archipelago motivated playing larger seaborne powers against each other, and certainly motivated flattering the Dutch visitors in the vain hope that they might assist the hard-pressed domains.

There might be other ways to approach indigenous perspectives. While there are hardly any early Timorese texts, there is a body of oral traditions from the fifty-odd domains of East Timor. While a Timorese domain was small, it was not chaotic or unstructured (though often beset by internal disputes). Many domains known to sixteenth- and seventeenth-century sources were political realities far into the twentieth century, and have some relevance even today. Anthropologists have elucidated their relatively complicated hierarchical structure, which usually includes a "king," an executive regent, vassal lords, and genealogical headmen at the village level (Schulte Nordholt 1971). Like in many African kingdoms, history telling was entrusted to appointed experts, and stories were transferred through a ritual language.

Can anything be known by way of oral transmission of a time that is more than three centuries removed from us? The answer is no doubt yes, as amply shown by genealogical history preserved on Rote and Savu, and to some extent Solor, Alor, and West Timor. The VOC records give proof that people and events as far back as the mid-seventeenth century have been commemorated through the generations. The anthropologist James Fox (1979), working with Rotenese genealogical history, has assumed that tradition tends to stabilize a set of "facts" soon after the occurrence of the event—A is succeeded by his son B, B is forced to hand over his power to brother C, and so on. From these facts a number of stories evolve, which may vary substantially from spokesman to spokesman. Another prominent feature with oral traditions is their concern with origins. A set of legendary stories explains the emergence of the traditional order in a given society: the origin of the ruling clan, the reason why certain clans are assigned this function or that, the contacts with neighboring polities, etc. From this point of view, we may expect Portuguese intruders in the stories.

We are not disappointed in this. A comprehensive unpublished manuscript by the Australian researcher Peter Spillett (1999) contains systematic interviews with tradition experts all over Timor. Additional materials have been collected by Shepard Forman (1977), Bishop Belo (2011) and others. It appears from these accounts that the various petty kingdoms usually do have an idea of the first coming of the Portuguese. Nevertheless, the circumstances vary a lot, not surprising regarding the fragmented political map of early Timor. Some regard them as coming from Larantuka, others from Makassar. When they land on Timor, they have peaceful commercial intentions in a few cases. There are also a number of accounts of the introduction of Christianity through Catholic fathers, an event of sometimes seminal importance in the collective memory. Mostly, however, the foreigners come as conquerors. Their initial attempt of conquest is not always successful; some stories end with the local defenders returning home with the heads of the Portuguese conquistadors. The local princely families occasionally trace their ancestry back to the foreigners from Larantuka; curiously enough, this applies to Vemasse (Ade) which was badly hit by the first wave of invasion in 1668—an event not remembered as far as I have been able to find out (Forman 1977: 107).[12] A complication with oral stories is that they are not chronologically fixed. Even if the stories may be founded on actual events, they could conceivably refer to any period of Portuguese conquest from the seventeenth to the early twentieth century.

Moreover, the Portuguese are not the only foreign visitors to be remembered. While the East Timorese narratives contain almost nothing about the Dutch, they are the more verbose about the Muslim seafarers from Makassar. Several accounts say that the Makassarese arrived before the Portuguese, which is historically consistent with their invasion in 1641, almost three decades before the Portuguese onslaught. Judging from the data collection of Peter Spillett, they occupy at least as much space in the narratives as the Portuguese do. To an extent the tradition experts may have told Spillett what he wanted to hear, due to his interest in early voyages from Sulawesi, but the Makassar stories are also known from other materials.[13] In the accounts they stand in a less frightening, more communicative position vis-à-vis the locals. Although they wage war on the Timorese in a few cases, even in concert with the Portuguese, they mostly stand out as traders. They occasionally settle on the island, marry daughters of rulers, and even start dynasties. The Makassarese were Muslims, but this is not an issue in the narratives. This can be complemented by recent archaeological research that has identified graves in eastern Timor-Leste known as *batu makassar*, which display some striking similarities with graves from South Sulawesi in the seventeenth century. They suggest a degree of Makassarese influence on Timorese culture in the period, implying that seafarers from Sulawesi might have been more important in terms of political allegiance than the Portuguese for long periods (McWilliam et al. 2012: 276).

Consequences

The precise chronology of Portuguese penetration will probably always be vague and tentative, but this is of somewhat limited concern to us. More relevant is the question of the consequences of the conquest phase. Ruling over large territories is rather untypical of the Portuguese realm in Asia, which tended to consist of *fortalezas* at strategic coastal places. However, governance on Timor followed its own logic. Not least, one should note the ethnic mixture and strong localization of the Lusophonic group in the region. Interracial marriage and cultural inclusion of locals occurred all over Portuguese Asia, but here it was pronounced. The weak ties with the Estado da Índia meant that Eurasian or Asian so-called Black Portuguese actually governed the place, although white Dominican priests also wielded influence. The leading officers, *capitão mor*, were included in local networks and alliances. Matheus da Costa married an Amanuban princess from West Timor. His rival and eventual successor António Hornay seems to have married, first, a descendant of a previous *capitão mor* and, second, a lady from Belu in Central Timor.

These circumstances had consequences both for the political control over East Timor and for the economic exploitation of the area. To elucidate this we once again have to explore the nature of the sources. The Iberian documents do not tell us much about the way Black Portuguese rule was implemented on a local level, but there are a few precious accounts. A letter by the merchant-adventurer Francisco Vieira de Figueiredo from 1664 mentions how Vieira made agreements with the West Timorese kingdoms Amanuban, Amarasi, and Amakono (Sonbai) where the kings received lands and honors in exchange for tributes in sandalwood to the Crown of Portugal, in fact to the local Portuguese. This left them with a fully autonomous position (Boxer 1967: 87–90). Another account from 1697 gives a few more particulars:

> On this island there is a common rumour, well known in the area, that the land has got many mines of gold, mercury, sulphur, iron, copper and tambaca [copper alloy]. Without lying, I can tell that one may obtain gold and tambaca in the rivers, so it is certainly an island of minerals. The people of this island are inclined to laziness, since they do not perform more work or cultivate more land than just barely sufficient for their subsistence. However, it was seen in the time of António Hornay that since he knew how to govern them, they remained obedient to his governance. Nevertheless, the foreigners who are on the island at this time do not make anything but disturbing, grumbling about and showing repugnance towards the governance of Goa.
>
> The *capitão mor*, or the governor, tenentes, captains and further officers who have always governed this land, do not receive any other provision than what the *capitães mores* give them, namely to acquire some sandalwood and furthermore a pension which they take from the kings of these lands, getting every year a fee called tutay, which consists of a certain number of baskets with rice, a certain number of pigs and other similar things, more or less for their sustenance and their residences. (Matos 1974: 216–17)

These remarks are presumably valid for the old Portuguese sphere in West Timor as well as the new territories in East Timor. The contrast between the two half-islands is hinted in another Portuguese report from 1696:

> This island of Timor consists in two parts, and two nations. The one where the sun sets is called Vayquenos. In this part live two emperors

with their lands, kingdoms and jurisdictions. The first emperor is Am-
ave. He fled to the Dutch and found assistance in Kupang at the western
point of the island. ... One of the lands of this emperor is Babau in
the vicinity of Kupang. This site is one of the best on the island, and
is depopulated. Those from Kupang tried to settle it during the time of
[the Portuguese leader] Francisco Hornay who immediately destroyed
it. ... The second emperor in the Vayquenos section is Sunubai whose
predecessors were traitors as Amacono. ... This emperor has his lands,
kingdoms and jurisdictions which are in a peaceful situation.

In the part [of Timor] where the sun rises, the first [kingdom] is
called Camanassa, and the second Vayaly. Both have their lands, kingdoms and jurisdictions, and both serve the Portuguese and Christians
faithfully, and are vassals of His Majesty, and never rebel against the
vassals of the said lord who reside here [in Lifau]; and because they
live far away, they are not nominated nor spoken to in this court. (Belo
2011: 13)

Here the west seems to be a political hotbed where Portuguese and
Dutch interests clash and interfere in local dynastic politics, while the
east largely appears to run its own business. However, it still does not
appear how the relatively small Black Portuguese group, numbering
perhaps a few thousand people, could control an extensive area that
stretched from Flores to easternmost Timor. A VOC missive from 1679
provides us with details not found in the Portuguese sources.

In this year the Dutch had spoken to people from Mena on the
north coast. They related that a Captain da Silva was posted in Ade
with forty or fifty soldiers. There were still two companies of the same
strength at the Belunese coast west of Ade. Their power was estimated
at twenty-three banners of forty to fifty men, provided with shotguns.
Adding to these were the men of the *capitão mor* Hornay. Every year
around March he would bring them from Flores. Together with refugees from Dutch Rote, free Africans ("kaffers"), Timorese Christians,
and Portuguese slaves, they amounted to about one thousand men.
Altogether the forces controlled by Hornay amounted to more than
two thousand soldiers with firearms. Among these, there were few or
no Europeans, since the few white Portuguese stayed in the trade-ori-
ented stronghold Lifau. The underlings of Hornay were allocated all
over the island by their leader, mostly along the coastline, in order
to keep watch against any uprising and to counteract any external
power appearing there.

The informers also told the Dutch that a Makassarese ship had arrived to Mena some six months previously. The crew announced to the
local Portuguese that Sili Saba, the expelled prince of Ade who had
settled in VOC-affiliated Wetar, had come over to Timor again to regain

power with VOC assistance. This brought some commotion, but the
seafarers were bested for spreading lies. The Makassarese skipper was
hanged while the rest of the seamen escaped to their ship and took to
the sea. As the Dutch commented, it was unclear whether these people had come to trade in beeswax or if they had really been told by Sili
Saba to spread this rumor (Generale missiven 1971: 273–74).

The report points to a method of governance previously used in
West Timor, namely placing small multiethnic garrisons in the various domains to keep them in obedience. A desperate sense of harsh-
ness also permeates the Portuguese polity: the unfortunate captain
is hanged for spreading rumors, which (as it turned out) were not
even true. Other reports suggest methods of overcoming resistance
that are strikingly reminiscent of those of the late colonial period. A
missive from 1692 relates that two domains situated two days travel
from Lifau tried to cut the ties to their overlord. However, Hornay reacted quickly. A few Portuguese soldiers were dispatched and supposedly drummed up twenty thousand native auxiliaries—probably a
much-exaggerated figure. The overwhelming force attacked the rebels
in their settlements and fortifications, and a complete holocaust followed. Of an original manpower of one thousand men, no more than
ten supposedly survived the fury of the onslaught (Generale missiven
1975: 458–59). The same pattern of fighting Timorese with Timorese
was repeated until the early twentieth century, and practiced by Portuguese and Dutch alike. While trained musketeers were awe-inspiring
in the low-technology societies of eastern Indonesia and Timor, they
were rather few in number. Using the efforts of native clients was necessary to keep the VOC and Portuguese polities running. At the same
time, there is no evidence that Portuguese rule amounted to anything
more than the small garrisons; also well known, a tight control over
the domains in Dutch and Portuguese Timor only commenced in the
early twentieth century.

Not surprisingly, Iberian sources tell at least a minimum about religious issues in East Timor. Christianity must have made at least a
superficial impact as the religion of the victors. A Franciscan account
from 1670 tells of two padres who stayed at Cutubaba for about a
month and were subsequently invited by the Portuguese naval commander (*capitão do mar*), who was based in Manatuto, to administer
the holy sacraments. This place was momentarily without a chaplain,
who had gone to Luca in the southeast, where the queen had recently
asked to become a Christian. In Manatuto the two Franciscan padres
managed to persuade a nephew of the local king to accept baptism on
his deathbed. The padres then continued their mission in Ade, whose

king also neared his death. They baptized the king who reportedly expired while pronouncing the name of Jesus. Some other people who were converted were entrusted to their Portuguese godfathers for further instruction (Teixeira 1957). The utterly limited resources for religious dissemination are highlighted in this account, but also the common missionary practice to target the highest-ranking in local society. When the first white governor arrived in 1702, he made contact with dozens of petty kings with Catholic Portuguese names (Matos 1974: 336–37).

The other side of the story is the economic. The Black Portuguese conquest was to an extent a response to the fall of Makassar and the new VOC initiatives, but apart from strategic reasons there were also economic aspects. Their realm was very much a trade-based one where the precious sandalwood was accompanied by some other items such as beeswax, slaves, turtle-shell, and small quantities of gold. Traders arrived to Lifau from Macao, Siam, and a few other places, and the Dutch were allowed to join in after 1663. The VOC records give sometimes quite circumstantial accounts of the Lifau trade. Sandalwood was cut in various places of the island and brought to Lifau by land or sea to be traded there. The records sometimes specify that vessels with sandalwood arrived to Lifau from the "Belunese coast," a vague concept that could denote Central or Central-East Timor.

It nevertheless seems that most of the accessible resources of sandalwood were found in the western part of the island—a very strong incentive for the early Portuguese penetration there. The aforementioned Dutch scouting expedition in 1665 found good resources of beeswax in several East Timorese domains: Ade, Manatuto, Lacló, Cailaco, and Mateyer. Sandal trees grew in the inaccessible and mountainous regions. There may have been resources in the interior, but the great labor of moving the wood to the coastal sites restricted foreign interests. A goldmine was supposedly found in Laloy, perhaps Laleia, and some gold found its way from there to Mateyer and finally into the hands of the Portuguese.[14] There were much-advertised stories of a "copper mountain" in Ade that fired European imagination until the nineteenth century, when it turned out to be illusory (Hägerdal 2007). Finally, the political and ethnic fragmentation made for a certain supply of slaves in the eastern domains. Slave trade was common among Western as well as indigenous groups in Southeast Asia, and few if any moral objections can be found in materials from the seventeenth and eighteenth centuries. The need for unfree manpower was on the rise in the second half of the seventeenth century, not least in the coastal port towns of Java (Tarling 1999: 136).

Historical Trends

A comparison between the different categories of source materials is frustrating but instructive. Preserved Portuguese sources tend to emphasize other things than the VOC sources do. East Timor might have seen its ruthless Pizarro or Cortés—Matheus da Costa and António Hornay immediately come to mind—but their bloody exploits do not give subject matter to a William Prescott. Events of obvious importance mentioned in the one archive are passed over in silence in the other. In order to appreciate them we must read the texts along the grain, elucidating their role in the early colonial milieus of maritime Asia. Preserved Portuguese pieces, a tiny fraction of what once must have been, mainly concern relations between Timor and the Estado da Índia or the missionary organizations. They reflect the diminishing resources of the Estado during much of the seventeenth century that let the world of Timor follow its own trajectory. The VOC archive, on the other hand, is the heritage of a commercial-cum-colonial organization that systematically explored all possibilities of profitable trade in maritime Asia (Tarling 1999: 16). While the company was steadily based in West Timor since 1653, East Timor flares up in the documents from time to time when possibilities of commercial influence present themselves.

But our investigation also envisages ways out of tyranny of the archive. Timorese oral tradition abounds with encounters with foreign groups, which play seminal roles in the self-perception of the various kingdoms. Taken together, these indigenous claims to reality are not dismissed that easily: they view the historical landscape in holistic terms that the fragmentary archival sources miss. The collective memory suggests some of the lines of confrontation and cooperation in the post-contact period, and of matters that the Europeans seldom documented, such as the Makassarese influences. Modern archaeological methods further serve to elucidate themes hinted at in written or oral sources, as seen in the recent findings about fortifications and graves.

The oral record reminds us that colonial processes cannot be reduced to the impact of European groups, but that part of their roots must be sought in economic and political structures in Africa and Asia as well. The narratives tell of Portuguese ancestors of princely families, include them in ritual acts, point out the graves of clerics as sites of devotion, and so on. In the same way, the contemporary sources point at the strong localization of the Portuguese. Few of the people involved in the conquest phase of the seventeenth century were "white," and most of them may not have had any European blood in their veins. The defiant reply of the Black Portuguese to the white governor in 1702 gives an idea about the attitude of the conquerors of East Timor, somewhere along the continuum between colonialism and indigenous governance:

> They protested that they were friends and brothers in arms of the King Our Lord, denying him the name of vassals; and they wished to constitute an independent republic to decide therewith the election of a government and dispose of the fruits of the island as they wished, without His Majesty having more than the name of king. As an excuse for their intent they declared that their forebears had conquered it and not the Portuguese arms, and that they had to defend what was theirs. (Matos 1974: 235).

Hans Hägerdal is professor of history at Linnaeus University, Sweden. Much of his research has addressed questions of colonial encounters and contact zones in Asian contexts, and the problem of overcoming Eurocentric bias in the use of historical sources. Presently, he is pursuing a project about early modern European-indigenous relations in Maluku (Indonesia) at Linnaeus University Centre for Concurrences in Colonial and Postcolonial Studies. He is also involved in an Amsterdam-based network studying slavery and slave trade in the Indian Ocean World. Among his publications are *Lords of the Land, Lords of the Sea: Conflict and Adaptation in Early Colonial Timor, 1600–1800* (2012), *Held's History of Sumbawa* (2017), and *Savu: The History and Oral Traditions of an Indonesian Island* (2018).

Notes

1. Sherlock 1980 contains 280 pages with something like 3,000 titles. A huge amount of books and articles has been published since, a large extent of which are political and development studies.
2. VOC 2285 (1733), f. 188–90, sub 13 May 1669. The king of Portugal at that time would have been the king of Spain, Philip III.
3. VOC 2285 (1733), f. 182–83, sub 16 December 1668.
4. VOC 1240 (1662), f. 887.
5. VOC 1187 (1651), f. 637.
6. VOC 2285 (1733), f. 179; Generale missiven 1968: 619–20.
7. VOC 2285 (1733), f. 188–90.
8. VOC 1275 (1670), f. 663.
9. See the letter from the missionary Frei Miguel de São Tomás from 1691: "I was also present at the conquest of half the island of Timor, which was made vassal by Matheus da Costa in the name of Your Majesty; the kings

and chiefs all offered their lands to the Loyal Crown of Your Majesty. And since the Dutch eagerly tried to expel us three times, I was present in the company of the said captain who received a bullet in his left leg in the defense of the island" (Leitão 1948: 259). This vague information appears to allude to the expansion in about 1670, and also to the Dutch campaigns in 1655, 1656, and 1657.

10. VOC 2285 (1733), f. 214–16.
11. For a similar rumor about East Timorese preference for the Dutch, see Speelman, "Notitie," H 802, KITLV Archive, p. 52.
12. The alleged Larantuquiro ancestry of some royal families, including Vemasse and Ossu (Belo 2011: 264), and the presence of Catholicized military detachments along the coast after 1670 may give some color to the hypothesis of Dana Rappoport (2011) that there were cultural connections between the Lamaholot world (Larantuka-Solor Islands) and easternmost Timor in the form of musical idioms.
13. See, for instance, some of the oral narratives included in *Sejarah raja-raja 2007*.
14. VOC 2285 (1733), f. 192–99.

References

Archival Sources

Nationaal Archief, The Hague

VOC
1602–1799   Archive of the Vereenigde Oost-Indische Compagnie (VOC), access number 1.04.02.

KITLV Archive, Leiden

1669   Speelman, Cornelis, "Notitie." H 802.

Published Sources

Barrkman, J. 2009. "Indian Patola and Trade Cloth Influence on the Textiles of the Atoin Meto People of West Timor." *Archipel* 77: 155–82.

Belo, C. F. X. 2011. *Os Antigos Reinos de Timor-Leste (Reys de Lorosay e Reys de Lorotoba, Coronéis e Datos)*. Baucau: Tipografia Diocesana Baucau.

Biermann, B. 1924. "Die alte Dominikanermission auf den Solorinseln." *Zeitschrift für Missionswissenschaft* 14: 12–48, 269–73.

Blussé, L. 1996. "The Vicissitudes of Maritime Trade: Letters from the Ocean Hang Merchant Li Kunhe, to the Dutch Authorities in Batavia (1803–09)." In *Sojourners and settlers: Histories of Southeast Asia and the Chinese*, edited by A. Reid, 148–63. Honolulu: University of Hawaii Press.

Boxer, C. R. 1947. *The Topasses of Timor.* Amsterdam: Koninklijke Vereeniging Indisch Instituut.

———. 1967. *Francisco Vieira de Figueiredo: A Portuguese Merchant-Adventurer in South-East Asia, 1624–1667.* The Hague: M. Nijhoff.

———. 1968. *Fidalgos in the Far East, 1550–1770.* Hong Kong: Oxford University Press.

de Castro, A. 1867. *As possessões Portuguezas na Oceania.* Lisboa: Imprensa Nacional.

Corpus diplomaticum. 1931. *Corpus diplomaticum Neerlando-Indicum, Deel 2: 1650–1675.* The Hague: M. Nijhoff.

van Dam, P. 1931. *Beschryvinge van de Oostindische Compagnie: Tweede boek, Deel 1.* The Hague: Nijhoff.

Diamond, J. 1997. *Guns, Germs and Steel. A Short History of Everybody for the Last 13,000 Years.* London: Vintage.

Durand, F. 2006. *Timor 1250–2005; 750 ans de cartographie et de voyages.* Toulouse: Arkuiris.

de Erédia, M. G. 1997. *Erédia's Description of Malaca, Meridional India, and Cathay.* Kuala Lumpur: MBRAS.

Forman, S. 1977. "East Timor; Exchange and Political Hierarchy at the Time of the European Discoveries." In *Economic Exchange and Social Interaction in Southeast Asia: Perspectives from Prehistory, History and Ethnography,* edited by K. L. Hutterer, 97–112. Ann Arbor: Center for South and Southeast Asian Studies, University of Michigan.

Fox, J. J. 1977. *Harvest of the Palm: Ecological Change in Eastern Indonesia.* Cambridge, MA: Harvard University Press.

———. 1979. "'Standing' in Time and Place: The Structure of Rotinese Historical Narratives." In *Perceptions of the Past in Southeast Asia,* edited by A. Reid and D. Marr, 10–25. Singapore: Heinemann.

———. 1982. "The Great Lord Rests at the Centre: The Paradox of Powerlessness in European-Timorese Relations." *Canberra Anthropology* 5: 22–33.

———. 1988. "The Historical Consequences of Changing Patterns of Livelihood on Timor." In *Contemporary Issues in Development,* edited by D. Wade-Marshall and P. Loveday, 259–79. Darwin: Australian National University.

———. 1991. "The Heritage of Traditional Agriculture in Eastern Indonesia: Lexical Evidence and the Indications of Rituals from the Outer Arc of the Lesser Sundas." In *Indo-Pacific Prehistory 1990.* Vol. 1: *Papers from the 14th IPPA Congress,* edited by P. Bellwood, 248–62. Yogyakarta: IPPA.

Generale missiven. 1960. *Generale missiven van Gouverneurs-Generaal en Raden aan Heren XVII der Verenigde Oost-Indische Compagnie.* Vol. 1: 1610–38. The Hague: Nijhoff.

———. 1964. *Generale missiven van Gouverneurs-Generaal en Raden aan Heren XVII der Verenigde Oost-Indische Compagnie.* Vol. 2: 1639–55. The Hague: Nijhoff.

————. 1968. *Generale missiven van Gouverneurs-Generaal en Raden aan Heren XVII der Verenigde Oost-Indische Compagnie*. Vol. 3: 1656–74. The Hague: Nijhoff.

————. 1971. *Generale missiven van Gouverneurs-Generaal en Raden aan Heren XVII der Verenigde Oost-Indische Compagnie*. Vol. 4: 1675–85. The Hague: Nijhoff.

————. 1975. *Generale missiven van Gouverneurs-Generaal en Raden aan Heren XVII der Verenigde Oost-Indische Compagnie*. Vol. 5: 1686–98. The Hague: Nijhoff.

Gunn, G. 1999. *Timor Lorosae: 500 Years*. Macau: Livros do Oriente.

Hägerdal, H. 2007. "A Note on Ade." *Bijdragen tot de Taal-, Land- en Volkenkunde* 163: 556–58.

————. 2012. *Lords of the Land, Lords of the Sea: Conflict and Adaptation in Early Colonial Timor, 1600–1800*. Leiden: KITLV Press.

Lape, P. V. 2006. "Chronology of Fortified Settlements in East Timor." *Journal of Island and Coastal Archaeology* 1: 285–97.

Leitão, H. 1948. *Os Portugueses em Solor e Timor de 1515 a 1702*. Lisboa: Tip. da Liga dos Combatentes da Grande Guerra.

————. 1952. *Vinte e Oito Anos de História de Timor (1698 a 1725)*. Lisboa: Agência Geral do Ultramar.

de Matos, A. T. 1974. *Timor Português 1515–1769: Contribuição para a sua História*. Lisboa: Faculdade de Letras da Universidade de Lisboa.

McWilliam, A. 2007. "Looking for Adê: A Contribution to Timorese Historiography." *Bijdragen tot de Taal-, Land- en Volkenkunde* 163: 221–38.

McWilliam, A., D. Bulbeck, S. Brockwell, and S. O'Connor. 2012. "The Cultural Legacy of Makassar Stone in East Timor." *Asia Pacific Journal of Anthropology* 13-3: 262–79.

Munslow, A. 2003. *The New History*. Harlow: Longman.

Newitt, M. 2005. *A History of Portuguese Overseas Expansion, 1400–1668*. London: Routledge.

O'Connor, S., A. McWilliam, J. N. Fenner, and S. Brockwell. 2012. "Examining the Origin of Fortifications in East Timor: Social and Environmental Factors." *Journal of Island and Coastal Archaeology* 7: 200–218.

Pigafetta, A. 1923. *Relation du premier voyage autour du monde par Magellan, 1519–1522*. Anvers: Gust Janssens.

Rappoport, D. 2011. "The Enigma of Alternating Duets in Flores and Solor (Eastern Indonesia)." In *Tradition, Identity, and History-Making in Eastern Indonesia*, edited by H. Hägerdal, 130–48.Växjö & Kalmar: Linnaeus University Press.

de Roever, A. 2002. *De jacht op sandelhout: De VOC en de tweedeling van Timor in de zeventiende eeuw*. Zutphen: Walburg Pers.

Roque, R. 2010. *Headhunting and Colonialism: Anthropology and the Circulation of Human Skulls in the Portuguese Empire, 1870–1930*. New York: Palgrave Macmillan.

de Santa Catharina, L. 1866. *História de S. Domingos: Quarta parte*. Lisboa: Panorama.

Schulte-Nordholt, H. G. 1971. *The Political System of the Atoni of Timor*. The Hague: Nijhoff.

Sejarah raja-raja. 2007. *Sejarah raja-raja Timor dan pulau-pulaunya*. Kupang: Dinas Pendidikan dan Kebudayaan.

Sherlock, K. 1980. *A Bibliography of Timor*. Canberra: Australian National University.

Spillett, P. 1999. "The Pre-colonial History of the Island of Timor Together with Some Notes on the Makassan Influence in the Island." Manuscript, held by Museum and Art Gallery of the North Territory, Darwin.

Tarling, N. (ed.). 1999. *The Cambridge History of Southeast Asia*. Vol. 1, pt. 2: *From c. 1500 to c. 1800*. Cambridge: Cambridge University Press.

Teixeira, M. 1957. *Macau e a sua Diocese IV: A Diocese de Malaca*. Macau: Tip. Do Orfanato Salesiano.

Valentijn, F. 1726. *Beschrijving van Oud en Nieuw Oost-Indiën*. Vol. 3. Dordrecht and Amsterdam: Joannes van Braam and Gerard onder de Linden.

Wadu, J., et al. 2003. *Sejarah pemerintahan Kabupaten Timor Tengah Selatan*. Penfui: Lembaga Penelitian Universitas Nusa Cendana.

Widiyatmika, M. 2007. *Lintasan sejarah bumi cendana*. Kupang: Pusat Pengembangan Madrasah.

Chapter 9

READING AGAINST THE GRAIN

ETHNOGRAPHY, COMMERCIAL AGRICULTURE, AND THE COLONIAL ARCHIVE OF EAST TIMOR

Andrew McWilliam and Chris J. Shepherd

Introduction

The landmark publication *Writing Culture: The Poetics and Politics of Ethnography* (1986) signaled a major shift in the practice of anthropology as a research discipline. Marking both a critical rethinking of the representational practice of ethnography, oftentimes expressed as a reflexive and ethical turn, it simultaneously expanded the potential and possibility of ethnography as an interdisciplinary approach to knowledge. Loosed from their disciplinary moorings, critical applications of ethnography provided an innovative lens for discovering otherness and difference across the whole sweep of human endeavor. Clifford called it a hybrid textual activity that traversed genres and disciplines (Clifford and Marcus 1986: 26). Championed in fields as diverse as cultural studies, literature, history, and even advertising, the distinctive intimate, social perspectives of ethnography have become widely popularized in scholarship and reimagined in the process (see Marcus 1995, 2002, as well as Pachirat 2011 for a more recent creative application).

As part of these transformations, the meaning of ethnography has also become more complex. No longer grounded solely in fieldwork, although this association continues to dominate, it has made a significant concession to the place of background history. Just as history has benefitted from the ethnographic lens (e.g. Brobower-Strain 2012), so ethnography has become far more historicised in three specific senses. First, historians now frequently combine history with ethnographic fieldwork just as field ethnographers expand their critical lens into history (e.g. Abercrombie 1998; Anderson 2008). Second, historians have adopted ethnographic tenets by paying more attention to emic or insider perspectives that complement or counter more conventional outsider views (Roque 2010a). And third, there has been a greater appreciation of the historical value of field ethnographies undertaken in the past (Shepherd 2019). Ethnohistory, postcolonial critique, and the anthropology of cultural memory (Holzman 2006) have arisen as manifestations of this synthesis of history, ethnography, and anthropology/ethnology and have served as the context for emergence of ideas such as local agency, history from below, reading against the grain, and history-as-cultural-memory.

Often however, it is left to the reader to decipher what is actually meant by ethnography in any given context. In this chapter, we employ multiple senses of the term as we take up the challenge posed by Ricardo Roque, namely to consider how former colonial-era encounters and ethnographies contribute to shaping scholarly understandings and how they might impact more widely on the generation of postcolonial interpretations of the history and anthropology of East Timor. We are urged to view the rich and complex Portuguese archival history of East Timor as a laboratory for wider reflections on the virtues and vices, connections and discontinuities between colonialism, post-independence, post-colonialism, and ethnography.[1] But field ethnography and historical investigation rarely come together seamlessly. Indeed, this chapter is premised on a stark disjuncture between "ethnography-as-fieldwork" undertaken in the final decade of Portuguese Timor (1966–75) and the particular facets of the Portuguese archive on Timor that concern plantation agriculture; the first tells us nothing about the second (for reasons that are treated in detail below). This disjuncture is articulated in the structure of this chapter. In the first two sections we attend to the question of ethnography. In the latter sections we explore what the archival sources can tell us that ethnographies cannot.

Our field-based ethnographic work in East Timor, at least initially, has been driven by concerns of a contemporary nature, in particular the aftermath of the Indonesian occupation and the remarkable achievement of independence. Like many other anthropologists, we were attracted to the novel possibilities for ethnography following what Geoffrey Gunn has described as the "ethnographic gap" and the near absence of field-based social enquiry during twenty-four years of militarized Indonesian rule (1975–99). Our research efforts over the past decade and a half have been directed to appreciating Timorese experiences of the recent past and their sustained efforts to restore rural livelihoods and rebuild a much-disrupted sociality damaged by war. However, just as all good ethnography requires a historical sensibility, we have both become conscious of the need for a more informed sense of social life in Portuguese Timor and the long history of colonial rule that has contributed so much to shape East Timorese society today. In the process, and with different objectives, we have been drawn to the various Portuguese *arquivos* and extensive colonial documentation for guidance in this regard. We have made separate visits to the extensive collections held in Lisbon and Macao, which has facilitated a much richer appreciation of the contemporary complexity of Timor, even as it raises at least as many questions as it answers—a subject to which we will return in due course.

Ethnography and History

The sunset period of Portuguese colonial rule in Timor (1960–75) saw an influx of enthusiastic French- and English-speaking anthropologists who arrived in the colony to pursue intensive, field ethnography among the diverse language communities of the territory. As David Hicks has noted, the advent of this new wave of professional anthropology was made possible through the combined efforts of French researcher Louis Berthe and Ruy Cinatti, the influential Portuguese poet, civil servant, and "amateur" ethnographer. Cinatti was an avid supporter of anthropology, especially following his period of study with Rodney Needham at the Institute of Social Anthropology at Oxford University. Hicks himself initiated long-term fieldwork in Viqueque in 1966, also through Cinatti's support and sponsorship (Hicks 2011: 5). From then until 1975, Portuguese Timor attracted numerous pioneering and intensive ethnographic projects among the diverse language communities of the territory. Examples include Louis Berthe's own work among Bunak speakers on the western border in conjunction with partner Claudine Friedberg; Brigitte Renard-Clamagirand studied Kemak speakers of Marobo in highland Bobonaro; and Henri and Maria Campagnolo (Portuguese students then based at the Sorbonne) conducted linguistic and anthropological research among Fataluku in Lorehe during the late 1960s. Later, American researchers arrived: Elizabeth Traube worked with Mambai in Aileu from 1972 to 1974; around the same time, Shepard Forman with Makassai in Baguia; and in the closing year of Portuguese Timor, Toby Lazarowitz, a student of David Hicks's, who undertook research among Makassai and (so-called) Kairui communities for his PhD dissertation (1980).[2]

These studies greatly expanded the available body of detailed ethnographic knowledge of Timorese societies and contributed significantly to opening up East Timor to international scholarship. But despite these achievements, the latter-day observer is struck by the paucity of references those ethnographers made to Portuguese documents in their respective publications. Exemplary in this respect is the 1980 volume *The Flow of Life*, edited by James Fox, that featured four ethnographic chapters on the indigenous communities of East Timor, all of which were contributions of the aforementioned ethnographers, but none of whom referenced existing Portuguese historical or anthropological works. In her classic work *Cosmology and Social Life* (1986), Elizabeth Traube makes no mention of any earlier Portuguese documents or studies. Similarly, David Hicks, in his book *Tetum Ghosts and Kin* (1976), mentions just one Portuguese work, Fr. Artur De Sá's *Textos em Teto da Literatura Oral Timorense* (1961).

Given the lengthy involvement of Portuguese researchers and colonial administrators in the production of official records, reports, commentaries, and memoirs on their service in the colony, much of it retained in the extensive Portuguese archives, the absence of references to this body of work is surprising. But it does raise the question why these sources were of no apparent use to the anthropologists of the 1960s and 1970s. How could it be that the long experience of Portuguese colonialism was of no consequence to an understanding of contemporary social formations? Certainly, questions of language and accessibility of sources at the time may have played a part. However, the most persuasive response, it seems to us, lies in the nature of the questions that these anthropologists were asking and, the corollary, that there was little in the Portuguese record of relevance to those specific enquiries.

On the first point, the surge in interest for detailed ethnographies of the societies of Portuguese Timor and neighboring islands was very much fueled by the fashionable theories of structuralism and its variants pursued in Anglo-French and American anthropology. This extended to explorations of the mythic and ideological basis for political and social organization as well as to the popularity of kinship and alliance theory where the agnatic societies of Portuguese Timor were illustrative of variant forms of symmetric and asymmetric prescriptive alliance, and complementary dualism in the prominent

symbolic categories of cultural life.[3] Thus, the role of the anthropologists in their different interpretive ethnographic quests[4] during this
period was very much attentive to the internal dynamics and category
relationships of single-language communities under study. These approaches tended to favor synchronic rather than diachronic perspectives and were therefore not predisposed to an examination of the role
and impact of colonial history.[5]

But that is only part of the answer. The other important element
here is that there was little Portuguese research material available of
direct relevance to their studies. David Hicks noted in response to our
queries on this matter:

> My *Tetum Ghosts and Kin* [book] does not include any of the Portuguese
> sources on the Tetum from Viqueque subdistrict only because I did not
> have any sources. Although mine is a structural approach, had there
> been any such information, I would have used it were it relevant to
> what I was writing. (Personal communication 2013).

Until quite recently, Portuguese social science had little grounding in
anthropology as we currently know it. Consequently, with few excep-
tions, Portuguese researchers prior to the 1960s did not pursue the
kind of focused, intensive, and sustained ethnographic research characteristic of modern field anthropology. Hicks (2011: 5) reinforces
this point when he writes that

> by . . . 1966 . . . a substantial amount of ethnographic work had al-
> ready been carried out in *Timor Português* but, with the exception of
> [Antonio de] Almeida, none had been conducted by professional eth-
> nographers and even they had not employed local languages to obtain
> their facts. Nor, with the exception of Almeida e Carmo and Gomes, had
> anyone studied any single community intensively.

The result was that most Portuguese studies of colonial subjects and
customary communities overlooked local Timorese perspectives on
their own social practices and their interpretive significance. Rather,
they tended to view the enterprise through the colonial lens of observed traditions, of the *usos e costumes* (customs and traditions) and
usually translated through the medium of local language assistants.
The result of that approach is that there are precious few Timorese
voices to be heard across the Portuguese archive (James Fox, personal
communication), and there are also no detailed ethnographic studies
of the kind that provide useful comparative perspectives for contemporary anthropology.[6]

We might, however, highlight one striking exception to the apparent disinterest in Portuguese documentary material in English- or

French-language publications during the late colonial period, namely the geo-ecological study by Joachim Metzner, *Man and Environment in East Timor* (1977), the fieldwork for which was undertaken over the period 1969–70. Metzner's study presents a unique analysis of the ecosystem of the Baucau-Viqueque corridor extending in a north-south transect across East Timor. In the process, he draws on dozens of Portuguese sources covering a wide range of subjects, including history, agriculture, forestry, general development, colonial taxes, government planning, language, and custom. His publication is a notable exception to English-language anthropology of the time, but perhaps by its very exceptionalism it demonstrates precisely the point that French[7] and American anthropologists were exploring forms of indigenous ethnographic knowledge for which there were few comparative precursors in the Portuguese collected archive.

Bridging the Ethnographic Gap:
New Questions, Archival Prospects

The tumultuous withdrawal of the Indonesian government from East Timor in late 1999 brought to an end the tight restrictions on independent field research that had prevailed for more than two decades. This unexpected openness in the political climate encouraged the attention of a younger generation of social-science researchers[8] who brought with them a whole set of new ideas, questions, and research frameworks with which to address what were clearly rich possibilities for ethnographic enquiry in East Timor. These possibilities included "greenfield ethnography" in areas that had not previously been studied in the earlier period of the 1960s and 1970s as well as novel comparative research directions exploring the impact of Indonesian occupation and the adaptive resilience of indigenous customs in the context of nation-building. Over the last twenty years, these twin orientations have attracted a steady stream of anthropologists (as well as other social scientists) to Timor-Leste from across the world and, not least, Portuguese researchers, resulting in an emerging interest in the research potential of the colonial archives of Timor Português. Ricardo Roque's fascinating monograph, *Headhunting and Colonialism* (2010), stands as a recent exemplar of this ethnohistorical trend and highlights precisely the kind of post-colonial historical critique that informs this volume.

Our own experiences mirror this growing trend of excavating colonial archives for insights and perspectives on Portuguese rule in East

Timor and, by extension, the adaptive responses of customary communities to the shifting imperatives of colonial governance. In a number of publications, particularly since 2007, we have drawn extensively on archival documents, colonial reports, and various historical and ethnographic writings to explore some of the historical antecedents of Timorese social and cultural practices. One of us, Andrew McWilliam, has taken particular interest in historical references to, and accounts of, the far eastern region of Timor, known as Ponta Leste, where he has been pursuing long-term anthropological research. The region retains a rich repertoire of mythologies and narrative accounts of engagements with outsiders such as the Portuguese (often referred to as Monarquia), and diverse trading interests, including those of Dutch, Makassar/Buton, and even Papuan contacts over the long period of colonial entanglement (e.g. McWilliam 2007a, 2007b). Chris Shepherd has focused more on development ethnography in contemporary Timor-Leste, which by and by incited a historical interest in the agricultural development and environmental past across Portuguese and Indonesian colonialism (Shepherd 2014, 2019).

In this conjunction of interests, we collaborated on a series of studies into plantation histories of East Timor, particularly coffee, which has been the most successful and extensively planted commodity in the country (see Shepherd and McWilliam 2013, 2014). Given the strong promotional role that successive Portuguese colonial regimes played in developing the sector, there is, understandably, considerable commentary and reportage on shifting developments in the estate crop sector. In this respect official reports and articles in the various government bulletins (such as the *Boletim de Comércio, Agricultura e Fomento* and the *Boletim da Agência Geral das Colónias*) provide a direct representation of colonial thinking during those times and the policies and programs promoted to generate economic returns from the chronically impoverished colony.

Although the collective body of Portuguese colonial writings is extensive, it is often patchy or fragmentary, particularly in relation to the earlier period of colonial history. Attempts to source early colonial government references and commentaries on the District of Lautem, for example, are generally unsuccessful until one reaches the early decades of the twentieth century, and even then the record is relatively thin. Apart from scattered references in published histories (e.g. Correia 1935, Leitão 1948, Matos 1974) the main Portugal-sourced information from pre-1900 Lautem comes from Pélissier's (1996) compilation of Portuguese reports on the various Timorese rebellions and punitive military responses that characterized so much of

Timorese - Portuguese relations during the nineteenth century. References to and commentaries on Portuguese development efforts and government activities in Lautem certainly expand in the various official *Boletim* coinciding with and following the success of the 'so-called' pacification wars (1896–1912). But it is still the case that more information can often be gleaned from non-Portuguese sources in this part of Timor, through Dutch archives and various commentaries of international observers such as George Windsor Earl (1852) and Henry Forbes (1885 [1989]).

In considering why this might be the case, we note the rueful remark of the justly renowned Ruy Cinatti (1964:1830), who made the point that

> the Portuguese have been known to be more ready for action than for writing; and that when they did write 'they concerned themselves with politics and history at the expense of the description of the physical world and material culture, which they regarded as less important.

Ironically, the politics and history that the Portuguese did address were focused almost exclusively on Portuguese activities and their fortunes rather than any attempt to analyse conditions and practices among the Timorese themselves. This is consistent with the comments of that great chronicler of Portuguese history in Timor, C.R. Boxer (1948:50), who speaks of the 'conquistador and clerical mentality' that was directed more 'to action than recording." Geoffrey Gunn (1999), who is credited with bringing Portuguese archival history to an English-speaking audience, has similarly noted that, ' [I]t is certainly not the case that Timor has been neglected in Portuguese letters, but just that few of the massive histories and compilations of documents went beyond a Portugalizing perspective' (1999:23).

These observations, in our experience, are general features of colonial reporting and not least in the colonial materials covering the plans and fortunes of the plantation sector in Portuguese Timor. Nevertheless, the records also provide a rich source of insight and information on colonial attempts to reconfigure the economic and agricultural landscape. In the process, they highlight the perennial concerns of successive Portuguese governors to generate revenues from the remote and impoverished half-island colony, and thereby justify continued support and subsidy from the metropole. From the mid-nineteenth century and reporting on successive attempts to expand plantation agriculture, the collective archive can be variously read as a sustained racialist discourse on the redemptive moral benefits of forced labour; as institutionalized forms of violence expressed in shifting regimes of power and as the reproduction of class distinctions including forms of inherited privilege and dependency (Shepherd and McWilliam 2013). As ever, the evaluations and reflections on the achievements of their efforts rarely extend to exploring Timorese perspectives or concerns. By and large the portrayals of Timorese involvement in the sector tend to be critical and dismissive of the various deficiencies and "perfidious" nature of their Timorese subjects. In this respect, the plantation archive is an ironic marker of the colonial gaze that works to disguise or subsume Timorese agency in favor of the unquestioned objectives of the civilizing mission. But despite this general effacing of Timorese voices, we have found much value in reading against the grain of this material to reflect on its implications for rural Timor-Leste colonial society and its historical legacy.

Given the sheer size of the archive, however, we limit our reflections here to a small selection of records that offer specific insights and interpretive challenges for the historian of rural agricultural development in Portuguese Timor. While we present the materials chronologically over the period 1860 to 1975, the focus lies on the Republican period from 1910 to 1925, which boasts the greatest density of provocative materials. Of particular interest is the extraordinary historical details and insights made available through the *Boletim de Comércio, Agricultura e Fomento da Província.*

Plans and Posturing in the Nineteenth- and Early Twentieth-Century Plantation Archive

The nineteenth century archival literature on plantations in Portuguese Timor can leave the researcher disappointed if seeking accessible and detailed descriptions of how cultivation was organized in practice and, by extension, how power was distributed between the Portuguese and the indigenous kingdoms (*reino*). This is disconcerting given that coffee plantations were introduced into Portuguese Timor as early as 1815[9] (Clarence-Smith 1992) and expanded significantly but most unevely over the twenty-five years from 1860 to 1885. The available writing of the period is mainly prescriptive, that is planning takes precedence over descriptions of previous plantation accomplishments or current activity. Forging big plans and publishing them seemed to drive Portuguese colonialism forth as much as it helped to secure the careers of ambitious governors and administrators. Conversely, casting a discomforting light on poor results was much less rewarding. As Clarence-Smith (1985) has observed, Timor occupied a quasi-mythical and romantic space of Portuguese imperialism-nationalism, and the sober realities of Portuguese ineptitude in Timor were best ignored.

Afonso de Castro's manuscripts, written during his governorship (1859–63), and subsequently collated under the title *As Possessões Portuguezas na Oceânia* (2010 [1867]), exemplify this tendency to look forward rather than retrospectively. Amid a vivid imaginary of Dili as an international port city and a population of "civilized natives" cultivating well-tended coffee, Castro's projections and calculations are a magnificent illustration of wishful colonial thinking. But beyond the figures and the outlines of a bureaucratic structure established for the task of coffee promotion, we find few clues as to how exactly, where, and to what extent these plans were executed. We do know that providing seed, incentives, and technical advice was the key to a modest increase in colonial coffee production in the 1860s. Yet one may assume that, given the endemic weakness of the Portuguese military and the feeble administrative reach of government, extending the coffee frontier into the autonomous *reinos* (petty kingdoms, or what Castro called *pequenas repúblicas*) was largely a question of inducement rather than force. In any event, there is simply insufficient documentation on plantations during the period in question to read much against the grain and obtain interpretive purchase.

However, in his masterwork *Timor en Guerre* (1996), French historian René Pélissier does offer the reader a sense of the extent to which control over coffee production and trade prefigured decades of conflict that transpired between the colonial authorities and the indigenous *reinos* from the mid-nineteenth century. The Portuguese always struggled to secure the coffee taxes they demanded, and the coffee harvest often ended up in the hands of others, usually the itinerant Chinese population and opportunistic Dutch traders. Relying predominantly on military reports, Pélissier's accounts of colonial warfare, culminating in the bloody pacification campaigns of the late nineteenth and early twentieth centuries, may be read as an alternative or counternarrative of coffee. It is also the story of Timorese responses—both military and agricultural—and underscores Roque's (2010a) characterization of Colonial Timor as involving a "parasitic interdependency" that prevailed between the Portuguese and the *reinos*, according to which power shifted temperamentally between the sides but never definitively in favor of one or the other. We might add that this interdependency was not excessive, and permitted the *reinos* to maintain a considerable degree of distance and autonomy. We also assume that the logistics of indigenous coffee plantations were little known to the colonial authorities in Dili, much less accounted for, and can take Castro's dispirited comments at face value when he wrote, "Our empire on this island is nothing but a fiction" (cited in Fox 2000: 16).

In the absence of more detailed accounts, we are left to infer that the Portuguese successfully promoted coffee cultivation in some *reinos* but struggled to maintain control over their operation, while the indigenous rulers (*liurai*) appropriated the coffee harvest to suit their economic and cultural ends (see Shepherd and McWilliam 2013). As Roque (2010b) has demonstrated, the colonial government was not only weak in practice but also in disarray amid internal corruption and disobedience, a situation that persisted well into the 1890s. It is in this context that we can interpret a series of letters penned by José dos Santos Vaquinhas (1881, 1882, 1883, 1887), garrison major of Macau and Timor and correspondent for the newly inaugurated Geographical Society of Lisbon. They were published in the society's *Boletim da Sociedade de Geographia de Lisboa*. Vaquinhas's principal and more optimistic message was that Timor was not nearly as insalubrious and dangerous as it was reputed to be (see also Roque 2012). It could well accommodate European settlers and represented, on the contrary, an ideal location to establish a large-scale agricultural company. If we read not so much against the grain but between the lines here, one may surmise that Vaquinhas sought solutions to the seemingly intractable problem of *liurai* power over the coffee trade through a new system of colonial economic organization and governance, for which an influx of white settlers was deemed necessary.

The precursor to this economic solution, however, was necessarily a military one. After Celestino da Silva assumed office as governor in 1896, a succession of brutal pacification campaigns deploying "divide-and-conquer" tactics contained the power of influential *liurai* and made them increasingly dependent on the Portuguese. Forced labor for public works, including roads and state plantations, was introduced. All the while, the natives were increasingly subject to the "tools of statecraft" that followed in the wake of military success. Celestino restructured the *reinos*, inaugurated a census, kept statistics on population numbers, and introduced an ambitious *capitação* (head) tax in 1906, which replaced the notoriously ineffective and much resented *finta* tax. All of these administrative measures and regulations pertaining to forced labor, taxes, and the many obligations of the indigenes are chronicled in meticulous detail in the *Boletim Oficial do Governo da Província de Timor*, a bulletin printed four times a month (from 1875 to 1975 available online). They have also been described and analyzed by historians, including Geoffrey Gunn, Luna de Oliveira, and F. A. Figueiredo among others.

What we do not find in the *Official Bulletins*, or any other historical source for that matter, is any considered exposition of how Timorese strategies of resistance shifted as Portuguese achieved dominance. For Timorese resistance appeared in new guises and expressions; for example, *liurai* found new, more subtle ways to retain power and the allegiance of indigenous commoners. If the people could not avoid forced labor, they could at least resist demands by slowing their work pace. The latter can be deduced from the early twentieth-century literature, when debates over whether the native population could be domesticated and civilized for plantation purposes became a major preoccupation of governors, administrators, and military officers (see for example Duarte 1944; Magalhães 1909). Frustrated plantation owners also took up their pens to point out the unique deficiences of "the Timorese man" (Garcia 1901; Silva 1910). For some observers, the indigenous workforce was a permanent liability, and attracting settlers (Chinese or European) the only plausible option; for others, "the Timorese man" was perfectly redeemable, as Magalhães (1909) went to great lengths to argue.

Celestino, like Vaquinhas, favoured large-scale plantation estates managed by Europeans, and a half dozen such plantations were opened as the pacification campaigns proceeded. The largest and most enduring of these estates was Celestino's own Sociedade Agrícola Pátria e Trabalho (SAPT) in Ermera district. As both Clarence-Smith (1992) and Gunn (1999) observe, historians will find themselves struggling to understand the details of plantation operations. The SAPT in particular, Clarence-Smith notes, was "a state within a state," barely penetrable by outsiders and subject to its own laws. Only in retrospect, after Celestino had retired and the Portuguese monarchy collapsed (1910), did it come to light that Celestino had his own answer to what was widely regarded as the problem with indigenous labor: the SAPT had used captives from the pacification wars as slave labor. The subsequent scathing denunciatory exposé that was published under the pseudoym of "Zola" is generally considered to be authored by António Pádua Correia, a Republican and colonial official.

What this case illustrates is that we cannot read the archival sources on Portuguese Timor independently of either political events in Portugal or the corruption that prevailed inside Timor. Both in the metropolis and in the colonies, governments closely managed information to present Portuguese colonialism in a positive light, and they suppressed information that reflected poorly on their administration.

As Roque (2010a) observes, colonial governance and the taking of "patrimonial benefices" for high-ranking officials went hand in hand.

Imperial Republicans and Scientific Plantations

The publication of Magalhães's opus, *Memória Descriptiva dos Recursos Agrícolas da Possessão Portugueza de Timor*, ushered in a new period of enthusiastic and less censured writing on Timor. In this fifty-page document, Magalhães covers many topics in unprecedented detail: the layout of private and state plantations that existed at the time; the aims and organization of the new government plantation in Liquiça (the Granja Eduardo Marques); the current and prospective conditions of indigenous labor; and the crop configuration, tools, and practices associated with "traditional agriculture." Magalhães proposed that plantation development should proceed through both scientific methods and the scientific management of the indigenous labor force, with better conditions for the workers.

Alberto Osório de Castro's *Flores de Coral: Poemetas e Impressões da Oceânia Portuguesa* (first published in Dili in 1910) is another important source of plantation information for the period. A section following the colonial magistrate's poetry, titled "A região do café e das grandes plantações europeias de Timor," tells of his journey in April 1909 to the European coffee plantations west and southwest of Dili (the SAPT; Sociedade Perseverança in Banitur; Sociedade Agrícola Comercial e Industrial de Timor in Hato-Lia; and the Companhia de Timor in the *reino* of Ermera) with Celestino da Silva's successor, Governor Eduardo Marques. The purpose of the trip was to investigate the potential for converting the new plantation of Cai-toco-Loa (established by the aforementioned Magalhães) into an experimental station. Osório de Castro was clearly influenced by Magalhães's ideas on indigenous labor (evidently they spent some time locked in conversation), but they disagreed on the extent of the damage that had been caused by the coffee leaf rust. *Flores de Coral* offers interesting reflections on the viability and prospects of the European plantations; Osório de Castro contemplated the possibility of drawing them all together to form one large agricultural company but, somewhat in contradiction, he also foreshadowed a future Republican preference for indigenous smallholder production. *Flores de Coral* now appears in volume 1 of Osório de Castro's collected works (Castro 2004); it also forms the basis of the refined and rearranged *A Ilha Verde e Vermelha de Timor*, first published in 1943 (Castro 1996 [1943]).

The arrival of the Republicans in Timor and their enlightened ideas, spearheaded by Magalhães, Castro, and the short-term governor Eduardo Marques, gave rise to the establishment of the Direcção dos Serviços de Fomento Agrícola e Comercial (henceforth the Department of Agriculture). This came at a time of unbridled enthusiasm for the agricultural potential of the wider Portuguese colonies, especially in São Tomé and Príncipe, both of which served as a model for Timor. This was not, moreover, an ordinary moment in the history of Timor, as the pacification of the indigenous population had finally been attained with colonial victory in 1912 over the Boaventura rebellion in Manufahi, and the lush and lightly populated south coast, in particular, brought the promise of riches to the colonial imagination. One key publication of the period, coauthored by the incoming governor Filomeno da Câmara (1911–17), underscores the new scientific approach to agriculture and the plan to diversify the plantation crops beyond coffee and coconut to include tea, cacao, cinnamon, vanilla, sisal, rubber, and various others. It was titled *Província de Timor: informações relativas aos jazigos de petróleo e à agricultura* (Branco and Câmara 1915).

Câmara's efforts (1911–17) led to feverish agricultural development in the newly pacified colony. He placed the military commanders under the expert authority of the Department of Agriculture, of which he was the ultimate authority. He expanded one state plantation (the Granja Eduardo Marques), created another in the defeated *reino* of Manufahi (the Granja República) and conceived of a new, democratic system of communal plantations that would see indigenous commoners dedicating themselves to cash-cropping, from which they and not their *liurai* masters would reap the benefits.

The Department of Agriculture, effective from 1913, produced its own publication, the *Boletim de Comércio, Agricultura e Fomento da Província de Timor* (henceforth BCAeF). The BCAeF is without question the most valuable archival source for understanding plantation development during the first Republican decade and makes this decade the best understood in the history of Timor's plantation programs. It comprises a series of bulletins printed bimonthly in Dili between 1914 and 1919, and biannually in 1920 and 1921. From 1914 to 1918, about one-third of the several thousand pages of BCAeF are filled with the stories of military commanders who presided over their respective *comandos militares*.

The commanders reported exuberantly on their efforts to encourage, force, or otherwise induce the indigenous population to raise as many coffee and coconut seedlings as possible and, subsequently, have them transplanted from nurseries to communal plantations, which numbered as many as one thousand by 1916. Several million coffee bushes and coconut trees were raised over this period. The commanders presented statistics and provided regular reports on the weather, the disposition of the natives, and the state of the crops—coffee, coconut, rice, maize, and manioc. Their reports also provide valuable glimpses into the strategies of promotion. For instance, we find that cash prizes and incentives (tools and seed) were offered to chiefs who excelled in plantation cultivation, penalities extended to those who did not, and prison sentences for those who flagrantly disobeyed the rules (such as trading with the Chinese outside authorized precincts).

More than any other historical source, the collective records of the BCAeF also reveal insights into the other side of the coin, namely the adaptive responses of the Timorese to the state's attempt to impose cash-cropping on their agricultural livelihoods. The texts make clear that the Timorese, to a greater or lesser extent, were able to pick and choose their planting strategies, appropriating interventions when favorable to their subsistence, commerical, or political interests, or otherwise refusing, circumventing, or disrupting them when they were not. "Even where there is apparent order and discipline, the indigenes can oppose our efforts with an invincible passive resistance, and the constant presence of Europeans is indispensible to give direction for even the tiniest of things," one commander reported candidly (BCAeF 1915[4]: 460). Scattered throughout the issues are the regular criticisms of the invidious character of the Timorese worker: leaving nurseries to overgrow, mishandling seedlings ("tearing plants out by the roots"), playing cards instead of tending crops, wilfully miscalculating yields to alleviate the heavy tax burden, hiding their buffalo to avoid the obligatory ploughing gangs, neglecting to space seedlings in order to meet quotas with minimal effort, making off with yields, and, when fed up, abandoning or burning the plantations. The lying, cheating, trickery, double-dealing, short cuts, sabotage, or simple indifference to colonial objectives all belonged to the art of resistance, at which its practitioners excelled (Scott 1985; Shepherd 2013). Even apparent compliance could in some circumstances serve indigenous ends.

In their diverse reports, the commanders also betray a general disregard for the realm of the sacred that Timorese describe as *lulik*. They quipped about what they saw as indigenous superstition and would not allow it to interfere with plantation objectives. There is abundant evidence in the BCAeF that commanders obliged locals to plant cash crops on "sacred lands" (Tetun: *rai lulik*), with often curious and unsettling consequences. When the crops failed, commanders witnessed locals undertaking a "fury of sacrifices" in fear of further ancestral-spiritual wrath, and given some commanders' eager expressions of vindication when crops thrived on those very sacred lands, the reader is left to wonder whether, deep down, commanders were themselves nervous that their transgressions of "*os lulics*" might see the spirits turn against them (see McWilliam, Palmer, and Shepherd 2014; McWilliam 2001).

One of the great challenges in reading the plantation archive is to determine to what extent indigenous populations were forced to clear *lulik* land set aside for spiritual reasons and then cultivate crops there; or whether they participated, perhaps keenly, in the reckless disenchantment of their country. Precisely how the historical clearing of *lulik* land took place in practice would be left entirely to the historical imagination, were it not for the remarkable testimony of one commentator that is so singular in its revelation that the original version has been published verbatim in a number of Portuguese sources, including Correia (1944). In the following summary we highlight the salient points.

In the account it is noted that the *indígenas* of Ossu region (Viqueque) considered as sacred (*lulik*) the great forest that covered one of their prominent mountains known as Mundo Perdido, so named by enthusiastic agriculturalist and self-same Portuguese governor Filomeno da Câmara. Upon seeing the massive forested mountain for the first time, the governor was fired with a vision of its transformation into a rich and lucrative coffee plantation. He addressed the gathered mountain inhabitants and urged their full cooperation and engagement in the project. They acted obligingly on his exhortation, and when he returned in due course, the *indígenas* had already undertaken the requisite and complicated rituals (*estilos*) required to placate the *lulik* spirits of the mountain in preparation for the great transformation. On the day of ceremonial commencement of the grand project, Filomeno was welcomed by the traditional leaders and the assembled population of the *reino*, the men ready with their machetes and axes to begin clearing, the women beating their festival hand drums in accompaniment. At that point the corpulent ruler (*régulo*) Dom Francisco of Ossu arose and addressed the governor and offered up as a sign of peace and cooperation the most *lulik* of ancestral relics that for generations had been stored inside the most important *uma lulik* of the *lulik* forests of Ossu. The object was a "fantastic rifle" (*espingardão*) that measured two and a half meters in length (cited in full in Shepherd and McWilliam 2014: 155)

The account of the clearing of sacred land in Ossu suggests that it took place under terms of persuasion, enticement, and mutual agreement rather than force, and that the wilful transgression of ritual injunctions and prohibitions was accompanied by ritual sanction and the full support of the Ossu ruler. It cannot be assumed, however, that this was always the case or that the authority of colonial command carried equal weight. Since Dom Francisco of Ossu's actions represented a special instance of *liurai* loyalty to the colonial government, we might hesitate to generalize his acquiescence, and the Timorese archive provides no definitive answers on this point.

The case of Mundo Perdido is not addressed at length in the BCAeF proceedings. But curiously, a few issues drawn from 1916 and 1917 reveal that the great plantations of Mundo Perdido that were carved out of the tropical forests were not thriving as anticipated. This experience was in fact widespread, particularly in the eastern part of the island where coffee plantings often languished. When faced with adverse results, commanders were quick to lay blame on environmental factors; nature proved to be as uncooperative as the natives, that the dry season was too long, the rains too torrential, the rats too voracious, and plant diseases too prolific. In the case of Mundo Perdido, the limestone soils were too alkaline. But the full extent of the soil-related catastrophe on Mundo Perdido, which resulted in the wholesale commercial failure of the coffee plantation, was not admitted until well after the Republicans had been ousted. Coffee expert J. A. da Silva Carvalho (1937) was the first to fully acknowledge the disaster and, by extension, the general failure of communal plantations under the Republican's zealous expansionary programs. Again, we observe that the received truth about plantation development in Timor is very much contingent upon political interests in Lisbon, and those same interests in Lisbon are intimately linked to how action in the colonies was represented and reflected back.

The BCAeF also provides considerable information on the circulation of crop varieties within Timor—from the European and government plantations to the *comando*-level plantations—and extended internationally to cover Portugal's African and Asian colonies, the Dutch East Indies, British Malaya, Indochina, and the Philippines. In fact, the BCAeF is so thematically broad and rich that the researcher of plantations in Portuguese Timor cannot help but feel some regret that the publication was suddenly terminated in 1921. The archives from 1922 to 1975 are much more superficial and sketchy on the details of agricultural interventions and practice.

Despite this return to desultory reporting, close reading offers up pockets of rich material. There are two dimensions of the colonial plantation push that barely receive mention in the BCAeF and yet are illuminated in curious ways through certain records located in the Arquivo Histórico Ultramarino (AHU). The first dimension relates to the question of land concessions granted or, as the case may be, not granted to non-Portuguese nationals. In one dusty box, we unearthed the peculiar case of Henry Blyth Manderson of Adelaide and William Kelly Smith, a Scottish resident of British Malaya.[10] These men applied for land concessions in 1922 and 1923, initially under the name of the Australian-registered Timor Development Company. In the first petition for one hundred thousand hectares in the far-eastern area of Fuiloro (Lautem), the pair proposed to have the indigenous population cultivate roselle hibiscus (*Hibiscus sabdariffa*) for fiber production, promising that under the direction of Australian overseers the indigenes "will be able to cultivate roselle with the same ease as they currently do maize." The application was rejected on account of indigenous reliance on the lands for extensive grazing.

In a second petition, Manderson and Kellie Smith requested twenty-five thousand hectares in the vicinity of the military post of Fatu-Berliu (Manufahi) for the cultivation of fiber plants, cotton, kapok, rubber, coconut, African palm oils, and palappa palms. A review made by the commander of Manufahi argued that "the private agricultural work of the *indígenas* would be impaired," and the application was similarly turned down in 1924. A third petition was William Kellie Smith's alone. Now a resident of Timor, he requested twenty-five thousand hectares once again at Fuiloro as well as a one-thousand-hectare quarantine precinct at the south-coast harbor of Loré (Vai-Lai-Vai), intending to import purebred cattle and stallions from Australia, cross them with their "stunted Timorese equivalents," and build a meatworks at Loré. "I have no desire to disturb the natives in their villages or to use their present grazing grounds," proclaimed Kellie Smith in anticipation of the authorities' decision against his favor, which was duly issued.

If the above case tempts us to believe that the Portuguese held some regard for the well-being of the indigenous population, the next case rather suggests the contrary. Contained in another box at the AHU is a folder whose hundred or so pages revolve around two reports that appeared in Dutch East Indies newspapers in 1929.[11] With information taken from the eyewitness accounts of a Javanese-Dutch rubber expert who was employed to apply his knowledge in Timor, the articles detail the conditions of twelve hundred inmates who labored on a prison plantation in Viqueque. The indigenous and deportee inmates allegedly lacked food and shelter, were subjected to horrendous punishments, and frequently perished due to starvation and disease. The

Ministry of Foreign Affairs in Lisbon demanded an official enquiry,[12] and while the subsequent investigation was able to refute all allegations, these materials point unequivocally to the existence of prison plantations and stand as the most graphic evidence available of the institutionalized violence that took place within them. Contrasting the case of the rejected applications for land concessions with the severe depredations suffered by indigenes on prison plantations, we might surmise that the Portuguese officials were assiduous in their defense of indigenous interests only when it suited them and were willing to go to extremes of degradation and violence in the pursuit of profits. But we also need to add a caveat, namely that the old rivals of the Portuguese on Timor, the Dutch colonial government, were often scathing of their counterpart's presence in Timor. So the allegations printed in Dutch East Indies' newspapers might well be as exaggerated as the findings of the official enquiry are defensive. Plantations in Portuguese Timor were inevitably drawn into the fray of colonial rivalries, and this bias is reflected in the collected archive.

Estado Novo: More Talk than Action

The documented history of Portuguese Timor in the 1930s marks "a return to discourse," with much discussion and criticism of the problems of state governance, most of which are blamed on the Republicans, and many ideas as to how past mistakes would be remedied under the Estado Novo. A series of papers presented at the Primeira Conferência Económica do Império Colonial Português epitomize this approach, leaving the reader to wonder what if anything was actually undertaken during the 1930s. We could cite here the work of Carvalho (1936a), which at least indicates that a body called the Agricultural Services existed at a time when the colonies were granted few resources from Lisbon.[13] However, it would not surprise us to learn that these Agricultural Services existed only on paper. With the Portuguese constantly on guard against the critical gaze of Dutch and English observers, the production of on-paper institutions, on-paper advancement of indigenous well-being, and on-paper civilizing of indigenous people was routine. Reading against the grain not only leads us to an appreciation of Timorese agency but also to one of the colonial propensity for dissembling and hubris.

The plantation drive resumed in the postwar period under the modern ideology of development. From the 1950s until the end of Portuguese colonialism, plantation cultivation grew more scientific and systematic, complementing the historical focus on coffee and a new focus on rice. The work of Helder Lains e Silva (1956) is an important postwar source. Silva not only belonged to the vanguard of this new scientific orientation, but he was arguably the first to grasp the manner in which indigenous groups had appropriated plantation cultivation in their distintictive way, indifferent to production yields but intent on minimizing labor inputs. Like Ruy Cinatti, Silva came to place value on indigenous logics—even "superstitions"—not common in the history of colonial Timor. But like many governmental discourses in Portuguese Timor, it is not clear that this meant very much in practice.

Under the technical direction of Silva and, initially, via the leadership of Ruy Cinatti (as chief of the Agricultural Services), a series of five-year development plans was implemented (1953–78).[14] The plans articulated ambitious proposals for plantation and other development, but successive reports and subsequent plans do not reveal much about how, and whether, the proposals were actually implemented. They do rather give the impression that all that was proposed was implemented as a matter of course; indeed, Shouton (2001) has argued that the colonial objective was to forge an image of Timor as a "scientific colony," which fused civilizing and rational planning. Reis's (2000) unpublished MA thesis, however, offers an excellent critical analysis of the very meager accomplishments that were realized under the developmental regime (1953–75). The plans say nothing of the social inequities in Timor and the privileges accorded *liurai* as part of the plantation promotion process. They are also notably silent on the forced labor regime that persisted until 1975 and the likely continuation of prison plantations.

Incidental to the five-year plans and the emphasis they placed on research as a precursor to program implementation were the more than one hundred scientific papers produced about Timor between 1950 and 1975 (Shepherd 2014). For the most part, these papers concerned the trialing of coffee and rice. Like the plans, the scientific papers omit any reference to the social conditions on Timor and the micropolitics of rice promotion that often flowed from these experiments. Yet they do provide a background to Metzner's (1977) singular geo-ecological study of the Baucau-Viqueque corridor, and in particular his account of south coast rice plantation development, in which three themes emerge: (1) the extent to which local *liurai* and village elders were able to profit from this large-scale development, (2) the reliance on a seasonal highland labor force, and (3) the struggle to contain both malaria and the indigenous interpretation thereof, namely, that spirits were resisting the residence of uplander communities in the lowlands (see Shepherd and McWilliam 2011). Apart from Metzner's work, and despite the veritable profusion of scientific papers, the period is characterized by a dearth of insightful works into the state of plantation agriculture and the labor practices of the Timorese within it. Given Portugal's postwar susceptibility to international criticism for the way it treated its indigenous subjects in the colonies, the strict control of information can be assumed. What we find in the archive is surely an effect of this political sensitivity at a time when pressure on Portugal to decolonize was intense and its full membership to the UN under debate. Research on plantations in Portuguese Timor thus reflects the concerns of an emerging international scrutiny on "human rights."

One final theme warrants brief mention. As early as the mid-1930s, Carvalho (1936b) recognized the correlation between coffee plantation density and the preponderance of poverty. Silva (1956) confirmed this same relationship in the 1950s. In 1970, F. M. Guerra produced one of the most damning reports on postwar development, arguing that over the course of a decade, food production had actually fallen by half just as coffee yields were about to reach a historical peak of twelve thousand tons per annum. The clear relationship between falling staple food production and a booming commercial coffee sector challenged the much-vaunted claims of the benefits of the civilizing mission of colonialism, which rather compounded the problem of rising poverty among the rural populations. In the case of Portuguese Timor, if not elsewhere, the long-cherished association between indigenous plantation work and the benefits of colonial paternalism proved once again to be a chimera based on flawed reasoning, wishful thinking, and willful exploitation of the native labor force.

Conclusion

Our selective excursion into the plantation archives of Portuguese Timor has sought to highlight the wealth of material for historians and ethnographers alike to generate detailed critical perspectives on the colonial past. Despite the comparatively and inevitably muted voices of long-suffering Timorese colonial subjects, their presence, adaptive responses, and strategic resistance can be discerned in the interpretive possibilities that emerge scattered among the diverse reports, candid admissions, and critical assessments of Portuguese administrators, military men, and colonial scientists who labored long to implement their imperial plans.

Anthropologist Clifford Geertz has highlighted the convergence of scholarly interests among historians and anthropologists in the following terms; namely, that "trying to understand people quite differently placed than ourselves, encased in different material conditions, driven by different ambitions and possessed of different notions as to what life is all about, poses very similar problems." For anthropologist and historian alike, "dealing with a world elsewhere comes to much the same thing when elsewhere is long ago as when it is far away" (2001: 120).

The notion that the past is a foreign country and therefore suggestive of an openness to historicized ethnographic enquiry requires both a sensitivity to cultural differences and a critical interpretive stance as to what is made explicit and what is elided or left unsaid in the documentary evidence at hand. Our explorations of the traces and trajectories of Timorese plantation ethnography filtered through the Portuguese archive highlight the possibilities and potential of a retrospective ethnography of plantation practice and an exploration of what Geertz has referred to as "the enmeshment of meaning in power" (2001: 128).[15]

Although the series of ethnographic studies that emerged in the late Portuguese period illuminates little about the plantation practice of the period or colonial relations more broadly, latter-day ethnographies can revisit the past through both archival exploration and the possiblities of living cultural memories. On a recent field trip to Remexio (Aileu district), for example, one informant was able to tell us with precision where the Celestino-era state coffee plantation was located (in the early 1900s) and describe something of the conditions of the plantation and his great-grandfather's role within it. Just how much of this testimony sheds light on historical events remains uncertain, but obviously the more recent the past, the more accessible it is to forms of nonmythologized recollection. And there is another, perhaps more important aspect to this source of knowledge. How the past is remembered today, and the local politics of memory, has been investigated in forensic detail in some areas of historical practice (e.g. CAVR 2005 or customary and colonial land tenure entanglements in Fitzpatrick et al. 2012) but overlooked in others such as plantation histories.

If memory is history remade in the present, this may provide yet another promising research direction to bring living memories and inherited knowledge to bear on the past. As intimated elsewhere (Shepherd and McWilliam 2013), recent elite proposals for large-scale plantations in contemporary East Timor, following development imaginaries that are not disimilar to those that existed a century earlier, are failing to excite popular trust or enthusiasm. While fears of broadacre, neocolonial, contemporary plantation plans may account for some of this reticence, the politics of memory and, to be sure, the memory of politics in the past arguably play an influential role. The case illustrates yet another ethnographic turn where history and otherness, to recall Geertz, may well be both "far away" and "long ago" but also here and now, and in the making.

Andrew McWilliam is professor of anthropology at Western Sydney University. He is a specialist in the anthropology of Southeast Asia with continuing ethnographic research interests in eastern Indonesia and Timor-Leste as well as northern Aboriginal Australia. Current research includes post-conflict social and economic recovery in Timor-Leste and an Australian Research Council (ARC)–funded project with Lisa Palmer (University of Melbourne) titled, *Spirit Ecologies and the Role of Customary Governance in Timor Leste*. Recent publications include coedited volumes *A New Era? Timor-Leste after the UN* (2015), *Land and Life in Timor Leste: Ethnographic Essays* (2011), and a coauthored monograph, *Property and Social Resilience in Times of Conflict: Land, Custom and Law in East Timor* (2012).

Chris J. Shepherd is an independent scholar affiliated with anthropology at the Australian National University. From Timor to the Andean countries, he researches indigenous cultures, history of science, rural development, mining, agrobiodiversity, resource management, colonial ethnography, professional anthropology, and animism. He is currently investigating transcendence tourism in Peru following a methodology of participant hallucination. He has two books on East Timor: *Development and Environmental Politics Unmasked* (2014) and *Haunted Houses and Ghostly Encounters: Animism and Ethnography in East Timor, 1860–1975* (2019). Liking story, he is testing another crossing in his writing on Timor: that of history and ethnography with fiction.

Notes

1. Confusion can arise in the use of terms, postcolonial and post-colonial. Hyphenated post-colonial and post-colonialism mean "after colonialism" (post-independence) while unhyphenated postcolonial and postcolonialism generally refer to the academic field and theoretical and interpretive styles as in those peculiar to postcolonial studies.

2. On the cusp of the Indonesian invasion, Sue Ingram from Australia had initiated her anthropology PhD field research in Laclubar (Manatuto), but within months she had to abandon these efforts as the curtain was drawn on this period of relative openness for ethnographic pursuits.

3. Illustrative texts include Rodney Needham (ed.), *Rethinking Kinship and Marriage* (1971), and *Right and Left: Essays on Dual Symbolic Classification* (1973). See also Lazarowitz's PhD thesis "The Makassai: Complementary Dualism in Timor" (1980), or James Fox's paper "Models and Metaphors: Comparative Research in Eastern Indonesia,' in *The Flow of Life: Essays on Eastern Indonesia*, ed. J. J. Fox (Cambridge, MA: Harvard University Press), 327–34.

4. What Keesing (1987) referred to as "symbolic anthropology."

5. Evans-Pritchard's was a prominent anthropological critic of the tendency he observed in much anthropology to ignore the value of historical documents and historical perspectives (1962 [1950]).

6. The same might be said for archaeology. The aforementioned António de Almeida, although producing extensive reports and published papers produced little of lasting worth in comparative or foundational archaeological studies (N. Oliveira, personal communication).

7. We include here the work of Maria Lameiras Campagnolo. Although Portuguese in origin, Lameiras Campagnolo is associated with the French grouping and its scholarly research frameworks. Her research was also written in French (e.g. Lameiras-Campagnolo 1975).

8. In addition, some of the veteran researchers from the 1960s and 1970s such as Elizabeth Traube and David Hicks returned to East Timor after 1999 to resume their interrupted research.

9. Although coffee was reportedly already known on Timor by 1734, following its spread from Yemen to the Dutch East Indies (Hägerdal, personal communication).

10. Letters and documents contained in folder "Concessões," AHU 1724-I 1c MU DGCOr Mc 1928.

11. "NuttigerWerk voor den Volkenbond: Uit Duister Portugeesh Timor; Behandeling van Gestraften en van Ned Ind Deskungige," *Surabaya Courant*, Saturday, 15 August 1929. A similar article appeared in *Java-Bode* on 12 July 1929.

12. Colónia de Timor, *Inquerito sobre o incidente entre o comandante militar de Viqueque e um pratico Javanez ocorrido em fevereiro de 1929*, Dili, March 1930, AHU 1724-I 1c MU DGCOr Mc 1928.

13. The administrator of Baucau in the 1930s, Pinto Correia, was perhaps the first to understand and appreciate the *lulik* realm, and his first book, *Gentio de Timor* (1934), although not anthropologically informed, was highly detailed and should stand as the first ethnography of Timorese traditions. He said nothing about plantations.

14. The Fifth Development Plan was due to terminate in 1978 but was of course abandoned after just two years of operation following the Indonesian occupation.

15. Reprising Clifford's comments that "cultural analysis is always en-meshed in global movements of difference and power" (1986: 22) and that ethnography offers a critical, reflexive, and contestable approach to understanding.

References

Abercrombie, T. 1998. *Pathways of Memory and Power: Ethnography and History among an Andean People.* Madison: University of Wisconsin Press.

Anderson, W. 2008. *The Collectors of Lost Souls: Turning Kuru Scientists into Whitemen.* Baltimore: The Johns Hopkins University Press.

BCAeF. 1915[4]. *Boletim de Comércio, Agricultura e Fomento da Província de Timor.*

Branco, J. E. C. C., and F. da Câmara. 1915. *Província de Timor: informações relativas aos jazigos de petróleo e à agricultura.* Lisbon: Ministério das Colónias.

Brobower-Strain, A. 2012. *White Bread: A Social History of the Store-Bought Loaf.* Boston: Beacon Press.

Campagnolo, H. 1979. *Fataluku I: Relations et Choix, Introduction méthodologique á la description d'une langue "non austronésienne" de Timor Oriental; Langues et Civilisations de L'Asie du Sud-Est et du Monde Insulindien 5.* Paris: Centre de Documentation et de Recherches sur L'Asie du Sud-Est et le Monde Insulindien (CeDRASEMI)/Centre Nationale de la Recherche Scientifique.

Carmo, A. D. de A. e. 1965. *O Povo Mambai—contribuição para o estudo do povo do grupo linguístico Mambai—Timor.* Lisbon: Instituto Superior de Ciências Sociais e Política Ultramarina.

Carvalho, J. A. da S. 1936a. "Bases destinadas a promover a íntima ligação entre as autoridades administrativas e os Serviços Agrícolas da Colónia." In *Primeira Conferência Económica do Império Colonial Português, Terceira Comissão, Colónia de Timôr,* 7 pp. Lisbon: Ministério das Colónias.

———. 1936b. "Bases destinadas a promover a demarcação na Colónia, de zonas de cultura para cada espécie cultural." In *Primeira Conferência Económica do Império Colonial Português, Terceira Comissão, Colónia de Timôr,* 5 pp. Lisbon: Ministério das Colónias.

———. 1937. "O café em Timor: Tese apresentada à Conferência Nacional do Café; Abril 1935." Thesis presented to the National Conference on Coffee, April 1935, Lisbon: Tipografia Viana.

de Castro, A. 2010 [1867]. *As Possessões Portuguezas na Oceania.* Whitefish, MT: Kessinger Legacy Reprints/Lisbon: Imprensa Nacional.

de Castro, A. O. 1996 [1943]. *A Ilha Verde e Vermelha de Timor.* Lisbon: Cotovia.

———. 2004. *Obra Poética.* Vol. 1. Lisbon: Imprensa Nacional-Casa da Moeda.

CAVR. 2005. *Chega! The Report of the Commission of Reception, Truth and Reconciliation, Timor-Leste.* www.cavr-timorleste.org.

Clarence-Smith, W. G. 1985. *The Third Portuguese Empire, 1825–1975: A Study in Economic Imperialism*. Manchester: Manchester University Press.

———. 1992. "Planters and Smallholders in Portuguese Timor in the Nineteenth and Twentieth Centuries." *Indonesia Circle* 57: 15–30

Clifford, J., and G. Marcus (eds.). 1986. *Writing Culture: The Poetics and Politics of Ethnography*. Berkeley: University of California Press.

Correia, A. P. 1935. *Gentio de Timor*. Lisbon: Agência-Geral das Colónias.

———. 1944. *Timor de lés a lés*. Lisbon: Agência Geral das Colónias.

Duarte, T. 1944. *Ocupação e Colonização Branca de Timor*. Porto: Educação Nacional.

Earl, G. W. 1853. *The Native Races of the Indian Archipelago: Papuans*. London: H. Bailliere.

Evans-Pritchard, E. E. 1962 [1950]. "Social Anthropology: Past and Present." The Marett lecture, *Man* 50: 118–24. Reprinted in *Essays in Social Anthropology*, London: Faber.

Fitzpatrick, D., A. McWilliam, and S. Barnes. 2012. *Property and Social Resilience in Times of Conflict: Land, Custom and Law in East Timor*. Farnham: Ashgate Publishing.

Forbes, H. O. 1989 [1885]. *A Naturalist's Wanderings in the Eastern Archipelago: A Narrative of Travel and Exploration from 1878 to 1883*. New York: Harper & Bros./Oxford: Oxford University Press.

Fox, J. J. 2000. "Tracing the Path, Recounting the Past: Historical Perspectives on Timor." In *Out of the Ashes: Destruction and Reconstruction of East Timor*, edited by J. J. Fox and D. Babo Soares, 1–27. Adelaide: C. Hurst & Co. Publishers.

Garcia, C. de P. 1901. "Algumas Palavras sobre a Colonização de Timor, Relatório Apresentado ao Congresso Colonial Nacional." In *Congresso Nacional: Actas das Sessões*, 73–83. Lisbon: SGL.

Geertz, C. 2001. *Available Light: Anthropological Reflections on Philosophical Topics*. Princeton, NJ: Princeton University Press.

Gomes, A. de P. ["Zola"]. 1911. *Timor: O Governo do General de Brigada do Quadro da Reserva José Celestino da Silva Durante 14 Annos: Latrocinios, Assassinatos e Perseguições*. Lisbon: n.p.

Gomes, F. de A. 1972. *Os Fataluku*. Lisboa: Instituto Superior de Ciencias Socias e Politica Ultramarina, Universidade Tecnica de Lisboa.

Guerra, F. M. 1970. *Alguns aspectos do desenvolvimento económico de Timor, vistos durante a visita de Sua Exª o Subsecretário de Estado da Administração Ultramarina aquela Província*. Lisboa: Ministério do Ultramar, Direcção Geral de Obras Públicas e Comunicações.

Hicks, D. 2011. "A Pesquisa Etnográfica no Timor Português." In *Ita Mau-alin . . . o livro do irmão mais novo: Afinidades Antropologicas em Torno de Timor-Leste*, edited by K. Silva and L. Soares, 31–45. Lisboa: Edições Colibri.

Holzman, J. D. 2006. "Food and Memory." *Annual Review of Anthropology* 35: 361–78.

Keesing, R. 1987. "Anthropology as an Interpretive Quest." *Current Anthro-pology* 28(2): 161–73.

Lameiras-Campagnolo, M. O. 1975. *L'habitation des Fatuluku de Lórehe (Timor Portugais)*. Paris: Thèse de doctorat de 3ème cycle, Université René Des-cartes, Sorbonne.

Lazarowitz, T. 1980. "The Makassai: Complementary Dualism in Timor." Un-published PhD diss., State University of New York at Stony Brook.

de Lencastre, J. G. 1929. "Aspectos da Administração de Timor." *Boletim da Agência Geral das Colónias* 5(54): 32–55.

Marcus, G. 1995. "Ethnography in/of the World System: The Emergence of Multi-sited Ethnography." *Annual Review of Anthropology* 24: 95–117.

———. 2002. "Beyond Malinowski and after *Writing Culture*: On the Future of Cultural Anthropology and the Predicament of Ethnography." *Austra-lian Journal of Anthropology* 13(2): 191–99.

Magalhães, F. da S. 1881. *Instrucções para a Cultura do Tabaco em Timor*. Macau: Tipografia Mercantil.

de Magalhães, A. L. 1909. *Memoria Descriptiva dos Recursos Agrícolas da Pos-sessão Portugueza de Timor*. Dili: Imprensa Nacional.

McWilliam. A. R. 2001. "Prospects for the Sacred Grove: Valuing *Lulic* Forests on Timor." *Asia Pacific Journal of Anthropology* 2(2): 89–113.

———. 2007a. "Harbouring Traditions in East Timor, Marginality in a Low-land Entrepôt." *Modern Asian Studies* 41(6): 113–43.

_____. 2007b. "Looking for Adê: A Contribution to Timorese Historiogra-phy." *Bijdragen Tot de Taal- Land en Volkenkunde* 163(2/3): 221–238.

McWilliam A. R., L. Palmer, and C. Shepherd. 2014. "Lulik Encounters and Cultural Frictions in East Timor: Past and Present." *Australian Journal of Anthropology* 25(3): 304–20.

Pachirat, T. 2011. *Every Twelve Seconds: Industrialized Slaughter and the Politics of Sight*. New Haven, CT: Yale University Press.

Pélissier R. 1996. *Timor en Guerre: le crocodile et les Portugais (1847–1913)*. Paris: Pélissier.

Reis, L. M. M. da S. 2000. "Timor-Leste, 1953–1975: O desenvolvimento agrícola na última fase da colonização portuguesa." Unpublished mas-ter's thesis, Universidade Técnica de Lisboa, Lisbon.

Roque, R. 2010a. *Headhunting and Colonialism: Anthropology and the Circu-lation of Human Skulls in the Portuguese Empire 1870–1930*. New York: Palgrave Macmillan.

———. 2010b. "The Unruly Island: Colonialism's Predicament in Late Nine-teenth-Century East Timor." *Parts of Asia: Goa, Macao, East Timor*, special issue of *Portuguese Literary and Cultural Studies* 17/18: 303–30.

———. 2012. "Mountains and Black Races: Anthropology's Heterotopias in Colonial East Timor." *Journal of Pacific History* 47(3): 263–82.

Scott, J. C. 1985. *Weapons of the Weak: Everyday Forms of Peasant Resistance*. New Haven, CT: Yale University Press.

Shouton, M. J. 2001. "Antropologia e colonialismo em Timor português." *Lusotopie*: 157–171.

Shepherd, C. J. 2014. *Development and Environmental Politics Unmasked: Authority, Participation and Equity in East Timor.* New York: Routledge.

———. 2019 *Haunted Houses and Ghostly Encounters: Ethnography and Animism in East Timor, 1860–1975.* Singapore: NUS Press.

Shepherd, C. J., and A. R. McWilliam. 2011. "Ethnography, Agency, and Materiality: Anthropological Perspectives on Rice Development in East Timor." *East Asian Science, Technology and Society: An International Journal* 5(2): 189–215.

———. 2013. "Cultivating Plantations and Subjects in East Timor: A Genealogy." *Bijdragen Tot de Taal Land -en Volkenkunde* 169: 326–61.

———. 2014. "Divide and Cultivate: Plantations, Militarism and Environment in Portuguese Timor, 1860–1975." In *Comparing Apples, Oranges, and Cotton: Environmental Histories of the Global Plantation,* edited by F. Uekoetter, 139–66. New York: Campus Verlag.

Silva, H. L. e. 1956. *Timor e a Cultura do Café.* Lisbon: Ministério do Ultramar.

Silva, J. C. M. e. 1910. *A Mão d'Obra em Timor: Breve memoria sobre o seu territorio, clima, producção, usos e costumes indigenas, industria, agricultura e commercio.* Lisbon: n.p.

Uekoetter, F. (ed.). 2014. *Comparing Apples, Oranges, and Cotton: Environmental Histories of the Global Plantation.* New York: Campus Verlag.

Vaquinhas, J. S. 1881. "Timor." *Boletim da Sociedade de Geographia de Lisboa* 2(9–10): 733–41.

———. 1882. "Timor." *Boletim da Sociedade de Geographia de Lisboa* 3(11): 747–49.

———. 1883. "Timor." *Boletim da Sociedade de Geographia de Lisboa* 4(6): 277–86.

———. 1887. "Colonisação de Timor." *Boletim da Sociedade de Geographia de Lisboa* 7(7): 453–61.

Chapter 10

ARCHIVAL RECORDS AND ETHNOGRAPHIC INQUIRIES IN VIQUEQUE

David Hicks

I shall only say further that I believe an interpretation on functionalist lines (of the present in terms of the present) and on historical lines (of the present in terms of the past) must somehow be combined and that we have not yet learnt to combine them satisfactorily.
—E. E. Evans-Pritchard, 1962

In this chapter I shall provide a case study in how I made use of archival documents and published materials in the ethnographic field research I carried out in Timor-Leste in the mid-1960s at the time it was the colony Timor Português, and on later occasions. Incorporating archival data or the results of research carried out in the past into contemporary ethnographic research directs us to the wider issue of how historical sources can be useful for social anthropologists and how ethnographic work can aid the historian.[1] In its more abstract considerations, therefore, this chapter concerns how diachronic and synchronic perspectives may be combined in their respective ways in helping to render institutions intelligible.[2]

My research in Timor Português /Timor-Leste can be summarized as follows. My total time in the field has amounted to roughly thirty months, beginning in 1966 with a stay that lasted nineteen months, fifteen months of which were spent in the *posto sede* of Viqueque *concelho* (district), about three months in the *posto sede* of Baucau *concelho*, and about a month in Dili and traveling in the eastern region of Lautem. I returned for a total of about two months over three shorter visits between 1999 and 2001, and then spent seven months, mostly in Dili, in 2005, followed by further visits of two weeks in 2007 and three weeks in 2009.

In this chapter, I describe the background to my first period in the field, discuss the extent to which archival and secondary sources were used during that first period of field research, and consider how my use of archival and secondary sources during my later field research compared with that initial time.

Background

My training in social anthropology was carried out at the Institute of Social Anthropology at the University of Oxford, where the chair of social anthropology was Professor E. E. Evans-Pritchard, who became my supervisor during the first year, 1962–63.[3] His approach to the study of social facts was profoundly influenced by the Durkheimian structural-functionalism school yet solidly grounded in history, as might be expected since his BA honors degree was in that discipline. His doctorate was in social anthropology, however, following his fieldwork among the Azande, and he established his reputation as a structural-functionalist with his classic monograph *The Nuer* (1940). This did not, however, prevent him from publishing *The Sanusi of Cyrenaica* (1949), a historical monograph on the Bedouin of Cyrenaica; his 1961 essay "Anthropology and History," which argued for the essential interdependence of the two disciplines of history and social anthropology, was a logical outcome of his dual inspiration. In that essay he quoted, with some approval, the historian F. W. Maitland, who contended that anthropology must choose between being history or being nothing, a precept Evans-Pritchard accepted with the proviso that it must imply that history must choose between being social anthropology or being nothing (Evans-Pritchard 1962: 64). This cross-disciplinary perspective readily appealed to me since my undergraduate degree had been in another discipline, geography.

A second personal influence upon the course my field research would take, in this case my ethnographic region, was Rodney Needham. Needham would later succeed Maurice Freedman, Evans-Pritchard's immediate successor, as chair of social anthropology. Although similar to that of Evans-Pritchard's, and like him steeped in the French *Année sociologique* tradition, Needham's theoretical direction owed more to the work of Claude Lévi-Strauss, while his ethnographic region of specialization was not Africa but the Indonesian archipelago. Moreover, he took a particular interest in what Lévi-Strauss had termed *échange générale*, which he redesignated "asymmetric prescriptive alliance." This was an institution to which the analytical tools of structural analysis could be especially usefully applied to render intelligible the holistic character of entire societies and exemplified what Marcel Mauss referred to as a "total social fact." Asymmetric prescriptive alliance is defined by the contraction of marriages between descent groups of varying degrees of segmentation, from clans, through lineages, to extended families, in interactive ties that may persist through generations. This institution is sometimes known as matrilateral cross-cousin marriage because, from a masculine perspective, in its simplest form it entails a man marrying a woman related to him as the daughter of a man who provided his father with his mother. The closest relative of this kind would be the daughter of his mother's brother, i.e. his first-degree matrilateral cross cousin, but would also include his second-degree matrilateral cross cousin, i.e. his mother's mother's brother's daughter, and his second-degree matrilateral cross cousin, and so on. According to the conventions of these systems, a person's descent group is linked by affinity to two categories of affines: those that supply his descent group with wives and those that take his father's sisters, sisters, and daughters as wives. A man's social universe consists of a triad: his own descent group (clan, lineage, or extended family), his wife-giving descent groups, and his wife-taking descent groups. Such systems provide excellent opportunities for a structural approach to studying social facts because their kinship terminologies and rules of marriage typically reflect this triadic structure and because notions of reciprocity, social status, material artifacts, indeed, entire social domains that encompass cosmological notions may be included in a single all-embracing structure. Wife-givers, for example, may be classified as superior to wife-takers; on communal occasions (e.g., the birth of a baby or when someone dies) when both affinal partners are present, wife-givers will be offered the same kind of ritual prestation (for example, buffalo meat) they received when their offspring were married, and their wife-takers will receive the same kind of ritual prestation (e.g., pigs), a classification that is integrated into the cosmological notions of their society. Furthermore, the house may serve as a microcosm of the indigenous universe and the lateral notions of left and right, colors like black and red, spatial contrasts like upper and lower and inside and outside, and moral qualities such as good and bad may be incorporated as elements of the system. So pervasive are these ramifications of the system that the society itself can be defined in its terms. The most comprehensive analysis of a society is that made on the Rindi of eastern Sumba by Gregory

Forth (1981), a student of Needham's. In Timor-Leste, asymmetric alliance occurs among many of its ethnolinguistic groups, including the Makassai, Mambai, and Naueti, and it is accompanied by various supplementary forms of marriage alliance, since asymmetric alliance is compatible with other forms of marriage alliance in the same society.[4] The various ethnolinguistic groups typically have their own term for their various categories of marriage, but throughout Timor-Leste the term one most frequently hears is *barlaque*, a generic denoting marriages according to local *lisan*,[5] which include both prescriptive and nonprescriptive unions.

Paradoxically, perhaps, although the topic of prescriptive alliance generated much attention in the mid-sixties, no substantial field research had yet been carried out by a fieldworker intent upon studying such systems or who had had the benefit of reading the often controversial views of those scholars who contributed to its theoretical implications, including Edmund Leach, David Schneider, and George Homans. Reliable ethnographic information was needed that might help resolve the theoretical issues of interest to social anthropologists at the time. As early as the middle of the nineteenth century the works of Henry Forbes (1884, 1885) indicated that asymmetric alliance occurred in Portuguese Timor, and so I decided to carry out my fieldwork in the colony.[6] I applied for a research visa and received one specifying that I work exclusively among one of the ethnic populations, the Tetum. A former Needham student, Ruy Cinatti, who had been instrumental in my obtaining a visa (see Hicks 2017), advised me that asymmetric prescriptive alliance was practiced among that population and suggested I used Viqueque as my base of operations.

Fieldwork (1966–67)

Although my work was to be focused in the Viqueque region, I used the Baucau *pousada* as a convenient home site for several months while a former Chinese shop that we had rented was being upgraded to serve as a house for my wife and infant son. From there we took the opportunity to introduce ourselves to the governor, in Dili, and embarked on a reconnaissance in Lautem *concelho*. Before arriving in Viqueque, accordingly, I had already collected ethnographic data on the Makassai and some on the Fataluku in the Lospalos area, where I photographed and sketched its celebrated elevated houses. We arrived in Viqueque *vila* (town) on 2 June 1966, and one of my tasks was to seek assistance from the local administration. Before coming to the town, I had not been able to find any detailed maps of the *posto sede*, one of the five *postos* (subdistricts) into which Viqueque *concelho* was divided, and had no notion of how many *povoações* (villages) there were in the vicinity of the town.[7] Nor did I have any information about the size of the population or data upon which to determine the population density. There was also the question of language, for I had learned in Baucau that the Makassai, Naueti, Kairui, and Wai Ma'a languages were also spoken in the subdistrict. Since I was interested in making my inquiries in villages that had been least influenced by the Catholic missionaries, I also needed to find out where Christianity had made least inroads.

I discovered that the administrative archives contained essential resources for my research. The most important were the census books (*Caderno do Recenseamento*), which were the product of the annual census carried out by local administrative officials in each subdistrict for the purpose of levying the annual head tax on members of the male population in good physical condition, aged eighteen to sixty, and livestock taxes on Bali cattle, buffalos, and horses (Metzner 1977: 6, 183–84, 211). The head tax amounted to 190 *escudos*, and the livestock tax was ten *escudos* per head of livestock. The first of the books bore the date 1946, and the administrator of Viqueque and his staff unhesitatingly placed each of them at my disposal.[8] On examination I discovered they included data on all households in Viqueque *vila* as well as in all the subdistrict's ten *sukus* and fifty-two *povoações*, making them amount to a kind of synchronic (single year) and diachronic (multiple years) "doomsday book" for the *posto sede*. Physically, the pages of each *caderno* were handwritten in ink on a set of double pages bundled together and held in place by a pair of bamboo slates. When I first visited the shed in which they were kept, I found piles of them displayed on the floor, the old ones faded into yellow, with some showing evidence of having provided rodents a meal. Still older ones had already done so or else were reduced by time to powder. Each *Caderno do Recenseamento* was registered the following information for each household in each *povoação*: the name and age of the (male) household head and those of his wife or wives, and his sons and daughters; the names of his father and mother; the number of the household's cows, buffalos, sheep, goats, pigs, horses, dogs, and their respective offspring, including their sexes; and the number of producing and nonproducing coconut and areca trees of the household. Besides the multiple uses this information had for my work, it relieved me from carrying out a census of my own. The Viqueque archive subsequently proved to hold documents that another visitor also held to be of considerable value. When the Indonesian army, the Angkatan Bersenjata Indonesia (ABRI), first set foot in Viqueque town several weeks after 7 December, its troops looted the shed of its documents, threw them into a pile, and burned them outside the administrative buildings (Soares 2005) in a public ritual perhaps intended to impress the people of Viqueque that the Portuguese colonial past had been obliterated and that their future needed no props from the past.[9] Figure 10.1 is a photocopy of a single sheet from the *recenseamento* carried out in 1946 in the *povoação* of Mamulak.

The archive also housed other kinds of information for which I had uses. There were maps of the district showing the administrative geography of the *posto sede* and the other four subdistricts and, in more detail, the location of all fifty-nine of the *posto sede's povoações*. Maps and the census data showed that the *posto sede* consisted of ten *sukus* and gave their respective population figures: Uma Kik (2,113), Caraubalo (2,042), Balarauin (2005), Bibi Leu (1,749), Uma Uain Craik (1,322), Uai Mori (1,213), Uma Uain Leten (1,171), Luca (993), Maluro (355), and Fatu Dere (325).

Another category of information was pure ethnography: three local myths and etymologies for the names of topographic features, such as hills, dated "1964." These documents may have been requested by the administration, and I found them in written form in the Portuguese language. Some of them had an attributed authorship. A story titled "Lenda da Lagoa Ola Bui Loe" carried the attribution "Luís Franco Ricardo." Another, titled "Lenda—Origem do Povo de Macalosso," lacked a signature of authorship but was dated 18 March 1964, as were two others. The first, the "Lenda da Origem de Uai Mori" (a *suku*

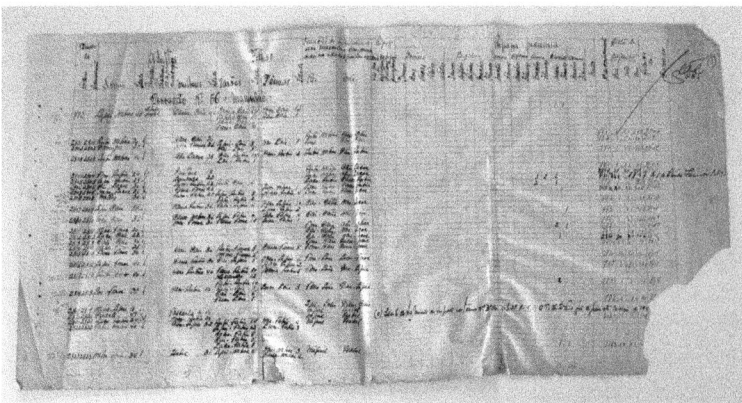

Figure 10.1. Specimen copy of *recenseamento* for 1946 showing page 1 entry for Mamulak *povoação*. Photo by the author.

in the *posto sede*) contained the information "Entregue pelo chefe do
suco do Uai-Mori senhor António da Costa Rangel," and the second
was titled the "O Monte de Hare-Meta e A Princesa Hare-Manek." I included the former narrative in an article titled "A Cairui Myth" (Hicks
1974: 124–30) and the latter in my monograph *A Maternal Religion*
(1984: 8–11). This Cairui text was, and perhaps remains, the only
example of a published narrative from this ethnic group. Another document provided the translation of the names of the *sukus* and of the
povoações within each *suku* from the vernacular into the Portuguese;
for example, the *suku* of Caraubalo was translated as "metade do buffalo." The inclusion of these narratives in the administration archives
was a very useful addition to the ethnographic information I was collecting at the time, but they would have been even more valuable had
they been transcribed in the original vernacular, with the Portuguese
translation provided. As it was, it was only the latter version that was
available to me. The texts I recorded in the villages were all in the
Tetum language. There was another document, dated 7 September
1964, that recorded "Produção Agrícola (em quilos) do ano de 1964"
for the *posto sede*, Lacluta *posto*, Ossu *posto*, Uato Carbau *posto*, and
Uato Lari *posto*. I would image there must have been hundreds, if not
thousands of such documents in the archives of the administration in
the colony. Most are now probably destroyed or otherwise lost.

Apart from this, I found nothing more. Nothing like a systematic
ethnographic study had been made anywhere in the entire *concelho*,[10]
so there was no "baseline" study that might have served as a point of
departure for the research I planned to carry out. The possibility of my
carrying out a comprehensive or extensive diachronic study was out
of the question. It had to be a synchronic perspective.

The Viqueque archive had no information on the distribution of
the local languages, Christianity, or asymmetric prescriptive alliance,
so another source was needed—this is where the 1966 *recenceamento*
was timely. In August, a team from the administration was scheduled
to travel around the *posto sede* collecting the information necessary
to complete that year's *recenseamento*, and the administrator invited
me to join the team. I have elsewhere given details of how this invitation came about (see Hicks forthcoming), so here I shall simply
describe the nature of the ethnographic information I obtained from
this enterprise and suggest its potential as a historical source. In addition to the ethnographic data I gathered by traveling with the team
to all ten *sukus*, I learned something of the geography of the *posto sede*
firsthand, appreciated the distances and nature of the terrain sepa-
rating the *sukus*, and, of course, came to know their locality. Further-

more, by putting my own questions to the residents of each *povoação*, I established that the subdistrict was predominately Tetum-speaking (8,356), with Makassai (3,204) second in terms of the number of its speakers, Kairui third (1,381), and Naueti fourth (347). I also learned that the *suku* of Caraubalo (the "half-buffalo"), whose *povoações* were sited in and around Viqueque *vila*, had proportionally the least number of Christian converts, a discovery that meant that I did not have to establish a new research site outside of the town. I also discovered that none of the Tetum villages in the subdistrict practiced prescriptive alliance. [11]

The terms of my visa permitted me to study the Tetum-speaking population of southern Timor only and excluded my carrying out detailed field inquiries among any of the other ethnolinguistic populations, and, having already established ourselves in Viqueque town, I was reluctant to travel further west to other Tetum groups that might have had prescriptive alliance. So I decided to remain where we were and began to subject the 1966 census figures to a more searching examination—I concentrated on Caraubalo *suku*, a *suku* that consisted of seven *povoações*: Mane Hat, Mamulak, Vessa, Has Abut, Cabira Oan, Lamaclaran, and Sira Lari.[12] With the census returns for each year giving me a synchronic picture of the household and *povoação*, I was able to assess the demographic character of the *suku* in diachronic terms by collating the returns for each year, and thereby add a historical dimension to my understanding of its social character.[13]

The three myths in the Viqueque archive were handwritten texts in Portuguese by two *chefes de suku*. Two narratives came from the Naueti *suku* of Maluro, and the other came from the Makassai *suku* of Wai Mori—they gave me some notion of the kind of narratives I could anticipate when I collected my own from Tetum speakers. Yet while they provided me with ideas as to the genre of tale available in the region and the motifs people expected to hear, my understanding of the narratives that I later collected on my own account benefited from my being able to hear them recited in the vernacular and witnessing the reactions of their listeners (laughing, tears, groans, silence, and the like). There was also the opportunity to question both tellers and audiences about the meaning of certain words, incidents, the significance of events or personalities in the tales, and what they understood the stories to mean. At times I took the opportunity to recite Tetum myths from the Samoro region of Manatuto, immediately to the west of Viqueque *concelho*, that Father Artur Basílio Sá had published in his *Textos em Teto da Literatura Oral Timorense*, which I had first encountered in Lisbon and which I took with me to Timor. These elicited responses that included codicils, exegeses, and other comments that furnished me with insights into how Tetum residents of Caraubalo thought about their oral literature.

Textos em Teto da Literatura Oral Timorense was one of my more important secondary sources, and although there were not many such works, there were a few that I discovered nonetheless, and as with Sá's book they provided me not only with ethnographic information in its own right but, as mentioned above, a research tool for eliciting responses from interlocutors. On my visit to the capital, I had acquired a copy of an issue of *Seara*, a journal published by the Diocese of Dili, that contained an article by Father Jorge Barros Duarte (1964) that described in a wealth of detail the system of asymmetric prescriptive alliance as the institution functioned among the Tetum communities of Samoro and neighboring Barique. While the marriage system of the Viqueque subdistrict Tetum differed significantly from that described in Father Duarte's article, when I recited to a Mamulak resident certain of the ritual verses recorded by Father Duarte that were spoken during the wedding ceremony, the villager immediately could relate to them. The ritual words accompanying weddings in his own village differed, but he spontaneously joined in as I recited them.

For Viqueque, however, no such published source was available that I might have used to guide my field inquiries, but there was a book, published in 1935, that did include some ethnographic material from Viqueque, though not specific to Tetum speakers or to Caraubalo *suku*. I had found it in the library of the Sociedade Geografia de Lisboa when I lived in Lisbon the preceding year (see Hicks forthcoming), and while in Baucau I was given a copy by an educated Makassai young man whose family, I believe, was of *liurai* rank. One day I asked him if he knew any local oral narratives, and he recited one. He told me he had read it in a book, *Gentio de Timor*, by Armando Pinto Correia. The following day he showed it to me. The author had served as administrator of Baucau before the Second World War, and his book consisted, for the most part, of a compilation of ethnographic information on, among other topics, kinship, ritual, and oral literature that he had collected on the Makassai of that *concelho*. For reasons that remain unclear to me, this book has received little attention by anthropologists who have written about the Makassai, though I found it a useful source of information for certain of my own writings on asymmetric alliance (see Hicks 1983)—when I mentioned it to Ruy Cinatti, he dismissed it as a collection of administrators' reports of no scholarly significance.[14] Given that my focus of research was in Viqueque and among the Tetum rather than the Makassai, the immediate interest *Gentio de Timor* had for me was that the book also included an ethnographic conspectus for each of the *concelhos* in the colony, collated from reports that fellow administrators of other *concelhos* had submitted to the governor, and there was some information on Viqueque. Unfortunately, Correia had not given the ethnolinguistic provenance of the ethnographic data he had marshaled from these reports, and so I could only use his information as a point of departure for the inquiries I was making in Caraubalo.

Fieldwork in 1999 (Two Visits)

It will be apparent from what I have said that, quite apart from the use I could put the ethnographic data I had collected to a synchronic interpretation of Caraubalo, my initial period in Viqueque enabled me to create a corpus of information that I could use when I returned to Timor at a later time—or that other ethnographers could use. I did return in July 1999 when my wife and I stayed in Dili for about a week to bring sundry items that we had been given by Timorese refugees and Catholic workers in Sydney for Timorese living under the Indonesian occupation and to renew acquaintances with friends. We were unable, for security reasons, to travel out of the capital, and so we did not manage to get to Viqueque. Upon my return to Stony Brook, I was invited to join a team that the Carter Center was sending to East Timor to monitor the plebiscite the following month, so, within a couple of weeks, I returned for the second time that year. On this occasion, though, I spent most of my time interviewing Timorese villagers, Timorese and Indonesian officials, representatives of NGO organizations, and members of the United Nations in Viqueque subdistrict.

One major change that struck me immediately as I drove down to Viqueque from the northern town of Ossu on the west bank of the River Cuha was how much the human and natural landscapes had altered. The physical space between the hamlets (*knua*) that line either side of the road had diminished, and the overwhelming number of houses made of concrete with tin roofs, which had not existed thirty-two years earlier, acknowledged the extent to which the population had exploded at the expense of the previous extensive tracts of woodlands that were now formidably reduced. This suburban stretch, however, did not extend into Viqueque town itself because a natural barrier—a steep hill through which a streamlet had cut a little gorge—still separated hamlets from the town. Houses now stood where woodland, savanna, and gardens had once hidden hamlets from those who passed by on the road. The names of the hamlets remained, but their appearance had profoundly changed. There was now a little bridge across the River Cuha linking the villages of Mamulak, Mane Hat, Cabira Oan, and Sira Lari on the western bank with the villages of Vessa and Lamaclaran on the eastern bank. Nevertheless, from both a social and a functional perspective the hamlets of Caraubalo *suku* merged into the urban center of Viqueque town, which greeted me, after I had rounded the aforementioned hill, with the shape of a huge statue of an Indonesian warrior erected after the Indonesian authorities had taken control of the town.

A large part of the reason for the population increase was that, as a result of the Indonesian policy of containing villagers in locations where they could be more closely supervised, the nine *sukus* located at a distance from Viqueque town had been emptied of their inhabitants, who had been forced to take up residence in and around the town. Thus did remote areas become deserted and the town overpopulated. A comparison of the Viqueque archive statistics from 1966 with those from today would show just how massive a surge occurred.

Fieldwork in 2001, 2005, 2007, 2009

Although my fieldwork in August 1999 concentrated on the plebiscite, I did manage to find some time to supplement my earlier collection of ethnographic data; however, when I returned in 2005, I had about seven months to engage in directed research of my own. Unlike the situation in 1966, I was now able to build upon a corpus of data that I had collected and published. Kinship, as such, was not one of my main research preoccupations now; I was more interested in social change, and one promising topic was local commerce and its sociological entailments. In the 1960s, much economic activity revolved around a biweekly market, the physical site of which was in the town center on the eastern side of and adjacent to the road from Ossu to the south shore. I had amassed a large amount of information on the economic and social nature of this institution during my first period of research, and I now had the opportunity to inquire into how market activities in the broadest sense had changed over the intervening decades. The results of my research resulted in an article in the *Bijdragen* that demonstrated how, between 1967 and 2005, radical adjustments had taken place in the commercial sphere. In 1967, commerce had been limited to about half a dozen Chinese shops and the biweekly marketplace, and whereas there had been no kiosks in the town, there were now dozens lining the road on either side, run by Chinese and Timorese. Within the context of market activities and using my existing data, I argued that space and time indexed social identity in very different ways in both periods (see Hicks 2012). Another second topic of research was population distribution. Interviews conducted in 2005 suggested that people were divided as to whether to return to their traditional *sukus* or remain in the town. By staying in Viqueque they could take advantage of its medical facilities, shops and kiosks, and the school, all of which were absent in the *sukus*. Some villagers would have liked to return since their social identities are to a significant degree derived from their birthplaces; but they preferred to remain in town because they enjoyed the facilities of town life. Also, in the case of at least one of the *sukus*, Uma Uain Craik, its *lisan* discourages residents from returning to their traditional *suku* unless their *liurai* has already done so. In 2009 the *liurai* had still not returned, but he continued to reside, apparently contentedly, in town.

I was not only able to make use of my unpublished ethnographic data collected in the sixties in my later research. As part of my research strategy in 2005, I showed the first edition of my book *Tetum Ghosts and Kin*[15] to villagers in Mamulak and Mane Hat to see what their reactions would be and to seek their help in correcting any mistakes I had made or amplifying my ethnographic data. Although they were unable to read the text, they could see the pictures and identify themselves and others, and I read out sections of the book to them. They did, indeed, find mistakes for me to correct, including the names of individuals in the photographs. Other things encouraged some villagers to add to what I had recorded or, in some cases, to bring me up to date with developments that had taken place since I first lived among them. By reciting some of the narratives that were in the book, I was able to provoke interest among them, and my audience commented on what I had recited and offered emendations and embellishments. I had had something of a prelude to this experience of the ethnographer's own monograph being the object of study several years earlier. In 1999, when I was waiting in the departure lounge in Dili airport, a young Timorese man approached me and asked if I were the author of the book *Roh Orang Tetum di Timor Timur*, the name the Indonesian translator had given the first edition of *Tetum Ghosts and Kin*. Upon my admission, he told me the book was used as a text in his school. The "ethnographic present," as ethnographers are wont to call the period during which they carried out their fieldwork, had become the "historical present" thirty-two years later.

Using one's own published works or unpublished data to cross-check the accuracy or to challenge one's interpretation is only possible, naturally, when one has first written or collected it. In 1966 I had nothing of my own to present to my informants, but with more publications and more ethnographic information, an interactive reflexivity becomes an increasingly profitable technique for amplifying one's reservoir of data as well as rendering them more intelligible. Let me give another two examples.

In Mane Hat village in the 1960s, I collected a narrative that, at the time, appeared to hold out scant possibility of being more than what it superficially seemed—an amusing folktale. It recounts the adventures of a pair of avian protagonists, one a friarbird and the other a bird known locally as a *kaoá*, who argue about how long day and night should be—i.e., whether each day should last one day or seven days—while eating around their hearth. The birds are so consumed by their selfish demands that they begin to hit each other. The *kaoá* is thrown in the hearth, his entire body blackened by the ashes, while friarbird has his head feathers ripped out, which, the story explains, is why today the *kaoá* is black and the friarbird has a light-colored head. As the narrator told me the tale, it elicited much amusement from the audience before we passed to the next tale. The fantastic fight between friarbird and *kaoá* remained unexamined in my fieldwork archives for three decades until I read an article by Dr. Gregory Forth (1992) that analyzed a set of similar myths from different parts of eastern Indonesia and concluded that the story was not only a narrative explaining the origin of their different avian traits and the present length of the day (twenty-four hours instead of seven days) but that it was also an etiological tale about the origin of death. Intrigued by Forth's unearthing a deeper meaning than I had suspected, I returned to a text to see if it might possess a more profound meaning than I had originally credited it with. My analysis confirmed Forth's suspicion. To test the interpretation I had now given the text, I took the opportunity of reading the tale to the household head of a *liurai* family we had been friendly with since 1966 and at whose guest house I stayed during fieldwork in Viqueque in 2009, adding my exegesis. She was very familiar with the story, and a relative of hers told me it was part of the local school curriculum. Both informed me that the tale was intended as an oral entertainment to amuse children; it was nothing more than a species of Aesopian just-so story.

My second example involves a myth the husband of this household head had written down for me in Tetum in December 1966 when he was fourteen years old, the first narrative I collected in the field.

The text describes the origin of his clan (*ahi matan*), which was called Tuna ("the Eel") and located in Mamulak village. His father, I believe, had dictated it to him for my benefit, and his son explained various things in the tale I did not understand. In 2005 when I recited the eel myth to a group of men that included the headman of Mamulak, he recognized it at once and narrated the story back to me, embellishing it such that its meaning was enriched for me.[16]

Between the time I left Timor in 1967 and when I returned in 1999, momentous events had, of course, reshaped Timorese life, and not only in commerce and population distribution. Even before I returned in 1999 I had decided to write a book on the twenty troubled months that marked the end of the Portuguese colonial empire and prepared the way for the recolonization of East Timor by the Republic of Indonesia (Hicks 2015). Over the course of these subsequent visits, I interviewed people in Dili and in various districts, including Viqueque, in order to assemble the information I needed, and I complemented my ethnographic inquiries with research in the archives of the Comissão de Acolhimento, Verdade e Reconciliação de Timor-Leste (the Commission for Reception, Truth and Reconciliation in Timor-Leste), more commonly known by its acronym, CAVR. CAVR had still to publish its monumental account of the history of 1974–75 and the Indonesian occupation, but some of the material it would eventually use for that publication was available in the form of a film record of public testimonies that participants in the events of 1974–75 had made about their experiences. The library also contained a copy of a film made by the Australian Clive Schollay, which depicts the progress of the war between the political parties in August–September 1975. It includes interviews in Ainaro subdistrict with such notables of the Fretilin political party as José Ramos-Horta and Alarico Fernandes at the time the Fretilin army was forcing the army of a rival party, the União Democrática Timorense, out of East Timor, over the international border and into Indonesian Timor. Both sources of information were essential resources for my book, and in some instances I had the opportunity of following up the testimonies given by the participants in the hearings by those who had given them, including Ramos-Horta and the former president of Fretilin, Francisco Xavier do Amaral. In addition, the information I obtained from the CAVR archives provided me with a context for interviews I had with residents of Viqueque town about their experiences during that time and during the twenty-four years of Indonesian occupation. Some of the interviewees were persons I had interviewed four decades earlier, and I took the opportunity during my inquiries to find out how they compared their new world with the Timorese world my wife and I had entered in the middle of the 1960s.

Conclusion

The documents that I found in the administration archives provided a mine of information, some of which I was eventually able to incorporate into two doctoral theses and my published work, and by including some of this material I was able to put a diachronic cast on certain aspects of it. But for the most part, because in 1966–67 the communities in which I carried out field research had had no recorded history available either in archives or in published form, I had little choice but to adopt a synchronic approach to make sense of their institutions. Now, however, with a wealth of ethnographic facts from that period, a comparison between contemporary institutions and those of that time is feasible, and synchronicity does not have to be our only means of making Caraubalo institutions intelligible. It almost goes without saying that a combination of a diachronic perspective and a synchronic perspective would yield a richer understanding than a single perspective allows. In the words of Lévi-Strauss (1958: 17, my translation):

> Moreover, when one limits oneself to the present moment in a society's life, one immediately falls victim to an illusion because everything is history. What happened yesterday is history. What was said a minute ago is history. Above all, one is unable to understand the present because only historical development allows one to weigh and evaluate the components of the present in their respective relationships.[17]

Acknowledgments

I wish to thank the following organizations for their help in funding my research at various times in Timor-Leste since 1966: the London Committee of the London-Cornell Project for East and South East Asian Studies, which was supported jointly by the Carnegie Corporation of New York and the Nuffield Foundation; the American Philosophical Society; and the J. William Fulbright Foreign Scholarship Board. At different times, Stony Brook University awarded me research leaves, and I acknowledge its consideration. I thank the following for their help when I was in Timor: Maria Rosa Biddlecombe, José Henriques Pereira, Rosa Maria da Costa Soares, and the many other Timorese villagers in Viqueque for the help they gave my wife and me.

David Hicks is a Life Member of Clare College, University of Cambridge, and professor of anthropology at Stony Brook University. He has carried out over thirty months of ethnographic research in Timor-Leste, starting in 1966 and, since the end of the Indonesian occupation, continuing to the present. His publications include *Tetum Ghosts and Kin* (1976, 2004); *Structural Analysis in Anthropology* (1978); *A Maternal Religion* (1984); *Kinship and Religion in Eastern Indonesia* (1990); *Rhetoric and the Decolonization and Recolonization of East Timor* (2015); *Cultural Anthropology* (with Dr. Margaret A. Gwynne) (1994, 1996); and *Ritual and Belief: Readings in the Anthropology of Religion* (1999, 2002, 2010), as well as articles in the *American Anthropologist*, the *Journal of the Royal Anthropological Society*, and the *Bijdragen tot de Taal-, Land- en Volkenkunde*, in addition to many anthologies.

Notes

1. In something like a parallel fashion, ethnoarchaeologists make use of analogies from contemporary populations to help understand populations that are now extinct and whose daily lives are now completely inaccessible.
2. Here I employ the term "institution" in the sense defined by Marcel Mauss (1968) as "public rules of action and *thought*" (my translation and emphasis).
3. I credit "E-P" with having had the most decisive influence on my career as a social anthropologist. I decided to study in Oxford after reading his article "The Teaching of Social Anthropology at Oxford" (1959) during my final undergraduate year at the University College of Wales at Aberystwyth, and the first anthropological monograph I ever read was *Witchcraft, Oracles among the Azande* (1937). It was E-P who accepted me into the Institute, and after my first year as his student, he offered me the position of graduate assistant there and was instrumental in my securing the Alan Coltart Scholarship at Exeter College. My gratitude to him is immense. He also introduced me to Rodney Needham.
4. The presence of this institution is not, of course, a *sine qua non* for structural analysis, as my monograph *A Maternal Religion* demonstrates.
5. For a discussion of the *barlaque*, see Duarte (1964) and Hicks (2010 and 2012b).
6. It was also known that asymmetric alliance existed in Indonesian Timor but research there for a British fieldworker was out of the question in the mid-nineteen-sixties owing to the *Confrontasi* that existed between Indonesia and Malaysia.
7. Besides the *posto sede* (the "seat" of the *concelho* where the administrator lived and from which the other *postos* were administered), Viqueque

concelho consisted of Lacluta *posto* to its northwest; Ossu *posto* to the north; Uato Lari *posto* to the east; and Uato Carabau *posto* to where the *concelho* abutted its neighbor, the Lautem *concelho*. A few statistics for the colony did exist in published form, and Duarte (1930: 114–15) provided the information that the kingdom of Viqueque (i.e. the *posto sede* minus the *suku* of Luca) and Luca kingdom numbered between them a total of 6,899 males and 6,341 females in 1927. There were 79 villages. In the same year Lacluta kingdom (i.e., Lacluta *posto*) contained 4,787 persons, made up of 2,651 males and 2,136 females. There were 25 villages.

8. Comparable archival material was made available to me by the Baucau administrator.
9. Before my wife and I left Dili after our return visit in 1999, a former administrative officer in Viqueque town gave me a photocopy of some of those very same documents I had copied (by hand) in 1966–67. They included three of the origin myths I transcribed and the etymologies. He had saved them from the flames. The map, which I reproduce here, was however lacking.
10. The administration also provided me with another source of information. I would go to the town's metrological office most days, and for the fifteen months I lived in Viqueque I would record the data that had been collected.
11. A quality they share with the Wehali Tetum of Indonesian Timor.
12. Sira Lari was a Makassai *povoação*, and its inhabitants practiced asymmetric alliance.
13. Other research commitments prevented and continue to prevent me from completing this task.
14. For a discussion of Cinatti's role in my research, see Hicks (2019).
15. Hicks (1976). A second, completely rewritten, edition was published in 2004, and it owes its different character, in part, to my later fieldwork.
16. On this occasion I acquired it, not as a written story transcribed on paper but on tape, using an instrument I wished I had possessed in 1966.
17. Quand, au surplus, on se limite à l'instant présent de la vie d'une société, on est d'abord victim d'une illusion: car tout est historie; ce qui a ete hier est histoire, ce qui a été dit il y a une minute est histoire. Mais surtout, on se condamne à ne pas connaître ce présent, car seul le développement historique permet de soupeser, et d'évaluer dans leurs rapports respectifs, les éléments du present.

References

Anonymous. 1964. "O Monte de Hare-Meta e A Princesa Hare-Manek." Unpublished typescript, Viqueque Administration, Viqueque *Concelho*, Portuguese Timor.

Correia, A. P. 1935. *Gentio de Timor*. Lisboa: Lucas & Co.

Duarte, J. B. 1964. "Barlaque." *Seara (n.s.)* 2 (3–4): 92–119. (Reditado com emendas como "Barlaque: casamento gentílico timorense." *Arquivos Centro Cultural Português* 14: 377–418. Paris: Fundação Calouste Gulbenkian, 1979.)

Duarte, T. 1930. *Timor (Ante-Câmara do Inferno?!)*. Famalicão: Tip. "Minerva."

Evans-Pritchard, E. E. 1937. *Witchcraft, Oracles and Magic among the Azande*. Oxford: Clarendon Press.

———. 1940. *The Nuer: A Description of the Modes of Livelihood and Political Institutions of a Nilotic People*. Oxford: Clarendon Press.

———. 1949. *The Sanusi of Cyrenaica*. Oxford: Clarendon Press.

———. 1959. "The Teaching of Social Anthropology at Oxford." *Man* 64: 121–24.

———. 1962. "Anthropology and History." In *Essays in Social Anthropology*, 46–65. London: Faber and Faber.

Forbes, H. O. 1884. "On Some of the Tribes of Timor." *Journal of the Royal Anthropological Institute* 13: 402–31.

———. 1885. *A Naturalist's Wanderings in the Eastern Archipelago*. New York: Harper Brothers, Franklyn Square.

Forth, G. 1981. *Rindi: An Ethnographic Study of a Traditional Domain in Eastern Sumba*. The Hague: Martinus Nijhoff.

———. 1992. "The Pigeon and the Friarbird: The Mythical Origin of Death and Daylight in Eastern Indonesia." *Anthropos* 87: 423–41.

Metzner, J. K. 1977. *Man and Environment in Eastern Timor: A Geoecological Analysis of the Baucau-Viqueque Area as a Possible Basis for Regional Planning*. Development Studies Centre Monograph no. 8. Canberra: Australian National University.

Hicks, D. 1974. "A Cairui Myth: Stony Brook." *Anthropologist* 1: 124–30.

———. 1976. *Tetum Ghosts and Kin: Fieldwork in an Indonesian Community*. Palo Alto: Mayfield Publishing. Indonesian edition published as *Roh Orang Tetum di Timor Timur*. Jakarta: Penerbit Sinar Harapan.

———. 1978. *Structural Analysis in Anthropology: Case Studies from Indonesia and Brazil*. St. Augustin: Anthropos Institut.

———. 1983. "A Transitional Relationship Terminology of Asymmetric Prescriptive Alliance among the Makassai of Eastern Indonesia." *Sociologus*, n.s. 33(l): 73–85.

———. 1984. *A Maternal Religion: The Role of Women in Tetum Myth and Ritual*. Monograph Series on Southeast Asia. Special Report No. 22. DeKalb: Northern Illinois University, Center for Southeast Asian Studies.

———. 1985. *Roh Orang Tetum di Timor Timur*. Jakarta: Penerbit Sinar Harapan.

———. 2010. "The Barlaque of Timor-Leste." In *Transition, Society and Politics in Timor-Leste*, edited by P. Castro Seixas, 115–22. Porto: Universidade Fernando Pessoa.

———. 2012a. "Indexing Social Space: Viqueque Market Place, 1966/2007." *Bijdragen tot de Taal-, Land- en Volkenkunde* 168(1): 55–73.

————. 2012b. "Compatibility, Resilience and Adaptation: The *Barlaque* of Timor-Leste." *Local-Global: Identity, Security, Community* 11: 124–37. Special edition, edited by D. Grenfell.

————. 2006. "How Friarbird Got His Helmet: Functional Reversal in an East Timor Narrative." *Anthropos* 101(2): 570–75.

————. 2015. *Rhetoric and the Decolonization and Recolonization of East Timor.* New York: Routledge.

————. 2017. "Research Past and Research Present: Doing Fieldwork in Portuguese Timor and Timor-Leste." In *Fieldwork in Timor-Leste: Understanding Social Change through Practice*, edited by M. Nygaard-Christensen and A. Bexley, 32–57. Copenhagen: NIAS Press.

Lévi-Strauss, C. 1958. *Anthropologie structurale.* Paris: Plon.

Mauss, M. 1968. *Oeuvres: 1. les fonctions sociales du sacré.* Edited by V. Karady. Paris: Les éditions de Minuit.

Rangel, A. da C. 1964. "Lenda da Origem de Uai Mori." Unpublished typescript, Viqueque Administration, Viqueque *Concelho*, Portuguese Timor.

Sá, A. B. 1961. *Textos em Teto da Literatura Oral Timorense.* Vol. 1. Lisboa: Junta de Investigações do Ultramar, Centro de Estudos Políticos e Sociais 45.

Soares, L. F. de G. 2005. Interview.

Chapter 11

THE *BARLAKE* WAR

MARRIAGE EXCHANGES, COLONIAL FANTASIES, AND THE PRODUCTION OF EAST TIMORESE PEOPLE IN 1970s DILI

Kelly Silva

Introduction

This chapter addresses a colonial controversy about marriage exchange in 1970s Dili. Retrospectively called after the Portuguese expression *guerra do barlaque* (*barlake* war), this controversy came to be considered, by at least one of the actors involved, a foundational event of East Timorese nationalism (Araújo 2012) because it brought to the fore opposing positions about local social life. Not by chance, from the debate marriage exchanges emerged as the most iconic institution of local societies, and its meanings and effects were considered condensed manifestations of the character of the East Timorese people.

The military bulletin *A Província de Timor*, the newspaper *A Voz de Timor*, and *Seara*, the Dili Diocese Ecclesiastical bulletin were the local media in which the *barlake* war gained public audience. All of them were colonial media, published in Dili, led by editors more or less commited to Portuguese government institutions or projects. In one way or another, each of these media published news about what was going on in the wider world beyond Timor; reported on local issues, including religious and civil government practices; and offered critical reviews on aspects and facts deemed typical of East Timorese societies (such as myths, rituals, institutions, etc.) (Paulino 2012, Fernandes 2014). Importantly, all these periodicals were directly (or indirectly, in the case of *Seara*) under close political surveillance by the PIDE (International and State Defense Police), the political police of the Salazar regime. The *barlake* war unfolded in two rounds, the first between the last months of 1969 and September 1970, the second between July and December 1973.

The *barlake* war was triggered by the publication of two literary pieces by Inácio de Moura, then a Portuguese civil servant in the colony. In these writings, the presentation for offering from wife-takers to wife-givers, so-called *barlake*, in order to seal a marriage was presented as a transaction that worked to comodify the bride, her feelings, and her subjectivity. This discourse of commodification was challenged by East Timorese intellectuals who, in general, argued that *barlake* was a very complex social process that could not be reduced to a commodity transaction.

Practices and discourses on marriage exchanges have been critical elements of the politics of custom in various colonial and postcolonial landscapes (Tonkinson 1982: 302; Filer 1985: 163; Jolly and Thomas 1992: 243–46; Thomas 1991, Keane 2007, Jolly 2015, among others). In colonial East Timor and elsewhere, missionaries, colonial administrators, and anthropologists have made various attempts to understand and/or control indigenous marital practices (Roque 2012, Fernandes 2014, Parise 2014; for an example of similar processes elsewhere, see Marksbury 1993). In the context of Papua New Guinea, for instance, Jorgensen (1993) and Carrier (1993) have discussed the various configurations and transformations of bridewealth (locally referred to as brideprice) among the Telefolmin and Ponam people, respectively. Both authors demonstrated that bridewealth is a dependent variable whose shape has responded to complex phenomena derived from colonial encounter and missionization during the twentieth century. Graeber (2011: 131) notes that by 1926, the League of Nations debated banning the practice on the grounds that it amounted to a form of slavery. British social anthropologists objected to the proposed ban, emphasizing the social meanings of such marital practices.[1] In the same decade, an important debate was underway in British social anthropology about the most appropriate word to describe marriage exchanges, considering their effects on sociality (Torday 1929; Driberg, Stoneham, and Cullen Young 1930; Evans-Pritchard 1931, among others). Later, scholars such as Lévi-Strauss (2003 [1949]), Goody (1973), among others, definitively set the consensus in anthropology, arguing that bridewealth is a social technology by means of which people negotiate rights in persons, identities, obligations, belonging, property transmission, power, and alliance relations, even if it is sometimes translated as brideprice (Thomas 1991). Therefore, the *barlake* war in East Timor constitutes one episode in a wider and long-term debate about how different collectivities organize their relations between animate and inanimate things in social life, a debate involving people from diverse origins and fostered by various political and epistemological projects.

The protagonists in the *barlake* war were people with a very distinctive profile in 1970s Dili. Although they disagreed about the meanings and consequences of customary marriage in East Timor, all of them claimed to be recognized as intellectual voices. Nevertheless, they had different social origins and trajectories. On the one hand, there were Portuguese-born agents—Inácio de Moura, Jaime Neves, and Luiz Filipe Thomaz—who nurtured a special interest in so-called "Timorese culture." All had served as officers of the Portuguese army when they first arrived in Timor; after their military service, they engaged in civil activities, either in Dili or in Portugal. However, their similar Portuguese origins and standing within the colonial administration did not imply similar positions on the *barlake* war, as demonstrated later. On the other hand, a group comprising self-styled native intellectuals—including Abílio Araújo, Xavier do Amaral, and Nicolau dos Reis Lobato—could be distinguished.[2] The position these native intelectuals took on *barlake* was to a considerable extent consistent with that of professional social anthropologists in the 1930s. Although originally from different parts of the country, all belonged to high-status houses in their home districts and received Western education in missionary institutions. Nicolau Lobato and Xavier do Amaral met at the Catholic Seminary of Soibada, where an important part of the East Timor upper classes was educated since the seminary's foundation in 1898. Abílio Araújo, in turn, studied at the Salesian School in Lahane, and then at the High-School Francisco Machado in Dili; in 1971, he went to Lisbon to study economics. After finishing their studies, all three engaged in different jobs and activities within the Portuguese colonial administration in Timor.[3] By 1974, after the Carnation Revolution in Portugal, they became active participants in the political events leading to the formation of political parties in Dili and to East Timorese struggle for independence. Xavier do Amaral was one of the founders of ASDT—Associação Social Democrata Timorense, later to become Fretilin—Frente Revolucionária de Timor-Leste Independente. Abílio Araújo was also a founding member of Fretilin: he drew up its first political program and manual and, during the brief 1975 Fretilin government, he became the first minister for economic and social affairs. Nicolau Lobato was the prime minister of the same government and, afterward, a prominent guerilla leader, until his death in 1978 at the hands of Indonesian soldiers. In the same brief context of 1975, Xavier do Amaral became the first president of the República Democrática de Timor-Leste.

The East Timorese actors in the debate were Christian-educated and linguistically qualified in the Portuguese language. In this liminal position, they could act as mediators between the Portuguese and Timorese worlds. Moreover, the fact that Araújo, Amaral, and Lobato were also recognized as so-called *assimilated* (*assimilados*) during the *barlake* war deserves attention. Established by the middle of the 1950s, the category *assimilado* was originally an official colonial category of citizenship to be "bestowed only" upon individuals with an indigenous cultural background who were considered (after strict evaluation) to have achieved a high degree of integration into the Portuguese cultural world. This category was applied to "natives" who did not follow local indigenous customs (*costumes*); had converted to Catholic Christianity; had received European education; spoke Portuguese; had a job, some possessions, or financial means to ensure their survival. In other words, *assimilados* were those who most successfully internalized a Western way of life and cosmology, in contrast to *pagan* native people. When the *barlake* war began in the 1970s, however, this citizenship status was no longer used in official state administration. Nevertheless, I believe the category and the social meanings it entailed were still significant in social life. For instance, the fact that Araújo, Amaral, and Lobato were widely acknowledged as *assimilados* gave them a special social authority to wage the *barlake* war almost on equal footing to the Portuguese officials. As *assimilados*, they could be perceived to be in possession of intellectual capacities similar to Europeans.

My approach to this colonial debate is inspired by ethnographic field research about marriage exchange, which I had been pursuing in Dili between 2008 and 2013. In addition to analyzing the current composition and social dynamics of marriage prestations, I was interested in understanding how they relate to a wider debate about the reproduction and government of customary practices in East Timor in the context of nation-building. As I argue elsewhere (Silva and Simião 2012), the colonial and postcolonial debates about customary practices provide important insights into the processes of social change and modernization in East Timor and other places. At the same time, analysis of these debates may unveil tensions, challenges, and contention structuring the making and unmaking of modernity, as Stoler (2002) has proposed. I argue that the transfer of wealth from wife-takers to wife-givers to arrange marriages has long been a main source of anxiety and tension in colonial and postcolonial governance because it calls into question key moral ideals and ontological perspectives upon which modern processes of subject formation are grounded. Customary marriage systems reveal another way to organize the relations between persons and things, very different from the opposing trend that marks certain Western cosmologies. Such institution allows for a certain symmetry between people and things, once valuables are offered in return for a bride. Such transactions have often been understood by outsiders as the purchase of a woman. Moreover, the dynamics of marriage prestations in social reproduction challenge the ideology of romantic individualism that feeds certain Euro-American expectations about marriage.

It was also in the course of my fieldwork in Dili that I came into contact with colonial writings on the topic of *barlake*. Some of my local interlocutors, who had grown up during the Portuguese period or who had been in close contact with institutional settings (such as the Catholic Church) that valued former Portuguese culture, frequently urged me to go back to earlier colonial literature. I was thus encouraged to read the works by Father Jorge Barros Duarte, Alberto Osório de Castro, and those of other colonial authors in order to understand what was at stake in marriage exchanges in the present. These instructions to penetrate the colonial archive led me to look closer into colonial literature. In effect, my interlocutors' advice is an indicator of the power and persistence of colonial knowledge in shaping representations of local practices, at least among formally educated Timorese people in Dili. In addition, it suggests that current controversies about *barlake* in Dili are structured by long-running anthropological fractures, involving government agents and local intelligentsia, and whose roots possibly date at least back to the 1970s. Knowledge disputes, moreover, are often intrinsically political, especially in a colonial setting (like 1960s–70s Dili) in which East Timorese nationalism was nascent. Thus it is no surprise that the controversies on *barlake* that took place in the 1970s came later to be understood as critical events in the rise of East Timorese nationalism.

The Dili-based controversy, I argue, was a form of epistemological and political project from which particular images of the East Timorese people and their sociality derived. When transfers of wealth at marriage were portrayed as a commodity exchange that materially benefited the bride´s relatives, they were characterized as a "barbaric" practice that reflected the "barbaric" character of those who performed it. However, when the offering of valuables from wife-takers to wife-givers is depicted as a means of social contract, and a device for alliance building and mutual recognition—which anthropologists have named gift-giving—the same transfers appeared as a "noble" practice that expressed the "noble" character of its practitioners. In addition, I contend that the colonial controversies discussed here were critical events by which the wider complexity of marriage exchanges in East Timor has been reduced in the Dili public space to one simple conception of *barlake* or *hafolin*. In the light of these discussions, it is possible that current public controversies about marriage exchanges are also a product of dillemas shaped, in part, by tensions discussed here.

This chapter is divided into four sections. First, I overview the theoretical debate about regimes of exchange. Second, I delineate the generative themes around which the *barlake* war developed. I also correlate what, following Latour (1994), I call purifying and antipurifying perspectives on marriage exchanges with the production of opposed discourses about East Timorese people. In the third section, I discuss the epistemological practices for legitimizing opposing perspectives about marriage exchanges. The resorts to colonial ethnographies and anthropology, etymological arguments, comparisons, and methodological procedures are identified as the tactics used by participants in the debate to support their positions. In concluding, I outline some possible relations of continuity between the colonial and postcolonial debates about *barlake*, taking into consideration my research about marriage exchanges in contemporary Dili (Silva 2018, 2019). I then hypothesize that the postcolonial debate on *barlake* retains the oppositional structure of the "*barlake* war."

Regimes of Exchange

I understand regimes of exchange as analytical categories for making sense of the diverse rules, expectations and effects involved in particular ways by which individuals and people transact valuables, rights in persons, or signs of recognition. The epistemological efforts in understanding such phenomena have provided three ideal types of regimes of exchanges: barter, commodity transactions, and gift-giving. Each of them is often associated with specific spheres of exchange (Bohannan 1955). I discuss below some characteristics of commodity transactions and gift-giving because they implicitly inform the *barlake* war.

Very briefly, the gift regime might be depicted as the one in which, by means of the exchange, people negotiate relations that are outside the immediate transaction (Strathern 1992). Things as well as human beings are treated as persons, as the valuables are bridges for producing and reproducing long-term relations between the people who exchange them. In the classic Maussian model, there is a sort of unity, a consubstantiality between the valuable exchanged and the giver that makes the first somehow inalienable and animate, endowed with a certain sort of agency. The value of the goods is measured by rank and not by price. The parts involved in the exchanges are mutually dependent and stand before one another asymmetrically (Gregory 1982: 41–70) and the equivalence of valuables is constructed in a long-term perspective. The offering of the gift is often taken as compulsory in the making of particular relationships.

Conversely, independence of the transactors and the presence of currency as a means to quantify and measure value are the main characteristics of the commodity regime. By comparison with the gift regime, where things are treated as persons, in commodity transactions, relations between people are experienced as relations between things. There is no consubstantiality between the transactors and the things exchanged, which makes the valuables alienable, inanimate, and subject to human actions. Their values are measured by price, and their equivalence has to be immediate (Gregory 1982: 41–70).

It is worth noting that all three regimes of exchange coexist in the social dynamic and are mobilized according to specific ends, even in the absence of all the variables associated with each of them (Thomas 1991). As Appadurai (1986) has argued, over the course of their social lives, particular objects may pass from one "regime of value" to another as they participate in different transactions. In fact, a particular exchange transaction may have the potential to be interpreted as a commodity or a gift transaction. Such ambiguity nurtures a certain anxiety among social actors, which triggers various social efforts to inscribe the transaction in a particular regime of exchange in order to produce certain social effects. In other words, people resort to social techniques to purify the potential ambiguity of their acts. I understand purification as defined by Latour (1994): the processes of and the search for separation by which the modern episteme projects ontological frontiers and limits between what are taken as diverse realms, beings and experiences of which social life is made up, such as the opposition between nature and culture, politics and knowledge, justice and power, humans and nonhumans, gift and commodity, among others.[4] Conversely, the antipurification perspective recognizes, at the outset, the hybrid nature of phenomena and the multiple mediations that bring them into existence.

The Politics of Knowledge in 1970s Dili

The *barlake* war was sparked by two literary works by Inácio de Moura: the poem "Mulher de Lipa, Feto Timor" and the short novel *Mau Curo e Bere Mau ou o Grande Amor de Cai Buti*, published in 1969 and 1973 respectively. Moura first arrived in Dili in 1965 to carry out his military service. By 1970, he had left his military career to become a civil servant at the Centro de Informação e Turismo de Timor (Timor Center for Information and Tourism). During the 1970s he published many articles and poems on what was called, in Portuguese colonial terminology of that period, *Timorese culture.*

Apart from Moura´s publications, the *barlake* war gained public visibility in three different media: the colonial newspaper *A Voz de Timor*, the military bulletin *A Província de Timor*, and the Dili Diocese Eclesiastic bulletin, *Seara*. In this period, Jaime Neves was the editor of *A Voz de Timor*. Like Moura, Jaime Neves first went to Timor as a Portuguese army officer. Later, he left military service to engage in civil administration. Besides his editorial activities, he also acted as anchor at the Emissora de Radio e Difusão de Timor (Broadcast Company of Timor); he was secretary of the Exchange Council (Conselho de Câmbios) and he acted unofficially as a lawyer (Luis Filipe Thomaz, personal communication). *A Província de Timor* was edited by Luis Filipe Thomaz, an erudite army officer who also taught Latin and Greek at the Seminary of Dare between 1970 and 1973. He was a nephew of the former president of Portugal, Américo Thomaz.[5] As will be discussed later, when the *barlake* war resumed in 1973, Luís Filipe Thomaz played a prominent role. At the time of the controversy, *Seara*'s editor was Father Manuel Andre Pinheiro. Its goal was to mediate the relations between the Vatican, the Portuguese State, and Catholic missionaries serving in Timor (Fernandes 2014) by informing each about the others.

In *Mulher de Lipa, Feto Timor*, Moura suggests that, in order to wed, East Timorese women had to sell their love in exchange for money and other material assets for their families. In response to the poem, Abílio Araújo wrote "Carta aberta ao Sr. Inácio de Moura" (Open letter to Inácio de Moura), published in *A Província de Timor* in 10 March 1970. Araújo's letter received several replies from Jaime Neves, published in a number of issues of *A Voz de Timor* between 22 March 1970 and 26 July 1970. In response to Neves, Abílio Araújo published "Onde está a verdade?" (Where is the truth?) in different issues of *A Província de Timor*. Meanwhile, Nicolau Lobato and Xavier do Amaral joined the debate.[6]

The controversy was structured around two opposing viewpoints backed by social actors who occupied distinct social positions in colonial Dili. On one side, colonial officials Inácio de Moura and Jaime Neves held that customary marriage in East Timor (which these actors generally encompassed under the terms *hafolin* or *barlake*) was a market operation in which women were sold. On the other side, East Timorese *assimilados*, like Abílio Araújo, Nicolau Lobato, and Xavier do Amaral, argued for a broader approach to this institution and contended that it did not function as a commodity exchange but as a socially complex and long-standing phenomenon essential to the reproduction of East Timorese societies. In 1973, the debate prompted by the publication of the aforementioned novel generated a heated argument between Inácio de Moura, Jaime Neves, and Luís Filipe Thomaz that gained public attention in *A Voz de Timor*.

At first glance, it would be tempting to portray the controversy as framed by an opposition between colonizers and colonized. But the scenario was much more complex. The fact that Thomaz was the editor of the military bulletin *A Província de Timor*, where all of Araújo´s criticisms of Neves and Moura were to be published, suggests that social boundaries in the colonial past were often blurred. It is important to note that Thomaz, himself also a colonial officer, took a position against Moura's narratives about *barlake*. Moreover, it is clear that as *assimilados*, Abílio Araújo, Nicolau Lobato, and Xavier do Amaral shared at least part of their classificatory system with their Portuguese interlocutors. This is why, I wager, it was so important for them to insist that there was no necessary contradiction between marriage for love (which they themselves arguably valued) and the presence of *barlake* in local sociality. Thus, the controversy cannot be reduced to an opposition between colonizers and colonized. Instead, it exposes an opposition within the local elite between those who claimed to possess a closer and emotional knowledge of the local dynamics of social reproduction and those who saw themselves as agents of a "civilizing mission" and thereby had a critical perception of some East Timorese institutions.

Differences also marked the life trajectories of Abílio Araújo, Xavier do Amaral, and Nicolau Lobato within the colonial society. Xavier, the oldest of the three, had been trained for the priesthood in Macau, a career that he eventually did not follow. After finishing his ecclesiastical studies, he returned to Timor to work as a teacher. Later, he got a position at the Dili customs house. Xavier was one of the founders of the União Desportiva e Recreativa de Díli (Sports and Leisure Union of Dili), a civil institution aimed at involving Timorese students from the Catholic missions in recreational activities. In such a place, local cultural practices were often praised, according to Luís Filipe Thomaz (personal communication). Until his death in 2012, Xavier do Amaral was known for his strong commitment to local traditions. Nicolau Lobato, in turn, was known in the institutions where he was trained as a brilliant student and a very devoted Christian. Economic limitations of his family of origin as well as his father's illness prevented him from following his dream of taking a law degree at the University of Coimbra, in Portugal. He served in the Portuguese army, where he was introduced to some African officers who made him familiar with the national liberation movements in other Portuguese colonies. Finally, after studying in Dare and Dili, eighteen-year-old Abílio Araújo was appointed administrator of the subdistrict of Hatohudo in 1968. In Dili, he taught music at the *Engenheiro* Canto Resende School where he composed his first musical pieces in Tetum. He then went on military service for two years, after which he received a scholarship to study in Portugal.

Retrospectively, according to Abílio Araújo (personal communication), the public debate about *barlake* in the 1970s launched the notion of *Maubere* as the political symbol of national pride and independence for Timor-Leste. The conthroversy provoked Portuguese-educated East Timorese who considered themselves *assimilados* to develop a positive approach towards local institutions, for the first time. Such an approach was later used in devising *Maubere* as an icon of Timorese-ness. Originally a proper name common among poor, illiterate and non-Christian Timorese, *Maubere* was used as a denigrating term in the colonial period. Only in the 1970s, under the influence of Fretilin, the term became a symbol for the exploited Timorese people in need of national liberation.

The Colonial Critique of Barlake *as a Commodity Exchange*

The challenge facing East Timorese women who supposedly wanted to marry *for love* was the primary political mover in the colonial criticism of *hafolin* or *barlake* (Moura 1969, 1973a). The material exchanges required for a marriage to take place were understood as a market operation that reduced women to commodities or even turned both the grooms and the brides into slaves (Neves 1970, 1970a, 1970c). These exchanges would respond only to the material interests of the bride's family members, with no respect for a woman's personal desires and expectations, eliminating a woman's freedom to choose whom to marry (Moura 1969, 1973a). In addition, traditional marriages were presented as one of the main causes of the allegedly submissive position of women in local societies (Neves 1970b, 1970c). Customary marriage was thus seen as an affront to women's dignity because it would prevent them from acting as individuals and making their own choices (Neves 1970d). The advertisement accompanying the release of Moura's book in 1973 described its plot as "a Timorese theme in which the author emphasises the hard but resounding victory of marriage for love over the complex setting of barlaque" (Moura 1973b).[7] The arguments articulated by Jaime Neves in the following debate reinforced this view:

> Hafolin is an agreement for purchase and sale with pre-set price. It does not entail any idea of dowry [*sic*]. *Barlaque* and *hafolin* are synonyms. (Neves 1970)

Araujo, and later Lobato, Amaral, and Thomaz, stood in opposition to this perspective. They argued that the material exchanges that composed *barlake* did not imply disrespect for a woman's feelings or for her freedom to choose her spouse. Therefore, there was no inherent opposition between *barlake* and marriage for love (Araújo 1970c). Marriage tactics aimed at preserving lineage status and rank were identified as the main constraint on a woman's will in a marriage arrangement (Thomaz 1973a). In addition, the material exchanges involved in *barlake* would not per se undermine the condition of women in society. Conversely, the larger the material exchanges between wife-takers and wife-givers, the greater the bride's sense of honor (Araújo 1970). From this perspective, the bride's sense of her own value, as well as the statuses of the families involved in the marriage, would be directly related to the amount of goods exchanged. The mutuality of the marriage exchanges as well as the long-lasting mutual obligations they created between wife-givers and wife-takers were also taken as an index that marriage prestations were not commodity transactions (Araújo 1970b). In Araújo's words:

> *Barlaque* is not the purchase and sale of women, because there is no subjection of the women's desire to their parents' greed. Barlaque is the bedrock of Timorese society. It is the reason why different "*cnuas*" and ethno-linguistic groups approach each other. It is the center from which different branches of the same family depart, making up an endless chain of kinship which seems non-sense to other people. (Araújo 1970c)

In contrast, Jaime Neves claimed to understand the essence of *barlake* itself. From his perspective, *barlake* should be analyzed in terms of the material transactions contracted at the time of wedding, that is, as an exchange of assets required for taking a woman in marriage. Thus oriented by a Western ontology in which things and persons are understood as incommensurable (Kopytoff 1986) and a person's value cannot be converted into material items or monetary amounts, Neves and Moura saw customary marriage as a moral outrage. The practice of circulating wealth from wife-takers to wife-givers in return for receiving a spouse feeds most of Neves's and Moura's perceptions of customary marriage as a market exchange; it further supports their negative evaluation of *barlake* as an inappropriate and barbaric trade in human beings, disrespectful of personal feelings.

In his attempt to identify the fundamental nature of *barlake* or *hafo-lin*, a sort of purification anxiety (Latour 1994) is, in my view, implicit in Neves's accounts of *barlake*. He and his team from *A Voz de Timor* were searching for the essence, the core of the traditional marriage system, attempting to make sense of it by itself without considering its effects and functions in social reproduction. The *barlake* ought to be one thing or another; it was inconceivable that it could have multiple meanings and functions simultaneously. This anxiety can be observed in statements like these:

> What is *barlake*, after all? A transtemporal act in obedience to a partic-ular ethic or a compulsory delivery of valuables, without the reciprocal will of the couple, through a previous negotiation between the bride's parents and the suitor, with the intervention of intermediaries. . . . We must examine the essence of customary marriage among the Timorese people. (Neves 1970)

From this approach, particular images of the East Timorese emerged that reflected and reinforced colonial civilizing projects. The animist character attributed to indigenous religious practices is pre-sented as the reason why the Timorese placed so much value on ma-terial exchanges for marriage purposes (Neves 1970, 1970a). Native people are portrayed (men, especially) as materialistic and selfish for allegedly valuing the material dimension of marriage over people's feelings and desires (Moura 1973a). The indigenous people were also presented as traders in human beings (Neves 1970), as, for instance, in a section of Moura's novel:

> As soon as the unwelcome visitors turned their backs, the *liurai* sum-moned his daughter Cai-Buti, who up until then had shut herself up in the room. In the presence of his wife and his other children, the *liurai* preached a tough sermon to Cai Buti, warning her that she would be bitterly punished at the slightest sign of mischief.
> "Do you want to marry a poor man, a wretched, mere farmer who has not even corn to eat during the year ?!," mocked her father. "Do

you want to stain the honor of our ancestors, giving yourself for free to a shameful commoner? . . . And do you want to repay your relatives for all the care they've given you, with poverty ?," continued the father. "So beware that the noble blood of our grandparents is the master of our house and that I am your master !!!," asserted the father in a heated way.

"But I like him so much . . ." retorted a sobbing Cai-Buti.

"Get out! Go away! Go to your room and leave it only when an honorable man comes to pay your barlaque," the father commanded. (Moura 1973b: 23)

Such negative cultural practices, these critics proposed, ought to be overcome by means of conversion to Christianity and access to Western education. The indigenous Timorese were considered fundamentally good people, in need of Christianization to develop their moral potential:

However, we cannot, help them [Timorese] rise to the century we live in by glorifying *camarruas, estilos* [rituals], *luliks*, lycanthropy and the *mate bian* [spirits of deceased relatives], which enslave their souls; and we cannot justify as "facts that people of advanced civilizations ignore" primitive customs that are offensive to the conscience of people of our time. Such customs put [the East Timorese] at a huge distance, in terms of thought and morals, from societies with higher religions. Let us, rather, do everything we can so that instead of ethnological and ethnographic curiosity, as with the Tupi and Bushmen, the Timorese people reach the heights of Christian life which characterizes the civilized man of our time. (Neves 1970: 3)

Opposing the Colonial Critique: Barlake *as Gift-Giving*

Opposing this purification anxiety were the narratives presented by Abílio Araújo, Nicolau Lobato, Xavier do Amaral, and Luis Filipe Thomaz. They proposed a more holistic approach to customary marriage and tried to demonstrate its character as a central institution through which various dimensions of local sociality were negotiated (Araújo 1970, Neves 1970c, Xavier 1970). In this perspective, they fostered a sort of antipurification position in the debate. For instance, Araújo (1970) introduced "Timorese natural marriage" as a social contract with broad consequences, organized through the system of *hafolin* (which implies the payment of bridewealth) *or habanin* (which implies the payment of bride service). For these authors, customary marriage was more a matrix for negotiating social life than a "thing-in-itself" (Araújo 1970c). All rejected socially decontextualized understandings of *barlake* or *hafolin*. In this view, there was no opposition between material goods and persons in marriage practices; instead, the exchange of wealth either created or reinforced social ties (Araújo 1970). Reacting ironically to Neves's first reply, Araújo (1970a) titled his article "Where Is the Truth?" Here he criticized the idea according to which *barlake* was a matter of "to be or not to be," and portrayed it as a complex institution that could not be considered from one single analytical perspective (Araújo 1970a).

At the same time, however, another sort of purification anxiety was, I believe, also implicitly present in the discourses of the East Timorese defenders of *barlake*. That conveyed a constant denial of the possibility that monetary or material gains might also be part of marriage exchanges. For them, gift exchange was what *barlake* was all about, and it had nothing in common with commodity transaction. Only inapropriate manipulations of gift-exchange practices would lead to consequences associated with commodity exchanges, such as the assumption that the valuables transacted do not have agency on their own. For these authors, market exchange was a specter they sought to keep at a great distance from *barlake*. "Comparatively," wrote Araújo, "one may say that even if someone carries out customary marriage with a view to monetary gains, this does not mean that such was the usage of our ancestors" (Araújo 1970a).

Araújo's, Lobato's, and Amaral's narratives produce other images of the East Timorese societies. First and foremost, they are depicted as complex social systems structured by distinctive principles of order that are not understandable from an exclusively Western mentality. Their narratives also suggest that women held a high status in East Timorese society given the indigenous awareness that social and biological reproduction relied on them. In these societies women would not be subordinated to the same degree as in African societies (Araújo 1970, Thomaz 1973). That they were called *feto maromak* (female god or divine woman) expressed their value.

Romantic love is also presented as a phenomenon of the local sociality to which people gave great attention in contracting marriages. The socially harmonizing effects of customary marriage are pointed out, and its potential to include personal desires and interests is emphasized. The offerings of goods from wife-takers to wife-givers are presented as signs of deference to the woman and a source of pride for the families involved. *Barlake* is said to be the most essential institution in the local sociality, and that from which all other social dynamics are derived (see Araújo 1970). In this perspective, the East Timorese people are presented as virtuous, comparable to more civilized people because of the values they held and celebrated.

With respect to the 1973 debate, Thomaz's criticism of Moura's narrative was very sharp. According to Thomaz, Moura misrepresented local societies by suggesting that a woman taken in marriage could be alienated to another man (Thomaz 1973). That suggestion contributed to a negative and distorted view of the East Timorese people and did not recognize that marriage arrangements were, and are, part of a complex system of social connections and obligations.[8]

Accordingly, for Luiz Filipe Thomaz, the main challenge that marriage exchange posed to Timorese social order was that it limited the use of livestock to ritual purposes, thus impeding cattle raising and subsequent economic development (Thomaz 1973c). Based on this rationale, Thomaz argued for a Christianization of customary marriage and for its regulation by the colonial state, which should establish the maximum expenses allowed in marriage practices (Thomaz 1973c).[9]

To sum up, in the late colonial context, the theme of marriage practices was generative of contrasting images of East Timorese people and society. If considered as a market operation, indigenous people emerge as barbaric and insensitive, in urgent need of civilization. In contrast, in the holistic, implicitly anthropological perspective of Thomaz, Araújo, Amaral and, Lobato, East Timorese social life is highly complex, difficult to understand for a Westerner unfamiliar with the local context. The position of women in the local system of prestige is also another important discursive mobilizer in the debate and an index of presence (or absence) of moral values. While Neves and Moura argued that *barlake* caused the social condition of women to be very low, equivalent to slaves or material goods, Abílio Araujo argued that the same practice emphasized women's fundamental role in social reproduction. Nevertheless, both sides in the debate recognized that these customary marriage practices were undergoing significant change (Araújo 1970a, Neves 1970c) and advocated, as in the case of Thomaz, stronger colonial control or even a Christianization of the institution (Neves 1970, Thomaz 1973c).

Epistemological Practices

Despite the various positions held by different actors in the debate, all those involved were mobilized by what we might call an anxiety of knowledge regarding the East Timorese people. The local practices of social reproduction were widely portrayed as a mystery, secret, or enigma that needed to be unveiled (Araújo 1970, Neves 1970a, Neves

1970c, Xavier 1970). Araújo recalled (personal communication) that the *barlake* war inspired him and his colleagues to pursue further research on Timorese traditional forms. From his perspective, the (mis) representation of *barlake* in Moura's narratives led him and a certain East Timorese elite to a journey of enlightenment and discovery of "authentic" traditional institutions that contributed to his nationalist feeling.

Regardless of the different positions in the controversy, those involved resorted to very similar epistemological practices to legitimate their different perspectives. All participants, in some way, resorted to the authority of etymology; of colonial ethnographies (namely, to ethnographies conducted by missionaries and colonial officials); of social science literature and methodology in order to support their respective points of view.

The Meaning of the Word Barlake

The Tetum word *barlake*, for instance, was scrutinized by both parties. It was believed that its original meaning could unveil its present-day uses. From this perspective, Abílio Araújo (1970) proposed that the word originated in the Malay words *ber* joined with *laki*, signifying "to get a husband." For Araújo, it supposedly signified the process of getting married from the woman's point of view, and accordingly he argued that *barlake* was not a market operation. In turn, based on Osório de Castro's works, Jaime Neves suggested that *barlake* would designate both the processes of a woman getting a husband and that of a man getting a wife (Neves 1970).

The uses and meanings of Tetum words like *sosa* (to buy), *hola* (to acquire), and importantly, *folin* (value; price) were also explored in the debate. Jaime Neves invoked the everyday uses of the question *folin hira?* (how much?) to learn the price of a good for sale in the market to support the view of *hafolin* as a purely commercial operation. The use of the same word—*folin*—in the context of both marriage negotiations and market transactions was presented as evidence that a market regime framed both phenomena (Neves 1970c).

By contrast, for Nicolau Lobato, it was a mistake to equate *hafolin* (to give/to fix a value) with *sosa* (to buy). He stated that no dictionary offered this equivalence and foregrounded the linguistic fact that the Tetum language had two different words to differentiate diverse ways of getting access to particular valuables. Instead of saying that someone would *sosa feto* (buy a woman), the only acceptable way to refer to getting a wife was *hola feto*. The word *sosa* could be used only for commodity transactions (Lobato apud. Neves 1970c).Against this perspective, Neves argued that the everyday usage of a word did not necessarily reflect its normative meaning or syntax. For this reason, he defended the translation of the expression *O hafolin hau, ka?* as "Do you buy me?" (Neves 1970c) when used in the context of marriage transactions. In fact, Neves was proposing a translation for a phrase that was never used.

Comparison was another strategy used to support arguments in the debate. To demonstrate the high status of women in Timorese societies, Araújo suggested that *barlake* was proof of the wealth that men (or their families) had to possess in order to gain access to women. This practice was compared to medieval jousts in which two knights fought to the death for the right to take a woman as wife (Araújo 1970). In rejecting this comparison, Neves (1970) suggested that the knights fought to take the women as slaves. Thus the comparison proposed by Araújo would either be inappropriate (since in the Middle Age the status of women was very low) or, if it was appropriate, the implication would be the inverse of what Araújo presumed. In another moment, it is Neves who uses comparison to support his criticism of *hafolin*. In his foreword to Moura's book (Neves 1973), Neves asserted that *barlake* was a traditional institution of Neanderthal man that needed to be eliminated in order to lead people to a Christian and civilized culture. Jaime Neves's comparative tactic was attacked by Thomaz (1973) as an unacceptable anachronism, given that the Neanderthal man was not considered a member of the *Homo sapiens* species.

The Use of Colonial Ethnographies

Another very important resource in the dispute on *barlake* was ethnographic knowledge produced by colonial administrators, missionaries, and academics alike. The citation of ethnographic accounts authored by either Portuguese Catholic missionaries or colonial administrators is constant throughout the controversy. For instance, against Araújo's argument that the literal translation for *ber/bar-laki* is "to get a husband," Neves turned to writings of the colonial judge, poet, and amateur ethnographer Alberto Osório de Castro, for whom, allegedly, *barlake* would mean to get a wife (Neves 1970). In the same article, the works of Father Laranjeiras, Jaime Ribeiro, Pinto Correia, Henry O. Forbes, and others are also quoted as means to support his understanding of marriage exchange as a market operation. In response, Araújo quoted Father Ezequial Pascoal's book *A Alma de Timor vista em sua Fantasia* (Pascoal 1967) according to which the complexity of Timorese marriage practices could not be easily understood given the reluctance of local authorities to share their knowledge (Araújo 1970a). Interestingly, Araújo (1970d) also highlights what he called an ethnographic mistake found in Neves's narratives that would considerably weaken their persuasiveness. In the article from 22 March, Neves (1970) asserts that the bride is exchanged for pigs. In response, Araújo stressed (correctly) that pigs are a gift given exclusively by the bride's family to the groom's. This basic ethnographic mistake is seen by Araújo as evidence of his opponents' fragile knowledge of the issue. Ethnographic accuracy was thus understood as a means to either strengthen or weaken the different positions in the debate.

The fact that some missionary ethnographers had referred to Timorese marriage exchanges using words such as *doação* (donation) or *dowry* (see Father Artur Basílio de Sá apud. Araújo 1970a) or even *gift* (Neves 1970c) compelled Jaime Neves to speak out on the issue. According to Neves, certain missionary accounts would use such words or invest in these perspectives for benevolent reasons. To keep their moral commitments with East Timorese people, the missionaries would lie about the meanings of *hafolin* or *barlake*. In Neves's view, anyone who considered customary marriage as something other than a commercial transaction was engaging in sentimental fantasies (Neves 1970, 1970a). "We tend to think that the euphemism employed by the good priest," he wrote referring to Pascoal's use of the term "donation," "must be a consequence of an act of charity. Love in his soul overcame the rigor of research. The repulsiveness of reality made him dodge the obstacle so as not to hurt the sensibilities of those who deny seeing the barlaque for what it is when uncovered" (Neves 1970a).

The lack of accuracy attributed to the missionary accounts of customary marriage by Jaime Neves suggests that the controversy was shaped by strategic readings of colonial knowledge. An affirmation was considered inaccurate the moment it challenged the effort at purification made by Neves and his team or threatened the metanarrative that defined marriage exchange as a market operation. The controversy was thus shaped by an ambiguous relationship with Portuguese colonial knowledge.

During the controversy, in different moments, critics of *barlake* suggest that Abílio Araujo, Xavier do Amaral, Nicolau Lobato, or the missionaries fell into romanticism in not recognizing that it entailed the selling of women (Neves 1970a, 1970c). Such romantic primitivism would prevent people from striving to emancipate indigenous people from their oppressive practices. That being so, it would be necessary to abandon this romantic view to lead people to civilization (Nota 1970).

The Authority of Professional Anthropologists

Academic anthropology was mobilized in the last rounds of debate. In 1970, a letter from the Portuguese ethnologist Viegas Guerreiro was adressed to Luis Thomaz, then the editor of *A Província de Timor*. Thomaz published the letter in the newsletter in order to support the view that *barlake* was not a commodity exchange. According to Luís Thomaz (personnal communication), Guerreiro's letter came as a response to Thomaz's request for his help in the debate. Thomaz asked the Portuguese academic authority to intervene in order to put an end to what was becoming an overly aggressive debate. Given the authority attributed to academic knowledge, the letter was used tactically by Thomaz to lead the debate to a successful closure. In that letter, Viegas Guerreiro quotes anthropologists such as A. R. Radcliffe-Brown and George Peter Murdock to support the view that "the bridewealth is a device for consolidating marriage. It is not a commodity transaction" (Guerreiro 1970).

In other instances of the debate, the authority of academic anthropologists was also mobilized to support arguments concerning methodological (in)accuracy. Thus, Jaime Neves (1970e) celebrated the alleged scientific skills of *A Voz de Timor* team in using what he considered to be the modern methods of anthropology and sociology. Although the consensus in anthropological theory since the 1930s was that marriage prestations were *not* commodity transactions, Neves's party invoked authors like Durkheim, Murdock, Radcliffe-Brown, Malinowski, and even the Brazilian Tales de Azevedo to display how well oriented, erudite, and up to date they were in engaging in the debate according to scientific criteria. The disagreements of their East Timorese interlocutors, in turn, were attributed to their lack of proper methodological training. Only inexperience would lead them to surrender to sentimental and literary arguments that lacked any scientific approach. East Timorese interlocutors are thus depicted as collectors of archaic traditions or "folklore":

> Our opponents, as we see, perceive the socio-cultural fact of barlaque as an expression of folklore, in an approach which is neither articulated with Ethnology nor Cultural Anthropology. They are describing, as incipient folklorists, marginal facts of the emotional life of the people, . . . that only incidentally relates to barlaque as a social institution. (Neves 1970d)

Not by chance, the tone and arguments voiced by Neves's team evoke one of the main tactics by which colonial rule produced its power effects: its self-proclaimed authority, in Stoler's words, "to designate what count as reason and reasonable ... one that, in turn, would profoundly affect the style and strategies of anticolonial, nationalist politics" (Stoler 2009: 57).

Against Neves and his team, Araújo and Amaral claimed that both literary and academic knowledge were insufficient to *truly* understand the indigenous institutions. An emotional closeness to the Timorese cultural worlds was required to comprehend their institutions. The absence of this intimacy would mislead people in their attempts to rationally understand local practices. An example would be the mistakes made by Neves and *A Voz de Timor* staff. They had not observed the subtleties of Tetum language, which had particular words to qualify exchanges framed by different regimes (*hola* and *sosa*, for instance): "The editor [of *A Voz de Timor*] goes on to assert that to translate thoughts it is necessary to master the language well," argued Xavier. "Vernacular-ness lies not only in the language or verbal expression itself, but also in the ways of feeling and thinking of each people" (Xavier 1970a). Xavier's (1970a) narrative in the controversy was thus shaped by a form of nativist ideology, an implicit claim that only people from East Timor could truly understand the local institutions or culture. This argument rationale is similar to one that fosters nationalism as a culturally rooted political project. Grounding their defense of *barlake* in a claim to emotional connection with the rural people, Timorese intellectuals—who, in fact, did not exclusively belong to either local-rural or metropolitan worlds—performed themselves as "insiders," attuned with what would soon be imagined as the *Maubere people*. It thus comes as no surprise that these colonial disputes of the 1970s can be considered today as critical events in the emergence of an East Timorese national consciousness.

Final Remarks

Barlake's potential to trigger controversies is not contained to the past. Contemporary marriage practices in Dili are strongly influenced by the contested character of this institution that continues to produce opposing perspectives about local sociality. In light of the *barlake* war, the postcolonial debate in Dili lacks novelty.

Current debates about marriage prestations among Dili elites are also framed by attempts to equate *barlake* or *folin* with either a commodity or gift regime of exchange, a phenomenon that is directly connected with the people's different trajectories of migration and interaction with the colonial powers established in Dili (see Silva 2010).

These contrasting understandings of *barlake* or *hafolin* are indicators of wider differences regarding East Timorese people and their social life. Broadly speaking, for those who consider *hafolin* to be a market exchange, indigenous people are uncivilized, irrational, and materialistic, who have not yet truly internalized the idea that people and things pertain to different ontologies and, as such, cannot be exchanged one for another. Based on that construction, indigenous people are turned, once again, into subjects of government, in need of discipline. On the other hand, those who see *hafolin* as a form of gift exchange have a more respectful perspective on local people and their sociality. *Barlake* is considered a means for establishing rules for social reproduction and for demonstrating respect and consideration. In this view, indigenous people are seen as capable of understanding how to foster dignity and how to forge appropriate relationships with ancestors and other supernatural agents. In addition, *hafolin* is also seen as a way to honor people's multiple ritual obligations.

It is also worth noting that contemporary debates about marriage exchange in Timor often revolve around the word *barlake*, exclusively. Despite the various gift-functions related to marriages (see, for instance Lazarowitz 1980; Barnes 1980; Hicks 1984, 2004 [1976]; Traube 1989; McKinnon 1991; Valeri 1994; Silva 2018; among others), they have been rhetorically reduced to *barlake* or *hafolin* in many colonial and postcolonial narratives (see also Fernandes 2014).

In the *barlake* war, both sides in the dispute explained *barlake* without taking into account the various moments and forms of exchange, as well as the distinct gift-functions that compose the marriage process as forms of negotiating rights in persons—phenomena later explored at greater length in ethnographic studies before and after the independence of Timor-Leste (apart from the references quoted above in this paragraph, see also Silva 2010, 2013, 2018; Niner 2012). This being so, it seems that such a controversy was one of the most important events responsible for the vernacularization and reduction of marriage prestations to *barlake* in Dili public space.

Acknowledgments

I am grateful to Elizabeth Traube and Ricardo Roque for their careful readings of earlier drafts of this chapter and for all their suggestions.

Kelly Silva is associate professor in social anthropology at the University of Brasília, and she has been carrying out fieldwork in Timor-Leste since 2002. Her main research interests relate to the invention, transposition, and subversion of modernity. She has published widely on politics, kinship, and religion in Timor-Leste, including the monograph *As nações desunidas: Práticas da ONU e a estruturação do Estado em Timor-Leste* (2012). She is currently a visiting fellow at the London School of Economics and Political Science.

Notes

1. I thank Elizabeth Traube for this reference.
2. In the first round of the *barlake* war, between 1969 and 1970, the articles here attributed to Xavier do Amaral were signed only as Xavier. According to Inácio de Moura and Luís Thomaz (personal communication) the author was Xavier do Amaral. However, in my view, because later on someone else named Jacob Xavier also took part in the debate, the authorship of these articles remains uncertain.
3. For further information about their biographies, see Araújo (2012).
4. Given such a theoretical frame, one might better understand why so much energy has been devoted to understanding the exchanges informed by the gift regime. The polyvalent character of the gift, its hybridity, challenges the purifying expectations for making sense of social acts as one thing or another, exclusively.
5. Later in life, Luís Filipe Thomaz became an important Asianist in Portugal and Europe.
6. Unfortunately, I could not access Nicolau Lobato´s article published in *Seara* during the completion of this chapter.
7. Given its brevity (no more than ten full pages), we should consider *Mau Curo & Bere Mau ou o grande amor de Cai Buti* a short story rather than a novel (see Thomaz 1973). The plot revolves around a love story between Mau Curo and Cai Buti who are not allowed to marry by Cai Buti´s father because they are from families from very disparate ranks. However, Mau Curo's close friend—Bere Mau—belongs to a high-rank family for whom Cai Buti´s father was happy to give his daughter in marriage. So, the narrative follows how Bere Mau takes Cai Buti in marriage for giving her in marriage for Mau Curo afterward.
8. The preclusion of "reselling" a spouse was a key theme in earlier anthropological rejections of the marriage-as-purchase model (Radcliffe-Brown 1950: 52 *apud.* Valeri 1994: 3).
9. Regulation of material and monetary spending for marriage-making have been used in different countries of Oceania in colonial and post-colonial times (Marksbury 1993). Recently, a joint governance initiative (shared by local and state authorities, nongovernmental agencies,

and the Catholic Church) target to control ritual expenses in Ermera, Timor-Leste, established the maximum value of US$2,500 for marriage exchanges (for a detailed discussion, see Silva 2014, 2016).

References

Appadurai, A. 1986. "Introduction: Commodities and the Politics of Value." In *The Social Life of Things: Commodities in Cultural Perspective*, edited by A. Appadurai, 3–63. Cambridge: Cambridge University Press.

Araújo, A. 1970. "Carta aberta ao Sr. Inácio de Moura." *A Província de Timor*, 10 de março.

———. "Onde está a verdade?" *A Província de Timor*, 02 de maio, 11–12

———. 1970b. "Onde está a verdade? (continuação)." *A Província de Timor*, 9 de maio, 8–9.

———. 1970c. "Onde está a verdade? (continuação)." *A Província de Timor*, 16 de maio.

———. 1970d. "Onde está a verdade? (continuação)." *A Província de Timor*, 23 de maio, 12–13.

———. 1970e. "Onde está a verdade?(final)." *A Província de Timor*, 30 de maio, 16–17.

———. 2012. *Autobiografia de Abílio Araújo*. Dato Siri Loe II. Lisboa: Alêtheia Editores.

Barnes, R. H. 1980. "Marriage, Exchange and the Meaning of Corporations in Eastern Indonesia." In *The Meaning of Marriage Payments*, edited by J. L. Comaroff, 93–122. New York: Academic Press.

Bohannan, P. 1955. "Some Principles of Exchange and Investment among the Tiv." *American Anthropologist* 57: 60–70.

Carrier, A. 1993. "Marriage Exchanges on Ponam Island, from 1920 to 1985." In *The Business of Marriage: Transformations in Oceanic Matrimony*, edited by R. A. Marksbury, 27–55. Pittsburgh, PA: University of Pittsburgh Press.

Driberg, J. H, H. F. Stoneham, and T. Cullen Young. 1930. "Bride-Price. Reviewed work(s)." *Man* 30: 74–76.

Dumont, L. 1983. *Essais sur l'individualisme: Une perspective anthropologique sur l'idéologie modern*. Paris: Seuil.

Evans-Pritchard, E. E. 1931. "An Alternative Term for 'Bride-Price.'" *Man* 31: 36–39.

Fernandes, A. J. M. 2011. *A cidadania de populações ultramarinas: o conceito de "indígena" na legislação colonial portuguesa (1926-1960)*. Working paper.

———. 2014. "Em searas do Timor Português: um estudo sobre as práticas de mediação da Diocese de Díli no período colonial (1949–1973)." Master's thesis, Universidade de Brasília.

Filer, C. 1985. "What Is This Thing Called 'Brideprice'?" *Mankind* 15(2): 163–83.

Foucault, M. 1980. *Power/Knowledge: Selected Interviews and Other Writings, 1972–1977*. New York: Pantheon.

Goody, J. 1973. "Bridewealth and Dowry in Africa and Euroasia." In *Bridewealth and Dowry*, edited by J. Goody and S. J. Tambiah. Cambridge: Cambridge University Press.

Graeber, D. 2011. *Debt: The First 5,000 Years*. New York: Melville House Publishing.

Gregory, C. A. 1982. *Gift and Commodity*. London: Academic Press

Guerreiro, V. 1970. "De novo o barlaque." *A Província de Timor*. 26 de setembro.

Hicks, D. 1984. *A Maternal Religion: The Role of Women in Tetum Myth and Ritual*. Dekalb: North Illinois University.

———. 2004 [1976]. *Tetum Ghosts & Kin: Fertility and Gender in East Timor*. Long Grove, IL: Waveland Press.

Humphrey, C., and S. Hugh-Jones. 1992. "Introduction: Barter, Exchange and Value." In *Barter, Exchange and Value: An Anthropological Approach*, edited by C. Humphrey and S. Hugh-Jones, 1–20. Cambridge: Cambridge University Press.

Jolly, M., and N. Thomas. 1992. "Introduction: The Politics of Tradition in the Pacific." *Oceania* 62(4): 241–48.

Jolly, M. 2015. "Braed Praes in Vanuatu: Both Gifts and Commodities?" *Oceania*. Special issue, *Gender and Person in Oceania* 85(1): 63–78.

Jorgensen, D. 1993. "Money and Marriage in Telefolmin: From Sister Exchange to Daughter as Trade Store." In *The Business of Marriage: Transformations in Oceanic Matrimony*, edited by R. A. Marksbury, 57–82. Pittsburgh, PA: University of Pittsburgh Press.

Keane, W. 2007. *Christian Moderns: Freedom & Fetish in the Mission Encounter*. Berkeley: University of California Press.

Kopytoff, I. 1986. "The Cultural Biography of Things: Commoditization as Process." In *The Social Life of Things: Commodities in a Cultural Perspective*, edited by A. Appadurai, 64–94. Cambridge: Cambridge University Press.

Latour, B. 1994. *Jamais fomos modernos*. Rio de Janeiro: Ed. 34.

Lazarowitz, T. 1980. "The Makassai: Complementary Dualism in Timor." PhD thesis, State University of New York at Stony Brook, New York.

Lévi-Strauss, C. 2003 [1949]. *As Estruturas Elementares do Parentesco*. São Paulo: Editora Vozes.

Marksbury, R. A. 1993. *The Business of Marriage: Transformations in Oceanic Matrimony*. ASAO Monograph 14. Pittsburgh, PA: University of Pittsburgh Press.

McKinnon, S. 1991. *From a Shattered Sun: Hierarchy, Gender, and Alliance in the Tanimbar Islands*. Madison: University of Wisconsin Press.

de Moura, I. de. 1969. *Mulher de Lipa, Feto Timor*. Jornal A Voz de Timor.

———. 1973a. *A Voz de Timor*. 13 de julho de 1973, p. 9.

———. 1973b. *Mau Curo e Bere Mau ou o grande amor de Cai-Búti*. Dili: Sociedade Editora de Timor Ltda.

Neves, J. 1970. "A propósito de uma carta aberta." *A Voz de Timor*, n. 514. 22 de março.

————. 1970a. "No desdobrar de uma carta aberta: Luz, mais luz!" *A Voz de Timor*, n. 522. 17 de maio.

————. 1970b. "No desdobrar duma carta aberta: Luz, mais luz!" *A Voz de Timor*, n. 523. 24 de maio.

————. 1970c. "No desdobrar de uma carta aberta: Luz, mais luz!" *A Voz de Timor*, n. 527. 21 de junho de 1970.

————. 1970d. "Ainda o barlaque. Palavras serenas." *A Voz de Timor*, n. 531. 19 de julho.

————. 1970e. "Ainda o barlaque. Palavras serenas." *A Voz de Timor*, n. 532. 26 de julho.

————. 1973. "Prefácio." In Inácio de Moura, *Mau Curo e Bere Mau ou o grande amor de Cai-Búti*. Dili: Sociedade Editora de Timor Lda.

Niner, S. 2012. Barlake: an Exploration of Marriage Practices and Issues of Women's Status in Timor-Leste." *Local Global*, Vol. 11. Pp. 138–53.

Parise, B. H. 2014. "Práxis epistemológicas e projetos de mudança social missionários no Timor Português: notas sobre a obra do Padre Jorge Barros Duarte." BA Hons monograph, Universidade de Brasília.

Pascoal, E. E. 1967. *A Alma de Timor vista em sua Fantasia*. Braga: Edição Barbosa & Xavier Ltda.

Paulino, V. 2012. "Representação identitária em Timor-Leste. Culturas e os media." PhD thesis, Universidade de Lisboa, Departamento de Letras.

Roque, R. 2012. "Marriage Traps: Colonial Interactions with Indigenous Marriage Ties in East Timor." In *Racism and Ethnic Relations in the Portuguese-Speaking World*, edited by F. Bethencourt and A. Pearce, 203–25. New York: Oxford University Press, Proceedings of the British Academy 179.

Said, E. 1990 [1979]. *Orientalismo: O Oriente como invenção do Ocidente*. São Paulo: Companhia das Letras.

Silva, K. 2010. "Riqueza ou Preço da Noiva? Regimes Morais em Disputa nas Negociações de casamento entre as elites urbanas timorenses." In *Lugares, Pessoas e Grupos*: *As Lógicas do Pertencimento em Perspectiva Comparada*, edited by W. Trajano Filho, 207–23. Brasília: Ed. Athalaia.

————. 2012. "Foho versus Dili: The Political Role of Place in East Timor National Imagination." *Realis—Revista de Estudos Antiutilitaristas e Póscoloniais* 1(2): 145–65, http://www.nucleodecidadania.org/revista/index.php/realis/article/view/28/37

————. 2013. "Negotiating Tradition and Nation: Mediations and Mediators in the Making of Urban Timor-Leste." *Asia Pacific Journal of Anthropology* 14: 455–70.

————. 2014. "O governo da e pela cultura: Complexos locais de governança na formação do Estado em Timor-Leste." *Revista Crítica de Ciências Sociais* 104: 123–50.

————. 2016. "Administrando pessoas, recursos e rituais: Pedagogia econômica como tática de governo em Timor-Leste." *Horizontes Antropológicos* 22(45): 127–153.

————. 2018. "Marriage Prestations, Gift Making, and Identity in Urban East Timor." *Oceania* 88(1): 127–147.

———. 2019. "Culture as Symbol: Customary Marriage Practices under Transformation in Urban Timor-Leste." In *Routledge Handbook of Contemporary Timor-Leste*, edited by A. McWilliam and M. Leach.

Silva, K., and D. Simião. 2012. "Coping with 'Traditions': The Analysis of East-Timorese Nation Building from the Perspective of a Certain Anthropology Made in Brazil." *Vibrant* 9(1): 360–81.

Stoler, A. L. 2002. *Carnal Knowledge and Imperial Power: Race and the Intimate in Colonial Rule*. Berkeley: University of California Press.

———. 2009. *Along the Archival Grain: Epistemic Anxieties and Colonial Common Sense*. Princeton, NJ: Princeton University Press.

Strathern, M. 1992. "Qualified Value: The Perspective of Gift Exchange." In *Barter, Exchange and Value: An Anthropological Approach*, edited by C. Humphrey and S. Hugh-Jones, 169–91. Cambridge: Cambridge University Press.

Thomas, N. 1991. *Entangled Objects: Exchange, Material Culture, and Colonialism in the Pacific*. Cambridge: Harvard University Press.

———. 1994. *Colonialism´s Culture: Anthropology, Travel and Governance*. Princeton, NJ: Princeton University Press.

Thomaz, L. F. 1973. "A propósito do recente livro do Sr. Inácio de Moura 'Mau Curo e Bere Mau.'" *A Voz de Timor*. 31 de agosto.

———. 1973a. "Ainda sobre a questão do barlaque." *A Voz de Timor*. 7 de Dezembro.

———. 1973b. "Ainda a questão do barlaque." *A Voz de Timor*. 14 de Dezembro.

———. 1973c. "Ainda a questão do barlaque." *A Voz de Timor*. 21 de Dezembro.

Toer, P. A. 1990 [1975]. *This Earth of Mankind* [original title *Bumi Manusia*]. New York: Penguin Books.

Tonkinson, R. 1982. "Kastom in Melanesia: Introduction." *Mankind* 13(4): 302–5.

Torday, E. 1929. "Bride-Price, Dower, or Settlement." *Man* 29: 5–8

Traube, E. 1986. *Cosmology and Social Life: Ritual Exchange among the Mambai of East Timor*. Chicago: University of Chicago Press.

Valeri, V. 1994. "Buying Women but Not Selling Them: Gift and Commodity Exchange in Huaulu Alliance." *Man*, New Series 29(1): 1–26.

Xavier [do Amaral]. 1970a. "Continuação de 'Nota de abertura a propósito de uma polêmica aberta': Barlaque—Venda e compra de mulher." *A Voz de Timor*, n. 527. 21 de junho.

———. 1970. "Nota de abertura. A propósito de uma polêmica aberta." *A Voz de Timor*, n. 521. 10 de maio.

AFTERWORD

GLIMPSES OF AN ETHNOHISTORY OF TIMOR

James J. Fox

The great value of this volume lies in the way that its various chapters fuse history and ethnography, exploring strategic perceptions of their intersection in the context of Timor-Leste. Contributors are ethnographers who have turned to history, or historians who have turned to ethnography. In either case, for most contributors, their starting points are current perceptions of the past, and their concerns are with how these perceptions have been formed and how they now shape the present. An added advantage for this volume is that several contributors, in particular Elizabeth Traube, Claudine Friedberg, and David Hicks, have been involved in fieldwork at an earlier period in their careers and are able to reflect on their personal perceptions of the recent past.

My intention in this postscript is not to comment on what has been written but to follow the theoretical leads that this volume offers by trying to bring together elements of ethnography and recorded history to construct a glimpse of an ethnohistory of Timor—primarily that of western Timor in contrast to eastern Timor.

I would like to adopt an island-wide view of Timor's past, consider some of the differences in what has occurred in eastern and western Timor, and ponder the ethnographic consequences of this past for the present. My approach, based on fragments from the past, is tentative, partial, and, at points, speculative.

My initial question is directed to what appears as the major ethnolinguistic difference between the eastern and western halves of the island of Timor. On the eastern side of the island—in Timor-Leste—there are more than a dozen distinguishable languages. In fact, there are reasonable linguistic grounds for extending this number, if one includes the small offshore island of Atauro, to more than twenty languages, and with these languages there would appear to be a corresponding number of distinct ethnic groupings.[1]

By contrast, in West Timor, there are—or were, before the exodus of East Timorese to the west in 1999—only a half dozen languages. Of these six languages, one, Helong, is a remnant language now found near the town of Kupang and on the offshore island of Semau; the second, Rotenese, is an intrusive language whose speakers were initially moved to Timor from the nearby island of Rote by the Dutch colonial government beginning in the early nineteenth century; the third, Bunak, is found on the border between East and West Timor and extends well into Timor-Leste; the fourth, Marae, is the language of a small Kemak-speaking group of migrants from the east who still cluster near the border with Timor-Leste.

There is, however, a substantial Tetun-speaking population on the south coast and in the central-north of West Timor—a linguistic population that also extends into the eastern end of Timor-Leste.

This leaves a single language, Uab Meto, spoken in a variety of dialects, as the dominant language of West Timor. This dominance of Uab Meto in the west compared to the diversity of languages in the east poses a problem for understanding the history of the island of Timor as a whole. On an island located in a region of linguistic complexity and populated for millennia, with a complex and varied landscape, the diversity of languages as found in East Timor is hardly surprising. However, the dominance of a single language across the major part of West Timor demands consideration and investigation.[2]

Shifting Trade from the South
to the North Coast of Timor

I have made one attempt (Fox 1988) to offer a possible explanation for this dominance by identifying some of the key factors in the historical expansion of the Atoin Pah Meto. Here I can only outline these factors. The important historical factors that have contributed to this dominance, it seems, derive from the presence of three foreign sources of influence who were located principally on the north coast of West Timor from the seventeenth century onward: the Portuguese at Lifao, the Dutch at Kupang, and the Chinese at Atapupu.

The early "Portuguese" were, for the most part, a mixed Portuguese-speaking, mainly native, population originating from Larantuka on Flores, known as the Topasses or, to the Dutch, as the "Black Portuguese." They were engaged primarily in obtaining precious sandalwood for trade into a maritime market that eventually carried this sandalwood to China. They began initially in the sixteenth century by visiting Timor to trade for and gather sandalwood. Eventually they established a permanent settlement at Lifao, creating an initial alliance with the first Meto ruler to convert to Christianity, the lord of Ambenu, in what is now the enclave of Oecusse.

Over time, the Topasses came to empower the Meto populations with whom they lived, married, and whom they intermittently led. Invoking Portuguese authority, these Topasses were able to stitch together links among local Meto rulers in a network of beneficial trading relations that gradually shifted earlier trading networks from the south to the north coast of Timor. Besides their trading connections and leadership, these Topasses provided a source of muskets, arming their core Meto supporters and directing them against the Dutch and, at times, against the Portuguese loyal to the viceroy at Goa who tried to assert their control in the west of Timor. The shift of a contingent of loyal Portuguese from Lifao to Dili in 1769 conceded much of West Timor to the authority of the Topasses and enabled the Meto to continue to expand.

The Meto obsession with the musket (*ken, kenat*) cannot be exaggerated. Until shortly after 1975, when the Indonesian government initiated a campaign to disarm the Meto of their muskets, it was rare to encounter any mountain Meto without a musket strapped to his shoulder. Dr. Solomon Müller's description dating from the early part of the nineteenth century captures this obsession:

> The trade in flintlock rifles is the most advantageous trade that can be conducted on Timor. . . . The rifle belongs, above all, to the most important piece of inheritance, to the costliest value that can pass from father to son: indeed a Timorese would often more easily and more happily do without house and livestock, even a wife and child, rather than without such a weapon. (1857: 2:234)

What is important to note is that the Meto were manufacturing their own muskets in different parts of their territory. The earliest site of manufacture is said to have been at Mutis-Bobnain, but other sites are remembered as well, as, for example, Hautkonob in Tautpah in the domain of Biboki. A few lines of a ritual recitation from Biboki to honor such ancient muskets kept as heirlooms within the house gives an ideal of their significance:

Ken upnapu, ken ateut humaf	Musket dispelling disaster, raising prestige
Nane uf ma matetu in tuakin	That comes from the source of life
Ken sakal ma'tani	Musket that holds great strength
Es on neik humaf ma in masan	That gives value and order to life . . .
Ken suf mese ma ken toe mese	Musket as one flower and one stalk
Kenat natuin in tusi ma in nono	Musket of order and custom
Kenat nun mafo ma kenat let mafo	Musket shaded by banyan and *dedap* trees
Kenat tamnau lasi	Musket that keeps promises
Ma kenat theuk leal	And musket that gathers followers.[3]

The Chinese were trading with Timorese for sandalwood from at least the fourteenth century. As their records (Rockhill 1915: 257–58) and that of Duarte Barbosa's 1518 account (Dames 1921: 195–96) indicate, this Chinese trade provided three main sought-after goods: porcelain, textiles, and iron tools. The Chinese traded from various locations on the north coast, but much of this trade seems to have centered on the small north coast port of Atapupu.

This independent trade continued particularly in West Timor through the nineteenth century and into the twentieth, even as some Chinese came to settle in the towns of Kupang and Dili. In the nineteenth century, much to the chagrin of the Dutch, the Chinese traders were given protected passage to journey into the interior where they continued to supply muskets and iron tools to the West Timorese (see Fox 2000: 21).

The Dutch were latecomers, managing to establish their outpost at Kupang at the far western end of Timor in the middle of the seventeenth century. This settlement was beleaguered by the Topasses and their Meto allies. The Dutch East India Company made one ill-fated attempt in 1656 to send an armed force out from Kupang and into the interior. Under their most distinguished general, Arnoldus de Vlaming van Oudtshoorn, this show of force ended in total destruction and a monumental disgrace. Thereafter the Dutch clustered in Kupang surrounded by loyal allies, several of whom were populations whose rulers had fled the Topass-led Meto alliance

Hemmed in within their settlement on the bay of Kupang, the Dutch, however, provided the Timorese with a key ingredient that helped to propel their demographic expansion. This ingredient was maize, which eventually changed the livelihood patterns of the Meto. A Dutch missive from the governor-general of the Company, dated 1672, ordered the planting of maize in Kupang. By 1699, William Dampier, who was refused access to Kupang and instead had to anchor in Kupang Bay, reported extensive planting of maize by the local population at a distance from Kupang (Dampier 1703 [1939]). In just over a quarter of a century, maize had become a critical subsistence crop for the local Meto (Fox 1977: 76). Maize came to replace foxtail millet and sorghum, which had been earlier basic stables (Fox 1992), demanding a more extensive, shifting agriculture that was made possible by the use of iron tools—iron digging sticks, machetes, and simple hoes.[4]

The Meto Expansion

When and how often these ingredients—muskets, maize, and iron tools—came together in west Timor to fuel the Meto expansion may never be definitely determined. They may have come together with other elements at different locations at different times. There was never, however, just one Meto migration from a single center, though indeed a variety of such "origin centers" are recognized. Instead, the Meto migration in West Timor involved a countless number of mini-movements crisscrossing the landscape in all directions, often backtracking and re-tracking again. The Meto retain memories of the populations who preceded them, referring to them by the general term *Melu* and often giving them specific names at particular locations. To this day, Meto migrations are recounted at the clan (*kanaf*) level and are spoken of as the separate journeying of a specific clan as embodied in its name—the *kanaf*-name—spreading through the land, encountering other clans, stopping and then continuing on again. Headhunting was part of this expansion and served to separate as well as unite local groups.

Much of this basic process continues to the present and is part of the social landscape of West Timor. Ethnographically this is—and probably was—predominately a movement of young males either in search of new lands to open or in search of settlements in which to settle, to marry, and eventually to come to control. The genius of the Meto social organization is in its multiple ways of assimilating the labor it needs to continue to expand (Fox 1999).

It is important to recognize that when these Meto migrations were taking place from the mid-seventeenth through the nineteenth centuries there was minimal direct armed interference from the Dutch. The Dutch were largely uninterested in what was happening at the local level in the mountains of West Timor. What authority they claimed to have secured by their "contracts" with different rulers was indeed nominal. The Dutch East India Company and the early colonial government that replaced it regarded Timor as an unprofitable and there-fore a commercially unimportant island. Dutch presence had to be maintained, however, to counter Portuguese influence.

This relative indifference by Dutch colonial authorities contrasts with the annual expeditions organized, orchestrated, and led by the Portuguese that directed local populations under their recognized rul-ers into war against other populations in an ever-shifting alliance of East Timorese allies and enemies. René Pélissier has superbly docu-mented this period from 1847 to 1913 (Pélissier 1996), and Ricardo Roque (2010) has brilliantly elaborated upon its celebration.

These historic conditions have their consequences for the contem-porary ethnography of Timor. On both sides of Timor, the domains (the former *reino* in East Timor and the former *keradjaan* in West Timor) are made of named clans (I prefer the term "origin groups"). In the west, the majority of these domains are Meto, and their clan struc-tures consist of an arrangement of named Meto *kanaf* whose trail of origin stretches beyond the domain and often across several domains.

By contrast, if one takes just the most closely related Central Ti-morese languages—Mambai, Tokodede, Kemak, and Welaun—they are divided among many domains (*reino*) that are composed of "eth-nically" distinct origin groups, whose traditions of origin are more circumscribed and localized.

In broad ethnographic terms, Timor-Leste is a nation of distinct ethnic groups whereas in West Timor there is a growing sense of a widespread Meto identity both politically and socially.

Tetun Ritual Precedence

These ethnohistorical considerations, however, so far as they go, prompt other questions about the ethnic composition of the island as a whole. Crucial to these considerations are the Tetun-speaking populations who have bequeathed to the nation-state of Timor-Leste a variant form of the language.

When, in 1522, the last surviving ship in Magellan's fleet put into port on the north coast of Timor, the chronicler of that historic voyage, the Italian Antonio Pigafetta, reported, among other things, that the island of Timor was ruled from its south coast by four brother kings whose habitations were Oibich, Lichsana, Suai, and Cabanazza. It is difficult to identify "Oibich" with Wehali, which has long been consid-ered the ritual center of the Tetun; yet Suai and Camanasa, even the designation Lichsana, are identifiable to this day (Pigafetta 1969).[5]

All these places belong to the "Female Land" (*Rai Feto*) of Timor. In the cosmogenic origin narrative, as told in Wehali, this is the source land of all the Tetun (Therik 2004). It is designated as socially "matrilineal" because women own all the land and all the houses on the land. These houses exchange males among themselves. As such, the *Rai Feto* is the motherland for all other Tetun populations. In the Wehali narrative, the first "sister" remained at the source but sent her brothers out to populate the land.

Following from this account, this Tetun migration of Wehali was to the north and, more significantly, to the east (referred to as *Likusaen*) reaching as far as the fabled, once-powerful domain of Luca in Viqueque in eastern Timor. In the Meto narratives, one younger brother who was sent west from Wehali became the bright, mysterious stranger who was installed as Lord Sonbai on Mount Mutis to become the "stranger king" of the Meto—their silent, resting source of authority (Fox 2008: 203–4). Wehali's own Maromak-Oan was similarly a silent ruler, but one who derived from Wehali's beginnings.

In Timorese understanding, Wehali's authority was established before that of Meto dominion and was given precedence as such. Tribute, including sandalwood, flowed to Wehali and its sister domains. It is interesting to note that the Tetun exodus from the Tetun female land was eastward, not westward. The Tetun migration to the west of the female land may have been checked by the Meto. The Tetun migration eastward was based on a different subsistence base, relying more on the extensive cultivation of mung beans/green grams (*fore*) than sorghum or millet, and this cultivation system benefited from the second rainy season that affects the south coast of Timor-Leste.[6]

There are few documents that shed light on this early history. One of the earliest is of singular significance in that it points to the importance of Tetun authority on Timor in the seventeenth century. On 2 February 1626, after a brief visit to Kupang, the French-speaking Swiss Protestant Captain Elie Ripon, sailing on behalf of the Dutch Company, put into Camanasa (Camenasse) on the south coast of Timor to establish a trading relationship and to pay respects to the Emperor (*l'empereur*) of the island.[7] His account gives us hints of Tetun rule at the time.

The emperor at Camanasa had a dozen wives, each in her own "royal house," and the emperor spent much of his time visiting each in succession. He would dine and spend the night at a different house and would otherwise pass his time with a court of some fifty elite nobles *(gentilhommes: hommes d'élection)*. There was a "king at Suai" (*Sueys*) but Ripon did not have the time to visit him since he had to return urgently to the Dutch fort on Solor.

Ripon makes clear that there was a great trade in sandalwood through Camanasa. Trees were collected, including their roots, and brought to Camanasa in readiness for the traders who came to gather this wood. The wood was exchanged for gold and Indian textiles as well as for rice, which was imported—Ripon claims that it was brought from Borneo or the Philippines—and eaten regularly at court with a variety of meats and "delicious tubers" ("d'une sort de racine qui sont assez bonnes") along with an abundance of palm wine. Ripon also reports that those guarding the emperor were reasonably good soldiers. Their arms were cutlasses, shields, lances, and spears ("Les armes son coutelas, rondaches, javelines et dards.") He makes no mention of muskets, the weapon that was to propel the Meto expansion.

Sixteen years later, in 1642, the Fidalgo Francisco Fernandez, who was born on the island of Solor, is reported to have led a band of ninety musketeers across Timor, striking first at the center of the dominion of Sonbai and then marching on to attack the Tetun center at Wehali. This decisive act, followed by the equally decisive defeat of the Dutch forces in 1656, enhanced Topass influence among their allies, allowing them to play a greater role in local Meto politics, particularly in the Sonbai area. It also gave prestige to the formidable Dominican priests who came to preach on Timor and, in the process, to complicate relations between the white and black Portuguese (see Hägerdal 2012: 316ff). William Dampier's succinct description of the situation of the Topasses at Lifao in 1699 is instructive:

> These [the Topasses] have no Forts, but depend on their Alliance with the Natives: And indeed they are already so mixt, that it is hard to distinguish whether they are *Portugueze* or *Indians*. Their Language is Portugueze; and the religion they have, is Romish. They seem in Words to acknowledge the King of Portugal for their Sovereign; yet they will not accept any Officers sent by him. They speak indifferently the Malayan and their own native Languages, as well as Portugueze. (1703, reprinted 1939: 171–72)

That the Topasses were using Portuguese and a mix of their own native languages—probably a combination of Uab Meto and some dialect of Lamaholot as spoken in Larantuka—is hardly surprising. More significant is the fact that Dampier notes that the Topasses were also using Malay. As traders in sandalwood, the Topasses had successfully inserted themselves into a network of trade that extended throughout eastern Indonesia and beyond. Timor was part of this trading network well before their arrival, and Malay was the *lingua franca* of this network. Captain Elie Ripon has provided conclusive evidence of this use of Malay. He quotes the greetings of the emperor at Camanasa as he entered the palace: "Tabai, bania, bania, baita pungnia sodara." This is recognizable as the distinct eastern dialect of Malay that was in use at the time: "Tabea banya banya, beta punya saudara: Many, many greetings [to] my brother."[8]

Comparative Comments: Western and Eastern Timor

Instead of contrasting the two halves of Timor, it is perhaps more pertinent to contrast the two European powers that eventually divided the island. Although the Dutch, regarded as "Father-Mother Company" (*Ama-Ina Kompani*), were an authoritative presence, it is hard not to conclude that the Portuguese were, from the very outset, more engaged as participants in the political and ritual dramas of the Timorese. Both Elizabeth Traube and Ricardo Roque make this clear in their contributions in this volume and in their other writings.

Roque, in his chapter, shows how similar both Portuguese and Timorese were in their processes of myth creation. Focusing on the death of Francisco Duarte at Atabai, they reduced an event to a name, place, and selected anecdote, and then rebuilt these elements into new, powerful, but significantly different legends. Judith Bovensiepen's chapter provides a similar ethnohistorical examination in the local context of the *reino* of Funar, as does the paper by Susana de Matos Viegas and Rui Graça Feijó in a missionary context in Lautem.

At the same time, Claudine Friedberg, the late doyen of Timorese studies, reminds us all that in attempting to construct the past, we are dealing with malleable sources. If her considered judgment that the *Bei Gua*—the great narrative of the Bunak population—embraces more than migrations of the Bunak and indeed includes Tetun migrations within its purview, we must all proceed with clear caution in dealing with our oral sources. This is the same message that the master historian of the Dutch archives, Hans Hägerdal conveys in his chapter in pointing to the potential of the archives for further interrogation.

Importantly, Andrew McWilliam and Chris Shepherd offer a critical reminder to focus as well on colonial intervention at the agricultural level, emphasizing the historical significance of the introduction of plantations in East Timor, something for which there was no equivalent in West Timor. Finally, the chapters by David Hicks and Kelly Silva give attention to Timor's recent history and the value of archives for enlightening ongoing contemporary research.

This book is a superb collection that opens many possibilities for further research in the future. Research on the ethnohistory of Timor has only just begun.

Acknowledgments

I would like to acknowledge the help of my colleagues James Grieves, Chuck Grimes, and Gregor Neonbasu for help with matters of translation and thank them for their assistance.

James J. Fox is currently emeritus professor at the Australian National University and adjunct professor at the University of Indonesia. He has an AB degree from Harvard University and BLitt and DPhil degrees from Oxford University. He first visited the island of Timor in 1965 and has written extensively on the anthropology, linguistics, and history of the island. His book, *Harvest of the Palm* (1977) dealt with the social and ecological history of Timor, with particular reference to the western side of the island. With Dionisio Babo Soares, he has edited a book on East Timor, *Out of the Ashes: The Destruction and Reconstruction of East Timor*, which is available as an ANU Press publication (http:// https://press.anu.edu.au/).

Notes

1. The Portuguese researcher, M. E. de Castro e Almeida (1982) claimed to identify some thirty-one distinct languages in Timor.
2. A linguistic complication in East Timor is the greater number of non-Austronesian-speaking populations, especially at the eastern end of Timor-Leste, some of whom, such as the Makassai, are in effect expanding and assimilating Austronesian-speaking populations. It is possible that there may once have been non-Austronesian-speaking populations in West Timor, but the Meto expansion has left few traces of this possibility.
3. These are just a few lines excerpted from a long ritual recitation recorded by my former student, Fr. Gregor Neonbasu. He intends to publish this recitation and others as part of his continuing investigation of the oral traditions of Biboki (Neonbasu 2011).
4. Maize eventually spread throughout the island of Timor and has become a basic staple for its population. What is important here is its historical priority and its great importance for Meto expansion, whose expansive swidden agriculture has changed the landscape of West Timor (see Ormeling 1955).

5. The Dutch researcher H. G. Schulte Nordholt identified Oibich with Wewiku, the executive domain of Wehali referred to by the dual name, Wewiku-Wehali (1971: 160). The connection is indeed plausible. *Oe* in Meto is *We* or *Wai* in Tetun, meaning "water." Oebich becomes Webich (i.e., Wewiku).

6. For a more extensive discussion of the diversity of crops grown on Timor and their history, see Fox 2003.

7. It is worth noting that the Dutch East India Company's "Treaty of Paravicini" signed in 1756 accorded the ruler of Wehali the title of kaiser on Timor and recognized Wehali's dominion over twenty-eight other named domains on Timor.

8. The use of the term *tabea* for "greetings" and *beta* for the first-person singular instead of *saya* are two clear markers of this eastern Malay dialect, which is still spoken in Kupang today (see Jacob and Grimes 2003).

References

Almeida, M. E. de C. 1982. *Estudo Serológico dos Grupos Etnolinguísticos de Timor-Dili (Sistema ABO)*. Lisboa: Instituto de Investigacão Científica Tropical.

Dames, M. L. (ed.). 1921. *The Book of Duarte Barbosa*. London: The Hakluyt Society.

Dampier, W. 1703 [1939]. *A Voyage to New Holland in the Year 1699*. London: The Argonaut Press.

Fox, J. J. 1977. *Harvest of the Palm: Ecological Change in Eastern Indonesia*. Cambridge, MA: Harvard University Press.

———. 1983. "The Great Lord Rests at the Centre: The Paradox of Powerlessness in European-Timorese Relations." *Canberra Anthropology* 5(2): 22–33.

———. 1988. "Historical Consequences of Changing Patterns of Livelihood on Timor." In *Northern Australia: Progress and Prospects*. Vol. 1: *Contemporary Issues in Development*, edited by D. Wade-Marshall and P. Loveday, 259–79. Canberra: Research School of Pacific Studies, Australian National University.

———. 1992. *The Heritage of Traditional Agriculture among the Western Austronesians*. Canberra: Occasional Paper, Department of Anthropology, Australian National University.

———. 1999. "Precedence in Practice among the Atoni Pah Meto of Timor." In *Structuralism's Transformations: Order and Revisions in Indonesia and Malaysia*, edited by L. V. Aragon and S. Russell, 3–36. Tucson: Arizona State University, Program for Southeast Asian Studies, Monograph Series Press.

———. 2000. "Tracing the Path, Recounting the Past: Historical Perspectives on Timor". In *Out of the Ashes: Destruction and Reconstruction of East Timor*, edited by J. J. Fox and D. B. Soares, 1–29. Adelaide: Crawford House Publishing and London: C. Hurst & Co. [Reprinted: ANU Press, 2003]

————. 2003. "Drawing from the Past to Prepare for the Future: Responding to the Challenges of Food Security in East Timor." In *Agriculture: New Directions for a New Nation, East Timor (Timor-Leste)*, edited by H. da Costa, C. Piggin, C. J. da Cruz, and J. J. Fox. 101–10. Canberra: Australian Centre for International Agricultural Research.

————. 2008. "Installing the 'Outsider' Inside: The Exploration of an Epistemic Austronesian Cultural Theme and Its Social Significance." *Indonesian and the Malay World* 36(105): 201–18.

Hägerdal, H. 2012. *Lords of the Land, Lords of the Sea: Conflict and Adaptation in Early Colonial Timor, 1600–1800*. Leiden: KITLV Press.

Jacob, J., and C. E. Grimes. 2003. *Kamus Pengantar Bahasa Kupang*. Kupang: Artha Wacana Press.

Middelkoop, P. 1938. "Iets over Sonba'i, het bekende vorstengeslacht in Timor." *Tijdschrift voor Indische Taal-, Land- en Volkenkunde* 78: 392–509.

Müller, S. 1857. *Reizen en onderzoekingen in den Indische Archipel, gedaan op last der Nederlandsch-Indische Regeering, tusschen de jaren 1828 en 1836*. Leiden: Fredrik Muller.

Neonbasu, G. 2011. *We Seek Our Roots: Oral Tradition in Biboki, West Timor*. Studia Instituti Anthropos No. 53. Fribourg: Academic Press.

Ormeling, F. J. 1955. *The Timor Problem: A Geographical Interpretation of an Underdeveloped Island*. Groningen: J. B. Wolters.

Pélissier, R. 1996. *Timor en guerre: le crocodile et les portugais, 1847–1913*. Orgeval: Ed. Pélissier.

Pigafetta, A. 1969. *Magellan's Voyage: A Narrative Account of the First Circumnavigation*. Translated and edited by R. A. Skelton. New Haven, CT: Yale University Press.

Ripon, C. 1997. *Voyages et aventures aux Grandes Indies 1617–1627*. Présentation et notes: Yves Giraud. Paris: Éditions de Paris.

Rockhill, W. W. 1915. "Notes on Relations and Trade of China with the Eastern Archipelago and the Coasts of the Indian Ocean during the Fourteenth Century. *T'oung Pao* 16: 236–71.

Roque, R. 2010. *Headhunting and Colonialism: Anthropology and the Circulation of Human Skulls in the Portuguese Empire 1870–1930*. New York: Palgrave Macmillan.

Schulte-Nordholt, H. G. 1971. *The Political System of the Atoni of Timor*. Verhandelingen KITLV 60. The Hague: Martinus Nijhoff.

Therik, T. 2004. *Wehali, the Female Land: Traditions of a Timorese Ritual Centre*. Canberra: Research School of Pacific and Asian Studies.

INDEX

encroachment, 245–47;
independence, 4, 6, 49, 143;
languages, 340; as new nation
state, 2
tokens (*rota*), 205, 206, 219–28,
223–28
ton terel (the sharing of goods
produced in common) marriage,
85
Topasses, 2, 21, 34, 346
topogeny, 25
topographic features, myths, 299
traders, 2, 342, 343
traditional rulers, 143
traditions: Mambai, 50; Mambai
(narratives), 53–56; narratives,
51
transactions, 318–19, 322–25. *See
also* marriage
Traube, Elizabeth, 7, 14, 26, 27, 96,
181, 193, 194, 268, 269, 339
triadic structure, 296
troops, 57
tropes, 110
truth from fiction, determining, 24
tyranny, 260

Uab Meto language, 340
ubdaida nor fortuna (luck and
fortune), 54
UDT (Timorese Democratic Union),
65
UDT (União Democrática
Timorense), 131
ukun (political power), 141, 142,
147
Underworld, 78
União Democrática Timorense, 307
United States, missionaries, 179
University of Oxford, 295

UN transitional administration
(UNTAET), 49
upper Lamaknen, 84
Upperworld, 82

Venus, 78
Vereenigde Oost-Indische
Compagnie (VOC), 247, 249–52,
257, 258, 260
Viegas, S. M., 31, 32
village (*suco*), 131
Viqueque: archives, 294–312;
rebellion (1959), 64, 100, 101,
220
Volksgeist, 156

Wagner, Roy, 16
warfare, 58, 108–11
wars of Funar, 134–39
wealth, 78
Wehali, 79, 81
West Timor, 256, 257, 258
Wiener, Margaret, 18
wife-givers, 317
wife-takers, 317
women: boar wives, 83; forms of
marriage, 84–87
World Below, 83, 84
World War II, 32, 100, 183, 184.
See also Japanese occupation
(1942–44)
worldwide indigenous strategy, 51
*Writing Culture: The Poetics and
Politics of Ethnography* (Clifford,
Marcus), 266
written records, 33

Ximenes, Pedro, 220

Zbyszewski, Georges, 218

www.ingramcontent.com/pod-product-compliance
Lightning Source LLC
Chambersburg PA
CBHW070609030426
42337CB00020B/3723